THE ROOTS OF
BACKPROPAGATION

Adaptive and Learning Systems for Signal Processing, Communications, and Control

Editor: Simon Haykin

Werbos / THE ROOTS OF BACKPROPAGATION: From Ordered
Derivatives to Neural Networks and Political Forecasting

THE ROOTS OF BACKPROPAGATION

From Ordered Derivatives to Neural Networks and Political Forecasting

PAUL JOHN WERBOS

A WILEY-INTERSCIENCE PUBLICATION

JOHN WILEY & SONS, INC.

NEW YORK / CHICHESTER / BRISBANE / TORONTO / SINGAPORE

Library of Congress Cataloging in Publication Data:

Werbos, Paul J. (Paul John), 1947–
        The roots of backpropagation: from ordered derivatives to
    neural networks and political forecasting / Paul John Werbos.
        p.   cm. — (Adaptive and learning systems for signal
    processing, communications, and control)
        Published simultaneously in Canada.
        Originally presented as the author's thesis (Ph. D.—Harvard,
    1974).
        "A Wiley-Interscience Publication."
        Includes bibliographical references and index.
        ISBN 0-471-59897-6 (cloth : alk. paper)
        1. Neural networks (Computer science)   2. Regression analysis.
    3. Prediction theory.   I. Title.   II. Series.
    QA76.87.W43   1993
    003.5—dc20   93-23159
                                                                  CIP

Foreword

As the first publicly distributed version of Paul Werbos' 1974 Harvard doctoral dissertation, *Beyond Regression,* this book has significant historical value. The work has far greater value, however, than merely as a historical reference. Indeed, the thesis, accompanied by the updated supplementary material in this volume, continues to provide an instructive account of the development of the fundamental learning rule that is now known as "backpropagation." Further, the thesis is a fascinating narrative of applications of that mathematical learning method to a broad class of difficult prediction problems in the social sciences. The fact that the work was developed nearly 20 years ago simply makes the reading even more inspiring.

After some prefatory material that frames the work in an appropriate historical perspective, Werbos immediately (Chapter Two) develops his algorithm for efficiently calculating derivatives, which he has defined as "dynamic feedback" and which we all now call backpropagation. The mathematics is clearly developed and easily understood. The work is rigorous and complete. What results is an enlightening account, starting with simple difference equations, of the development a powerful learning rule.

With the development of the backpropagation learning algorithm complete, Werbos engages in the main thrust of the work, thoughtful discussions of its application to prediction problems. The insights gained since its original publication serve to better interpret its utility and to extend its value to previously unexplored classes of problems (notably, for example, its application to artificial neural networks).

Since the popularization of backpropagation and all of its relatives in the 1980s, there have been countless articles and a fair number of texts that describe the application of backpropagation to difficult estimation and prediction problems. Typically, these applications focus on a concrete engineering or scientific goal; for example, detecting military targets in noisy thermal images or controlling a structure in the presence of an unknown noise disturbance. Far more abstract social science problems are considered, however, in the original portions of this work. The fact that these discussions predate the more modern, less ambiguous investigations illustrate Werbos' clever perceptions about predictive theories.

The entertaining reading that follows links dynamic feedback to problems in national assimilation, Skinner's behavioral models, political mobilization, questions of ethics and rational behavior, and internal telecommunication patterns in Norway, to name a sample few. Werbos' work is remarkable in that it shows the application of the same fundamental learning rule to diverse classes of problems.

I am sure readers of this book will enjoy it, not merely as a historical record, but also as an instructive essay describing the development of the most popular learning rule in use today and as a fascinating journey through its applications to difficult and interesting socio-economic phenomena.

BERNARD WIDROW
Professor of Electrical Engineering
Stanford University

Preface

Simon Haykin, the editor of this series, offered to publish my 1974 Ph.D. thesis, *Beyond Regression*, because this thesis has become something of a classic reference in the neural network and engineering world. The thesis is now recognized as the original source of *backpropagation*, which is now the most widely used algorithm by far in the neural network world. Also, the thesis *communicates* that algorithm to an audience with *no prior understanding* of neural networks; it is divided up, de facto, into chapters written for regular engineers, for statisticians, and for political scientists (mirroring the thesis review committee). Chapters 7 to 10 are also important, because they strengthen both the historical and the pedagogical value of this book.

In actuality, the thesis contains much more than the basics of backpropagation. My real aim in the thesis was to translate some of the vast goals of the general systems and cybernetics movements into a tangible mathematical reality: to initiate a whole body of new mathematical tools capable of generating deeper theoretical understanding and practical applications across a whole range of topics, ranging from neuroscience and engineering to economics[1] and political forecasting,[2] with relevance to the deepest issues faced by human society and human individuals. The thesis gave an example of the use of these tools, by applying them to a model of nationalism and social communications proposed by Karl Deutsch,[3] by turning it into a working forecasting model, while enriching it with greater detail. The thesis also discussed the issue of how to go beyond behaviorism, in building social sciences that account for the phenomenon of *intelligence*.

In 1974, these goals seemed incredibly ambitious for a mere graduate student. However, the great blossoming of the neural network field as a large, organized intellectual disciple (or "interdiscipline") since 1987 has made it possible for many people, including myself, to build on the ideas developed

---

[1] G. DeBoeck, ed., *Trading on the Edge: Neural, Genetic, and Fuzzy Systems for Chaotic Financial Markets,* Wiley, New York, 1994.

[2] A. Gore and M. Lloyd, in *Campaign and Election*, in preparation for 1994 submission.

[3] K. W. Deutsch, *Nationalism and Social Communications*, MIT Press, Cambridge, MA, 1966.

in the thesis and expand their applications in many directions. Also, the formulation of backpropagation in the thesis is the logical basis for fast automated differentiation (FAD), which has begun to excite interest in the more classical numerical world; by integrating such FAD programs into new designs based on backpropagation, it now seems as if the learning capabilities available for neural networks can be extended for easy use with a wider class of models, such as econometric-style models, conventional engineering models, finite element models, or production rule systems interpreted via fuzzy logic. Applications of this kind already exist but require serious technical skills. Connections have been developed between this mathematics and many strands of human psychology—cognitive science, experimental psychology or conditioning systems, and humanistic studies of psychology and social psychology. Finally, neural network methods based on backpropagation have gone back to the original domain of application studied here: the forecasting of economic[1] and political[2] variables, which has also proved highly successful. Many of these studies, cited in the Introduction can be understood without the highest level of mathematical sophistication.

These new developments have required many new techniques and refinements, based on the work of many people, which rise much higher than the foundations presented here. However, it is surprising for me to look back on my thesis and see how many of the most recent developments are echoed—sometimes briefly and sometimes at length—in this document written in 1974.

The Introduction will describe some parts of this history in more detail, in order to put the thesis (Chapters 1–6) and applications (Chapters 7–10) into perspective. It will provide citations to related sources and explain how this work relates to more advanced possibilities for future developments. First, I will describe backpropagation or derivative calculations as such; then I will describe optimization and prediction tools emerging from the thesis and from backpropagation; and, finally, I will discuss linkages to larger social and psychological issues, in a way that I hope is accessible to social scientists. (Both in the thesis and in the Introduction, the social scientist may want to jump over some of the earlier mathematically oriented discussion.)

For completeness, I should add that all this work—both the thesis and the more recent advanced work cited here—could easily have been lost in obscurity, even after 1987–1988. The neural network community and I have a very deep debt to five individuals—David Parker, Bernard Widrow, Stephen Grossberg, Nick DeClaris, and Richard Sutton—who helped us through that period.

PAUL JOHN WERBOS

Washington, D.C.

Contents

Introduction

This book shows how the lowly concepts of *feedback* and *derivatives* are the essential building blocks needed to understand *and replicate* higher-order phenomena like learning, emotion, and intelligence at all levels of the human mind, including the social level. It shows how a relatively new way of computing derivatives—now called "backpropagation"—plays a crucial role in new systems that perform tasks like automatic modeling and prediction, pattern recognition, function approximation, and optimal decision, control and planning. Some of these systems are based on artificial neural networks (ANNs); others are not. As discussed in the Preface, these system designs have *dual use*—as *engineering tools* now used for tasks ranging from reducing pollution through to political forecasting, and as *models* of intelligence.

This book presents a unified approach to this range of topics. Unfortunately, the people studying these various topics have all developed different vocabularies, and have different attitudes towards mathematical details. Reflecting this diversity, the book contains some sections written for the highest-level generalists, and others containing specific pseudocode and equations for people who need to see all the details.

The next part of this Introduction provides a general outline of the book. It describes how the different chapters fit together and fit into the needs of different audiences. The following section explains in general terms how this new mathematical concept—"backpropagation" or "ordered derivatives"—opens up the possibility of a scientific understanding of intelligence, as important to psychology and neurophysiology as Newton's concepts were to physics. The remaining sections put this book into context, by describing more of the history and by providing citations to more advanced work which builds on the fundamentals given here; they do this for the three main topics of this book, in order:

1. Derivative calculation and backpropagation as such, with an emphasis on neural networks.

2. Modeling (prediction and system identification) and intelligent optimization.

3. The methods and foundations of social science and psychology.

A GUIDE TO THIS BOOK

Part One—Chapters 1 through 6—is my 1974 Harvard Ph.D. thesis, the original source for true backpropagation. Chapter 7 contains a 1981 conference paper, also of historical and conceptual significance. Chapters 8, 9 and 10 contain more recent papers, describing the most important developments of the past few years in a tutorial fashion. Recent work on detailed circuits in the brain is discussed briefly and cited, but not included, because of its highly specialized prerequisites.

The entire thesis was written for a Harvard committee containing a political scientist, a statistician, and two applied mathematicians. However, Chapter 2 was scrutinized most carefully by the mathematicians, Chapters 3 and 4 by the statistician, and Chapters 5 and 6 by the political scientist.

Chapter 1 is a general summary. Chapter 2 explains the original backpropagation algorithm, which I then called "dynamic feedback." It also describes a number of possible applications, particularly in modeling or prediction and in optimization. Chapter 2 presents backpropagation as a *general* method, which could be applied to simple artificial neural networks (ANNs) or to any *other* ordered nonlinear system. (It also defines what an ordered system is.) Chapter 3 *applies* backpropagation to the general problem of vector ARMA estimation, which—according to conventional statistical theory—is the proper way to do prediction and modeling when the data we use may be corrupted by measurement noise. Chapters 2 and 3 both try to start out at a relatively low level, and build up gradually to formal proofs which are inherently more difficult. Those proofs are *not* a prerequisite to the remainder of the book.

Chapter 4 describes simulation studies showing how new *robust* methods for prediction over time perform better than the usual methods (ordinary least squares *or* ARMA) still in use by most social scientists and by most neural networkers. This chapter was written at the request of Dr. Mosteller, a statistician, but should be straightforward in any case.

Chapters 5 and 6 were written for the "behavioral scientist"—the psychologist or social scientist. Chapter 5 presents my own views of behavioral science (as of 1974), ranging from the role of backpropagation and neural networks, through to long-term theories of history and their value to the decision maker. (The last section of this Introduction gives an update.) Chapter 6 provides a detailed empirical study of Karl Deutsch's theory of nationalism and social communications, using the modeling tools (based on backpropagation) given earlier in the thesis; this chapter includes both an extension of Deutsch's model, and a test of alternative modeling tools based on real empirical data, further supporting the conclusions of Chapter 4.

The conference paper in Chapter 7 was, in my view, a key link in the causal chain from my thesis to the actual use of backpropagation in the neural network field. (See the later part of this Introduction.) It provides a compressed discussion of three main topics: (1) alternative forms of backpropagation, useful for calculating second derivatives and for time-forwards calculations (called "forwards propagation" by some researchers); (2) the use of backpropagation in providing various kinds of *sensitivity analysis* information, crucial to the users of economic models; (3) the use of backpropagation as part of a *reinforcement learning system*, a kind of neural-network optimization system with specific parallels to specific parts of the brain.

Chapter 8 provides a more straightforward, step-by-step tutorial on how backpropagation is used in neural network engineering today. Many engineers have told me that Chapter 8 is the most straightforward tutorial in existence on backpropagation for them, and that it provides certain advanced capabilities—crucial to many applications—which are missing or even muddled up in other popularized accounts. They have also told me that Chapters 8 and 9 are crucial as prerequisites to other sources, such as the *Handbook of Intelligent Control*, which provides the technical details of the most advanced neural net designs for modelling and control in existence, along with the details of many engineering applications [14].

Chapter 9 provides a relatively less technical overview of "neurocontrol"— the study of neural networks that make decisions or control engineering systems. This chapter mentions engineering applications, but it also mentions how the brain itself is a neurocontroller.

Many papers on neural networks emphasize the dozens upon dozens of applications now on the market; for example, the everyday modem is based on work by Widrow, which is an important precursor to backpropagation. Chapter 9 places more emphasis on applications in the pipeline which could have a big impact on human society, in the context of long-term historical trends (as discussed in Chapter 5). On the positive side, neurocontrol could provide the extra capability needed for a big reduction in the cost of space travel which, in turn, would help permit a Rostow-style economic takeoff in space. It could help solve the complex integration and control problems involved in the transient cycles and startup of fuel cell cars, which might in turn free the world from its dependence on oil. On the negative side, the dangers depicted in movies like *Terminator 2* are more realistic than one might imagine.

Chapter 10 comes back full circle to the human mind, to the basic issues in psychology which inspired all of this work in the first place. Many of us believe that this is the real payoff to this entire enterprise. Chapter 10 provides a deeper, more intuitive explanation of backpropagation, which can be useful even in engineering applications. It also provides a condensed discussion of a very wide range of issues, which may merit a careful line-by-line consideration by those of us concerned with humanistic psychology.

LEARNING AND BACKPROPAGATION AS KEYS TO THE BRAIN

This section explains how new developments in mathematics and engineering—including backpropagation—make it possible to create a "Newtonian revolution'' in our understanding of intelligence as it exists in the human brain. It will focus on the brain itself—on neuropsychology—because that is the area where theory and experiment have the greatest chance to come together in a precise way in the near future, and because later parts of this book already deal with the larger aspects of human intelligence. As this book goes to print, crucial new experiments are now being reported or initiated; but, because of inertia and overspecialization, both in universities and in government, it is far from clear that this opportunity for a Newtonian revolution will in fact be grasped.

The analogy here is to Issac Newton. Before Newton, physics (or ''natural philosophy'') was essentially an anecdotal science, a very complex melange of historical ideas and empirical observations, without any true unification— like neuroscience today. Newton's new mathematical concept—the *derivative*—was the key to Newton's laws of gravity, which in turn *created* physics as a modern science. Before Newton, natural philosophy *described* nature; after Newton, there were laws of physics used to *explain* nature.

Can we uncover mathematical laws for intelligence in the brain, laws which could play the same role as Newton's laws did in physics, both in unifying and simplifying the subject?

At first glance, most neuroscientists would regard this as a rather wild idea for us to think about today. Most neuroscientists have become overwhelmed by the mind-numbing complexity of the literature on the brain, including the literature on the dynamics of thousands upon thousands of local circuits in the dozens upon dozens of the species they study very carefully. A few researchers have even tried to translate their despair into a general, fundamental principle: if the information content in any *one* brain—the brain under study—is as great as the capacity of the brain trying to study it, then it is impossible for the second brain to hold all that information. Based on this principle, they argue that a scientific understanding of the brain is impossible.

What would Newton have said about this despair? Certainly, the complexity of the human brain at any one time is very great. But so is the complexity of the *entire physical universe*, which is what the physicists study. Newton did not find a clever way of summarizing all our knowledge about the *present state* of the universe; instead, he *changed the focus of attention* toward an effort to understand the *dynamic laws* which *govern* the state of the universe, as it changes over time. The *catalog* of neural circuits—including the recurrent connections and dynamics at any one time—will always be too complex for a human to absorb in full. But the *laws of learning*—the dynamic principles which *change* the strengths of connections between cells (and other long-term parameters)—are a very different matter.

Dozens and dozens of studies of ''plasticity'' or learning have shown that the *higher* centers of the brain—centers like the cerebral cortex, which are responsible for higher intelligence—have a highly flexible and uniform (''modular'') kind of structure. One part of the cortex will learn to take over the functions of another, if it is given the right inputs; for example, cells in temporal cortex (which normally performs language functions in humans) can learn to develop edge detecotrs, when they are hooked up to visual inputs. We should *not* expect that the mathematical laws of learning are the same for *different* organs of the brain, such as the cerebral cortex and the cerebellum, even when similar molecules are involved; however, we can expect that the same basic laws will apply across all cells of similar types within each major organ. *The effort to undestand these laws of learning will be the basic foundation of our Newtonian revolution, if in fact that revolution happens.*

What is the role of engineering and of backpropagation—the use of our new kind of derivative—in that revolution?

In the past, the neural network community has mainly been divided into three or four subgroups, who use similar-looking models at times, but often find it difficult to understand each other because they use *totally different standards of validation* for their models. Biological modellers usually consider how well their models fit local-circuit physiological data. Psychologists (including cognitive scientists) usually study how well their models replicate a few selected aspects of human or animal behavior, at an aggregate input–output level. Engineers study how well different designs actually work in learning to perform difficult tasks. Humanistic psychologists would ask how well different models would fit their direct knowledge of what goes on in their own minds and in the minds of others. Yet a true description of human intelligence should meet *all four validation criteria*. The human brain *works*, as a highly capable engineering system, at least after learning; this is an extremely important piece of information, which we need to exploit to the utmost when developing models.

Chapters 9 and 10 explain in more detail why backpropagating itself is crucial in building any system—artificial or natural—that *works* in certain tasks (like planning or optimization over time) which the human brain does handle. Those chapters, and the following section, cite more detailed discussions of relevant biological experiments. Among the important recent experiments are those showing that NO acts as a reverse transmitter, the work by Sclabassi showing that conventional LTP experiments suppress the nonlinear capabilities of the hippocampus, and the work by David Gardner apparently demonstrating backpropagation-based learning in Aplysia. Among those in the pipeline are engineering-style tests of learning by cells in (co)cultures, such as inferior olive cells at Northwestern University and Purkinje cells trained to learn time-lags at the University of North Texas. Crucial as this work may be, it is still only a small beginning.

HISTORY AND CAPABILITIES OF BACKPROPAGATION

This thesis uses the term "dynamic feedback" to describe a method which is now called "backpropagation." No one I know is sure where the word "backpropagation" comes from; however, some people speculate that someone reading a draft of the popularized version of backpropagation in Rumelhart and McClelland [1] noticed a vague, qualitative similarity to an earlier algorithm developed by Rosenblatt, which Rosenblatt had called "backpropagation." The term appears in the index of that book, but not in the chapter it refers to. Whatever the disadvantages of the term, it is now widely used, and there is no point in trying to change it. The essence of backpropagation is the idea of calculating derivatives efficiently, through calculations that work their way backward from the outcome variables of interest.

My own work in the neural network field—like that of Grossberg [2] and of many other pioneers in the field—was inspired by the classic book of D. O. Hebb, *The Organization of Behavior* [3]. Hebb's book contained a wide variety of insights, some of which go beyond what most of today's researchers seem to be aware of. The core of his book was the idea that neuroscience could be developed into a true science by focusing on the simple laws of *learning* or *adaptation*, which underlie the more complicated experimental data in which scientists often get lost. This idea is discussed further in Chapter 5 and in Madhavan et al. [4]. The Grossberg school of thought essentially took Hebb's early hypothesis about learning and translated it directly into differential equation models fully consistent with classical neuron dogma. However, in 1964, when I read Hebb, I quickly (too quickly!) concluded that Hebb's rule basically calculated correlation coefficients in situations where something like regression coefficients or causal models were needed; thus I began a search for an alternative approach, rooted more firmly in concepts from statistical theory and optimization. My goal was to construct something like a general theory of intelligent systems, inspired by Minsky's discussion in Feigenbaum and Feldman [5], by Freud, and by other concepts related to reinforcement learning. Actually, my very first goal after reading Hebb was to understand how people's concepts about political systems might *change* in response to appropriate actions; in other words, I was interested in the deep foundations of human learning and adaptation, as it might affect large-scale social decisions.

By 1967, I had hit on the idea of translating Freud's notions about "psychic energy" or "cathexis" into a mathematical design, involving a backward flow of value measures in a reinforcement learning system, built up from model neurons slightly modified from those used by Widrow and Rosenblatt and Minsky in the 1960s [6]. I submitted the basic ideas for publication in 1967, and it came out in 1968 [7]. (The close connection between Freud and backpropagation is described in Chapter 10, which stresses the relationship between *values* and *derivatives*; also see Madhavan et al. [4].) While the intuition was all there in the 1968 paper, the key details needed for a working intelligent system were not.

In 1968, I had the privilege of taking courses at Harvard from Y. C. Ho of the Harvard Committee on Applied Mathematics, whose well-known textbook on control theory [8] certainly deepened my understanding of dynamic programming and influenced my thinking on reinforcement learning. In later years, LeCun [9] showed that it is possible to *derive* backpropagation from certain ideas in that textbook; however, the derivation in my thesis (Chapter 2, Section 2.12) is even more direct and general, starting from concepts like substitution and expression, which are fundamental to all rigorous mathematical proofs [10]. Jacobson and Mayne [11] described ideas in control theory somewhat closer to backpropagation, but still without saying how to *take advantage* of complex sparse structure—the true basis of backpropagation (and of large-scale problems in most of the real world).

By 1970–1971, I had crystallized the basics of a new mathematical model of intelligence, linking backpropagation and reinforcement learning together. However, the resulting scheme was relatively complex and difficult for the Harvard Committee to evaluate. (I have copies of that thesis proposal in my files, if anyone is interested.) Then, to make the idea simpler, I proposed pulling out a small piece of that theory and building multilayer perceptrons built up from *differentiable* model neurons, using backpropagation to adapt the weights. (This idea was later popularized by Rumelhart, Hinton, and Williams [1]; however, Chapter 8 may provide a more straightforward tutorial on the subject, with citation to important work by Parker and others.) There was considerable skepticism about this idea in the Harvard Committee on Applied Mathematics (which was *not* arguing that they should take credit for the idea), reinforced by my inability to get support from anyone on the MIT faculty with an interest in neural networks. Some of those discussions appear very amusing in retrospect but are probably of little interest to most readers.

Ironically, my career was saved through the intervention of Professor Karl Deutsch, whom I had worked for over the summer at Harvard, in a project which also involved Professor Dick Chadwick. Initially, I worked for Deutsch simply because his ideas about subjects like war and peace [12] seemed very promising, and also because he had written a book advocating what amounts to a neural network framework for analyzing political systems [13]. He proposed that I try to apply my theory of intelligence in some way to political forecasting, using his model of nationalism as a starting point. (Note that his *concepts* about nationalism were far richer than the two-equation model in the appendices of his book; Chapter 6 of my thesis provides a somewhat more complete mathematical articulation of the original concepts.) This was accepted by the Committee on Applied Mathematics, with the tacit understanding that I would be applying something like the more conventional statistical methods, drawing on concepts from Box and Jenkins whose multivariate extensions had not yet penetrated the social sciences. (As far as I know, they still have not.)

I still remember the deep pain in my stomach on the day when I discovered that the algorithms in the book by Box and Jenkins led to a huge increase in computational costs—way beyond my limited computer budget—for reasonable sized multivariate models. I remember exclaiming to myself in frustration that I could make an entire brain work in $o(N)$, and asking *why* I would have to use $o(N^6)$ for such a simple structure. It was then that I hit on the idea of *generalizing* backpropagation to the case of an arbitrary nonlinear differentiable structure—the core idea in Chapter 2 of the thesis. Some people have called this "generalized backpropagation."

Actually, the thesis generalized backpropagation *only* to the case of ordered or "feedforward" systems. It clearly specifies how to handle time lags as well. (Economists would say that Chapter 2 discusses systems with "time-lagged endogenous variables," which neural network people would refer to as "time-lagged recurrent networks (TLRNs)" [14].) However, in 1981, when working at the U.S. Department of Energy, I figured out how to *generalize* backpropagation to the case of implicit systems (which economists call "simultaneous equation models" and neural network people call "simultaneous-recurrent networks" [14].) In effect, I found a way to join my original notion of backpropagation together with "adjoint" methods pioneered by Oak Ridge National Laboratory. This resulted in a new sensitivity analysis tool, able to pinpoint model parameters that destabilize the outputs of econometric forecasting models. For a variety of political reasons, the publication of this method and its first application was delayed until 1988 [15]. A more straightforward discussion of how to implement this generalization may be found in White and Sofge [14], and a flowchart appears in Madhavan et al. [4]; however, Chapter 8 in this book provides additional background, which may be important in implementing (and debugging) the generalization. There is now good reason to believe that simultaneous-recurrent networks are crucial to higher-order intelligence—to "chunking," "planning," symbolic reasoning, and the like [4, 14, 34].

For historical reasons, some neural network researchers like to describe neural networks as differential equations, rather than using the simple $t/(t + 1)$ formulations that I stress both here and elsewhere. When backpropagation is applied to neural networks, the differential equation formulations usually confuse the two different types of recurrence (simultaneous versus time-lagged), which have very different properties and uses [14]. The results are disastrous, in most cases, even in the hands of famous people. On the other hand, some people, like NASA/JPL, have used differential equations very well to describe neural network chips that are carefully controlled, so that they represent simultaneous-recurrent systems only, with no internal memory, embedded within larger systems that could provide memory and other functions through external connections. See White and Sofge [14] for more details on how to embed networks within networks, when building intelligent systems.

Since 1974, ARMA-related methods have grown much more popular in engineering. However, they still have identifiability problems in the multivariate case (as noted in Chapter 3). They are essentially a special case of the TLRNs discussed in Chapter 8 of this book and Chapter 10 of [14].

Another generalization of some importance is the generalization to calculating second derivatives, described very briefly in Chapter 7. The notation used in calculating such derivatives can be extremely confusing; therefore I now recommend the notation and procedures given in White and Sofge [14, Chapter 10].

The idea of *applying* backpropagation to artificial neural networks appears only obliquely in Chapter 5 of the thesis (again, because of skepticism in the Committee); however, I did go on and describe "dynamic feedback" in several subsequent papers [16–18], which explicitly linked the idea to models of intelligence and the brain. Still, Chapter 7 in this book, when it first appeared as a major conference paper in 1981, was the first paper to truly expand at length on the importance of this algorithm in neural networks, with reference to perceptrons, Grossberg, and specific circuits in the brain. It is my belief that this paper—which I distributed rather widely (including a lengthier version that went to my reviewing official, Charles Smith, at DOE)—was the crucial spark that set off the chain of events leading to the use of this method by a larger audience. (See Chapter 8 for citations to other authors.)

Note, by the way, that some of the footnotes in Chapter 5 of the thesis proposed that backpropagation may be implemented in the human brain through backward flows in the microtubules, an idea that I have elaborated on [19] and that has received further support from Hameroff, Dayhoff, and others [20]. These footnotes have been collected into a new Section, 5.5.1; however, the text has not been altered, except for very light copy editing to conform with the publisher's standards.

In this thesis, I mostly used backpropagation in combination with (scaled) steepest descent methods; however, a wide variety of other gradient-based methods have been used in later work [14]. See White and Sofge [14] as well for the relations between backpropagation and other designs used in pattern recognition problems.

The thesis noted that backpropagation was implemented in the TSP software system at MIT and was planned for a more general implementation; however, while the TSP ARMA command was disseminated somewhat, the more general capabilities were caught in the middle in a management conflict and never happened.

OTHER MATHEMATICAL TOOLS IN THE THESIS

My 1974 thesis was not just a document on backpropagation, by any means. Backpropagation may be as important and as all-pervasive as derivatives, but—like derivatives—it is essentially a low-level tool or phenomenon. The study of intelligence also requires some understanding of higher-level concepts, like optimization over time and prediction.

In the realm of prediction, the "measurement-noise-only" or "pure robust" method described in the thesis is essentially the same as "simulation path" methods in economics, which were developed at about the same time. Simulation path methods aroused great interest in economics but died off quickly, mainly because of the computational cost. However, with backpropagation and modern computers, computational cost is not that much of a problem.

In Chapter 2 of the thesis, I noted that the pure robust method has certain limitations, and I proposed the idea of a "relaxation method" for the general case. In 1977, I proposed a way of implementing that method [16], which never worked out empirically; however, in 1978 [18], I found a variant of that method which did work.

Almost all neural network predictions to date have been based on very simple maximum likelihood approaches. In 1987, I proposed that the pure robust method and relaxation method be used in neural network forecasting as well [21]. In 1990, I even wrote out the detailed equations for how to do that [22] and suggested a modified neuron model— the "sticky neuron"—to make such networks more stable over time and more able to represent systems with slowly changing time-varying parameters. But none of this was implemented until Professor McAvoy, Chairman of the Chemical Engineering Department at Maryland, agreed to a collaborative project in this area. That collaboration documented an order-of-magnitude reduction in forecasting error for about half the real-world chemical processes to which it was applied [14] and significant improvement in the other half. Also, I was able to penetrate [14] more deeply into the theoretical issues raised in Chapter 2 of the thesis and develop new concepts, which could provide the basis for better forecasts in the future. McAvoy's follow-up in this area has resulted in several truly real-world applications.

All these exercises in robust estimation have focused on the problem of reducing *forecasting* error. There is a further problem in trying to model the *structure of noise* in a complex, nonlinear world. The section on pattern analysis in Chapter 2 of the thesis presents an important approach to this problem, elaborated on in my 1977 paper [16]. Only in 1991 did I find the time (and ability) to translate this concept into a well-defined mathematical design, coupled with a partial proof of statistical consistency in the multivariate linear case [14]. This new development was still based on maximum likelihood concepts, suggesting the need for further research on how to combine it with robustness.

The area of *optimization over time* has also seen substantial progress over the last few years [14, 23]. There are two major kinds of approaches useful in optimizing a *large* dynamic system: the backpropagation of utility and "adaptive critic" designs (or approximate dynamic programming). Chapter 2 of the thesis gives an example of the backpropagation of utility through time. Chapter 7 discusses some adaptive critic ideas (e.g., GDHP), which had also been mentioned in my earlier papers [16–18]. In actuality, the adaptive critic or "reinforcement learning" designs are the only ones that have a serious hope of reproducing true brain-like real-time intelligence. They are described in detail in White and Sofge [14] and in a recent paper by myself [23] and explained intuitively in Madhavan et al. [4]. To achieve brain-like intelligence, one must *combine* the power of adaptive critics *together with* model-based designs using backpropagation; Chapter 10 discusses the basic ideas involved and their close connection with Freud's original concepts.

LINKS TO LARGER SOCIAL AND PSYCHOLOGICAL ISSUES

Dozens of research approaches or paradigms have been proposed over the years in the social sciences and psychology. Four global, representative approaches are:

1. The *descriptive approach*, in which the researcher simply accumulates lots of facts, anecdotes, and data, without performing any deep cause-and-effect analysis or evaluation. Many management consultants have described this as "data" without "information."

2. The *classical or normative approach*, which attempts to build up a rational hierarchy of values in a kind of top–down fashion. One starts with global principles from ethics and epistemology. One then deduces long-term social values by combining such principles with analysis of long-term historical trends and possibilities. And one proceeds by trying to develop a cause-and-effect understanding at ever more practical levels, translating basic values step-by-step into guidance for decision-makers of all kinds. This approach tries to be eclectic, in drawing on information from all sources—verbal, quantitative, and intuitive.

3. The *pure microeconomic approach*, which starts out by developing a simplified mathematical model of human motivation, like utility maximization, and tries to develop insights into the efficiency of different social arrangements, based on *conceptual* mathematical models (which may never be translated into *empirical* models).

4. The *behaviorist approach*, which restricts itself to developing predictive quantitative models describing measured variables over time.

My own research has been motivated by the normative approach, which tries to be of maximum possible utility to real decision-making. Like the microeconomists, I have tried to develop mathematical tools leading to conceptual models, which can be used to *link* behaviorist analysis *and other sources of information* to important policy questions; however, I have hoped that we could broaden the range of tools, and the depth of analysis of psychology, to the point where the word "economics" would be misleadingly narrow.

Chapter 5 of the thesis addresses these issues but tends to use somewhat abstract language, simply because it is hard to address deeply held attitudes in a direct and decisive way without eliciting defensive reactions that close off serious reflection.

To begin with, Chapter 5 addresses some of the common methodological problems that occur even *within* behaviorism and descriptivism (which are arguably the dominant approaches in political science departments today).

Descriptive studies have long been useful as sources of raw data or questions, for use in later stages of analysis. However, when they are treated as an end in themselves—as an approach to analysis—they lead to substantial problems.

Descriptivism is often used as an excuse for analysts to argue that they are drawing *no conclusions* about cause-and-effect or values, and that there is therefore no danger of their drawing false conclusions of that sort. However, as the management consultants say, "data" are not the same as "information." (Actually, I present a more detailed taxonomy in a 1986 paper [24], which extends the idea of "data" versus "information" into a classification closer to the kinds of data/information that may exist in the mind.) All too often, people draw conclusions about cause-and-effect from information that they see in descriptive studies, and this often tends to be misleading for reasons well known to statisticians—the need for control variables, the need to discriminate between causation and correlation, and so on. Government agencies are especially guilty here, because descriptivist rhetoric is often a useful excuse for covering their managers and avoiding the need for difficult analysis, even though their reports often try to convey some degree of relevance (justifying funding) by highlighting "interesting" facts (which tend to impinge on values or beliefs about cause-and-effect).

In a 1990 article [25], I describe alternative ways to develop utility functions for energy decisions; the first few pages—describing the common approaches now used in government—may seem a bit bizarre to those who have not experienced first-hand what can happen when people try to establish that they are not really part of a decision-making process. A major cause of this problem is the idea that all real decisions are supposed to be made by political appointees, who, in turn, do not have time for global long-range analysis; however, the corporate culture varies considerably from agency to agency (and from appointee to appointee) on such matters. (In case the reader is tempted to infer something incorrect, I would like to stress that neither the Department of Energy nor the National Science Foundation fits the extreme form of the problem which I am highlighting here.)

A careful analysis of how one uses quantitative data to analyze cause-and-effect relations still leads to the emphasis on *prediction*, stressed in Chapter 5. As Chapter 5 notes, the emphasis on prediction was essential to learning some important empirical lessons in the thesis. However, it extends well beyond the thesis. In econometrics, for example, people often use adjust R-squared measures within constraints, and so on, which tend to lead to very impressive-looking theories; however, the leading theories of that type may turn out to be gross misrepresentations of the empirical real world when one tests them against whole-systems multiperiod prediction. In a recent publication [26], I give an example of this, in the development of a model of the industrial sector for the U.S. Department of Energy. There are many other examples in the literature as well. In the same publication [26], I also describe efforts—in collaboration with the Stanford Energy Modeling Forum—to find the way to best combine technology and microeconomic insights with more refined behaviorist methodologies.

For those interested in the larger, normative questions, Chapters 5 and 10 may be of special interest.

Strictly speaking, the normative approach begins with questions of philosophy—ethics and epistemology—which are not addressed in the thesis. In ethics, one seeks to define goals that can be used in a coherent way to define *rational* actions; this, in turn, tends to lead toward an approach that defines a global, integrative value measure or utility function [27, 28]. The idea of utility maximization is more controversial in social science, but I will argue later that it is still defensible, if interpreted in a very careful way, related to reinforcement learning.

In psychology, the reinforcement learning view basically splits up the most important issues into two parts: (1) the study of motivation, which describes where our utility functions U come from, and (2) the study of intelligence, which describes how brains and other systems *learn* to optimize U over time. (There are other issues in neurophysiology, of course, but these are the most crucial ones in this context.)

The study of intelligence bears directly on epistemology—the effort to understand the basis of human learning and knowledge; it seeks to understand the *actual* roots of the *actual* learning (or "induction") that occurs in our minds, both at the preverbal and verbal level. From an existential point of view, one might argue that these are the only roots we really have. Chapter 10 of the book edited by White and Sofge [14] describes how quantitative researchers from a number of fields have taken basic questions in epistemology and translated them into more definite mathematical versions, important to the design of actual systems capable of learning. The emphasis is on the *preverbal* level, but other chapters and later work make the connection to symbolic reasoning as well.

The study of motivation bears directly on ethics, but there are many controversies here.

First, the idea of describing the mind as a utility maximizer still remains quite controversial, despite the work of Von Neumann and Simon and so on. It is very fashionable to discuss the examples of *irrationality* [28] which are observed in human behavior; however, such examples can be understood as the *inevitable* result of a system evolved to *learn* to optimize as well as possible, within the *constraints* of what is possible in a working intelligent system with finite computational resources [4]. In behaviorist psychology, it has been observed that there are two major "classes" of conditioning experiments: (1) "Skinnerian" experiments, which fit very nicely the idea that the organism maximizes "primary reinforcement" over time [19], and (2) "Pavlovian" experiments, which appear to require a different paradigm. However, Baird and Klopf [29] have shown that a simple reinforcement learning model can explain *both* the 18 most important Skinnerian experiments *and* the 18 most important Pavlovian experiments; in other words, the real-world imperfections of a working system that *learns* to maximize utility over time can in fact explain the main imperfections observed so far. There is much more work to be done, of course, to explain further experiments and to use more complex models, but the viability of the approach has been established empirically. In fact, very basic considerations about Darwinian evolution suggest [7, 30] that evolution would tend to develop brains that optimize some measure of evolutionary success, subject to the limitations of the computing hardware available.

Second, many readers would argue that this approach *assumes* that the human mind and the human brain are essentially identical. However, I have argued that this approach is still worthwhile, no matter which view one takes on the mind–body problem; a variety of alternative views exist. There is no doubt that such issues have normative implications. (See [20] and Chapter 10.)

Third, there is the question of how we can learn something *about* the utility or reinforcement functions that evolve in Darwinian selection (which itself may be thought of as a kind of general mathematical phenomenon). Ironically, in my pre-thesis oral examination, I defended *two* topics—the theory of motivation and its long-term implications, and a theory of intelligence. Most of the discussion and interest at the time focused on the first of the two.

By now, the emerging field of "sociobiology" has captured many of the relevant insights, though some of the packaging and secondary developments are controversial. The key lesson from the models of sociobiology, in my view, is that the utility functions that would result from Darwinian evolution involve some (varying) degree of *altruism*; one may think of them as something like a weighted sum of the well-being of different organisms, where the weights depend on a number of factors. (*Sociobiology* tends to highlight factors like kinship and similarity, but potential future contributions to the tribe of different individuals would presumably enter in as well, in certain environments.) It is now known empirically that major genetic changes in expressed motivation can occur in as few as 10 generations [28], which may have some link to observed historical cycles, as hinted at in Chapter 5. The ethical implications of this are discussed in Chapter 10, again with several variants.

No matter which variant one picks, I would describe the mind as a system that attempts to achieve the most distant possible horizon in decision-making; in other words, I would describe it as a system that attempts to maximize U over an infinite time horizon, subject to uncertainties that force what look like finite horizons—in practice, horizons that have a natural tendency to expand as the organism reduces uncertainty through learning. (Again, this follows from a view of Darwinian evolution.)

The ethical ideal of foresight—motivated either by my concepts or by Christianity or Islam—does create problems for traditional microeconomics. Traditionally, perfect foresight is associated with a zero real discount rate. One can still rationalize positive real interest rates even on the basis of ethical foresight, but there are certainly some major policy implications [25], which do impinge on policy regarding energy and the environment. Long ago [31], it was pointed out that a "rational" economic actor, responding to a 15% real interest rate, would always choose the extinction of the human race over its continuation, if the former were accompanied by 8 years of doubled consumption between now and the end of the human race 8 years later. Ethical foresight would try to encourage economic policies that prevent the invisible hand of the marketplace from making that kind of decision. Unfortunately, in the real world, low interest rates sometimes encourage high debt ratios, which can bind the hands of future generations and *reduce* effective foresight; therefore implementing such a policy is no trivial matter.

In general, if one truly believes that the human race is at a kind of "crossroads" in terms of long-term social evolution (as suggested in [25, 32, 33] and Chapter 5), a rational human being committed to ethical foresight would redirect all of his or her action toward maximizing the probability of our going down the right fork in the road (except to the extent that there are additional spiritual considerations, which are assumed to outlast the human species.) (See Chapter 10 and [20].) This point was made using unfelicitous language in a 1979 paper by myself [18] (language so strong as to be somewhat misleading in regard to the role of government); however, the logic remains valid, and my later discussion [32] may be a better formulation of what it really leads to in practical terms. This, in turn, provides the long-term strategic values required for a proper assessment of more mid-term and short-term policy issues, informed by knowledge from behaviorist studies, from technology analysis, and from a better understanding of the human actors who pervade the process.

REFERENCES

1. D. Rumelhart and J. McClelland (eds.), *Parallel Distributed Processing*, MIT Press, Cambridge, MA, 1986.

2. M. Commons, S. Grossberg, and J. Staddon (eds.), *Neural Network Models of Conditioning and Action*, Lawrence Erlbaum Associates, Hillsdale, NJ, 1991.

3. D. O. Hebb, *The Organization of Behavior*, Wiley, New York, 1949.

4. P. G. Madhavan et al. (eds.), *Neuroscience and Neural Networks: Efforts Towards and Empirical Synthesis*, INNS Press/Erlbaum, Washington, D.C., forthcoming.

5. E. A. Feigenbaum and J. Feldman, *Computers and Thought*, McGraw-Hill, New York, 1963.

6. M. Minsky and S. Papert, *Perceptrons*, Expanded Edition, MIT Press, Cambridge, MA, 1988.

7. P. Werbos, The elements of intelligence, *Cybernetica (Namur)*, No. 3, 1968.

8. A. Bryson and Y. C. Ho, *Applied Optimal Control*, Ginn and Co., 1969.

9. Y. LeCun, Une procedure d'apprentissage pour reseau a seuil assymetrique, in *Proceedings Cognitiva 1985*, Paris, June 1985.

10. A. Church, *Introduction to Mathematical Logic*, Princeton University Press, Princeton, NJ, 1953.

11. D. Jacobson and D. Mayne, *Differential Dynamic Programming*, American Elsevier, New York, 1970.

12. K. W. Deutsch, *Nationalism and Social Communications*, MIT Press, Cambridge, MA, 1966.

13. K. Deutsch, *The Nerves of Government*, Glencoe Free Press, Westerville, OH, 1966.

14. D. White and D. Sofge (eds.), *Handbook of Intelligent Control: Neural, Fuzzy and Adaptive Approaches*, Van Nostrand, New York, 1992.

15. P. Werbos, Generalization of backpropagation with application to a recurrent gas market model, *Neural Networks*, Vol. 1, pp. 339–356, October 1988 (submitted August 1987).

16. P. Werbos, Advanced forecasting for global crisis warning and models of intelligence, *General Systems Yearbook*, 1977 issue.

17. P. Werbos and J. Titus, An empirical test of new forecasting methods derived from a theory of intelligence: the prediction of conflict in Latin America, *IEEE Transactions SMC*, September 1978.

18. P. Werbos, Changes in global policy analysis procedures suggested by new methods of optimization, *Policy Analysis and Information Systems*, Vol. 3, No. 1, June 1979.

19. P. Werbos, The cytoskeleton: why it may be crucial to human learning and to neurocontrol, *Nanobiology*, Vol. 1, No. 1, 1992. Originally presented as a conference paper in January 1990 at the NATO workshop organized by S. Hameroff.

20. K. Pribram (ed.), *Rethinking Neural Networks: Quantum Fields and Biological Evidence*, International Neural Network Society (with Erlbaum), Washington DC, 1993; see also D. Gardner, Backpropagation and Neuromorphic Plausibility in *WCNN93 Proceedings*, Erlbaum, 1993, and *The Neurobiology of Neural Networks*, MIT Press, 1993.

21. P. Werbos, Learning how the world works: specifications for predictive networks in robots and brains, in *Proceedings of the SMC Conference*, IEEE, New York, 1987.

22. P. Werbos, Neurocontrol and related techniques, in A. Maren (ed.), *Handbook of Neural Computing Applications*, Academic Presss, Orlando, FL, 1990.

23. P. Werbos, Neurocontrol and elastic fuzzy logic: capabilities, concepts and applications, *IEEE Transactions on Industrial Electronics*, April, 1993.

24. P. Werbos, Generalized information requirements of intelligent decision-making systems, in *SUGI 11 Proceedings*, SAS Institute, Cary, NC, 1986. (A revised version, somewhat more readable, is available from the author.)

25. P. Werbos, Rational approaches to identifying policy objectives, *Energy: The International Journal*, March/April 1990. To be reprinted in J. Weyant and T. Kuczmowski (eds.), *Engineering–Economic Modeling Handbook*, Pergamon, Tarrytown, NY, 1993.

26. P. Werbos, Econometric techniques: theory versus practice, *Energy: The International Journal*, March/April 1990. To be reprinted in J. Weyant and T. Kuczmowski (eds.), *Engineering–Economic Modeling Handbook*, Pergamon, Tarrytown, NY, 1993.

27. J. Von Neumann and O. Morgenstern, *The Theory of Games and Economic Behavior*, Princeton University Press, Princeton, NJ, 1953.

28. H. Raiffa, *Decision Analysis: Introductory Lectures on Making Choices Under Uncertainty*, Addison-Wesley, Boston, 1968.

29. L. Baird and E. H. Klopf, Extensions of the associative control process (ACP) network: Heuristics and provable optimality, in *Proceedings of the Second Inter-*

national Conference on Simulation of Adaptive Behavior (Hawaii 1992), MIT Press, Cambridge, MA, 1993. Extensions of this paper and a companion paper by Klopf et al. have been submitted to *Adaptive Behavior*, for publication in 1993.

30. E. O. Wilson, *Sociobiology: The New Synthesis*, Harvard University Press, Boston, 1975.

31. Freeman, *Energy: The New Era*, Anchor Books, Landover Hills, MD, 1974.

32. P. Werbos, Energy and population: transitional issues and eventual limits, in L. Grant (ed.), *Elephants in the Volkswagen: Facing the Tough Questions About Our Overcrowded Country*, Freeman, New York, 1992.

33. A. Gore, *Earth in the Balance: Ecology and the Human Spirit*, Houghton Mifflin, Boston, 1992.

34. P. Werbos, Supervised learning: can it escape its local minimum? In *WCNN-93 Proceedings*, Erlbaum, 1993.

PART 1

THESIS

Beyond Regression

New Tools for Prediction and Analysis In the Behavioral Sciences

PREFACE

The initial impetus for this thesis came from a suggestion by Professor Karl Deutsch, my thesis supervisor, that I look more closely at the prediction of national assimilation and political mobilization, by use of the Deutsch–Solow model; his comments have been of major help to me with all the empirical work on nationalism and in revising the original structures of Chapters 5 and 6. The earlier work reported in Section 6.2 of Chapter 6 was carried out under his supervision and support, through a research project funded by the Cambridge Project. I have been surprised more than once by the sensitivity and receptiveness of his intuition, in suggesting areas of research that looked unworkable at first but that led in the end to useful and surprising innovations. The opinions expressed in Chapter 5, however, remain my own responsibility, particularly in their more bull-headed aspects.

Professor Mosteller, in the Harvard Statistics Department, has helped by introducing me to current work on robust estimation, by suggesting the use of simulation tests, and by monitoring the general content of the first four chapters. Professors Anderson and Bossert, of the Committee on Applied Mathematics, and Professor Dempster, of the Harvard Statistics Department, have helped me to find a more orderly way of presenting the mathematical ideas here—help that was sorely needed in the summer of 1973. I thank the Cambridge Project, and its sponsors at ARPA, not only for all the computer time used in this research and in its documentation, but also for the opportunity to translate some of these ideas from theory into operational systems without the extensive delays more common in such research; without their support, this research could never have been accomplished.

The personal and financial conditions that led to the completion of this thesis were rather complex, and debts are owed to more individuals than should properly be cited here. Certainly I have a strong debt to my parents in this respect; a debt to Richard Ney, whose ideas on the stock market financed a large part of my activity during this period; a moral debt to Professor Nazli Choucri of MIT, who, in a brief discussion in the spring of 1973, encouraged me to continue this work; a debt to a colleague, Gopal Krishna, for helping me see more clearly that the psychological hurdles I faced at first were not totally unique; a debt to Dr. Karreman, of the Bockus Research Institute, who, in one of those 1960s programs to encourage high school students, connected with the Moore School of Electronics at the University of Pennsylvania, got me started asking questions about the phenomenon of intelligence, questions that led me to the dynamic feedback concept, which was applied only later to formal statistics.

SYNOPSIS

This thesis provides a broad, coherent exposition of a new mathematical approach to social studies and to related fields.

This work began as an attempt to apply the classical techniques of statistics and econometrics to the Deutsch–Solow model of nationalism, in order to turn this model into a workable tool for predicting the political future. In the course of this effort, it became clear that the usual statistical methods do a poor job in fitting dynamic models to real-world data, if we judge these models by their ability to make good predictions across time. It also became clear that newer and better methods would not be feasible economically, unless we could also invent less expensive algorithms. Thus the goals of this thesis are fivefold: (1) to describe new ways of fitting models to data; (2) to define new algorithms that make these methods feasible; (3) to introduce evidence for the superiority of these methods, both for real-world and for simulated data; (4) to discuss the applications of these ideas, in broad terms, to social and even biological sciences; and (5) to discuss the new work on nationalism, which has led us in these directions.

Let us begin with the first three goals.

I have studied not one, but two, new approaches to fitting models to data. First, I generalized the work by Box and Jenkins on "ARMA" processes, or "mixed *auto*regressive *moving average*" processes. Chapter 3 discusses the mathematics of this approach in detail. It shows how an ordinary, multivariate autoregressive process, observed by way of "noisy" data (i.e., data measured with random measurement errors or conceptual distortions), becomes a "vector ARMA" process. It then shows how to apply "dynamic feedback" to estimate the coefficients of such processes, at much lower costs than were possible previously; the resulting computer program is now available to the public through the MIT Cambridge Project Consistent System. In Chapter 5, I discuss why this approach is important for quantitative political science.

In studies of simulated data, the ARMA approach generally yielded only half as much error as regression did in estimating the coefficients of a simple model; it was more efficient in making use of limited data and it led to less systematic bias. However, with real-world data, the ARMA approach did little better than regression in making long-term predictions; the error distribution curves for ARMA are only about 10% smaller than those for regression, and the curves are uniformly close to each other.

After reexamining these empirical results and the theory of maximum likelihood itself, I formulated a new, more radical, and more successful approach to the fitting of models. In essence, the idea is to maximize long-term predictive power *directly*, over the known data, instead of maximizing formal likelihood. Formally, this idea rests on the a priori expectation that many social processes are governed by relatively deterministic underlying trends, obscured both by measurement noise and by transient deviations of great complexity. The qualitative, political basis of this idea is discussed in Chapter 5. Sections 2.7 and 2.11 of Chapter 2 discuss the statistical basis.

The "measurement-noise-only" approach strongly outperformed both ARMA and regression, over both real-world and simulated data. It outperformed ARMA most strongly in the most complex simulated processes, which seem most representative of the real world. According to the error distribution graphs, the new method cuts in half the errors in long-term predictions of real-world variables; the biggest reductions occur with those variables, such as national assimilation, and with those cases, near the middle of the distributions, for which the simple models of the first half of Chapter 6 can do an adequate job of prediction.

These empirical results for the new approach came from special computer programs, which exploited the simplicity of the models under study. In Chapter 2, I discuss how the algorithm of "dynamic feedback" can be used to estimate more general "measurement-noise-only" models, at minimal cost, especially for models that are very intricate, nonlinear, and non-Markovian; I also discuss how the algorithm can fit more conventional models, can optimize policy, and can perform "pattern analysis" — a dynamic alternative to factor analysis. "Dynamic feedback" is essentially a technique for calculating derivatives inexpensively, for use with the classic method of steepest descent. In Section 3.4 of Chapter 3, and in Section 6.3 of Chapter 6, I discuss how the experience here with steepest descent has led to new ways of adjusting the "arbitrary convergence weights" of steepest descent; these methods speeded up the process of convergence by a large factor. Section 2.13 discusses extensions of these methods for the general, nonlinear case.

From a practical point of view, the applications of such mathematical ideas in the social sciences remain controversial. The extreme positions of "behaviorism" and "traditionalism" remain popular; divisions still exist between quantitative and verbal studies of social behavior. In Chapter 5, I describe how these new mathematical tools might fit into the broader context of social studies and political decision-making. From a utilitarian and Bayesian point of view, I suggest a methodological approach intermediate between "behaviorism" and "traditionalism," in which the different frameworks might be integrated more closely with each other. In sketching out the possibilities for such an integrated framework, I also point out that the algorithms of Chapter 2, taken as part of "cybernetics," have a direct value as paradigms, to help us understand the requirements of the complex information-processing problems faced by human societies and by human brains. Mention is also made of possible applications to other fields, including ecology.

Finally, Chapter 6 presents some empirical and analytic work on nationalism.

In Sections 6.2 and 6.3, I discuss the success of some long-term predictions of national assimilation and mobilization, by use of the Deutsch–Solow model. Table 6.8, for example, gives the average errors in predicting the *percentage* of population assimilated, over time periods on the order of 30 years; these errors are uniformly distributed between 0% and 2%, except for four outliers (20% of all cases) at 2.68%, 3.08%, 3.09%, and 6.21%. The failures of these predictions are also informative; they give a picture of those external factors that really do have the power to divert the processes of assimilation and mobilization from a steady course. I have tabulated the predictions of the "robust" method for the years 1980, 1990, and 2000; these predictions are subject to caveats discussed in Section 6.3.

In Section 6.4, more complex models of nationalism are synthesized by drawing together ideas from the literature on this topic and ideas from social psychology. The future possibilities of these models, in verbal and quantitative analysis, are sketched out briefly. These models attained high levels of "statistical significance" and led to noticeable improvements in long-term prediction in empirical tests described in Section 6.5; however, these tests, based on classical estimation routines, are regarded as preliminary. The communications concepts of Section 6.4, as applied in Section 6.5, also yielded an explanation of one of the inconsistencies observed with "gravity models" in previous research; this explanation was validated empirically.

The MIT Cambridge Project has begun implementing the algorithms of Chapter 2.

1

General Introduction
and Summary

The original purpose of this research was to apply the classical techniques of statistics and econometrics to the Deutsch–Solow model of nationalism, in order to turn this model into a workable tool for predicting the political future. In the course of this research, it became clearer and clearer that the usual statistical methods do a poor job in fitting dynamic models to real-world data, if we judge these models by their ability to make good predictions across times. Furthermore, it became clear that newer and better methods would not be feasible, economically, unless we could also develop new, less expensive algorithms. Thus the goals of this thesis are fivefold: (1) to describe new ways of fitting models to data; (2) to define the new algorithms that make these methods feasible; (3) to introduce evidence for the superiority of the methods (see Table 4.1 and Figures 6.1–6.4); (4) to discuss the applications of these ideas, in broad terms, to social and even biological sciences; and (5) to discuss the new empirical work on nationalism, which has led us in these directions.

Let me begin by discussing the first three goals.

Strictly speaking, I have studied not one, but two, new approaches to fitting models to data in political science. The first approach was essentially an extension of work by Box and Jenkins on ARMA processes, or mixed *auto*regressive *moving-average* processes. Chapter 3 discusses the mathematical statistics of this approach in detail. It begins by pointing out that an ordinary, multivariate autoregressive process, observed by way of data that were not measured perfectly accurately (i.e., measured with random measurement errors or conceptual distortions), turns into a "vector mixed autoregressive moving average process." It then proceeds to show how the algorithm of "dynamic feedback," discussed in Chapter 2, can be applied to estimate the coefficients of such a process at a lower cost than was possible with previous methods; the resulting procedure has been tested and made available to the general user as part of the MIT Cambridge Project Consistent System. In Chapter 5, I discuss why this approach seemed important in quantitative political science.

In studies of simulated data, this approach did quite a bit better than the best form of regression. In Table 4.1, one can see that the average estimates ("av") produced by "arma," for the coefficients of a simple model, were much closer to the true values than were those of "reg" in the 12 cases studied; this implies much less systematic bias. Also, the dispersion of the "arma" estimates was about half as much as that of "reg" on the whole; this implies less random error in estimation or, in other words, greater practical efficiency in making use of limited data. However, in studies of real-world data, the long-term predictions by this method were only slightly better than those by regression; for example, in Figures 6.1-6.4, one can see that the error distribution curve for ARMA is only about 10% smaller in area than that for regression, and that the curves are uniformly close to each other.

After reexamining the empirical results of this research, and the concepts of maximum likelihood themselves, I arrived at a new, more radical, and more successful approach to the fitting of models. In essence, the idea is to maximize long-term predictive power *directly*, over the known data set, instead of maximizing formal likelihood. Formally, this idea rests on the a priori expectation that many social processes are governed by relatively deterministic underlying trends, obscured both my measurement noise and by transient deviations of a very complex sort. The qualitative, political basis of this idea is discussed in Chapter 5. The statistical basis is discussed in Sections 2.7 and 2.11 of Chapter 2.

The "measurement-noise-only" approach performed much better than both ARMA and regression, on both real-world and simulated data. In Table 4.1, "ext" is markedly superior to "arma" in estimating coefficients; in the text of Chapter 4, I note that this superiority is greatest for the simulated data generated by the more complex processes (11 and 12), processes that may be more representative of the real world. In Figures 6.1-6.4, the measurement-noise-only approach, described as the "robust" approach, had much lower distributions of error than ARMA or regression did in long-term prediction. If one allows for the spread of the vertical axis in these graphs, one can see that the robust method cuts the long-term prediction errors roughly in half; the biggest reductions occur with those variables, such as national assimilation, and with those cases, near the middle of the distributions, for which the simple models of the first half of Chapter 6 can do an adequate job of prediction.

The empirical results for the robust method were all based on special computer programs, designed to take advantage of the simplicity of the models under study. In Chapter 2, I discuss how the general algorithm of "dynamic feedback" can be used to estimate such measurement-noise-only models, at a minimal cost, especially for models that may be very intricate, nonlinear, and non-Markovian; I also discuss how the algorithm can be used to fit more conventional models, to optimize policy, and to perform "pattern analysis" — a dynamic alternative to factor analysis. The technique of dynamic feedback is essentially a technique for calculating derivatives inexpensively, to be used with the classic method of steepest descent. In Section 3.4 of Chapter 3, and in Section 6.3 of Chapter 6, I point out how practical experience with steepest descent in this context has led to new ways of adjusting the "arbitrary convergence weights" of steepest descent; these methods appear to have the power, in normal, practical situations, to speed up the process of convergence by a large factor. In Section 2.13, I mention a few generalizations of these methods, which may be helpful in the general, nonlinear case.

From a practical point of view, the applications of these and other mathematical approaches in the social sciences remain a subject of dispute. The extreme positions of "behaviorism" and "traditionalism" remain popular; a division still tends to exist between quantitative and verbal studies of social behavior. In Chapter 5, I describe how these new mathematical tools might fit into the broader context of social studies and political decision-making. From a utilitarian and Bayesian point of view, I suggest a methodological approach intermediate between "behaviorism" and "traditionalism," in which the different frameworks might be integrated more closely with each other. In sketching out what such an integrated framework might look like, I also point out that the algorithms of Chapter 2, taken as part of "cybernetics," may have some direct value as paradigms, to help us try to understand the requirements of the complex information-processing problems faced by human societies and by human brains. I also discuss the possibility of applying these approaches to other fields, such as ecology.

Finally, in Chapter 6, a few substantive conclusions emerge from the empirical and analytic work on nationalism. The relative success of the long-term prediction of national assimilation and mobilization, as shown in Tables 6.8 and 6.9, is some substantive interest; note, for example, that in predicting the *percentage* of population assimilated, over periods of time on the order of 30–40 years, the errors are uniformly distributed between 0% and 2%, except for four outliers (20% of all cases) at 2.68%, 3.08%, 3.09%, and 6.21%. The exact sources of weakness in these predictions are also of interest, insofar as they give a picture of those external factors that really do have the power to divert the processes of assimilation and mobilization from a steady course. In Tables 6.21 and 6.22, predictions are given for the robust method for the years 1980, 1990, and 2000; these predictions are subject to caveats discussed in Section 6.3. In Sections 6.2 and 6.3, all predictions are based on the Deutsch–Solow model, with minor modifications.

In Section 6.4, more complex models of national assimilation and mobilization are synthesized by drawing together ideas from the literature on this topic and ideas from social psychology. The future possibilities of these models, in verbal and quantitative analysis, are sketched out briefly. In Section 6.5, a preliminary test of the models is described. The main methodological conclusion of Chapter 6 is that the available tools for time-series analysis cannot cope adequately with the level of complexity represented by such models; however, in the preliminary tests, the models attained a high level of "statistical significance" and did have a noticeable value in improving long-term prediction. The communications concepts of Section 6.4, as applied in Section

6.5, also suggested a rational explanation of one of the inconsistencies observed with "gravity models" in previous research; this explanation was validated empirically.

In concluding this introduction, it would seem appropriate to describe what might come out of this work in the future. However, these possibilities are discussed in enough detail in each of the separate chapters. Still, it should be of general interest that the programming of the general algorithm of Chapter 2 is already underway at MIT, as part of the large-scale DATATRAN project on Multics, and is scheduled to be available to the social scientist in 1974.

2

Dynamic Feedback, Statistical Estimation, and Systems Optimization

General Techniques

2.1 INTRODUCTION

In recent years, social scientists and ecologists have become interested more and more in the use of mathematical models to describe the dynamic laws of the systems they study. Karl Deutsch and Robert Solow, for example, have proposed [1] the following model to predict the size of the assimilated population, A, and the unassimilated population, U, in a bilingual or bicultural society:

$$\frac{dA}{dt} = aA + bU,$$

$$\frac{dU}{dt} = cU, \tag{2.1}$$

where a, b, and c may be treated as constants, at least for medium lengths of time. The constant b represents the rate of assimilation, as a fraction of the people yet to be assimilated, per unit of time; a and c represent the natural growth rates of the assimilated and unassimilated populations, respectively. (See Section 2.14.1 for complete citations.)

Mathematical models may serve two general purposes in the social sciences. On the one hand, they may be used as a tool in verbal reasoning, as a technique for formulating one's assumptions and their consequences very clearly and very coherently; they may be used to construct paradigms, which, like meta-

29

phors, may be very useful but which are not meant to be taken literally. The "prisoner's dilemma" paradigm is a good example of such a model. (See Section 2.14.2.)

On the other hand, mathematical models may be used to make actual predictions of variables that can actually be measured; economists, for example, have long been in the business of predicting the GNP, as a number, from the use of equations originated by Keynes and Samuelson. These equations offer *different predictions* for the GNP, depending on one's assumptions about government spending and tax rates; thus they can be used not merely in prediction but in helping the government to choose a policy for spending and taxation, so as to maximize the real GNP. (Even the most elementary models used in economics tend to be used to generate tangible numerical prediction; for example, see Samuelson [2, Chapters 11–13]. More explicit predictive models may be found in Hickman [3].)

The major concern in this thesis is with the second type of model—predictive models, like the Deutsch–Solow model above. Given such a model, the social scientist would want to ask three questions: (1) How likely is it that the model is true empirically? (2) How can we measure the values of the constants in the model? (3) If the model is true, but if certain policy-makers could change some of the constants or even control some of the variables directly, what should they do in order to get the "best" results? The first two questions concern the problem of estimation, the core of classical statistics. The third question falls roughly into the area now called "control theory." All three questions can be answered by use of existing methods, but *only* for certain restricted classes of models. The main objective in this chapter is to present a more general method, to allow one to answer these questions for any explicit model, of any complexity, at a minimal cost in terms of computer time. More precisely, if a user specifics a model in terms of equations built up out of elementary operations and functions, known to a standard computer package, then my method could give this computer package the power to answer the three questions above, at a minimal cost. As more data become available in the social sciences and in ecology, and as models are developed that reflect the true complexity of the social systems themselves, the need for such a general method may grow greater and greater.

In this chapter, I plan to explain the dynamic feedback method, by building up examples of its most important applications; these examples will grow in complexity until, in Section 2.12, the general algorithm is presented explicitly. Thus in Section 2.3, I show how to reduce the cost of conventional nonlinear estimation. In Section 2.4, I show how the dynamic feedback method can cope with simple models with "memory"; even simple models of this type are difficult to handle by other methods. In Sections 2.5–2.7, I discuss the basic problem of induction, as seen by the statistician. This material prepares the reader for the discussion of more advanced applications in later sections and also in Chapter 3. In particular, in Section 2.7, I propose a new "robust" approach to estimation, which, *even for simple models*, calls for the use of the dynamic feedback method; later, in Section 2.11, I specify exactly which "models with memory" are used in this approach, and in Chapters 4–6 I discuss the evidence that this approach is worthwhile. In Section 2.8, I discuss the problem of estimation with complex noise models. In Section 2.9, I develop a radically new concept, "pattern analysis," for dealing with situations where the nonlinearities and complexities of a process defy the use of straightforward estimation; the application of this concept would include problems now dealt with by factor analysis or by pattern recognition techniques. Once a person has finished estimating a model, he/she may then wish to go on to use this model in formulating policy; in Section 2.10, I show how the dynamic feedback method can be used at that stage too to help one maximize the utility function of one's choice. Finally, in Section 2.13, I mention a few technical procedures, which can help speed up the convergence of a computer routine based on the dynamic feedback method.

2.2 ORDINARY REGRESSION

Let us begin by discussing the first two questions listed in Section 2.1, from the viewpoint of classical maximum likelihood theory.

How would we ascertain the "truth" of a model like the Deutsch–Solow model, Equations (2.1), if we were given the values of A and U every year for some nation, from 1901 to 1973? If we were given the values of the constants a, b, and c, then we could simply solve these equations, starting from the known values of A and U in 1901. In order to avoid having to solve a differential equation, we could rewrite the model in a simpler, but equivalent, form:

$$A(t + 1) = k_1 A(t) + k_2 U(t),$$

$$U(t + 1) = k_3 U(t), \tag{2.2}$$

where $U(t)$ means the value of U in the year t, and where k_1, k_2, and k_3 are all constants. In either case, we could predict A and U for 1902 through 1973, by starting from our knowledge of A and U in 1901 and using our model. We could compare the predictions of the model against the observed data. And we would discover that Equations (2.2) are simply false, as written; there would always be some difference between our predictions and the data, while Equations (2.2) do not allow for any such error. Equations (2.2) are completely deterministic. This complaint may seem like quibbling, but it is central to the classic concepts of statistics. In practice, admittedly, one may be more interested in the *predictive power* of a simplified model, rather than its formal statistical truth; however, in Section 2.7, I discuss this possibility as an extension of the more classical approach discussed here. At any rate, to construct a model that has some hope of being "true" in the social sciences, we need to express the idea that there will be a certain amount of unpredictable random noise in the system we are studying. Thus we might rewrite Equations (2.2) to obtain

$$A(t + 1) = k_1 A(t) + k_2 U(t) + b(t), \qquad (2.3a)$$

$$U(t + 1) = k_3 U(t) + c(t), \qquad (2.3b)$$

where $b(t)$ and $c(t)$ are random error terms, obeying

$$p(b) = \frac{1}{\sqrt{2\pi} B} e^{-(b/B)^2/2},$$

$$p(c) = \frac{1}{\sqrt{2\pi} C} e^{-(c/C)^2/2}. \qquad (2.4)$$

In other words, we do not know what $b(t)$ and $c(t)$ will be in advance; the probability that $b(t)$ will equal some particular value, b, is given by $p(b)$ in the formula. Strictly speaking, since b is a continuous variable, $p(b)$ is actually a probability *density* function; one may think of it as the probability that $b(t)$ lies between b and a nearby point, $b + db$, *divided* by the size of the interval, db.[1] These functions for the probability of b and c are simply the classic bell-shaped curve, or "normal distribution." The constants in front of the e ensure that the probabilities of the different values for b add up to 1, when the formula is integrated. The constants B and C, like the constants k_1, k_2, and k_3, need to be specified before the model is complete.

According to this elementary model, the probability of b (or c) is highest when b (or c) is zero; in other words, it is highest when the exponent is zero, instead of a negative number. When b gets to be a large number, positive or negative, in *proportion* to B, the exponent gets to be a large negative number, and the probability falls off very quickly. It should be emphasized that this simple model of noise, while standard, is far from the only possibility in this case; in Section 2.7, I mention a few other possibilities.

Once we have decided to formulate such a simple model, at least to start with, classical statistics can tell us exactly how to measure its "likelihood of truth" for any combination of the constants k_1, k_2, and k_3. In Sections 2.5 and 2.6, I discuss in more detail how it is possible for some statisticians to arrive at such strong statements; for the moment, however, I will relegate the theoretical abstractions to an end note (Section 2.14.3). Even on a very concrete level, one can get a feeling for the power of the classical approach.

---

[1] From a strict mathematical point of view, these "density functions" are actually "measures" or "distributions" rather than functions. Thus the notation db and dc should have followed Equations (2.4), for total rigor. Historically, this issue has not turned out to be of major importance; see the discussion at the end of Section 2.5, and the more rigorous discussion in Box and Jenkins [12, pp. 274–283].

Looking back at Equations (2.3), we may define

$$\hat{A}(t + 1) = k_1 A(t) + k_2 U(t)$$

and

$$\hat{U}(t + 1) = k_3 U(t).$$

$\hat{A}(t + 1)$ is simply the best prediction one could make for $A(t + 1)$, at time t, given our knowledge of $A(t)$ and $U(t)$ and given our model. From Equations (2.3) we get

$$b(t) = A(t + 1) - \hat{A}(t + 1),$$

$$c(t) = U(t + 1) - \hat{U}(t + 1). \tag{2.5}$$

Intuitively, one would expect that a model that gives us "good' predictions, $\hat{A}$, would be likelier to be true than a model that gives us "bad" predictions; one would expect that bigger errors, b and c, would imply a lower probability that the model is true. Indeed, when we look back at Equations (2.4), the only probability functions we have with this model, we can see that larger values of b and c would imply a lower probability. More exactly, as we look at these equations, we can see that the probabilities of these errors really depend on $(b/B)^2$ and $(e/C)^2$—that is, the size of the *square* of the error. As part of our model, we assume that the errors at different times are all independent of each other. Thus in order to combine all the different probabilities for different times, t, into one overall probability, it is legitimate to multiply them all together; this has the effect of telling us to add up all the exponents, the square error terms, $(b/B)^2$ and $(c/C)^2$, to get an overall measure of the probability of the model. Therefore we can measure the total effective size of the errors in Equation (2.3a) by

$$L_1 = \sum_t \left(\frac{b(t)}{B}\right)^2 = \frac{1}{B^2} \sum_t [b(t)]^2.$$

In order to pick the best value of k_1 and k_2, in our model, we do not have to account for the other part of the error, the c^2 term, since our choice of k_1 and k_2 does not affect Equation (2.3b). Indeed, to pick the best values of k_1 and k_2, in Equation (2.3a), we do not even have to worry about the value of B, since B does not appear in that equation; thus we can simply try to minimize

$$L = \sum_t [b(t)]^2. \tag{2.6}$$

Similarly, in Equation (2.3b), we can pick k_3 by minimizing the analogous function:

$$L' = \sum_t [c(t)]^2.$$

Note that we now seem to have two *separate* measures of truth, for (2.3a) and (2.3b) treated as independent equations. Formally speaking, we have found that the maximization of likelihood for the composite model, Equations (2.3) and (2.4), can be decomposed into the maximization of likelihood for (2.3a) and (2.3b) as separate equations, attached to the top and bottom equations of (2.4), respectively. This decomposition is due to the simplicity of the original model; it would *not* be valid for many more complex models. In Section 2.6, I will present more details of this decomposition with ordinary regression; in Chapter 3, however, the focus is on a class of standard statistical models, the "vector ARMA" models, for which such a decomposition is impossible, and for which an equation-by-equation estimation procedure cannot have statistical consistency.

Even in the simple case here, however, we have yet to specify how to pick k_1 and k_2 to minimize L in Equation (2.6). Let us begin by substituting into Equation (2.6) the value of $b(t)$ from Equation (2.3a):

$$L = \sum_t [A(t + 1) - k_1 A(t) - k_2 U(t)]^2. \tag{2.7}$$

Our problem, again, is to minimize L as a function of k_1 and k_2, while treating the measured data series, $A(t)$ and $U(t)$, as fixed. From basic calculus, we know that a function has its minimum, for variables k_1 and k_2, only at a point where its derivatives with respect to k_1 and k_2 both equal zero. In other words, if the derivative of L with respect to k_1 were *not* zero, but, say, $+10$, this means that L will change whenever we change k_1, and that the change in L will equal 10 times the change in k_1, roughly, for small changes in k_1; thus if we change k_1 by $-\frac{1}{100}$, then L would change by about $-\frac{1}{10}$, proving that it hadn't yet reached a minimum at our original choice of k_1 and k_2. Thus we can try to find values for k_1 and k_2 such that the derivatives of L with respect to both of these parameters will equal zero.

Differentiating, we get

$$\frac{\partial L}{\partial k_1} = \sum_t \frac{\partial}{\partial k_1} [A(t + 1) - k_1 A(t) - k_2 U(t)]^2$$

$$= \sum_t 2[A(t + 1) - k_1 A(t) - k_2 U(t)] \frac{\partial}{\partial k_1} [A(t + 1) - k_1 A(t) - k_2 U(t)]$$

$$= \sum_t 2[A(t + 1) - k_1 A(t) - k_2 U(t)] [-A(t)]$$

$$= -2 \left(\sum_t \{A(t + 1)A(t) - k_1 [A(t)]^2 - k_2 U(t)A(t)\} \right),$$

which we will try to set to zero. And we get a similar expression for $\partial L/\partial k_2$. Putting them together, we get two algebraic equations:

$$\sum_t A(t + 1)A(t) = k_1 \sum_t [A(t)]^2 + k_2 \sum_t U(t)A(t)$$

and

$$\sum_t A(t + 1)U(t) = k_1 \sum_t U(t)A(t) + k_2 \sum_t [U(t)]^2.$$

We can calculate these sums by looking at our data; we can solve these simple simultaneous equations for the variables k_1 and k_2 exactly, by classical algebra, or by using programs available on any computer. The procedure above is the procedure of classic multiple regression.

All this reasoning, however, supposes that we decide to look at a very simple model, like Equation (2.3a). It also assumes that the "errors," b and c, follow a normal distribution. There is nothing to stop us from using the same calculating procedure in cases where we do not expect the noise to be normal; from a classical point of view, this may still be equivalent to accepting the normal distribution as part of one's "simplified model," but the effects of such a "simplification" are far from obvious a priori.

Once again, this discussion has been based on the maximum likelihood point of view, which will be called into question in Section 2.7. For those who are concerned with predictive power, and not with the likelihood of truth as such, the success of various noise models depends less on their "truth" in the process at hand and more on the robustness of the associated estimation procedure; thus one may choose to regard the regression procedure described above as an independent algorithm, which can be derived from maximum likelihood theory but which is still a distinct object able to stand alone. From this point of view, then, the methods above do not *require* an assumption of a normal distribution.

What happens, however, if we move on to consider a more complex model? What would happen if we decided to change Equation (2.3a) itself? For example, in Equation (2.3a), we assume that the rate of assimilation, k_2, is constant in any given country. In reality, we know that this is unreasonable. If the "unassimilated" outnumber the "assimilated" by a large majority, they may feel very little pressure at all to assimilate; on the other hand, if they are a tiny isolated group, dependent on an economic world that is mostly "assimilated," then their rate of assimilation is likely to be higher than it otherwise would be. There are other factors involved, but, holding those factors constant, our model is likely to be "truer" and better if it accounts somehow for the power of percentage dominance.

How could we revise Equation (2.3a) to express this kind of effect? First, we need to find some kind of measure of "percentage dominance." The simplest and most obvious measure is the difference between the percentage of the population that is assimilated and the percentage of the population that is unassimilated. In order to avoid having to multiply everything by 100, let us look instead at the difference between the fraction that is assimilated and the fraction that is not. The fraction of the population assimilated equals, by definition, the ratio between the number of people assimilated, $A(t)$, and the total number of people, $A(t) + U(t)$; thus it equals $A(t)/[A(t) + U(t)]$. The fraction unassimilated equals $U(t)/[A(t) + U(t)]$; the difference between the two equals $[A(t)$

$- U(t)]/[A(t) + U(t)]$. Somehow, we wish to express the idea that an unassimilated person is more likely to assimilate if the "percentage dominance" of the assimilated population is larger. If we recall that k_2 was defined as the rate of assimilation per unassimilated population per unit of time, we may simply postulate that k_2, instead of being constant, will be larger if "percentage dominance," as defined above, is larger. For simplicity, we may consider the idea that k_2 is directly proportional to percentage dominance:

$$k_2(t) = k_2' \frac{A(t) - U(t)}{A(t) + U(t)}. \tag{2.8}$$

This time, k_2' is assumed to be constant. While the actual relation between k_2 and percentage dominance is not likely to be quite this simple, this equation still gives us some expression of the important qualitative idea that there is a strong and consistent positive connection between the two. To generate an *explicit* model of assimilation, we may substitute this equation back into (2.3a):

$$A(t + 1) = k_1 A(t) + k_2' \left(\frac{A(t) - U(t)}{A(t) + U(t)} \right) U(t) + b(t). \tag{2.9}$$

The second term on the right is an "interaction term," nonlinear in A and U. A great deal of fuss has been made about this kind of nonlinearity, with terminology such as "curvilinear regression," "polynomial regression," and even "spectral regression" often used [4, Chapter 6]. However, this kind of situation can be dealt with fairly easily. We can solve for $b(t)$, as before, to obtain

$$L = \sum_t \left[A(t + 1) - k_1 A(t) - k_2' \left(\frac{A(t) - U(t)}{A(t) + U(t)} \right) U(t) \right]^2. \tag{2.10}$$

As a function of k_1 and k_2', this is really the same kind of expression as Equation (2.7), with $U(t)$ replaced by a more complicated expression, which we might call $U'(t)$:

$$U'(t) = \frac{A(t) - U(t)}{A(t) + U(t)} U(t).$$

The derivatives with respect to k_1 and k_2 are the same, with a few "prime" signs interjected, and we wind up with the same algebraic equations to solve and almost the same sums to calculate. (We have to sum up $[U'(t)]^2$ and $U'(t)A(t)$ instead of $U(t)^2$ and $U(t)A(t)$.) In practice, one would normally begin by calculating the variable U' from one's existing data, and injecting it into a standard regression package to calculate the sums and solve the equations; in a computer package such as TSP, one could compute U' from one's previous data by use of the command GENR (generate), and issue a regression command (OLSQ) with U' and A as independent variables. What is essential in this example is that we continue to express $A(t + 1)$ as a linear combination of other variables, which are defined as specific functions of the available data.

2.3 NONLINEAR REGRESSION AND DYNAMIC FEEDBACK

However, if we want to move on to more interesting models of social phenomena, we will often find that we have to estimate constants that do not simply multiply an expression we already know how to calculate, like $U'(t)$; we will find that there are constants on the "inside" of the model. For example, in Equation (2.8) we said that k_2 is directly proportional to the dominance of A over U as a fraction of the total population. How do we know that it is a matter of direct proportionality? k_2 is the rate of assimilation, per unassimilated person per unit of time, as originally defined in Equation (2.3). In Equation (2.8), if U is 25% of the population, then $(A - U)/(A + U)$ will equal $\frac{1}{2}$; if U is almost 0, then $(A - U)/(A + U)$ will equal 1. Thus we assume that the rate of assimilation will always be twice as much in the latter case, as compared with the former case. But how do we know it is only twice as much? It might be four times as much. After all, the pressures on a tiny community, near 0%, may be much, much larger than on a community near 25%, which may be large enough to protect its own members, and to give them economic opportunities almost as great as they would find after assimilation. So instead of $(A - U)/(A + U)$, we might have written $[(A - U)/(A + U)]^2$ or $[(A - U)/(A + U)]^3$. Even without considering more complicated possibilities, it would be interesting to try to measure just how strong these effects are that we have been talking about. We may write

$$k_2(t) = k_2' \left(\frac{A(t) - U(t)}{A(t) + U(t)} \right)^{k_4},$$

where k_4, like k_2', is a constant that we would like to estimate. To turn this into an explicit model of assimilation, we substitute into Equation (2.3a):

$$A(t + 1) = k_1 A(t) + k_2' \left(\frac{A(t) - U(t)}{A(t) + U(t)} \right)^{k_4} U(t) + b(t). \qquad (2.11)$$

We can solve for $b(t)$ to get

$$L = \sum_t [b(t)]^2$$

$$= \sum_t \left[A(t + 1) - k_1 A(t) - k_2' \left(\frac{A(t) - U(t)}{A(t) + U(t)} \right)^{k_4} U(t) \right]^2. \qquad (2.12)$$

When we differentiate L and try to set the derivatives to zero, as before, we find a very unpleasant set of equations emerging:

$$A(t)A(t + 1) = k_1 \sum_t [A(t)]^2 + k_2' \sum_t A(t) \left(\frac{A(t) - U(t)}{A(t) + U(t)}\right)^{k_4} U(t),$$

$$U(t)A(t + 1) = k_1 \sum_t A(t)U(t) \left(\frac{A(t) - U(t)}{A(t) + U(t)}\right)^{k_4}$$

$$+ k_2 \sum_t \left[U(t) \left(\frac{A(t) - U(t)}{A(t) + U(t)}\right)^{k_4}\right]^2,$$

$$0 = \sum_t \left\{2\left[A(t + 1) - k_1 A(t) - k_2' \left(\frac{A(t) - U(t)}{A(t) + U(t)}\right)^{k_4} U(t)\right]\right.$$

$$* \left.\left[k_2' U(t) \left(\frac{A(t) - U(t)}{A(t) + U(t)}\right)^{k_4} \log \left(\frac{A(t) - U(t)}{A(t) + U(t)}\right)\right]\right\}.$$

(Note that we use the asterisk to indicate multiplication, as in FORTRAN.) To solve these three equations as functions of k_1, k_2', and k_4 is not only a difficult exercise in algebra, but it would appear to be impossible. There are many equations in algebra for which there simply exist no "closed" solutions—that is, no solutions that can be expressed in terms of the ordinary "vocabulary" of mathematics [5, p. viii]. Thus in order to devise computer routines to handle this contingency, we must use routines that give numerical *approximations* to the constants k_1, k_2', and k_4; we must estimate k_1, k_2', and k_4 by a numerical technique of successive approximations, rather than an exact solution. This is the classic problem of "nonlinear estimation." A similar problem can even arise when dealing with more sophisticated linear models.

There are two well-known methods for dealing with the problem of nonlinear regression. The simplest, and perhaps the best,[2] is the method of "steepest descent." [6, pp. 161–162]. When we try to maximize L, as a function of k_1, k_2', and k_4, we may not be able to solve for

$$\frac{\partial L}{\partial k_1} = 0, \quad \frac{\partial L}{\partial k_2'} = 0, \quad \text{and} \quad \frac{\partial L}{\partial k_4} = 0.$$

However, if we start off with reasonable guesses for all the constants k_1, k_2', and k_4, then we can *differentiate* Equation (2.12), plug in our guesses, and see

[2]Alternative techniques exist, but those listed by Wasan are second-order: they require the calculation of second derivatives, which are more numerous than first derivatives and may be expensive to calculate. The Marquadt algorithm, the better-known alternative, assumes that the likelihood function is quadratic, an assumption not made in this thesis. Also, it incurs heavy costs in other ways. Section 2.13 proposes a procedure for handling the convergence difficulties cited by Wasan, for variations on the theme of steepest descent; for multivariate ARMA(1, 1) estimation, at least, convergence times have been reasonable.

if the derivatives happen to equal zero; if so, chances are good that we have guessed the best values. (With classic regression, when we had two simple equations in two unknowns, k_1 and k_2, there would only be one solution in the usual case, and there would always be a minimum for L; therefore we could be fairly certain that the derivatives were zero only at the minimum. With very complex formulas, we simply have no way of being sure about this.) If the derivatives are not zero, then we can guess new values for our constants, values that will make L smaller. If $\partial L/\partial k_1$ is positive, then we can decrease L by decreasing k_1; if $\partial L/\partial k_1$ is negative, then we can decrease L by *increasing* k_1. If $\partial L/\partial k_1$ is close to zero, then k_1 is probably close to its best value; if $\partial L/\partial k_1$ is far away from zero, then k_1 is probably further off. Thus we can create a new guess, $k_1(n + 1)$, better than the old guess, $k_1(n)$, by changing k_1 in *proportion* to $\partial L/\partial k_1$, but in the *opposite* direction:

$$k_1(n + 1) = k_1(n) - C\,\frac{\partial L}{\partial k_1},$$

where C is some positive constant, and where we calculate the derivative by using our *old* guesses, $k_1(n)$, $k_2'(n)$, and $k_4(n)$. We also calculate the derivatives and then the new guesses for k_2' and k_4 also. Once we have our new guesses for k_1, k_2', and k_4, we can go back to Equation (2.12), to see if we really have gotten a smaller value for L. If we have, then we can start again from our new guesses, to check the derivatives, and so on. If *not*, then C must be too large. If C is small enough, the definition of the derivative assures us that L can be predicted as well as we like by looking at just the first derivative; therefore for *some* C small enough, we know that our new guesses will have a smaller L than our old guesses. If we find ourselves making C smaller and smaller, from guess to guess, then we may eventually quit, when C is so small that we aren't changing the constants very much. Hopefully, this will mean that our approximations are very close to the ideal values. In Section 2.13 a few ways to speed up the convergence of this classical technique are suggested.

As we look back at Equation (2.12), it is clear that the biggest problem is in actually doing all this work: we have to calculate the derivatives of a very complicated looking expression, L, and we have to calculate the exact numerical values of these derivatives for many different values of the constants k_1, k_2', and k_4. Even worse, in most cases there is the question of who the "we" is who will do all the work. Classical regression can be done automatically for the social scientist, at a low cost, by a computer program; the social scientist need only load in his/her data and specify the choice of variables. Who is to do the differentiating here? The social scientist? In BMD, one of the biggest computer packages for use in social science and biology, there is only one "nonlinear regression" routine, added into the X-Supplement [7, p. 177]; this routine requires the social scientist to write his/her own FORTRAN programs *both* for the function $A(t + 1)$ *and* for all its derivatives. It is reasonable to ask a social scientist to understand the logic behind a formula like (2.11); it seems rather unreasonable to ask him/her to carry out elaborate differentiations and write and debug his/her own FORTRAN programs, for every such model being investigated. Also, this approach could become expensive in terms of computer time, depending on the user's ability to devise low-cost ways of calculating the derivatives. There is a second possibility: the user could be asked to specify a FORTRAN program to calculate $A(t + 1)$, as a function of $A(t)$, $U(t)$, k_1, k_2', and k_4; the program would then go on to calculate the derivatives numerically, by changing k_1 a little bit, and seeing what happens to $A(t + 1)$. At each time, for *each* constant, the computer would have to carry out calculations as expensive as calculating $A(t + 1)$; with many constants, this could multiply the cost many-fold. Besides BMD, in the two nonlinear regression routines easily available in Cambridge—TSP-CSP [8] and TROLL/1 [9]—the social scientist has a more convenient way to get the work done. In these two systems, the scientist need only specify the model in terms of a "formula," such as

$$A(t + 1) = k1 * A(t) + k2 * U(t) * (((A(t) - U(t))/(A(t) + U(t))) ** k4).$$

This is the same as Equation (2.11), but with FORTRAN conventions used to make it possible to put everything on one line, and with error terms left implicit. (Single asterisk means multiplication, double means raising to a power.) This formula then gets translated by the computer into a list of simple expressions. This list of expressions would normally look something like Table 2.1, with the explanation column on the left removed; such a list is called a "Polish string." The categories of operation allowed on such a list depend on the arbitrary choices of the systems programmers. In some systems, there are function names reserved for user-supplied FORTRAN subroutines; in other systems, there are functions corresponding to model neurons, for use in statistical pattern recognition, et cetera. It is already possible for a computer to calculate the symbolic derivatives of a formula by manipulating formulas that have been broken down like this; however, that process becomes quite expensive, if we have many parameters to differentiate against.

The easiest way to calculate these derivatives is by a simple use of dynamic feedback. Now we know that

$$L = \sum_t [b(t)]^2$$

and

$$\frac{\partial L}{\partial k_1} = \sum_t \frac{\partial}{\partial k_1} ([b(t)]^2).$$

To calculate $\partial L/\partial k_1$, we need only calculate $(\partial/\partial k_1) ([b(t)]^2)$ for *each* time, and add up these derivatives over time. We want to know the effect on the error, $[b(t)]^2$, of *changing*, say, k_1, while we keep our data (i.e., $A(t)$, $A(t + 1)$, $U(t)$) constant, and while we keep the other parameters (k_2', k_4) constant.

TABLE 2.1 Table of Operations for Equation (2.11)

Actual Variable	Variable Number (Address)	Category	Major Source	Minor Source
$A(t + 1)$	13	Sum	12	11
$k_1 A(t)$	12	Product	3	1
$k_2' U(t) \left(\dfrac{A(t) - U(t)}{A(t) + U(t)} \right)^{k_4}$	11	Product	10	4
$U(t) \left(\dfrac{A(t) - U(t)}{A(t) + U(t)} \right)^{k_4}$	10	Product	9	2
$\left(\dfrac{A(t) - U(t)}{A(t) + U(t)} \right)^{k_4}$	9	Power	8	5
$\dfrac{A(t) - U(t)}{A(t) + U(t)}$	8	Ratio	7	6
$A(t) - U(t)$	7	Difference	1	2
$A(t) + U(t)$	6	Sum	1	2
k_4	5	Parameter	—	—
k_2	4	Parameter	—	—
k_1	3	Parameter	—	—
$U(t)$	2	Given	—	—
$A(t)$	1	Given	—	—

In Table 2.1, let us define the "ordered derivative" of $[b(t)]^2$ with respect to variable number i to be the change we get in $[b(t)]^2$ in proportion to the change in variable i, *when we hold all the previous variables constant*. For $(\partial/\partial k_1)$ $[b(t)]^2$, this definition doesn't give us anything new; the ordered derivative, $(\partial^+/\partial k_1) [b(t)]^2$, is the same as the ordinary partial derivative, $(\partial/\partial k_1) [b(t)]^2$. But for the other variables, it gives us something new to calculate.

Now suppose we want to know the total effect on $[b(t)]^2$ of *changing* variable #7 by a small amount. Changing variable #7 will have a direct effect on only *one* variable, later in the system—variable #8. (See Table 2.1). Thus if

$$X_7' = X_7 + d,$$

where d is a small number, X_7 is variable #7, and X' is the value after our changes, we will produce the following direct effect on later variables:

$$X_8' = \frac{X_7'}{X_6'} = \frac{X_7 + d}{X_6} = X_8 + \frac{d}{X_6} \quad (X_6 \text{ held constant}).$$

If we are calculating backward from the top of the table, we already know $(\partial^+ / \partial X_8) ([b(t)]^2)$: we already know the ratio between $[b(t)']^2 - [b(t)]^2$ and $X_8' - X_8$. Let us call that ratio, or derivative, S_8. Thus we know, for small values of g, that if $X_8' = X_8 + g$, then $b'^2 = b^2 + S_8 g$. Now we just found out, for small d, that if $X_7' = X_7 + d$, then $X_8' = X_8 + d/X_6$; thus if we write $g = d/X_6$, we know that this change in X_8 will lead to a *total* change in $[b(t)]^2$ of $S_8 d/X_6$. (Before, when we measured S_8, we assumed that X_7 would be held constant. However, when we vary X_7 and hold the earlier variables constant, there is no way that this change can affect anything later on, except by way of X_8.) Thus we deduce that

$$S_7 = \frac{S_8}{X_6}.$$

In more sophisticated language, this is an example of

$$\frac{\partial^+}{\partial X_7} ([b(t)]^2) = \left(\frac{\partial^+}{\partial X_8} ([b(t)]^2)\right) \frac{\partial f_8}{\partial X_7},$$

where f_8 is the function $X_8 = f_8(X_7, X_6) = X_7/X_6$. Now let us consider a more complicated example. In Table 2.1, X_2 has a direct effect on *three* variables higher in the table—X_{10}, X_7, and X_6. When we start to vary X_2, we have to account for the total effect of all *three* of the changes it introduces directly on these other variables. Thus we get

$$S_2 = S_{10} \frac{\partial f_{10}}{\partial X_2} + S_7 \frac{\partial f_7}{\partial X_2} + S_6 \frac{\partial f_6}{\partial X_2}$$

$$= S_{10} X_9 + S_7(-1) + S_6(+1).$$

Of course, X_2 is simply $U(t)$; the reader, differentiating Equation (2.12) with respect to $U(t)$, would also arrive at three terms, equal to the three terms here, but the work involved would be rather tedious. To make it explicit how we begin this downward calculation, let me point out how to get S_{13}:

$$S_{13} = \frac{\partial^+}{\partial \hat{A}(t + 1)} ([b(t)]^2)$$

$$= \frac{\partial^+}{\partial \hat{A}(t + 1)} ([A(t + 1) - \hat{A}(t + 1)]^2)$$

$$= -2[A(t + 1) - \hat{A}(t + 1)].$$

One way to operationalize all this is to start from the top and, for every variable, to look at all its direct connections to variables higher up. An easier way, in practice, is to *pass down* from the top all the information to variables *below them* and also directly connected to them; the effect is exactly the same, but the order of computations is easier to deal with. We can start out, in our example, by setting S_1 through S_{12} equal to zero, and plugging in S_{13} as above. At S_{13}, we note that we have a "sum"; thus we *add* S_{13} to S_{12} and to S_{11}, to account for the direct effect of X_{12} and of X_{11} on $[b(t)]^2$. Then we are done; we go down to S_{12}. At S_{12}, we know that all the later effects of X_{12} have already been added into S_{12}, and that our value for S_{12} has been calculated completely. At S_{12}, we encounter a product, $X_3 X_1$. Thus we add $S_{12} X_3$ to S_1, and $S_{12} X_1$ to S_3. We go down to S_{11}. We encounter another product. We add $S_{11} X_{10}$ to S_4, and $S_{11} X_4$ to S_{10}. We go down to S_{10}. And so on. At the end, we really look only at S_5, S_4, and S_3, the derivatives we wanted for the steepest descent method. The mathematical basis of these operations is the theorem, for a set of ordered functional relations $X_i = f_i(X_{i-1}, X_{i-2}, \ldots, X_1)$, that

$$\frac{\partial^+ X_n}{\partial X_i} = \sum_{j=i+1}^{n} \frac{\partial^+ X_n}{\partial X_j} \cdot \frac{\partial f_j}{\partial X_i}, \tag{2.13}$$

a theorem to be discussed in Section 2.12. For each line of the list, as we go down, we have only two calculations to perform at most, one for the "major source" and one for the "minor source"; thus the total number of calculations needed for each time, t, will equal only $2n_x$, where n_x is the total number of variables on the list. The total cost will be $2n_x T$, across all times, to get *all* the derivatives we want, regardless of how many parameters there are. Note that to go *up* the list, starting from $U(t)$ and $A(t)$, requires one calculation per line of the list; thus the total cost, merely to compute all the $\hat{A}(t+1)$ for a given model, will equal $n_x T$, the same order of magnitude. I assumed above that we had already carried out this latter calculation, so that the values of the X_i were already known; given that we have to find L for each guess, not just the derivatives of L, there is no extra cost in first calculating the X_i and L.

In practice, one can imagine three ways that a systems programmer might want to use the generalized form of the dynamic feedback method. First, the programmer might simply write a subroutine, to do the calculations specified above directly, on the table of operations for some model. Second, the programmer might write one subroutine to look at one table of operations, and to specify the calculations required by the dynamic feedback method for this table, in another table of operations; he/she might write a second subroutine to prune away all unnecessary and redundant operations from this table. The relative advantages of these methods would depend heavily on the characteristics of the model being studied, on the number of time periods and calculations of derivatives to be performed, and even on machine characteristics. Finally, one might imagine the possibility that the operations on a table like Table 2.1 will someday be grouped into "layers," groups of operations that can be performed in parallel on a computer capable of parallel processing. On such a machine, one could perform the operations at a given set of S_i in parallel, using the same procedures as above, as long as none of the corresponding X_i depend directly on each other as input sources. In short, one could use any system of stratification that was adequate for calculating the X_i. This possibility is restricted, however, by the requirement that several processors would have to be able to add something to the same machine word (S_i for i on the next lower layer), at the same time, with the result that this word would be increased by the sum of all the numbers added.

2.4 MODELS WITH MEMORY

Now with a firm mathematical basis for these procedures—Equation (2.13)—we can extend them still further. The models discussed so far have all been rather conventional "Markovian" models; in other words, they give us a prediction of $A(t + 1)$ as a function of $A(t)$ and $U(t)$. We could add in $A(t - 1)$ and $U(t - 1)$ as dependent variables, without changing much, because we would still have a distinct table for every time t, giving $A(t + 1)$ as a function of a manageable number of variables. Suppose, however, that we have a model with "memory." In economics, for example, there is a model of consumer behavior, which states that consumers spend money not in proportion to their *current* income but in proportion to the *permanent income* [15, pp. 20–31] that they expect to average in their lifetimes. (Friedman's [10] discussion leaves open somewhat the question of how permanent income is determined; the simplified model used as our example assumes a simple exponential learning process, based on actual income.) The model states that the perceived permanent income is adjusted slightly, from year to year, in response to actual income. Thus we obtain the following model:

$$C(t) = k_1 Y_p(t) + b(t), \tag{2.14a}$$

$$Y_p(t) = (1 - k_2)Y_p(t - 1) + k_2 Y_A(t), \tag{2.14b}$$

where C is consumption, Y_p is permanent income, Y_A is actual annual income, and $b(t)$ is an error term. Note that statistics will normally be available here for C and for Y_A, but *not* for Y_p. However, this is still what we would call an "explicit" or "phenomenological" model. Given estimates for $Y_p(t)$ and data for $Y_A(t)$, the model tells us exactly how to calculate $Y_p(t + 1)$ and how to predict $C(t)$. To calculate the $Y_p(t)$, for all times t, and to make predictions for the $C(t)$, we need to start off, at time $t = 1$, with some estimate of $Y_p(0)$; this estimate we can treat as an external constant f the model, like k_1 and k_2, to be estimated by the statistician (us). (From $Y_p(0)$ and $Y_A(1)$, Equation (2.14b) tells us how to calculate $Y_p(1)$; then we can calculate $Y_p(2)$ from $Y_p(1)$ and $Y_A(2)$, then $Y_p(3)$ from $Y_p(2)$ and $Y_A(3)$, and so on.)

To minimize the sum of the errors squared, L, is much harder in this case than with our complicated-looking model in Equation (2.11). To calculate $\partial L/$

∂k_1 here, it is not enough to set up separate tables, like Table 2.1, for each time t, and add up the $(\partial/\partial k_1)[b(t)^2]$. Equation (2.14b) establishes a *connection* between the unknown variables, Y_p, at all different times. However, we *can* set up a large table to include *all* the different values of $Y_p(t)$ and $C(t)$ across different times; this will be like taking the separate tables for each time t, tables like those implied by Table 2.1, and putting them together into one large table. In this large table, we can show the relations that exist across time. Suppose that we have data for C and Y_A from time 1 to time 4. We get a big table, as shown in Table 2.2.

TABLE 2.2 Table of Operations for Equations (2.14)

Actual Variable	Variable Number	Operation Category	Major Source	Minor Source(s)
L	37	Sum	36	28,20,12
$[b(4)]^2$	36	Product	35	35
$b(4) = C(4) - k_1 Y_p(4)$	35	Difference	34	33
$C(4)$	34	Input	—	—
$k_1 Y_p(4)$	33	Product	32	1
$Y_p(4)$ [see Equation (2.14b)]	32	Sum	31	29
$k_2 Y_A(4)$	31	Product	30	2
$Y_A(4)$	30	Input	—	—
$(1 - k_2) Y_p(3)$	29	Product	24	4
$[b(3)]^2$	28	Product	27	27
$b(3) = C(3) - k_1 Y_p(3)$	27	Difference	26	25
$C(3)$	26	Input	—	—
$k_1 Y_p(3)$	25	Product	24	1
$Y_p(3)$ [see Equation (2.14b)]	24	Sum	23	21
$k_2 Y_A(3)$	23	Product	22	2
$Y_A(3)$	22	Input	—	—
$(1 - k_2) Y_p(2)$	21	Product	16	4
$[b(2)]^2$	20	Product	19	19
$b(2) = C(2) - k_1 Y_p(2)$	19	Difference	18	17
$C(2)$	18	Input	—	—
$k_1 Y_p(2)$	17	Product	16	1
$Y_p(2)$	16	Sum	15	13

TABLE 2.2 Table of Operations for Equations (2.14) (Continued)

Actual Variable	Variable Number	Operation Category	Major Source	Minor Source(s)
$k_2 Y_A(2)$	15	Product	14	2
$Y_A(2)$	14	Input	—	—
$(1 - k_2)Y_p(1)$	13	Product	12	4
$[b(1)]^2$	12	Product	11	11
$b(1) = C(1) - k_1 Y_p(1)$	11	Difference	10	9
$C(1)$	10	Input	—	—
$k_1 Y_p(1)$	9	Product	8	1
$Y_p(1)$	8	Sum	7	5
$k_2 Y_A(1)$	7	Product	6	2
$Y_A(1)$	6	Input	—	—
$(1 - k_2)Y_p(0)$	5	Product	3	4
$1 - k_2$	4	Difference	0	2
$Y_p(0)$	3	Parameter	—	—
k_2	2	Parameter	—	—
k_1	1	Parameter	—	—
1	0	Input	—	—

With a given set of constants—$Y_p(0)$, k_1, and k_2—and with a given a set of data, we can calculate "forward in time," or *upward* in this table, to calculate every one of the "actual variables," including L, the total error. To calculate $\partial L/\partial k_1$, we can calculate *backward*, just as we did before with Table 2.1, from the top of the table to the bottom. This time, however, it is easier to see where to start:

$$S_{37} = \frac{\partial^+ L}{\partial X_{37}} = \frac{\partial L}{\partial L} = 1.$$

This time, with L itself on top instead of $[b(t)]^2$, we get a simpler result at the end:

$$S_1 = \frac{\partial^+ L}{\partial X_1} = \frac{\partial L}{\partial k_1},$$

$$S_2 = \frac{\partial^+ L}{\partial X_2} = \frac{\partial L}{\partial k_2},$$

$$S_3 = \frac{\partial^+ L}{\partial X_3} = \frac{\partial L}{\partial Y_p(0)},$$

exactly the quantities we need to apply the steepest descent method. For each line of the table, except for the top, there are only two sources, or no sources; thus to go back from the top line to the bottom line requires only two operations per line, at the most. For a very large table, with n_x lines *for each time* t, and with T periods of time, this amounts to $n_x T$ lines, and $2n_x T$ operations in all, to get all the derivatives of L. Remember that to go up the table, to calculate L, we had to carry out one operation per line—$n_x T$ operations in all. No matter how complex the model, if the functional relations across time are explicit enough that they can be put into formulas that the computer can translate into a table, like Table 2.2, then "dynamic feedback" can be used to calculate all the derivatives in one pass.

As a practical matter, one may wonder just how explicit is "explicit enough." In general, the procedure above allows us to calculate the derivatives backward down any ordered table of operations, as long as the operations correspond to differentiable functions. In order for us to use this method then, the primary requirement is that we be able to specify the model well enough to construct such a table. This is the *same requirement* that applies when we wish to use a model forward in time, to make a prediction of the future, without having to solve a complex set of nonlinear algebraic equations in every time period. In general, in the existing computer packages (including FORTRAN compilers), any formula expressed in the following form can be parsed into a table of operations (a "Polish string") generating the variable $X_i(t)$ from operations performed on the arguments:

$$X_i(t) = f_i \text{ (arguments)},$$

where f_i is a function made up by nesting basic operations known to the computer package; for example

$$X_i(t) = W(t-1) * Y(t-1) + k + \sin(Z(t) - 1)).$$

In order for a *set* of such formulas to be converted into a table of operations, we need only find an ordering of the variables to be computed, $X_i(t)$, such that the arguments used in calculating $X_i(t)$ are calculated before $X_i(t)$ itself is; the table of operations to calculate $X_i(t)$ can simply be inserted on top of the table already built up to calculate variables earlier in the causal ordering. If the arguments of f_i included only constants, parameters, and values of variables at $t - n$, for all f_i, with n always greater than zero for endogenous variables, then this requirement would be satisfied automatically. Otherwise, an ordering of the variables $X_i(t)$ would have to exist, with the later expressed as functions of the earlier. Global things to be calculated, such as the sum of a utility function or a loss function over time, can always be inserted on top of the table of calculations, as long as we specify formulas for calculating them as a function of sums across time or the like. Indeed, even if one had a set of implicit equations, so that one had to use algebraic solution methods instead of explicit calculation in order to carry out a simple prediction of the future from given parameters, then one could easily calculate the matrix of partial derivatives for those equations, to be used in *conjunction* with the algebraic solutions generated for prediction, to allow one to carry out the dynamic feedback estimate. However, simulations of this sort are both expensive and outside the major realm of interest here.

Parenthetically, one might note that there is a certain difference between the operations needed to specify the generation of a random number and the operations needed to calculate the associated loss function. Estimation by dynamic feedback requires the specification of loss functions. In the case where the unobserved random numbers are generated by a rather complex process, the translation between the two forms of specification may not be easy. However, if the losses one is concerned with are the discrepancies between the actual and predicted values of known variables, the specification of an explicit loss function should present no problem to the user of a computer package. The corresponding model would be suitable for predicting the future but may not be quite as suitable for stochastic simulations of the future, in some cases. In such cases, however, the method of pattern analysis, to be discussed in Section (2.9), may help reduce the distance between the two forms of specification.

2.5 NOISE AND THE CONCEPT OF THE TRUTH OF A MODEL IN STATISTICS

Up until now, we have avoided one other aspect of statistical estimation: the problem of *noise models*. In our old model, in Equations (2.3) and (2.4), we assumed a simple equation to predict $A(t + 1)$, and a simple bell-shaped curve for the distribution of the errors, $b(t)$. In the last three sections, we have considered more and more complex models to predict things. However, we have stayed with the old idea of minimizing the square of the error, an idea based on the old bell-shaped normal distribution. We have begun in this way only with great reluctance, and only for the sake of exposition. In fact, if we admit that most processes in human society and ecology do contain important elements of randomness, then we must admit that Equation (2.4) is just as much a part of our original model as Equation (2.3). Equation (2.4) is not an "assumption that must be proved true before we can use classical techniques"; like Equation (2.3) itself, it is part of a simple, approximate model, to be *evaluated* for its predictive power. Unfortunately, there has sometimes been a tendency in social science and ecology to formulate ever more complicated models to predict things, *without* an explicit model of the random element; the "errors" are sometimes regarded as something unpleasant, that one faces up to at the end of one's research, after one has formulated a model of what is interesting.

Statisticians, on the other hand, have long since passed the stage of "minimizing least squares" or of "minimizing error" in general. The idea of measuring the "probability of truth" of a model was mentioned earlier, as was the problem of how to estimate the probability of truth of a model, *given* a set of data observations. The traditional "maximum likelihood" school of statistics, as represented by Carnap and Jeffreys and the more recent Bayesian schools both agree that this is simply equivalent to the following problem in conditional probabilities[3]: how do we estimate the probability of the truth of a model, conditional on our having made a certain set of observations? Formally, the conditional probability of A given B, $p(A|B)$, is defined to equal $p(A$ and $B)/p(B)$. From this follows Bayes' law:

$$P(A|B) = \frac{P(B|A)P(A)}{P(B)}.$$

Statisticians have applied this law to deduce

$$P(\text{model}|\text{data}) = \frac{p(\text{data}|\text{model})p(\text{model})}{p(\text{data})} \tag{2.15}$$

This equation does not say that the "data" and the "model" have to be expressed in purely mathematical terms; as a result, the equation has led to enormous controversy among both statisticians and philosophers. It is a general equation telling us how to determine the probability of truth of any sort of theory; thus its relevance to the social and natural sciences goes well beyond the question of statistical methods proper. The calculations on the right involve two terms of real interest—$p(\text{data}|\text{model})$ and $p(\text{model})$. The term $p(\text{data})$ is the same for all models and does not help us to evaluate the *relative* probabilities of truth of different models, except perhaps indirectly (as in Section 2.14.4). The term $p(\text{data}|\text{model})$ represents what statisticians have traditionally focused on: how well the data "fit" the model, defined as the probability that these particular data would have been generated if the model were true. The term $p(\text{model})$ refers to *the probability of the model before any data have been observed at all*; it is our *a priori* probability distribution. The philosopher Immanuel Kant [14] long ago asserted that "empirical induction" is impossible, without some system of a priori assumptions (the "a priori synthetic") with real information content to them; the choice of $p(\text{model})$ would constitute such a system of assumptions.

More recent philosophers, such as Carnap and Jeffreys [11], have tried to preserve the more popular attitudes of pure empiricism and positivism, by sug-

[3]The most fundamental source for this viewpoint is [11]. Discussions of its direct applications to statistics may be found in [12, pp. 250–252] and in Kendall [13, p. 150].

gesting that p(model) should be "equal" (a priori) for all different models. Thus p(data|model) would be the only term left to consider, in measuring probabilities of truth. Their suggestions have been carried over to the field of statistics, where they are now orthodox practice [11–13]. (See also Wasan [6, pp. 150–152], Anderson and Bancroft [15, p. 101], and Hays [16, pp. 816–821, 841–842].) This approach is normally referred to as the "maximum likelihood approach." In more recent years, however, many members of a new school of statisticians, the Bayesians, have grown in their opposition to this orthodox procedure. They have pointed out that p(model) $= k$, with the same k for all models, is a very strong assumption, just as strong as any of the alternatives. In most practical problems, the social scientist would have some reason to expect some models to be likelier than others, even before running a statistical analysis. Thus they suggest that a user of statistical programs should be asked to *specify* his/her a priori probability distribution as the first step of any statistical analysis[4]; *then* the computer program can account for *both* p(model) *and* p(data|model), in picking out the model with the highest probability of truth. From a broader perspective, one might say that the Bayesians are proposing a procedure for allowing the social scientist to account for two *different* kinds of data—statistical data and verbal data he/she has from other sources. This still leaves open the question of where the initial p(model) should come from, a question that we can avoid in this context.[5]

The Baysesians may be right in principle, but in practice the orthodox procedures may remain a sensible way to design computer statistical packages. The social scientist, when reading the output of a computer, would normally expect that this output reflects only the ability of different models to *fit* the actual data; in deciding what he/she finally believes about the world, he/she can *then* account for the verbal data. This does require that the social scientist understand what "standard errors" mean, in ordinary regression, so that he/she can get some idea of the variety of models consistent with the statistical data. It also suggests that a direct printout of the *relative probabilities of truth* of different models, over the given data, would be a useful feature to have. In brief, it requires the development of an intuition regarding the relation of mathematics to social processes, an intuition strong enough to sustain the balanced assessment of probabilities. This does place a burden on the social scientist. On the other hand, the extreme Bayesian alternative—to ask a social scientist to encode his/her intuition into a few normal distributions and to ask for a more complete faith in what comes out of a computer—would seem to place a much heavier burden on the social scientist. It would tend to deemphasize the learning experience that usually occurs at the end of a statistical analysis, when

[4]See later chapters in Hays [16]. See also Lindley [17], and Schlaifer [18, Chapter 13], Hogg and Craig [19, pp. 208–209], Wasan [6, p. 184, definition 5, and subsequent discussions], and Box and Tiao [20]. The two computer programs generally available in Cambridge for Bayesian estimation are described in Brode [18] and in Schlaifer [21].

[5]In this area, too, the traditional formulation by Carnap and Jeffreys is under question. See Shimony [22, p. 100], Solomonoff [23], and Barker [24].

the social scientist tries to relate all the things that came out of the computer to what he/she knows in the real world; if this experience is what develops a balanced intuition in the first place, it should not be given a diminished role. In Chapter 5, the importance of this type of experience to the actual application of statistical methods in the social sciences is discussed in detail. Furthermore, the verbal knowledge of a social scientist will not normally fit a simple distribution. Even if it did, few "intuitive decision-makers" can express their intuition at all reasonably in terms of probability distributions, even in simple cases, without extensive training in that task [25]. While there is more that could be said on both sides of this particular issue, the orthodox approach would seem quite adequate for the purpose of the present context.

The dynamic feedback algorithm, which is being discussed here, can actually be applied to Bayesian estimation as easily as to conventional estimation. In the examples and applications given here, the more orthodox procedures are followed. However, I will refer back, on occasion, to the concept of "prior probabilities" when this is appropriate.

In concluding this section, I would like to note, for the sake of the mathematician, that Equation (2.15), when used in statistics, is normally used to give the probability *distributions* of a continuous family of models rather than a discrete probability. Strictly speaking, such distributions are not even functions; they are actually "measures," and they would normally be written as the product of a function times an explicit measure, like $d\theta$, where θ is a parameter of the model. In Equation (2.15), however, the choices of measure used for the data cancel out; thus it is not of intrinsic importance, as long as we are consistent in the units we use to record the data. The choice of measure for the model is one more aspect of the problem of specifying p(model), an aspect discussed by the sources referred to above. In general, however, one would not expect the maximum likelihood choice of parameters to be affected very strongly by the choice of measure, unless the standard error for these parameters indicated a large uncertainty and probably a low statistical significance in any case.

2.6 ORDINARY REGRESSION AND THE MAXIMUM LIKELIHOOD APPROACH

Previously, in Section (2.2), when I discussed how to measure the "probability of truth" of the Deutsch–Solow model, I glossed over the basic questions discussed in Section 2.5. In Section 2.2, I discussed two different "measures" of the probability of truth: one for Equation (2.3a) and another for Equation (2.3b); all the rest of the discussion focused on Equation (2.3a), an equation to predict a *single* variable, $A(t + 1)$. When discussing a single equation, to predict a single variable from known data, it makes some kind of sense simply to add up all the square errors $[b(t)]^2$ across time and use the sum as a measure of how good the equation is. However, what do we do if there are *two* equations and *two* sets of errors? How do we combine the two different error terms to measure the validity of the model as a whole? With the Deutsch–Solow model, I could pick out the best values for k_1 and k_2 without answering these questions, because the two equations were essentially independent, and because I assumed that the two error terms, b and c, each had their own probability distributions independent of each other (Equation (2.4)). But I had to avoid the question of how to measure the validity of the model as a whole. Now, using the concepts of Section 2.5, we can come back to answer this question. Let us define the relative probability of truth, P, of any model as

$$P = p(\text{data}|\text{model}),$$

the probability that we would have observed the data we have observed, if the model were true. More precisely, this "probability" is actually a probability density, as are the other "probabilities' in this section. For simplicity, let us assume, with the Deutsch–Solow model, that we only have data for three years, 1958, 1959, and 1960, in one country. Writing out the data explicitly, we are trying to measure

$$P = p(A(1960),\ U(1960),\ A(1959),\ U(1959),\ A(1958),\ U(1958)|\ \text{model}),$$

which, by classic probability theory, equals the product

$$P = p(A(1960)|U(1960),\ A(1959),\ U(1959),\ A(1958),\ U(1958),\ \text{model})$$

$$*\ p(U(1960)|\ A(1959),\ U(1959),\ A(1958),\ U(1958),\ \text{model})$$

$$*\ p(A(1959)|\ U(1959),\ A(1958),\ U(1958),\ \text{model})$$

$$*\ p(U(1959)|\ A(1958),\ U(1958),\ \text{model})$$

$$*\ p(A(1958),\ U(1958)|\ \text{model}).$$

Now our model, Equation (2.3), predicts $A(1960)$ as a function of $A(1959)$ and $U(1959)$; once these data are given, the other data will not affect the probability of $A(1960)$ as given by the model. The same is true for $U(1960)$, and so on. Thus we can simplify our expressión:

$$P = p(A(1960)|\ A(1959),\ U(1959),\ \text{model})$$

$$*\ p(U(1960)|\ U(1959),\ \text{model})$$

$$*\ p(A(1959)|\ A(1958),\ U(1958),\ \text{model})$$

$$*\ p(U(1959)|\ U(1958),\ \text{model})$$

$$*\ p(A(1958),\ U(1958)|\ \text{model}).$$

Once we are given values for $A(1959)$ and $U(1959)$, how do we determine the probabilities of the possible values for $A(1960)$? The *most likely* value of

$A(1960)$, according to Equations (2.3) and (2.4), is the one with $b(1960) = 0$, that is, $A(1960) = \hat{A}(1960)$, which equals $k_1 A(1959) + k_2 U(1959)$. But *any* value for $A(1960)$ would be consistent with Equations (2.3), for some value of b. Values of $A(1960)$ far away from $\hat{A}(1960)$, however, would imply large values of b, which, according to Equations (2.4), are not as likely as small values of b. To determine the probability of any given $A(1960)$, *given* $A(1959)$ and $U(1959)$, we need only look at the probability of the value of b needed to generate the combination.

$$p(A(1960)|\ A(1959),\ U(1959),\ \text{model}) = p(b(1959)|\ \text{model})$$

$$= \frac{1}{\sqrt{2\pi}B} \exp\left[-\frac{1}{2}\left(\frac{b(1959)}{B}\right)^2\right].$$

And similarly for $A(1959)$, $U(1960)$, and $U(1959)$. Thus we get, in summary,

$$P = p(b(1959)|\ \text{model}) * p(b(1958)|\ \text{model}) * p(c(1959)|\ \text{model})$$

$$* p(c(1958)|\ \text{model}) * p(A(1958),\ U(1958)|\ \text{model}),$$

which, by equation (2.4), equals

$$\left\{\frac{1}{\sqrt{2\pi}B}\exp\left[-\frac{1}{2}\left(\frac{b(1959)}{B}\right)^2\right]\right\}\left\{\frac{1}{\sqrt{2\pi}B}\exp\left[-\frac{1}{2}\left(\frac{b(1958)}{B}\right)^2\right]\right\}$$

$$* \left\{\frac{1}{\sqrt{2\pi}C}\exp\left[-\frac{1}{2}\left(\frac{c(1959)}{C}\right)^2\right]\right\}$$

$$* \left\{\frac{1}{\sqrt{2\pi}C}\exp\left[-\frac{1}{2}\left(\frac{c(1958)}{C}\right)^2\right]\right\}$$

$$* p(A(1958),\ U(1958)|\ \text{model}).$$

What do we do about the last term, representing our earliest data point, 1958? The usual practice is simply to ignore the final term on grounds that it is difficult to compute and contributes only one time-point worth of information; for long series of data, the importance of one extra point of information grows very small. In the social sciences, the argument for eliminating this term grows even stronger. This term, as usually interpreted,[6] requires us to compute the probability that *we would have started off* at a data point equal to $(A(1958),\ U(1958))$, if this initial data had been generated by the Deutsch–Solow model operating for an infinite length of time before the start of the available data. Normally, in the social sciences, one picks the start of one's data series for

---

[6]See Box and Jenkins [12, p. 247]. Note that the "Bayesian estimates" suggested on p. 252 of this reference and also the approximations suggested on p. 277, involve disregarding this term with or without small adjustments elsewhere.

one of two reasons: (1) one is trying to find a model to describe events in a *given historical period*, and one does not expect the model to be valid before the start of one's data series; or (2) the data are not available before a certain time, usually implying that some aspects of the social system were different beforehand. Furthermore, if one's model is not "stationary," as few social processes are, then the usual procedure for computing this term breaks down in any case.

On this basis, we get a relative probability density:

$$
P = \frac{1}{\sqrt{2\pi}B} \exp\left[-\frac{1}{2}\left(\frac{b(1959)}{B}\right)^2 \right] \frac{1}{\sqrt{2\pi}B} \exp\left[-\frac{1}{2}\left(\frac{b(1958)}{B}\right)^2 \right]
$$
$$
* \frac{1}{\sqrt{2\pi}C} \exp\left[-\frac{1}{2}\left(\frac{c(1959)}{C}\right)^2 \right]
$$
$$
* \frac{1}{\sqrt{2\pi}C} \exp\left[-\frac{1}{2}\left(\frac{c(1958)}{C}\right)^2 \right],
$$

which reduces to

$$
P = \frac{1}{4\pi^2 B^2 C^2} \exp\left\{ -\frac{1}{2}\left[\left(\frac{b(1959)}{B}\right)^2 + \left(\frac{b(1958)}{B}\right)^2 \right.\right.
$$
$$
\left.\left. + \left(\frac{c(1959)}{C}\right)^2 + \left(\frac{c(1958)}{C}\right)^2 \right] \right\}
$$

The interesting part of this formula is the exponent, the part that depends on b and c. In order to maximize p with respect to k_1, k_2', and k_4, we try to bring the negative number in the exponent as close to zero as possible. This number is essentially the *sum* of the errors squared, exactly what we tried to maximize before. Once we have done this, it is well-known that we can maximize P by picking B and C to equal the root-mean-square average of b and c, respectively.

2.7   THE NEED FOR SOPHISTICATED NOISE MODELS

In general, there is little reason to believe that the classic normal distribution, of Equations (2.4), will be a good model of the noise element in all social processes. Mosteller and Rourke [26], for example, have pointed out that "flukes" occur fairly often in real social data [27]. There may be many processes that normally plod along in a predictable sort of way, governed by a noise process $b(t)$ that fits a normal distribution and that never gets to be very large; every once in a while, however, the process may be hit by a fluke, which leads to changes much larger than one would have expected in the normal course of events. Suppose that p_1 is the probability, at any time, of getting a fluke. Then the probability distribution for $b(t)$ may actually fit the following kind of equation:

$$p(b) = (1 - p_1) \frac{1}{\sqrt{2\pi}B} \exp\left[-\frac{1}{2}\left(\frac{b}{B}\right)^2\right] + p_1 * \frac{1}{\sqrt{2\pi}B_1} \exp\left[-\frac{1}{2}\left(\frac{b}{B_1}\right)^2\right]$$

where B_1 is much larger than B. This equation states that most of the time—$(1 - p_1)$ of the time, to be precise—b will fit the same bell-shaped curve as before; *however*, when a "fluke" occurs, b will fit a much broader bell-shaped curve, leading to much larger values for b. One way to account for these effects is to use this probability formula explicitly, instead of the usual normal distribution, in one's noise model; it may be impossible to estimate B_1 accurately, but, if flukes are a serious problem, it may still be possible to estimate k_1 and k_2 more accurately and to show when P is larger for this kind of model.

Another source of noise, rarely handled explicitly in social science, is "measurement noise." In our discussion above, we talked about $A(1959)$ and $A(1960)$ as if we had available exact data for the true levels of assimilation in those years. We may have data, but there is good reason to believe that errors of different sorts occurred in the collection of these data. Even if the data were "perfect," in the sense of giving us a perfect measure of who speaks what language when, for example, they may still not be giving us a perfect measure of the underlying concept of assimilation, as governed by Equations (2.3). Let us define $U(t)$ as the true size of the unassimilated population, and $U'(t)$ as the *measured* size of the unassimilated model. Then we might modify Equation (2.3b) by writing

$$U(t + 1) = k_3 U(t) + c(t), \tag{2.16a}$$

$$U'(t + 1) = U(t + 1) + d(t + 1), \tag{2.16b}$$

where c is the noise going on in the process itself and d is the measurement noise. The "process noise," c, is a random factor in the actual process (Equation (2.16a)), which determines the objective evolution of the *real variable* in which we are interested, U, *through time*. The "measurement noise," d, does not affect the objective reality, U, but only adds a factor of distortion to our measurement of U, our U'; $U' - U$, the difference between the measured value of U and the true value of U, equals the measurement error, d. Even if U' did represent an objective variable in its own right, but a variable different from the one we really postulate to govern the dynamics, then this mathematical structure would still apply.

Given that we do not know the true value of $U(t)$ at any time t, this model is not an "explicit" model; it does not tell us directly how to estimate $U'(t + 1)$ from earlier available data. (Note that the noise term, $c(t)$, makes it impossible to calculate later values of $U(t)$ from an estimate of $U(0)$.) However,

Box and Jenkins [12, pp. 121–124] have shown that this model is equivalent to the explicit model[7]:

$$U'(t + 1) = k_3 U'(t) * f(t + 1) - k_4 f(t),$$

where f is a noise process fitting a normal distribution. This model has a kind of "memory term" in it, $k_4 f(t)$, and may be estimated by use of the dynamic feedback method, as discussed in Section 2.4. In Chapter 3, I describe how this method can be specialized to deal with models of this general sort, with any number of dependent variables. Economists, like Cochrane and Orcutt, have developed techniques to deal with some of the secondary consequences of measurement noise, like the problem of serial correlation; however, in their original article [28], these authors made it quite clear the general problem of measurement noise is beyond the scope of their techniques.

This idea can be taken even further, if we wipe out the term for "process noise," and allow for the possibility of measurement noise only. In Equations (2.16), this would mean eliminating the term $c(t)$, while retaining $d(t + 1)$ and the other terms of the model; this would make Equations (2.16) an "explicit" model, with memory $U(t)$, similar to the example of Section 2.4. At first glance, this procedure sounds both unrealistic and totally inferior to the procedures of the paragraph above. Process noise does exist in most social and ecological processes; as long as we can account for both process noise and measurement noise, why should we limit ourselves to the second possibility only?

Let us begin by seeing what this process really entails. If we assume that there is no process noise at all, then we can start out from our initial estimates (or data) for our variables and solve our equations *exactly* to yield a stream of predictions for later data, right up to the end of our data set; these predictions account *only* for the data in the initial time period. Note that this is exactly what we were thinking of doing, early in Section 2.2, before we introduced the more "sophisticated" concept of ordinary regression. Also, note that this is what Jay Forrester's techniques [29] for "dynamic systems analysis" tend to involve, even though he prefers to judge the final fit of his models by eye rather than by computer. Above all, note that the practical value of social and ecological models usually lies in their ability to *predict* the situation at distant times, without requiring knowledge of intervening times in the future. (This includes, of course, the ability to predict the results of different policies.) Using our new procedure, we evaluate models by their ability to yield good predictions across long periods of time, not by their ability to predict across the smallest possible period of time; therefore we will generate models and coefficients better suited to the practical demands that will be placed on them. In order to estimate such models, we will have to resort to the dynamic feedback techniques of Section 2.4. The prior unavailability of such techniques offers at

---

[7]The formula here is a special case of Box and Jenkins'.

least some justification for the apparent disregard of empirical data in some of Forrester's [30] more interesting work[8]; however, if these estimation routines should become available soon at the Cambridge Project Consistent System, a more empirical analysis of these issues will become possible.

In short, the practical reasons for disregarding process noise can be very strong at times. From a theoretical point of view, however, the reasons are not so obvious. If we start with a given statistical process, governed by a given set of equations, then those equations themselves are the best possible basis for prediction, whether across one period of time or many. Thus "truth" implies predictive power. When we have a given set of data, the maximum likelihood method allows us to make use of *all* the information available—not just one measure, like long-term predictive power over the *given* data—to find the parameters and model closest to being "true."

The difficulty in this argument is that "closeness to truth," unlike "truth" itself, can be measured in many different ways. The Bayesian school of thought has begun to argue that this point too, should be accounted for in practical statistical routines [19, pp. 250–253]; however, their concepts of "loss function" do not fully encompass the concept of "long-term predictive power" here. As a practical matter, most models in the social sciences and in ecology are simplified, approximate models, which we do not expect to be "true" in any absolute sense; we only expect them to *approach* truth, or, more realistically, we expect them to give us predictions similar in a broad way to what we would predict if we knew the full truth. Even when these models contain a hundred variables or so, they will still be hundreds of times simpler than the complete systems that they represent. If there were an infinite quantity of representative data available, and if we had to choose between a limited set of models, *none of which are "true" in an absolute sense*, then the model that performs best on, say, predicting across 10 years of time, over these data, can also be expected to give us the best predictions of the future 10 years hence. In order to estimate such a model, we should indeed try to minimize the errors across 10 years, instead of following the conventional likelihood approach. In other words, if we wish to carry out an estimation that is "robust"—an estimation that will give us good predictions *despite* the oversimplification of one's model—then a *direct* maximization of predictive power is appropriate; that is exactly what our "measurement-noise-only" approach entails.

In reality, we will have to accept limits both on our choice of models and on the size of our data. We will have two sorts of information to use in evaluating the predictive powers of our models: (1) the long-term predictive power *as measured directly* over the available data and (2) general information about the "truth" of our model, as given by the maximum likelihood formulas. The first information is a direct measure of what we want to know. On the other

---

[8]The successor to Forrester's book is one by Meadows et al. [31]. The lack of empirical validation and other important aspects of this work are discussed in Cole et al. [32]. A few alternative approaches are sketched in Chapter 5.

hand, we only have a certain limited amount of this kind of information in our data. The second information does tell us something about how close our model is to "truth," which in turn tells us something about predictive power. When our total information is limited, statistical theory recommends that we make use of all information at our disposal, including both the "hard" and the "soft." Our problem, then, is one of a more practical nature: Which of the two sources of information should we emphasize, when we want to build a model suitable for medium-term and long-term prediction?

General guidelines for dealing with this problem will have to come from experience, experience with both ordinary procedures and with the new procedure suggested here. It should be clear, however, that the relative importance of process noise and measurement noise will vary from case to case. A direct comparison of the methods, say, in predicting the second half of one's data from the first half, would probably be desirable in most cases. When the major flaw in one's existing model lies in its inability to describe *measurement* noise accurately, then one would suspect the possibility that the unexplained portion of that measurement noise would be organized enough to be partly "predictable" from one's process variables and noise; this would lead to distortion of the parameters of the process proper. For models that have this problem, the best way to improve predictive power may be to avoid this distortion, by making sure that measurement noise is not falsely attributed to the process equations (i.e., to process noise); by falling back on a measurement-noise-only model, in which process noise does not exist at all, one can eliminate this distortion entirely. Once again, as noted earlier, the measurement-noise-only approach involves no distortion at all, insofar as it maximizes long-term predictive power directly; its weakness lies in the lack of formal statistical efficiency. When process noise is very large, and the neglect of process noise would appear to seriously weaken one's ability to make full use of one's data, then it would still be possible to compromise, by the relaxation methods to be discussed in Section 2.11; these methods, by allowing process noise, but by making it much more "expensive" to attribute randomness to process noise than to measurement noise, may reduce the false attribution of the latter to the former, while preserving an adequate level of statistical efficiency. It is conceivable that in social science, as in hard science, there will someday be a viable distinction between "practical" statistical work, where prediction is most important, and "theoretical" statistical work, where "truth" as such turns out to be a more effective guide to finding new variables and terms to use in one's models. However, once again, the practical values of these techniques will have to emerge from empirical work. The empirical work of this thesis, in Chapters 4 and 6, does provide a strong indication that the measurement-noise-only approach is superior to the pure maximum likelihood approach in the social science; this indication has been strong enough to totally reverse my own initial bias in favor of the classical approach. Still, the empirical studies here are only the beginning of a long process.

Finally, let us consider one other situation where the conventional approach

TABLE 2.3 Hypothetical Example of Ideal Types

Variable	Type 1	Type 2	Type 3
1	1	0	1
2	0	1	1
3	1	0	0
4	0	1	0

to noise is inadequate: the case of "ideal types." Very often, in social science, we run across variables like "Republican President" and "Democratic President," which do not tend to vary across a continuous spectrum; they tend to be simply "true" or "false." The error in predicting such variables would not follow a normal distribution, but the problem need not be overwhelmingly difficult. On the other hand, we often find societies falling into certain distinct "ideal types"[9], such as "traditional," "developed," and "transitional." We may find that a whole collection of other variables—political stability [34, pp. 114–118], aggressiveness, economic growth, and so on—depend heavily on which ideal type a society falls into. As an extreme example, let us imagine that there are three ideal types a nation might fall into, and that we have been studying four social variables that are all really determined by the current ideal type (see Table 2.3). If we predict that variable 1 will equal 1, and discover that it actually equals 0, then this last piece of information tells us exactly what to expect for variables 2, 3, and 4. If we already made predictions for variables 2, 3, and 4, then we would also know now exactly what errors to expect in these predictions. Thus there is a connection, though complex, between the "errors" in predicting different variables. If our example had been somewhat more complex, with a lot of nonlinearity and a certain amount of freedom to deviate from one's ideal type, it is clear that the correlations between the prediction errors of different variables could become hopelessly complex. According to maximum likelihood theory, as sketched briefly in Section 2.5, it is important to minimize the "right" measure of error, even when we estimate the coefficients we intend to use in making predictions of this process. The "right" measure is supposed to correspond to the actual noise process going on. If it does become important, in practice, that we do have such an accurate measure of error, and if the actual noise process is as complex as above, then we face serious difficulties in estimating any parameters at all. In our simple example, we could escape from these difficulties, by carrying out a simple factor analysis to detect the ideal types; then we could go on to study the ideal types only and disregard the original four variables. However, in the general

[9]The "ideal types" idea originated with Max Weber; a review of the early idea may be found in Rogers, [33].

case, a linear technique like factor analysis may not be enough; also, we may still want to consider the original variables, to account for whatever independent variation they have. In any case, it is clear that the conventional model of independent errors, following a normal distribution, cannot deal effectively with this kind of situation. The measurement-noise-only technique could conceivably reduce the difficulties here, but one would still expect a better model to emerge, if one could account for the complex interrelations of the process variables more explicitly.

In summary, in order to produce a "true" model of social process, which is also capable of yielding good predictions, one must have an accurate model both of the "predictive part," like Equations (2.3), and of the "noise part," like Equations (2.4); otherwise, the standard techniques of statistical estimation may yield unrealistic estimates of both. If one pursues an unbalanced approach, giving more weight to the "predictive" part than to the "noise" part, one may soon find oneself in a situation where the inaccuracies in one's noise model are so large that any improvements in the "predictive" part are reflected by little improvement, in any, in the statistical likelihood of one's model. The "models without process noise" discussed above can, at the very least, serve as detectors for this kind of difficulty.

2.8   HOW TO ESTIMATE EXPLICIT SOPHISTICATED NOISE MODELS

Suppose that we had decided to make the Deutsch–Solow model for assimilation more sophisticated, *not* by working on the "predictive" part, but by working on the "noise" part; suppose that we decided to account for the possibility of "flukes," as discussed previously. Then we might write the model:

$$A(t + 1) = k_1 A(t) + k_2 U(t) + b(t + 1)$$

$$p(b) = (1 - p_1) \frac{1}{\sqrt{2\pi B}} e^{-1/2(b/B)^2} + p_1 * \frac{1}{\sqrt{2\pi B_1}} e^{-1/2(b/B_1)^2} \quad (2.17)$$

Our problem is to try to maximize "P," which, as in the case of ordinary regression, will equal the product:

$$P = p[b(2)]p[b(3)]p[b(4)] \ldots p[b(T)],$$

where T is the last time period for which we have data. An easier way to approach this is by trying to maximize the logarithm of P:

$$L = \log P = \log p[b(2)] + \log p[b(3)] + \ldots + \log p[b(T)].$$

We are trying to pick out the best possible values for the parameters k_1, k_2, B, B_1 and p_1. As before, we can try to do this by using "steepest descent"; as before, this means trying to measure the derivatives, $\partial L/\partial k_1$ etc. As before, in Section 2.3, we can set up a table of operations for each time t, which corresponds to a table which would emerge from a computer program to analyze this model; this table is shown in Table 2.4.

We may use such a table, as before, to calculate all the derivatives required by the steepest descent method. We may compute $(\partial/\partial k_1) \log p(b(t+1))$, and

TABLE 2.4 Table of Operations for Equations (2.17)

Actual Variable	Variable Number	Operation Category	Major Source	Minor Source
$\log p(b(t+1))$	32	Logarithm	31	—
$p(b(t+1))$	31	Sum	30	25
$\dfrac{(1-p_1)}{\sqrt{2\pi B}} e^{-1/2(b(t+1)/B)^2}$	30	Product	29	16
$e^{-1/2(b(t+1)/B)^2}$	29	Exponential	28	—
$-\dfrac{1}{2}\left(\dfrac{b(t+1)}{B}\right)^2$	28	Product	27	1
$\left(\dfrac{b(t+1)}{B}\right)^2$	27	Product	26	26
$\dfrac{b(t+1)}{B}$	26	Ratio	20	9
$\dfrac{p_1}{\sqrt{2\pi B_1}} e^{-1/2(b(t+1)/B_1)^2}$	25	Product	24	13
$e^{-1/2(b(t+1)/B_1)^2}$	24	Exponential	23	—
$-\dfrac{1}{2}\left(\dfrac{b(t+1)}{B_1}\right)^2$	23	Product	22	1
$\left(\dfrac{b(t+1)}{B_1}\right)^2$	22	Product	21	21
$\dfrac{b(t+1)}{B_1}$	21	Ratio	20	8
$b(t+1) = A(t+1) - k_1 A(t) - k_2 U(t)$	20	Difference	6	19
$k_1 A(t) + k_2 U(t)$	19	Sum	18	17
$k_1 A(t)$	18	Product	5	11
$k_2 U(t)$	17	Product	4	10
$\dfrac{1-p_1}{\sqrt{2\pi B}}$	16	Ratio	15	14

TABLE 2.4 Table of Operations for Equations (2.17) *(Continued)*

Actual Variable	Variable Number	Operation Category	Major Source	Minor Source
$1 - p_1$	15	Difference	3	7
$\sqrt{2\pi}B$	14	Product	2	9
$\dfrac{p_1}{\sqrt{2\pi}B_1}$	13	Ratio	7	12
$\sqrt{2\pi}\,B_1$	12	Product	8	2
k_1	11	Parameter	—	—
k_2	10	Parameter	—	—
B	9	Parameter	—	—
B_1	8	Parameter	—	—
p_1	7	Parameter	—	—
$A(t + 1)$	6	Given	—	—
$A(t)$	5	Given	—	—
$U(t)$	4	Given	—	—
1	3	Given	—	—
$\sqrt{2\pi}$	2	Given	—	—
$-\dfrac{1}{2}$	1	Given	—	—

so on, by inserting $S_{32} = 1$ and working down the table as before to compute all the derivatives. The error model was complicated; therefore the table is long. We can compute $\partial L/\partial k_1$ simply by computing $(\partial/\partial k_1) \log p(b(t + 1))$ for all times t, from 1 to $T - 1$, and adding up all the results; this would be the same sort of operation as in Section 2.3. In brief, if our model of error is complicated, but explicit, then dynamic feedback can be used to estimate the parameters of our model. Note that if there had been *two* variables to predict, $A(t + 1)$ and $U(t + 1)$, then the *two* error terms $b(t + 1)$ and $c(t + 1)$ would appear somewhere in the middle of the table; if $p(b(t + 1), c(t + 1))$ were a function of *both* errors, a very complicated but explicit function, we could still have put together a table like this and used dynamic feedback. Also, if there were "memory" in the model, we could merge all these tables, for different times t, just as we did in Section 2.4. Note, however, that when the models become extremely complex, the choice of the initial guesses for our constants, to be used with the steepest descent method, becomes increasingly important; bit by bit, this problem becomes a subject worthy of attention in its own right, as our models grow in complexity.

2.9 PATTERN ANALYSIS

When ideal types or other systematic patterns are present, as in the example in Section 2.7, then it may be very difficult to formulate a good explicit model of noise, accounting for all the interrelationships between the errors in the predictions of different variables. A more natural way to handle such situations is by finding out what the ideal types are and trying to predict them instead of predicting our original variables. In order to do this, we must try to find a way to describe the data at time $t + 1$ in terms of a limited number of ideal-type variables. Our description should be "complete" in the sense that we can regenerate the original data at time $t + 1$ from knowing the ideal types, with minimum error. In the case of simple or only moderately complicated systems, with limited data available, we may use this approach as a way to reduce the number of variables, as we do with factor analysis. More generally, if we find that we have a large set of variables, heavily interconnected in a nonlinear way, we may try to find a set of "fundamental" variables that govern the behavior of all the original, more superficial variables in a more independent, more linear, and more comprehensible manner. The formulas that we use to estimate such variables might be considered to be "pattern detectors" or "feature detectors," in the language of pattern recognition. With a complex nonlinear system, the number of fundamental variables might actually be larger than the original number of variables; however, it would still be much smaller than the number of possible *system configurations*.

Let us imagine that we start out with a set of variables to study, $X_1, \ldots,$ $X_i, \ldots, X_n$, forming a vector, $\mathbf{X}$. We are looking for another set of variables, $R_1, \ldots, R_m$, forming a vector $\mathbf{R}$, which "governs" the vector $\mathbf{X}$ in the sense that it accounts for all the cross-correlation between the different components of $\mathbf{X}$. (More precisely, it accounts for the cross-correlation in the random disturbances applied to the different components of $\mathbf{X}$.) At every time $t + 1$, we wish to define these variables, $R_i(t + 1)$, as *functions* of the data at time $t + 1$, $\mathbf{X}(t + 1)$. More generally, we may allow them to be functions of $\mathbf{X}(t)$ and $\mathbf{R}(t)$ also; this would allow us to detect dynamic patterns, involving such phenomena as population growth or physical motion. Thus we may define

$$R_i(t + 1) = f_i(\mathbf{X}(t + 1), \mathbf{X}(t), \mathbf{R}(t)).$$

In trying to "find" or to "define" the fundamental variables, R_i, our goal is to adjust the parameters of the functions f_i to *fit the verbal requirements implied by our discussion above*. These requirements involve the dynamic relations of the R_i and X_i variables; thus we can fit the parameters of the functions f_i only within the broader context of fitting a dynamic model of the entire process.

The first of the requirements we must meet is that the $R_i(t + 1)$, *unlike* the original $X_i(t + 1)$, are generated by *independent* stochastic processes. Our dynamic model must include a description of each of these processes. Thus it must specify the probability distribution for each variable, $R_i(t + 1)$, as a function of $R(t)$ and $X(t)$; it must maintain the assumption that these probability distributions are independent of each other. Thus we may write

$$p(R_i(t + 1)| X(t), R(t)) = g_i(R_i(t + 1), X(t), R(t)).$$

These functions, g_i, like the functions f_i, are part of our model. Rather than assume that we start out with the "correct" g_i, we will try to adjust the parameters of the functions g_i and the parameters of the functions f_i, in order to make the model as a whole fit the data as well as possible. This procedure will presumably adjust the functions f_i to fit as well as possible the assumption of independence, which is built into this model.

Finally, we have a second verbal requirement to meet. We require the ability to regenerate the $X_i(t + 1)$ back again for $R(t + 1)$, with minimum possible error; as before, we can also allow the use of information from $R(t)$ and $X(t)$ in this procedure. In setting up equations to predict the $X_i(t + 1)$ from known values of $R(t + 1)$, $X(t)$, and $R(t)$, we are effectively just extending our dynamic model to predict a new set of variables. We want the value of $R(t + 1)$ to account for all the interdependence of the variables, $X_i(t + 1)$; thus once the value of $R(t + 1)$ is *known*, we want to be able to predict all the $X_i(t + 1)$ independently of each other. Therefore we want to extend our dynamic model to describe the probability distribution of each variable, $X_i(t + 1)$, as a function of $R(t + 1)$, $R(t)$, and $X(t)$; we want to maintain the requirement that each of these probability distributions is independent of all the others. Thus we may write

$$p(X_i(t + 1)| R(t + 1), R(t), X(t)) = h_i(X_i(t + 1), R(t + 1), R(t), X(t)).$$

These functions, h_i, like the functions g_i and f_i, are part of our model. In adjusting the parameters of all these functions to fit the data, we hope to adjust the parameters of the f_i to fit the assumptions of independence for *both* the g_i *and* the h_i.

Our objective, then, is to estimate the functions f_i, g_i, and h_i, so as to maximize the likelihood of this model as a whole. In order to do this, we could calculate the likelihood as we have with other models:

$$p(X(t + 1)| X(t), R(t), \text{model})$$
$$= p(X(t + 1)| R(t + 1), X(t), R(t), \text{model})$$
$$* p(R(t + 1)| X(t), R(t), \text{model})$$

(Note that, in this equation, we do not have to integrate over all possible values of $R(t + 1)$ on the right because the $R_i(t + 1)$ have been defined as definite functions of the other variables here; it is as if they were components of $X(t + 1)$, or, from another point of view, as if their probability distribution contingent on $X(t + 1)$, $R(t)$, and $X(t)$ were a Dirac delta function, which we have already integrated implicitly.) This yields a likelihood measure for a complete set of data:

$$L = \sum_t \log p(\mathbf{X}(t + 1)| \mathbf{X}(t), \mathbf{R}(t))$$

$$= \sum_t \left(\sum_{i=1}^n \log h_i(X_i(t + 1), \mathbf{R}(t + 1), \mathbf{X}(t), \mathbf{R}(t)) \right.$$

$$\left. + \sum_{i=1}^m \log g_i(R_i(t + 1), \mathbf{X}(t), \mathbf{R}(t)) \right)$$

$$= \sum_t \left(\sum_{i=1}^n \log h_i(X_i(t + 1), \mathbf{f}(\mathbf{X}(t), \mathbf{R}(t)), \mathbf{X}(t), \mathbf{R}(t)) \right.$$

$$\left. + \sum_{i=1}^m \log g_i(f_i(\mathbf{X}(t), \mathbf{R}(t)), \mathbf{X}(t), \mathbf{R}(t)) \right).$$

Using this likelihood function, we may construct tables, analogous to those used in Section 2.3 for log p, to let us calculate the derivatives of likelihood with respect to all our parameters, in the functions f_i, g_i, and h_i. Thus, once again, we may use the method of steepest descent to maximize likelihood.

It should be emphasized, however, that the likelihood function spelled out in the equation above was based on substitutions, which were, in some ways, arbitrary. From a formal point of view, the functions f_i, g_i, and h_i are somewhat redundant as model specifications; thus we have a certain amount of leeway in deciding how to combine them. When, as above, the functions h_i are adjusted in such a way that the f_i are considered to be fixed but effectively unknown functions, and in such a way that $\mathbf{R}(t)$ and $\mathbf{X}(t)$ are directly available to the h_i as arguments, then the resulting model will, as a whole, be at least as good as a simple model specifying the $X_i(t + 1)$ as independent functions of $\mathbf{R}(t)$ and $\mathbf{X}(t)$. In other words, even if the $R_i(t + 1)$ are totally ignored, a model fit in this way can achieve, at a minimum, the level of fit that would be achieved by a conventional model assuming independence. In order to get maximum value from this technique, however, one would want to adjust the definition of the f_i to increase the actual likelihood of the model as a whole, evaluated in terms of the *observed* data, $\mathbf{X}(t + 1)$, by themselves. It is likely that the constraint of having to assume independence at all levels, in order to minimize cost with a large number of variables, might not be consistent with achieving an absolute maximum of likelihood by this more strenuous criterion. Also, it is far from obvious that the procedure above is the best procedure for measuring likelihood, even subject to that constraint. The concepts of time-series analysis discussed elsewhere in this thesis required considerable theoretical and empirical work, before the pros and cons of specific algorithms began to seem clear; pattern analysis, which is a more subtle and potentially more powerful technique, will require at least as much development, both theoretical and empirical, to become useful in the future. Theoretical studies of the linear special case may be of particular value in the early stages of this development.

Even at this stage of research, however, it seems clear where the applications of pattern analysis will lie. Pattern analysis is essentially a generalization of the idea of factor analysis to the nonlinear dynamic case. The dynamic power of a proposed "principal factor" would appear to be a better measure of its importance than the variance it accounts for in static cross-sections; when time-series data are available, pattern analysis would appear to be a clearly superior strategy for evaluating the same set of parameters as with factor analysis. With many variables or long time-series, the nonlinear feature may also turn out to grow in importance; statistical pattern-recognition or satellite-collected data may both provide major applications for the possibility of nonlinearity here. In such highly complex systems, the massive number of variables may make the assumption of independence a necessity, both in terms of computational cost and in terms of avoiding models with more degrees of freedom than one could hope to estimate; pattern analysis may be essential to prevent excessive reductions of model likelihood as a result of that assumption. Also, with such systems, note that one does not have to restrict one's computer package to estimating functions—f_i, g_i, and h_i—whose form has been specified in advance by the user. One can provide an option for the computer to try out new tables of operations, automatically, by pruning out terms that contribute little and by evaluating the improvement in likelihood from adding new terms, chosen essentially at random. Finally, one should note that the assumption of independence may be especially valuable on machines that allow parallel processing; the one-to-one association between functions f_i and functions g_i, corresponding to the same components of **R**, may be of major importance in making pattern analysis operational on such machines.

2.10 OPTIMIZATION

In Sections 2.3 and 2.4, we saw how dynamic feedback can be used to minimize error; later on, we saw how it could be used to maximize probability. In general, the method of steepest descent can be used to minimize or maximize any function we please, as long as we can calculate all the derivatives. Dynamic feedback lets us calculate the derivatives, as long as our system of formulas is explicit. Therefore the dynamic feedback method can be used to minimize or maximize other things besides error.

Suppose, for example, that we have a simple model of the U.S. economy, something like

$$C(t + 1) = k_1 C(t) + k_2 Y(t + 1),$$

$$Y(t + 1) = a_1 P(t + 1),$$

$$P(t + 1) = P(t) + k_3 (P(t) - C(t)). \tag{2.18}$$

In this case, we are *not* trying to evaluate or estimate a model. We assume that the model has *already* been tested and that k_1, k_2, and k_3 have already been estimated by some kind of statistical procedure. C here represents consumption, Y represents personal income, and P represents production. With optimal government policy, all production capacity will be channeled to either consumption or to some kind of investment; a_1, the rate of taxation, determines how much goes to each. Our problem here is to find the "best" level for a_1. Suppose that we define "best" to mean the level of a_1 that maximizes consumption in the long term. Suppose that we start from a known position in year 1 and want to maximize the sum of consumption over the next 3 years. Then we may define our utility function, U, to equal $C(2) + C(3) + C(4)$. We may set up the table of calculations, shown in Table 2.5, which defines

TABLE 2.5 Table of Operations for Equations (2.18)

Actual Variable	Variable Number	Operation Category	Major Source	Minor Source
$U = C(2) + C(3) + C(4)$	29	Sum	28	21, 14
$C(4) = k_1 C(3) + k_2 Y(4)$	28	Sum	27	26
$k_1 C(3)$	27	Product	21	4
$k_2 Y(4)$	26	Product	25	3
$Y(4) = a_1 P(4)$	25	Product	24	1
$P(4) = P(3) + k_3(P(3) - C(3))$	24	Sum	23	17
$k_3(P(3) - C(3))$	23	Product	22	2
$P(3) - C(3)$	22	Difference	17	21
$C(3) = k_1 C(2) + k_2 Y(3)$	21	Sum	20	19
$k_1 C(2)$	20	Product	14	4
$k_2 Y(3)$	19	Product	18	3
$Y(3) = a_1 P(3)$	18	Product	17	1
$P(3) = P(2) + k_3(P(2) - C(2))$	17	Sum	16	10
$k_3(P(2) - C(2))$	16	Product	15	2
$P(2) - C(2)$	15	Difference	10	14
$C(2) = k_1 C(1) + k_2 Y(2)$	14	Sum	13	12
$k_1 C(1)$	13	Product	7	4
$k_2 Y(2)$	12	Product	11	3
$Y(2) = a_1 P(2)$	11	Product	10	1
$P(2) = P(1) + k_3(P(1) - C(1))$	10	Sum	9	5

TABLE 2.5   Table of Operations for Equations (2.18)   (Continued)

Actual Variable	Variable Number	Operation Category	Major Source	Minor Source
$k_3(P(1) - C(1))$	9	Product	8	2
$P(1) - C(1)$	8	Difference	5	7
$C(1)$	7	Given	—	—
$Y(1)$	6	Given	—	—
$P(1)$	5	Given	—	—
k_1	4	Given	—	—
k_2	3	Given	—	—
k_3	2	Given	—	—
a_1	1	Parameter	—	—

how U is to be calculated up from the parameter and the constants of this problem. In order to maximize U by the method of steepest ascent, we need only calculate $\partial U/\partial a_1$, the derivative of U with respect to the parameter we have to control. We may calculate the derivatives of $U = X_{29}$, as before, by using the method of dynamic feedback on the table of operations, Table 2.5. We may start with $S_{29} = \partial U/\partial X_{29} = 1$; then, if we calculate derivatives down the table, as before, S_1 will equal $\partial U/\partial a_1$. Our original model was very simple in this example; however, it should be clear that even a complicated nonlinear model, involving many control parameters, could be translated into a table like Table 2.5, by computer, if the model is "explicit" in the sense of Section 2.4.

In the example above, we have described a problem that does not quite fit the standard format used most often in control theory. It is a problem in what we would prefer to call "systems optimization" or "dynamic systems optimization." Problems of this type have been discussed by Jacobsen and Mayne [35], as a device for overcoming some of the difficulties of optimization under conditions of uncertainty; in the social sciences, however, this formulation may have substantive advantages over the more standard formulation, which are worth pointing out here.

In the case above, for example, we tried to pick the best possible value for a_1, a *constant* in the nation's taxation system. In standard control theory, one would usually look at $a_1(t)$, the taxation rate *at each time*, and try to find the best possible schedule of tax rates for different years. In principle, the second way is better, but only if it is feasible politically to change the tax rates up and down every year. In practice, governments trying to follow conventional Keynesian policies, adjusting tax rates every year, have encountered serious political problems and problems of timing; thus there has been great interest in "automatic adjustment" factors [2] and in other system parameters that can be adjusted to improve economic performance *without* forcing us to change policy too often. Thus "systems optimization" has something worthwhile to offer the policy-maker, above and beyond its mathematical convenience.

The methods here could also be used in conventional control theory problems. In our example, we could try to pick the best values for the *three* parameters, $a(2)$, $a(3)$, and $a(4)$, by putting all three at the bottom of our table and calculating back

$$\frac{\partial U}{\partial a(2)}, \quad \frac{\partial U}{\partial a(3)}, \quad \text{and} \quad \frac{\partial U}{\partial a(4)}.$$

Jacobson and Mayne [35] have shown how steepest ascent methods, very similar to ours, can also be used in cases where noise terms appear in the model.[10] The dynamic feedback method allows us to calculate $\partial U/\partial a_i$ in cases where the dynamic laws of the system are arbitrarily complex and where the interconnections in time may stretch over several time periods; it allows us to exploit the internal structure of the model, as spelled out in a table, in order to calculate back all the derivatives in one pass, at a cost much lower than with separate differentiations. Otherwise, however, the methods discussed by Jacobson and Mayne for making use of $\partial U/\partial a_i$, in systems optimization, are very general and do not require further elaboration here.

2.11 THE METHOD OF "RELAXATION" WITH MEASUREMENT-NOISE-ONLY MODELS

In Section 2.7, the possibility of "measurement-noise-only" models were discussed, which are at the opposite pole from the usual regression models, which may be characterized as "process-noise-only" models. Between these two poles is a whole spectrum of more moderate techniques. Let us suppose that one has a simple model of some process, defined by the equations

$$X_i(t + 1) = f_i(X_1(t), \ldots, X_n(t)), \quad i = 1, n \qquad (2.19)$$

Using the classical regression approach, we would tack on a normal noise term, $a_i(t)$, to the end of these equations, to arrive at the stochastic model:

$$X_i(t + 1) = f_i(X_1(t), \ldots, X_n(t)) + a_i(t).$$

We would estimate the parameters in this model by trying to minimize the square errors:

$$L_i = \sum_t [X_i(t + 1) - f_i(X_1(t), \ldots, X_n(t))]^2, \qquad (2.20)$$

---

[10]Samuelson [2, p. 345] begins a discussion of this topic; his own attitude is more partial to the traditional Keynesian approach, but his discussion clearly indicates that automatic adjustment factors have been of great interest to some economists.

after we substitute in for the *measured* values of $X_i(t + 1)$ and $X_j(t)$. In effect, this would imply minimizing the square error for predictions over *one interval* of time.

With the measurement-noise-only models, we would normally include, in the list of parameters to be estimated, the values of $Y_i(0)$, where Y_i is defined as the "true" value of X_i. Using Equations (2.19), we can predict the "true" value of $X_i(1)$—$Y_i(1)$—from our estimates of the $Y_i(0)$, and predict $Y_i(2)$ from the predictions of $Y_i(1)$, and so on. Using these long-term predictions, $\hat{Y}_i(t)$, we can try to minimize the errors:

$$L'_i = \sum_t [X_i(t + 1) - f_i(\hat{Y}_1(t), \dots, \hat{Y}_n(t))]^2.$$

From the viewpoint of maximum likelihood theory, these predictions, $\hat{Y}_i(t)$, may be viewed as the "estimates" of $Y_i(t)$, derived from the estimates $\hat{Y}_i(0)$ and from the assumption that Equations (2.19) are *exactly* true, with no noise, for the true values, $Y_i(t)$.

How can we find a viable compromise between Equations (2.20) and (2.21)? In Equation (2.20), we use the *measured* value, $X_i(t)$, to estimate the true values, $Y_i(t)$, for use as the arguments of f_i; in Equation (2.21), we use estimates, $\hat{Y}_i(t)$, based solely on updating our estimates for $Y_i(t - 1)$, that is, $\hat{Y}_i(t - 1)$, by use of Equation (2.19). The obvious compromise is to estimate $Y_i(t)$ by something half-way between the measured values, $X_i(t)$, and the estimates of $Y_i(t)$ that result from updating our estimates of $Y_i(t - 1)$. Thus we may define new estimates, $Z_i(t)$, of $Y_i(t)$ by

$$Z_i(t) = (1 - r)f_i(Z_1(t - 1), \dots, Z_n(t - 1)) + rX_i(t). \qquad (2.22)$$

Using these estimates, we may attempt to minimize the loss function:

$$L'_i = \sum_t [X_i(t + 1) - f_i(Z_1(t), \dots, Z_n(t))]^2. \qquad (2.23)$$

The $Z_j(0)$, like $Y_j(0)$, would be parameters to estimate. The constant r may be called the "coefficient of relaxation"; it is a kind of interest rate, which, when large, implies a greater concern for short-term prediction than for long-term prediction.

Note that the structure of Equation (2.22) looks similar to that of a filtering system, designed to yield a posterior estimate of the "true" value of $\mathbf{X}$, given both a prior expectation and an actual measurement. In the field of engineering, a great deal of work has been done on the problem of designing an optimal filtering system, to deal with vectors $\mathbf{X}$ that result from noisy measurements of a linear process, which has been completely specified in advance. It is well known that the best way to update one's estimates, in this situation, is not by the independent equations (2.22), but by the matrix equations of the "Kalman filter" [36, p. 361]:

$$\mathbf{Z}(t) = \mathbf{f}(\mathbf{Z}(t - 1)) + K(t)[\mathbf{X}(t) - H(t)\,\mathbf{f}(\mathbf{Z}(t - 1))],$$

where K and H are time-varying matrices determined by

$$K(t) = P(t)H^T(t)R^{-1}(t),$$
$$P(t) = [M^{-1}(t) + H^T(t)R^{-1}(t)H(t)]^{-1},$$
$$M(t + 1) = \phi(t)P(t)\phi^T(t) + G(t)Q(t)G^T(t),$$

and where H, R, G, and Q are all characteristic matrices of the linear process, a process that may be specified:

$$\mathbf{X}(t) = H(t)\mathbf{Y}(t) + \mathbf{b}(t),$$
$$\mathbf{Y}(t + 1) = G(t)\mathbf{Y}(t) + \mathbf{c}(t), \tag{2.24}$$

with R and Q the covariance matrices of the noise vectors $\mathbf{b}$ and $\mathbf{c}$, respectively. The details of these equations are beyond the range of the discussion here. One should note that the linear processes of Equation (2.24) are essentially the same as those to be discussed early in Chapter 3; it will be shown there that processes of that general sort can be dealt with exactly by use of the ARMA approach, whose practical limitations are discussed in Chapters 4–6. However, even if the Kalman filtering equations were derived for a limited class of linear processes, one might expect them to be an improvement over Equations (2.22), on the theory that they can be used to perform the same function, somewhat more rationally, as part of our system of robust estimation. In this case, one would adjust the matrices H, R, and Q in an ad hoc sort of way, just as one would adjust the relaxation constant r, rather than estimate them all beforehand by use of the maximum likelihood technique on some version of the simple questions (2.24). However, this use of the Kalman filter brings three difficulties with it, which make it a subject for future research rather than present systems design: (1) the need to adjust three matrices, H, R, and Q, automatically requires a much greater development of the theory of robust estimation than does the need to adjust a single constant, r, by hand; (2) the sheer complexity of the Kalman equations would impose heavy costs on the systems programmer; and (3) even given a rational approach to estimating the matrices H, R, and Q, one would presumably need a huge quantity of data to estimate so many parameters, in addition to all the parameters of one's model.

2.12 THE ORDERED DERIVATIVE AND DYNAMIC FEEDBACK

The traditional formalism used for dealing with partial derivatives was evolved to deal with the problems of geometry and of physical science. In those fields, one normally deals with functions defined over a fixed set of coordinate variables; even when one changes one's choice of coordinates, one is usually making a clear-cut shift from one set to a second set. In the social sciences, however, one normally deals with a complex web of functional relations and variables. This web will often have a *causal ordering* associated with it. Thus when we say that $x_{t+1} = f(y_t, z_t)$, we not only mean that a relation exists between the variables y_t, z_t, and x_{t+1}; we also tend to mean that the variables y_t and z_t "cause" x_{t+1} to equal what it does, and that x_{t+1} is causally "later" than y_t and z_t. We will often be interested in asking what changes will follow, *later*, if we change a given variable by a small amount *at a given time*. Clearly, this question calls for us to calculate some kind of partial derivative. In order to deal with this kind of situation, as easily as we now deal with situations in physical science and geometry, we need to define a new formalism for this kind of partial derivative.

Let us begin by imagining that we have a well-ordered set of variables, x_1, $x_2, \ldots, x_n$, with each variable x_i obeying a functional relation:

$$x_i = f_i(x_{i-1}, x_{i-2}, \ldots, x_1).$$

Let us define a new set of functions, F_i, recursively:

(i) $F_n(x_n, x_{n-1}, x_{n-2}, \ldots, x_1) = x_n$

(ii) $F_{i-1}(x_{i-1}, x_{i-2}, \ldots, x_1)$

$$= F_i(f_i(x_{i-1}, x_{i-2}, \ldots, x_1), x_{i-1}, x_{i-2}, \ldots, x_1)$$

(In other words, F_i expresses x_n as a function of the variables x_i, $x_{i-1}, \ldots, x_1$, arrived at by substitution into higher F_j's.) Let us define the ordered derivative of x_n as follows:

$$\frac{\partial^+ x_n}{\partial x_i} = \frac{\partial F_i}{\partial x_i}, \quad n \geq i \geq i_0,$$

where the derivative on the right is evaluated by traditional procedures, holding constant all the variables $x_{i-1}, \ldots, x_1$. We may further define

$$\frac{\partial^+ x_n}{\partial x_i} = \frac{\partial F_{i_0}}{\partial x_i}, \quad 1 \leq i \leq i_0.$$

Theorem

$$\frac{\partial F_j}{\partial x_i} = \sum_{k=j+1}^{n} \frac{\partial^+ x_n}{\partial x_k} \cdot \frac{\partial f_k}{\partial x_i} \quad \text{for} \quad \begin{matrix} i_0 \leq j < n \\ 1 \leq i \leq j \end{matrix}.$$

We can prove this, for any given i and n within the acceptable range, by induction on j downward from $j = n - 1$ (down to $j = i$). Let us begin by considering the initial case, $j = n - 1$. In this case, our general claim reduces to

$$\frac{\partial F_{n-1}}{\partial x_i} = \frac{\partial^+ x_n}{\partial x_n} \cdot \frac{\partial f_n}{\partial x_i}.$$

From our definitions of F_n and of F_{n-1}, this reduces immediately to

$$\frac{\partial f_n}{\partial x_i} = \frac{\partial x_n}{\partial x_n} \cdot \frac{\partial f_n}{\partial x_i},$$

which is clearly true.

Now, to complete our proof, we need only prove the formula for $j \geq i$ and $j \geq i_0$, on the assumption that it is true for $j + 1 < n$. Let us begin by going back to the definition of F_j:

$$F_j(x_j, x_{j-1}, \ldots, x_1) = F_{j+1}(f_{j+1}(x_j, x_{j-1}, \ldots, x_1), x_j, \ldots, x_1).$$

In order to make this more explicit, we may write it as follows:

$$F_j(x_j, x_{j-1}, \ldots, x_1) = F_{j+1}(s_{j+1}, s_j, s_{j-1}, \ldots, s_1)$$

where

$$s_{j+1} = f_{j+1}(x_j, x_{j-1}, \ldots, x_1),$$

$$s_i = x_i, \quad 1 \leq i \leq j.$$

By the conventional chain rule for partial differentiation,

$$\frac{\partial}{\partial x_i}(F_j(x_j, x_{j-1}, \ldots, x_1)) \quad ,$$

$$= \sum_{k=1}^{j+1} \left(\frac{\partial}{\partial s_k}(F_{j+1}(s_{j+1}, \ldots, s_1)) \right) \left(\frac{\partial s_k}{\partial x_i} \right)$$

$$1 \leq i \leq j$$

Now for $k \leq j$, our definitions of s_k as a simple function of the x_i clearly tell us that $\partial s_k / \partial x_i$ equals 1 if $k = i$, and zero otherwise. For $k = j + 1$, our definition tells us that

$$\frac{\partial s_k}{\partial x_i} = \frac{\partial f_{j+1}}{\partial x_i}.$$

Thus the sum on the right in the equation above may be evaluated to give us a new equation:

$$\frac{\partial F_j}{\partial x_i} = \left(\frac{\partial}{\partial s_{j+1}} (F_{j+1}(s_{j+1}, \ldots, s_1)) \right) \frac{\partial f_{j+1}}{\partial x_i}$$

$$+ \frac{\partial}{\partial s_i} (F_{j+1}(s_{j+1}, \ldots, s_1)).$$

Give that our remaining derivatives with respect to the s_i do not involve the expression x_i anywhere, and given that the s_i have been defined in such a way as to equal the x_j for $1 \le i \le j + 1$, the value of these expressions will not change if we substitute in the letter x for every occurrence of the letter s. Thus we obtain

$$\frac{\partial F_j}{\partial x_i} = \frac{\partial F_{j+1}}{\partial x_{j+1}} \cdot \frac{\partial f_{j+1}}{\partial x_i} + \frac{\partial F_{j+1}}{\partial s_i}.$$

Now from the induction hypothesis we were given that

$$\frac{\partial F_{j+1}}{\partial s_i} = \sum_{k=j+2}^{n} \frac{\partial^+ x_n}{\partial x_k} \cdot \frac{\partial f_k}{\partial x_i}.$$

From our definition of the ordered derivative, this is merely

$$\frac{\partial F_j}{\partial x_i} = \frac{\partial^+ x_n}{\partial x_{j+1}} \cdot \frac{\partial f_{j+1}}{\partial x_i} + \sum_{k=j+2}^{n} \frac{\partial^+ x_n}{\partial x_n} \cdot \frac{\partial f_k}{\partial x_i}$$

$$= \sum_{k=j+1}^{n} \frac{\partial^+ x_n}{\partial x_n} \cdot \frac{\partial f_k}{\partial x_i},$$

which establishes our contention for the case j, and which, by induction, proves the contention as a whole.

Corollary 1. *If $i_0 \le i \le n$,*

$$\frac{\partial^+ x_n}{\partial x_i} = \sum_{k=i+1}^{n} \frac{\partial^+ x_n}{\partial x_k} \cdot \frac{\partial f_k}{\partial x_i}.$$

This follows immediately from setting $j = i$ in our theorem, and exploiting the definition of the ordered derivative.

Corollary 2. If $1 \le i \le i_0$,

$$\frac{\partial^+ x_n}{\partial x_i} = \frac{\partial F_{i0}}{\partial x_i} = \sum_{k=i0+1}^{n} \frac{\partial^+ x_n}{\partial x_k} \cdot \frac{\partial f_k}{\partial x_i}.$$

Note that $F_{i_0}(x_{i_0}, \ldots, x_i)$ is the function that expresses x_n as a function solely of the "external parameters," x_{i_0} through x_1. If x_n represents something like "likelihood," L, and if the "external parameters" represent constants of the model and fixed data, then F_{i_0} expresses likelihood as a function of these parameters. When we are trying to maximize likelihood "as a function of these parameters," we are trying to maximize L *expressed as* F_{i_0}. Thus when we ask about $\partial L / \partial k_1$ in that context, we are really asking about $\partial F_{i_0} / \partial k_1$.

Note that the concept of "ordered derivative" does not really depend on the exact choice of order $x_1, x_2, \ldots, x_n$. Suppose that x_i is really "simultaneous" with $x_{i+1}, x_{i+2}, \ldots, x_{k+1}$, in the sense that it is not really an argument of the functions $f_{i+1}, f_{i+2}, \ldots, f_{k+1}$. Then, in our chain rule above, the derivative $\partial f_j / \partial x_i$ is zero for j of $i + 1$ through $k - 1$; thus the actual value of the ordered derivative, as given by those formulas, will not be affected by our arbitrary decision to treat these variables as if they were "later" than x_i in the causal ordering. The ordered derivative would appear to be defined with respect to the general causal ordering, a weak ordering of our lattice of variables, rather than the strong numerical order chosen to represent it. For our purposes, however, it is not necessary to establish such generality, since we need only justify a calculating procedure based on the definite numerical ordering chosen for our tables.

As a practical matter, all of the "working back" of the derivatives cited earlier might be carried out by one standard computer subroutine, called on by simple "main programs" within one's computer package to carry out estimation and optimization for models of all different sorts. Other possibilities have been mentioned briefly in Section 2.3. Model specification could be allowed either in terms of standard TSP formulas or in terms of Forrester-style DYNAMO expressions. In principle, the standard subroutine(s), set up to allow optimal control calculations, would also allow maximum-likelihood estimation of "hidden variables" in *implicit models*; however, the use of this provision should probably not be encouraged, except in those cases where a theoretical understanding exists of its potential value.

2.13 VARIATIONS ON THE STEEPEST ASCENT METHOD FOR EFFICIENT CONVERGENCE

The discussion of the dynamic feedback method throughout this chapter depends on the assumption that the derivatives calculated by this method can be used as the input to the steepest ascent method, in minimizing or maximizing various types of functions. In practice, however, I have found great difficulty in getting adequate convergence with the classical steepest ascent method in early experiments with ARMA estimation, to be discussed in Chapter 3. This experience seems to be in line with the general impressions of other people in the community who have used the method. It is possible, however, to bring the convergence rate up to reasonable standards by use of "variable metric techniques" and related methods.

In Section 2.3, we alluded briefly to the constants C to be used in the steepest ascent method; in the discussion, there was never any reason to require that C be the same for all the parameters a_i. In the "variable metric" approach, one simply chooses different constants, C_i, for different parameters. Thus one would write

$$a_i^{(n+1)} = a_i^{(n)} + C_i \frac{\partial U}{\partial a_i} (\mathbf{a}^{(n)}).$$

This equation specifies that our $(n + 1)$st estimate of the parameter a_i will equal our nth estimate, plus C_i times the derivative with respect to a_i of the function U, which we are trying to maximize. (The derivative is calculated, of course, from our current set of estimates, $\mathbf{a}^{(n)}$.) This approach has become fairly popular in some quarters.

Ideally, if one had all the second derivatives available, one might use the classic Gaussian method:

$$\mathbf{a}^{(n+1)} = \mathbf{a}^{(n)} - A^{-1}(\nabla U),$$

where ∇U is the vector $\partial U/\partial a_i$ and A is the matrix of the second derivatives, $\partial^2 U/\partial a_i \partial a_j$. To pick the constants C_i above, one might try to pick them to form as close an approximation as possible to the Gaussian equation here. Thus one might try to approximate

$$C_i = -1 \left(\frac{\partial^2 U}{\partial a_i^2} \right).$$

In order to generate a low-cost, order-of-magnitude estimate, S_i^*, of

$$\left(\frac{\partial^2 U}{\partial a_i^2} \right) = \left(\frac{\partial^2 U}{\partial x_i^2} \right),$$

one might carry out another feedback calculation down our tables of operations:

$$S_i^* = \sum_{j=i+1}^{n} \left[\left(\frac{\partial f_j}{\partial x_i} \right)^2 S_j^* + \left(\frac{\partial^2 f_j}{\partial x_i^2} \right) S_j \right], \tag{2.25}$$

where S_j is the ordered derivative of U with respect to x_j, as computed by the procedures of Section 2.3, and the rest of the notation here comes from Section 2.12. The term on the left-hand side of the expression to be summed preserves the sign of the "estimated" second derivatives, as we go down from the S_j^* to S_i^*. The term on the right, however, risks a change of sign; it might either be eliminated or else cut off to equal zero whenever it tries to go too far in an abnormal direction, if we choose to avoid this risk. In the case of a maximization problem, the normal sign for the second derivatives is negative. If we write

$$C_i = -w/S_i^*,$$

then, if the $(n + 1)$st estimate turns out to be inferior to the nth, we can simply reduce the unsubscripted constant w and try again. This method is guaranteed eventual convergence to a local maximum, as we adjust w back and forth, for exactly the same reasons that the classical method is guaranteed convergence as C is adjusted back and forth; given that we have imposed measures to keep the signs of the S_i^* negative, we may invoke the definition of the derivative, just as we did in Section 2.3. In the case of ARMA estimation, a similar though more specialized approach has turned out to be quite successful. While I have not run across this particular form of the variable metric approach in the literature, I have heard rumors that something similar may have attracted attention elsewhere in statistics; however, it would be difficult to believe that Equation (2.25) itself, which is based on a procedure related to dynamic feedback, has been used in this general form.

In situations where the number of variables is great, and many iterations are required in any case, one can imagine an additional provision, "convergence learning," to try to make the constants C_i better approximations to the choice that would lead to the fastest convergence. One may set

$$C_i = -w\theta_i/S_i^*,$$

where θ_i is increased when the parameter $a_i^{(n)}$ seems to be moving systematically in one direction from estimate (n) to estimate, and where it is decreased when $a_i^{(n)}$ seems to be oscillating. One might, for example, multiple θ_i by $1 + C$, for some positive C, when $\partial U/\partial a_i$ calculated at $a^{(n+1)}$ has the same sign as $\partial U/\partial a_i$ calculated at $a^{(n)}$; one might divide it by $1 + C$ when the signs are opposite. As before, if the sign of θ_i is positive, one is still assured of eventual convergence to a local maximum. Insofar as each of these factors θ_k is essentially an adjustment factor for our approximation of $\partial^2 U/\partial a_k^2$, we might even use it in Equation (2.25), to divide those terms in our summation on the right which involve entries X_j in our table of operations, which use the parameter a_k as a "source variable."

In order to define these procedures in more detail, it would be necessary to have some way to evaluate the many alternative possibilities in these directions; insofar as these procedures are all aimed at the practical goal of speeding up convergence it would seem best to evaluate them by way of practical experiments, when the necessary computer routines become available.

2.14 ENDNOTES TO CHAPTER 2

2.14.1 Citations on Deutsch-Solow Model

Note that the letter U is used instead of D in the revised version of the model. Also note that several versions of this model have appeared in print. The version here, in all fairness, was actually taken directly from Hopkins, Raymond, and Carol, "A difference equation model for mobilization and assimilation processes" (unpublished works). A copy of this paper was provided by Professor Deutsch and described as containing the final revision of the model. This revision appears, in difference equation form, in Hopkins and Raymond [37]. The reasons for the revisions to earlier versions are described in Hopkins and Raymond [38, p. 381].

2.14.2 Discussion of Prisoner's Dilemma

The "prisoner's dilemma," in its original form, is a simple two-person game in which each player has two options from which to choose: to betray or not to betray the other player to the police. If neither player is betrayed, both pay a slight penalty (a small jail sentence). If one is betrayed, then he/she pays a heavy penalty, but the other escapes all penalty. If both betray each other, both pay a fairly heavy penalty. The structure of this game has been used as a paradigm for certain arms races, in which the self-interest of each player, paradoxically, may lead both into a competition in which both of them enjoy less security and have less money left over then if both had shown restraint [39].

2.14.3 Fine Points on Maximum Likelihood Theory

More precisely, classical maximum likelihood theory specifies a unique log likelihood measure of goodness of fit, for the simple model above, *including the normal noise distribution as part of the model*. This measure of fit is a special case of what is described in more detail in Section 2.6, based on the concepts of Section 2.5. From a conservative Bayesian point of view, this measure is taken to be the logarithm of the probability of truth of a model, conditional on the observed data, assuming a prior probability distribution that is "flat" when described in terms of the coefficients of the model as written, and relying on the space of these coefficients and of the data as encoded to provide us with the measures over which these probability distributions are defined.

In a sense, this criterion provides a meaningful estimate of the *relative* probability of truth of the coefficient values considered, subject to the constraint that the model is assumed to be "true," for some value of the coefficients, in whatever sense it is possible for a statistical model to be "true." One of the primary objectives in this thesis is to point out tangible, correctible deficiencies in the classical idea of looking for "truth" as such, in statistical dynamic models; in Chapter 5, I point out that verbal models and statistical models are subject to similar difficulties in basic matters. (Statistical models in a very hard science, such as pure physics, may be different, however.) In Section 2.7, where the new alternatives are discussed on a theoretical level, it is emphasized that these approaches to the practical prediction of time series can be understood as an offshoot of the more general and more coherent Bayesian philosophy of induction, as briefly sketched in Section 2.5. The maintenance of this connection is especially important to the social sciences, where the Bayesian framework has many applications beyond those of explicit data analysis; for example, see Raiffa and Howard [40].

2.14.4 Possible Significance of Pr(Data) Term

In the philosophy of science, there is occasional reference to the "cosmological principle" that we expect p(data) for the observed data to end up reasonably large, once a full spectrum of theories has been studied. In other words, one expects that the observed data will not be an unusual local coincidence, according to a "true" theory; one expects that data, as observed from earth in particular, are likely to be typical of data observed elsewhere. Such an additional assumption would not be necessary, or even logical, if we felt that we had p(model) available for the full range of possible models, along with p(data| model). However, when we ask about the probability that new models, as yet unformulated, may turn out to be valid, the "cosmological principle" does have something to tell us.

REFERENCES

1. K. W. Deutsch, *Nationalism and Social Communications*, rev. 2nd ed., MIT Press, Cambridge, MA, 1966, Appendix V.
2. P. A. Samuelson, *Economics: An Introductory Analysis*, 4th ed., McGraw-Hill, New York, 1958.
3. B. G. Hickman, *Econometric Models of Cyclical Behavior*, National Bureau of Economic Research, 1972.
4. M. Ezekiel and K. A. Fox, *Methods of Correlation and Regression Analysis*, 3rd ed., Wiley, New York, 1959.
5. O. Postrikov, *Foundations of Galois Theory*, Pergamon Press, New York, 1962.
6. M. T. Wasan, *Parametric Estimation*, McGraw-Hill, New York, 1970.
7. W. J. Dixon, *BMD Biomedical Computer Programs: X-Series Supplement*, University of California Press, Berkeley, June 1972.
8. J. Brode, *Time-Series-Processor—TSP*, available from Project Cambridge, MIT,

5th floor, 575 Technology Square, Cambridge, MA 02139. A manual for the revised version of TSP may be forthcoming in the MIT Press.

9. *TROLL/1 Primer*, available from National Bureau for Economic Research, 9th floor, 575 Technology Square, Cambridge, MA 02139.

10. M. Friedman, *A Theory of the Consumption Function*, Princeton University Press, Princeton, NJ, 1957.

11. R. Carnap and R. C. Jeffreys, *Studies in Inductive Logic and Probability*, University of California Press, Berkeley, 1971.

12. G. E. P. Box and G. M. Jenkins, *Time-Series Analysis: Forecasting and Control*, Holden-Day, San Francisco, 1970.

13. M. G. Kendall and A. Stuart, *The Advanced Theory of Statistics*, 2nd ed., Hafner Publishing Co., New York, 1970, Vol. 2.

14. I. Kant, *A Critique of Pure Reason*. Meikle, J. M., tr., C. E. Tuttle, 1934.

15. R. L. Anderson and T. A. Bancroft, *Statistical Theory in Research*, McGraw-Hill, New York, 1952.

16. W. L. Hays, *Statistics for the Social Sciences*, 2nd ed., Holt, Rhinehart and Winston, New York, 1973.

17. D. V. Lindley, Professor Hogben's crisis—a survey of the foundations of statistics, *Applied Statistics*, Vol. 7, No. 3, pp. 186–198, 1958.

18. H. Raiffa and R. Schlaifer, *Applied Statistical Decision Theory*.

19. R. Hogg and A. Craig, *Introduction to Mathematical Statistics*, 3rd ed., Macmillan, London, 1970.

20. G. E. Box and G. Tiao, *Bayesian Inference in Statistical Analysis*, Wiley.

21. R. Schlaifer, *User's Guide to the AQD Programs*, Harvard Business School, Boston, MA, Part III, p. 18.

22. A. Shimony, Scientific inference, in R. Colodny (ed.), *Nature and Foundation of Scientific Theories*, University of Pittsburgh Press, 1970.

23. R. Solomonoff, "Mathematical foundations of induction." Manuscript available in 1964 at the MIT Artificial Intelligence Laboratory from Professor Minsky.

24. S. F. Barker, The role of simplicity in explanation, in F. Feigl and G. Maxwell (eds.), *Current Issues in the Philosophy of Science*, Holt, Rinehart and Winston, New York, 1961.

25. M. Alpert and H. Raiffa, "A progress report on the training of probability assessors." Available in 1971 as an unpublished manuscript from the office of Professor Raiffa in the Littauer Building, Harvard University, Cambridge, MA 02138.

26. C. Mosteller and R. E. Rourke, *Sturdy Statistics: Nonparametric and Order Statistics*, Addison-Wesley, Reading, MA, 1973.

27. W. Tukey, A survey of sampling from contaminated distributions, in I. Olkin et al. (eds.), *Contributions to Probability and Statistics: Essays in Honor of Harold Hotelling*, Stanford University Press, Stanford, CA, 1960, pp. 448–485.

28. D. Cochrane and G. H. Orcutt, Application of least squares regression to relationships containing autocorrelated error terms, *Journal of the American Statistical Association*, p. 34, March 1949.

29. J. W. Forrester, *Industrial Dynamics*, MIT Press, Cambridge, MA, 1961.

30. J. W. Forrester, *World Dynamics*, Wright-Allen Press, Cambridge, MA, 1971.

31. D. H. Meadows, D. L. Randers, and W. Behrins, *The Limits to Growth*, 3rd printing, Signet Books, New York, 1972.

32. H. S. D. Cole, C. Freeman, K. L. R. Pavitt, and M. Jahoda, *Models of Doom: A Critique of the Limits to Growth*, Universe Books, New York, 1973.

33. R. E. Rogers, *Max Weber's Ideal Type Theory*, Philosophical Library, New York, 1969.

34. I. K. Feierabend, L. Rosalind, and T. Gurr (eds.), *Anger, Violence and Politics*, Prentice-Hall, Englewood Cliffs, NJ, 1972.

35. D. Jacobson and D. Mayne, *Differential Dynamic Programming*, American Elsevier, New York, 1970. See especially Chapter 6.

36. A.E. Bryson, Jr. and Y.-C. Ho, *Applied Optimal Control*, Ginn and Co., Waltham, MA, 1969.

37. R. Hopkins and Raymond, Projections of population change by mobilization and assimilation, *Behavioral Science*, p. 254, 1972.

38. R. Hopkins and Raymond, Mathematical modeling of mobilization and assimilation processes, in H. Alker, K. Deutsch, and A. Stoetzel (eds.), *Mathematical Approaches to Politics*, Elsevier, New York, 1973.

39. A. Rapoport, *Fights, Games and Debates*, 2nd printing, University of Michigan Press, Ann Arbor, 1961.

40. H. Raiffa, *Decision Analysis: Introductory Lectures on Making Choices Under Uncertainty*, Addison-Wesley, Reading, MA, 1968.

3

The Multivariate
ARMA(1, 1) Model

Its Significance and Estimation

3.1 INTRODUCTION

In recent years, the ARMA model for statistical processes has become very popular both in industry and in certain parts of the social science community. This popularity is due partly to the landmark book by Box and Jenkins, *Time Series Analysis* [1], which places emphasis on the application of ARMA models for predicting future values of time-series variables. Using their approach, one fits a separate model to each variable of interest, a model of the variable as a mixed *Auto*Regressive *Moving Average* process of some very complex order; one uses these models, variable by variable, to make predictions of the future.

The emphasis here is quite different. My concern, from the beginning, was with studying the interaction *between* different variables—national assimilation and communications, as described in Chapter 6—rather than with the prediction of time-series in isolation from each other; univariate studies were carried out only to help evaluate methods for dealing with the more general case. With "causal analysis" of this sort, where many variable must be considered together, multiple regression still is the most popular technique by far. (Section 3.6.1 substantiates this).

Nevertheless, one of the theorems of Box and Jenkins—that the presence of errors in data collection can turn a simple regression process into an ARMA process—can be generalized very easily to the multivariate case, as will be shown later. Thus one might think of multivariate ARMA analysis as generating the same coefficients as a multiple regression analysis, but "corrected" for the effects of measurement errors. In Chapters 4–6, I discuss the empirical work which has convinced me that such measurement noise is not only common, but may also have a drastic effect in reducing the quality of predictions of a model fit by ordinary regression.

In practice, there are two difficulties with using the generalization of the ARMA model to the multivariate case. First, and most important, is the sheer computational difficulty of estimating a full, multivariate ARMA model (a "vector ARMA" model). Hannan [2] in 1970 described the current techniques in this area as follows: "Though there are, no doubt, circumstances in which a vector mixed moving-average autoregressive model will give a much better fit with a given number of constants than either a moving-average or autoregressive model (i.e., ordinary regression), the computational complications are so great that it can be doubted whether the more complicated model will be used, and we do not feel that the techniques at the present stage are sufficiently near to being practically useful to be included in this book." In 1973, Professor George E. Box, of Box and Jenkins, mentioned to me that the heavy orientation of his own work to the univariate case was due in large part to such difficulties. In Section 3.3 I describe the application of the dynamic feedback algorithm, described in Chapter 2, to overcome this difficulty; Section 3.4 contains a detailed description of the computer routine, now available to social scientists from Hawaii to London, that I have written to use this method in estimating multivariate ARMA processes.

Second, and more persistent, is the difficulty of "too many degrees of freedom" with ARMA models. If, in *addition* to accounting for many variables at once, we *also* added "higher-order" terms, as discussed by Box and Jenkins, the numbers of parameters in these models could become hopelessly large; such higher-order models could be estimated by a variant of the algorithm below, but the substantive value of the estimates would be questionable. In practice, however, our interest in the ARMA model does not lie int its capacity for being made ever and ever more complicated; our interest is in the possibility of accounting rationally for the problem of "measurement noise," the problem of errors in measuring and indexing the underlying variables which one is trying to study. Thus the discussion is restricted here to considering "white noise" (random noise, uncorrelated with itself across time but *possibly* correlated from variable to variable at the same time) in the process of measurement; all the ARMA models to be discussed are of the variety which Box and Jenkins would call ARMA(1, 1) models. While the degrees of freedom problem makes it impractical in most cases to consider more complex, more realistic models of measurement noise, it is hoped that the difference between accounting for measurement noise and not accounting for it at all would be enough to overcome most of the problems of real-world prediction. However, as pointed out in Chapter 1, this hope has only been partly realized; given the impracticality of adding too many degrees of freedom to these models, my current opinion is that the "robust method" described in Sections 2.7 and 2.11 of Chapter 2 will be crucial to any further progress with real-world problems.

Let us now define more precisely what is meant by an ARMA(1, 1) model. Box and Jenkins [1, p. 76] define an ARMA(1, 1) process z_t as a stationary process governed by the scalar equation

$$z_t = \phi z_{t-1} + a_t - \Theta_1 a_{t-1}, \tag{3.1}$$

where a_t is a random normal noise process of covariance σ_a^2, and where t is the time period. (Recall from Chapter 2 that "random" means that the processes has no correlation with itself across time, or with other processes in the system at earlier times.) Also, note that we are treating t as a subscript here solely because this is the way it appears in Box and Jenkins.

By contrast, the classic autoregressive model may be written, in the univariate case,

$$x_t = \phi x_{t-1} + a_t. \tag{3.2}$$

The term a_t in this equation refers to "process noise," to a random impulse that will affect the true value of x at time t, and thereby affect later values of x as well. In practice, however, the measured data, which we may call z_t, may differ from the true values of the variable we are trying to study, which we may call x_t. The difference between the true value and the measured value, $z_t - x_t$, may be called "measurement noise." If we postulate that this measurement noise, like the random impulses that govern x_t itself, is a random process, then we arrive at the following modification of the classic regression model (3.2):

$$x_t = \phi x_{t-1} + b_t,$$

$$z_t = x_t + c_t, \tag{3.3}$$

where both b_t and c_t are normal random noise processes with zero means and with no correlation between each other.

Box and Jenkins [1, p. 30] have pointed out that any stationary process, z_t, such as the z_t of Equation (3.3) or (3.1), may be completely characterized by knowledge of its correlation function (or, more precisely, its autocovariance), Z_T, across time:

$$Z_T \triangleq E(z_t z_{t-T}).$$

This equation states that Z_T is *defined* to equal $E(z_t z_{t-T})$; $E(z_t z_{t-T})$, in turn, is the notation that will be used to indicate the "expected value" or "mean value," across all times t, of the product $z_t z_{t-T}$ throughout the statistical process under study. Box and Jenkins argue, in the context of discussing general processes which include Equations (3.3) as a special case, that the autocorrelation function of the z_t in Equation (3.3) has the same characteristics as that of z_t in Equation (3.1); therefore they conclude that the former statistical process, as a generator of z_t, is equivalent to a process of the second kind. (The special case is defined by $q_1 = q_2 = 1$ and $d = 0$ in [1, pp. 121—124]). In other words, a z_t generated by a process such as (3.3) will appear to obey a phenomenological equation such as (3.1).

More precisely, Box and Jenkins ask us to consider the following process, in connection with Equations (3.3):

$$w_t = z_t - \phi z_{t-1} = (x_t + c_t) - \phi(x_{t-1} + c_{t-1})$$

$$= (\phi x_{t-1} + b_t + c_t) - \phi x_{t-1} - \phi c_{t-1}$$

$$= b_t + c_t - \phi c_{t-1}. \tag{3.4}$$

From the randomness of b_t and c_t, it is clear that the autocorrelation of this process will be zero for time intervals T larger than 1. From this information, and from the Gaussian character of the process, they conclude immediately that w_t is itself a simple moving average process of order 1, representable as

$$w_t = a_t - \theta_1 a_{t-1},$$

for some θ_1 and some random process a_t. If we recall the definition of w_t in Equation (3.4) and substitute, we find that the z_t from Equations (3.3) obeys an equation representable as (3.1). Those readers who have difficulty with this equivalence should refer back to Box and Jenkins.

In the social sciences, however, most dynamic processes of interest involve more than one variable. Fortunately, it is easy to generalize the definitions and results above to the multivariate case, by treating sets of variables as vectors. Thus we can define a multivariate ARMA(1, 1) process as a process that obeys

$$\mathbf{z}_t = \mathbf{a}_t + \theta \mathbf{z}_{t-1} + P \mathbf{a}_{t-1} \quad (\theta \text{ and } P \text{ matrices}), \tag{3.5}$$

where $\mathbf{a}_t$ is a vector random process, obeying a multivariate normal distribution[1]:

$$p(\mathbf{a}_t) = \frac{1}{\sqrt{(2\pi)^n \det A}} \exp\left(-\tfrac{1}{2} \mathbf{a}_t^T A^{-1} \mathbf{a}_t\right), \tag{3.6}$$

where A is the covariance matrix of this process, where the off-diagonal terms of A allow as to account for the possibility of cross-correlations in the noise process, and where n is the dimensionality of the vectors $\mathbf{z}$ and $\mathbf{a}$. We can also define a noisy time-series regression process as one obeying

$$\mathbf{x}_t = \theta \mathbf{x}_{t-1} + \mathbf{b}_t,$$

$$\mathbf{z}_t = \mathbf{x}_t + \mathbf{c}_t, \tag{3.7}$$

where $\mathbf{b}_t$ and $\mathbf{c}_t$ are random normal processes of dimensionality n, as was $\mathbf{a}_t$ above, with covariance matrices that we will call B and C. If we define $\mathbf{w}_t$ as

[1]See Box and Jenkins [1] Equation (A7.1.9), on p. 260.

$\mathbf{z}_t - \theta\mathbf{z}_{t-1}$, then the rest of Equation (3.4) goes through exactly as before, yielding a process with zero autocorrelation for $T > 1$, representable, as before, as a simple moving average process, that is, as $\mathbf{a}_t + P\mathbf{a}_{t-1}$. Thus Box and Jenkins' argument for equivalence goes through in its entirety, with equal validity, in the multivariate case.

The main concern in this chapter will be with the estimation of the coefficients in equations (3.5) and (3.6), for a given set of data, $\{\mathbf{z}_t\}$. However, since interest in Equation (3.5) and (3.6) comes from interest in Equation (3.7), one should investigate how to go back, *after* fitting a model of the form (3.5), to derive the coefficients of an equivalent model of the form (3.7). In the following section, the mathematical details of this process are elaborated. For the social scientist, however, the most interesting conclusion from this argument will be the equivalence between θ in Equation (3.5) and θ in Equations (3.7). Thus the θ_{ij} estimated by the ARMA estimation program itself may be thought of as "corrected" regression coefficients. Just as the usual regression coefficient, b_{ij}, is called a "*b* coefficient" or "beta coefficient," our "corrected regression coefficient," θ_{ij}, may be called a "theta coefficient"; in a similar way, our P_{ij} may be called a "rho coefficient."

3.2 THE RECONSTRUCTION OF A WHITE NOISE MODEL FROM A VECTOR ARMA MODEL

After fitting a vector ARMA(1, 1) model, a model of the form (3.5) and (3.6), how do we derive the coefficients of the equivalent model of the form (3.7), assuming that an equivalent model does exist? Recalling that Gaussian stationary processes are completely characterized by their autocovariance functions [1, p. 30], we may rephrase this question. For given values of θ, P, and A, in Equations (3.5) and (3.6), we wish to find values for θ, B, and C in Equations (3.7), such that the autocovariance matrices Z_n will be the same for the two processes, for all time increments, n. Let us use the notation θ to represent the θ in Equation (3.5), and ϕ to represent the θ in Equation (3.7); these two matrices will turn out to be equivalent to each other, but for now we must establish the equality.

The autocovariance matrix, Z_n, is defined as being made up of components, $Z_{n,ij}$, defined as follows:

$$Z_{n,ij} \triangleq E(z_{t,i}z_{t-n,j}),$$

where $z_{t,i}$ refers to the value of the ith component of the vector $\mathbf{z}_t$, the value of the vector $\mathbf{z}$ at time t; from another point of view, $z_{t,i}$ may be regarded as the value of the individual variable z_i at time t. Note that we have used the same notation here as in Section (3.1) to define the autocovariance. From this definition, we may immediately deduce that

$$Z_{n,ij} \triangleq E(z_{t,i}z_{t-n,j}) = E(z_{t-n,j}z_{t,i})$$
$$= E(z_{t,j}z_{t+n,i}) \triangleq Z_{-n,ji}$$

$$Z_n = Z_{-n}^T \quad \text{for all } n.$$

Thus if $Z_n^{(a)} = Z_n^{(b)}$ for our two processes **a** and **b**, for $n \geq 0$, then the equality will hold for $n \leq 0$, and vice versa; thus we need only consider $n \geq 0$ in determining equivalence.

From the randomness of a_t, b_t, and c_t, from the causal structure of our equations, and from our assumptions about the normal distributions governing these processes, we have

$$E(a_{t,i}a_{t+n,j}) = \delta_{n0}A_{ij} = \delta_{n0}A_{ji}, \tag{3.8}$$

$$E(b_{t,i}b_{t+n,j}) = \delta_{n0}B_{ij} = \delta_{n0}B_{ji}, \tag{3.9}$$

$$E(c_{t,i}c_{t+n,j}) = \delta_{n0}C_{ij} = \delta_{n0}C_{ji}, \tag{3.10}$$

$$E(a_{t,i}z_{t+n,j}) = 0 \quad \text{for } n < 0, \tag{3.11}$$

$$E(b_{t,i}z_{t+n,j}) = 0 \quad \text{for } n < 0, \tag{3.12}$$

$$E(c_{t,i}z_{t+n,j}) = 0 \quad \text{for } n < 0, \tag{3.13}$$

$$E(b_{t,i}x_{t+n,j}) = 0 \quad \text{for } n < 0, \tag{3.14}$$

$$E(c_{t,i}x_{t+n,j}) = 0, \tag{3.15}$$

$$E(b_{t,i}c_{t+n,j}) = 0. \tag{3.16}$$

Note that δ_{ij}, the Kronecker delta, is defined as equal to 1 if $i = j$, and zero otherwise.

Let us begin by calculating the autocovariance matrices, Z_n, for an ARMA(1, 1) process as in Equation (3.5). To make our calculations more explicit, let us transform Equation (3.5) into

$$a_{t,i} = z_{t,i} - \sum_j \theta_{ij}z_{t-1,j} - \sum_j P_{ij}a_{t-1,j}. \tag{3.17}$$

Let us multiply Equation (3.17) on the right by $a_{t,k}$ and take the expectation of the resulting equation on both sides:

$$E(a_{t,i}a_{t,k}) = E(z_{t,i}a_{t,k}) - \sum_j \theta_{ij}E(z_{t-1,j}a_{t,k})$$
$$- \sum_j P_{ij}E(a_{t-1,j}a_{t,k}),$$

which, by Equations (3.8) and (3.11), reduces to

$$E(z_{t,i}a_{t,k}) = A_{ik} = A_{ki}. \tag{3.18}$$

Multiplying Equation (3.17) by $a_{t-1,k}$ and taking expectations, we obtain

$$E(a_{t,i}a_{t-1,k}) = E(z_{t,i}a_{t-1,k}) - \sum_j \theta_{ij} E(z_{t-1,j}a_{t-1,k})$$
$$- \sum_j P_{ij} E(a_{t-1,j}a_{t-1,k}),$$

which, by Equations (3.8) and (3.18), reduces to

$$E(z_{t,i}a_{t-1,k}) = (\theta + P)A. \tag{3.19}$$

Now let us multiply Equation (3.17) on the right by $a_{t-n,k}$, for $n > 1$:

$$E(a_{t,i}a_{t-n,k}) = E(z_{t,i}a_{t-n,k}) - \sum_j \theta_{ij} E(z_{t-1,j}a_{t-n,k})$$
$$- \sum_j P_{ij} E(a_{t-1,j}a_{t-n,k}),$$

which, by Equation (3.8) and by changing the arbitrary origin of our expectation notation, reduces to

$$E(z_{t,i}a_{t-n,k}) = \theta E(z_{t,j}a_{t-n+1,k}),$$

which, by induction starting from Equation (3.19), gives us

$$E(z_{t,i}a_{t-n,k}) = \theta^{n-1}(\theta + P)A \quad \text{for } n > 0. \tag{3.20}$$

Now let us multiply Equation (3.17) on the right by $z_{t-n,k}$, for $n > 1$:

$$E(a_{t,i}z_{t-n,k}) = E(z_{t,i}z_{t-n,k}) - \theta E(z_{t-1,j}z_{t-n,k})$$
$$- PE(a_{t-1,j}z_{t-n,k}),$$

which, by Equation (3.8) and by change of origin in expectation, reduces to

$$Z_n = \theta Z_{n-1} \quad \text{for } n > 1,$$
$$Z_n = \theta^{n-1} Z_1 \quad \text{for } n \geq 1. \tag{3.21}$$

Multiplying Equation (3.17) by $z_{t-1,k}$, we get

$$E(a_{t,i}z_{t-1,k}) = E(z_{t,i}z_{t-1,k}) - \theta E(z_{t-1,j}z_{t-1,k})$$
$$- PE(a_{t-1,j}z_{t-1,k}),$$

which, by Equations (3.11) and (3.18), reduces to

$$Z_1 = \theta Z_0 + PA. \tag{3.22}$$

Multiplying Equation (3.17) by $z_{t,j}$, we get

$$E(a_{t,i}z_{t,j}) = E(z_{t,i}z_{t,j}) - \theta E(z_{t-1,j}z_{t,k})$$
$$- PE(a_{t-1,j}z_{t,k}),$$

which, by Equations (3.18) and (3.19) and our definitions, reduces to

$$A = Z_0 - \theta(Z_1^T) - P((\theta + P)A)^T,$$

which, by substitution from Equation (3.22), reduces to

$$A = Z_0 - \theta Z_0 \theta^T - \theta AP^T - PA\theta^T - PAP^T. \tag{3.23}$$

Equations (3.21) and (3.22) are clearly enough to determine the Z_n for $n > 0$, given A, P, θ, and Z_0.

From the stationarity of process (3.5), we know that the true variance matrix of $\{z_i\}$ does exist and must satisfy Equation (3.23), just as it is consistent with all the equations from which Equation (3.23) has originally been derived. From the stationarity of Equations (3.5) and (3.7), we may also deduce that both ϕ and θ have the property that there exist no nonzero matrices M such that $M = \theta M \theta^T$ or $M = \phi M \phi^T$. (Section 3.6.2 explains why.).

It is worth noting, however, that this property, which we make use of here, involves a much weaker assumption than that of stationarity. (Section 3.6.3 explains why.).

At any rate, from this property, we may deduce that the solution, Z_0, to Equation (3.23), is unique; if there had been two distinct solutions, Z_0 and Z_0', then $M = Z_0 - Z_0'$ would be a nonzero matrix violating our assumption for θ. At any rate, given our restriction on θ, Equations (3.21), (3.22), and (3.23) are sufficient to define the matrices Z_n as functions of θ, P, and A.

Now let us calculate the autocovariance matrices as functions of B, C, and ϕ. Let us rewrite Equations (3.7):

$$b_{t,i} = x_{t,i} - \sum_j \phi_{ij}x_{t-1,j}, \tag{3.24}$$

$$c_{t,i} = z_{t,i} - x_{t,i}. \tag{3.25}$$

Let us multiply Equation (3.24) by $b_{t,k}$ and take expectations:

$$E(b_{t,i}b_{t,k}) = E(x_{t,i}b_{t,k}) - \phi E(x_{t-1,j}b_{t,k}),$$

which, by Equations (3.10) and (3.15), reduces to

$$E(x_{t,i}b_{t,k}) = B_{ij} = B_{ji}. \tag{3.26}$$

Let us multiply Equation (3.24) by $b_{t-n,k}$, for $n > 0$:

$$E(b_{t,i}b_{t-n,k}) = E(x_{t,i}b_{t-n,k}) - \phi E(x_{t-1,j}b_{t-n,k}),$$

which, by Equation (3.9), by changes of time origin, and by induction, reduces to

$$E(x_{t,i}b_{t-n,k}) = \phi^n E(x_{t,i}b_{t,k}) = \phi^n B, \qquad (3.27)$$

where the last step comes from substituting Equation (3.26).
Now let us multiply Equation (3.24) by $x_{t-n,k}$, for $n > 0$:

$$E(b_{t,i}x_{t-n,k}) = E(x_{t,i}x_{t-n,k}) - \phi E(x_{t-1,j}x_{t-n,k}),$$

which, by Equation (3.14) and by induction, reduces to

$$E(x_{t,i}x_{t-n,k}) = \phi^n E(x_{t,i}x_{t,k}) = \phi^n X_0. \qquad (3.28)$$

Multiplying Equation (3.24) by $x_{t,k}$, we get

$$E(b_{t,i}x_{t,k}) = E(x_{t,i}x_{t,k}) - \phi E(x_{t-1,j}x_{t,k}),$$

which, by Equations (3.26) and (3.28), reduces to

$$X_0 = \phi(\phi X_0)^T + B = \phi X_0 \phi^T + B. \qquad (3.29)$$

Now let us shift to considering Equation (3.25), multiplying it by $x_{t-n,k}$, for $n \geq 0$:

$$E(c_{t,i}x_{t-n,k}) = E(z_{t,i}x_{t-n,k}) - E(x_{t,i}x_{t-n,k}),$$

which, by Equations (3.15) and (3.28), reduces to

$$E(z_{t,i}x_{t-n,k}) = X_n = \phi^n X_0. \qquad (3.30)$$

Multiplying Equation (3.25) by $c_{t,k}$, we get

$$E(c_{t,i}c_{t,k}) = E(z_{t,i}c_{t,k}) - E(x_{t,i}c_{t,k}),$$

which, by Equations (3.10) and (3.15), leads to

$$E(z_{t,i}c_{t,k}) = B_{ik} = B_{ki}. \qquad (3.31)$$

Multiplying Equation (3.25) by $z_{t,k}$, we get

$$E(c_{t,i}z_{t,k}) = E(z_{t,i}z_{t,k}) - E(x_{t,i}z_{t,k}),$$

which, by Equations (3.31) and (3.30), gives us

$$Z_0 = C + X_0. \qquad (3.32)$$

Multiplying Equation (3.25) by $z_{t-n,k}$, for $n > 0$, we get

$$E(c_{t,i}z_{t-n,k}) = E(z_{t,i}z_{t-n,k}) - E(x_{t,i}z_{t-n,i}),$$

which, by Equations (3.13) and (3.20), reduces to

$$Z_n = \phi^n X_0 \quad \text{for } n > 0. \tag{3.33}$$

Now our problem is to find ϕ, B, and C given θ, A, and P. Assuming that the Z_n are nonsingular, Equations (3.33) and (3.21) clearly tell us that

$$\phi = \theta. \tag{3.34}$$

To find B, let us begin by left-multiplying Equation (3.22) by $\theta^{-1} = \phi^{-1}$:

$$\theta^{-1}Z_1 = Z_0 + \theta^{-1}PA.$$

From Equations (3.33) and (3.34), this reduces to

$$X_0 = Z_0 + \theta^{-1}PA.$$

Let us left-multiply this by θ, right-multiply it by θ^T, and subtract the results from the original equation:

$$X_0 - \theta X_0 \theta^T = Z_0 - \theta Z_0 \theta^T + \theta^{-1}PA - PA\theta^T.$$

Substituting in from Equations (3.23) and (3.29), we get

$$B = A + \theta AP^T + PA\theta^T + PAP^T + \theta^{-1}PA - PA\theta^T$$

$$= A + \theta AP^T + PAP^T + \theta^{-1}PA \tag{3.35}$$

To find C, let us left-multiply Equation (3.32) by θ, right-multiply the result by θ^T, and subtract the result from Equation (3.32) proper:

$$Z_0 - \theta Z_0 \theta^T = C - \theta C\theta^T + X_0 - \theta X_0 \theta^T,$$

which, by Equation (3.29), reduces to

$$Z_0 - \theta Z_0 \theta^T = C - \theta C\theta^T + B.$$

By Equations (3.35) and (3.23), this gives us

$$A + \theta AP^T + PA\theta^T + PAP^T$$

$$= Z_0 - \theta Z_0 \theta^T$$

$$= C - \theta C\theta^T + (A + \theta AP^T + PAP^T + \theta^{-1}PA),$$

which reduces to

$$PA\theta^T = C - \theta C\theta^T + \theta^{-1}PA,$$

The above equation can be solved by

$$C = -\theta^{-1}PA. \tag{3.36}$$

As with Equation (3.23), our assumptions about θ lead to uniqueness in this solution.

In summary, Equations (3.34), (3.35), and (3.36) give us the values of ϕ, B, and C, respectively, necessary for construction of a model of the form (3.7), equivalent to a process known to fit Equations (3.5) and (3.6) for a given set of coefficients θ, P, and A. These values, however, may yet be insufficient; in other words, there may be no values of C, B, and ϕ able to yield an equivalence. Box and Jenkins' argument, cited earlier, states that processes of the form (3.7) will always have equivalents of the form (3.5); they did not state the converse. If θ, P, and A in Equation (3.36) should require that C not be a positive symmetric matrix—what a variance matrix is supposed to be—then we may conclude that our estimates of θ, P, and A contradict the hypothesis that the process at hand fits a model of the form (3.7). For the purposes of social science modeling, Equation (3.34) tells us that the θ coming out of an ARMA estimation can not only be used in forecasting but can also be treated as a description of the underlying social dynamics, ϕ. Therefore we have decided, in our statistical programs, to concentrate on the task of estimating this θ matrix, and the other ARMA coefficients, rather than adding routines to operationalize Equations (3.35) and (3.36). The terms "beta coefficient" and "b coefficient" are already widely used in describing the matrix elements of ordinary regression; therefore our computer routines call the θ_{ij} "theta coefficients" to emphasize the parallel with regression. The P_{ij} are called "rho coefficients," and the A_{ij} are simply called "error covariance."

3.3 THE ESTIMATION OF MULTIVARIATE ARMA PROCESSES

Now let us move on to the central question of this chapter: the estimation of multivariate ARMA(1, 1) processes. As pointed out in Section (3.1), it seems rather clear that techniques for multivariate ARMA estimation have not, in the past, been reduced to a computational cost approaching that of classical regression. One might have imagined that some kind of spectral techniques might exist in parts of the literature of which Hannan and Box and Jenkins are unaware. However, Jenkins is coauthor of one of the classic textbooks [3] on the application of spectral methods to statistics and has been fully aware of such recent developments as the fast Fourier transform.[2] Hannan's book [2] also

---

[2]Jenkins and Watts [3], on p. 313, refer to the Cooley–Tukey fast Fourier algorithm, developed in 1965.

indicates a full awareness of the possibilities for spectral analysis.[3] Engineers
have studied problems which are related but distinct (see Section 3.6.4).

Box and Jenkins [1] do present a technique for the estimation of ARMA
processes. This technique, while described in univariate terms, is phrased in
such a way that it extends very easily to the multivariate case; we will find,
however, that the extension involves costly computations. They begin with the
maximum likelihood technique, as described in Chapter 2. In other words, they
set themselves the task of maximizing

$$L = \log p(\text{observations} \mid \text{model}).$$

They note [1, p. 210] that the a_t in Equation (3.1) can be calculated as functions of θ_1, ϕ, and a_1, by use of the equation itself, and that the $\{a_t\}$ contain
all the information we have available about $\{z_t\}$, *given* θ_1, ϕ, and a_1. Thus
they write

$$L = \log p(a_1 \cdots a_T \mid \theta_1, \phi, a_1^*, \sigma_a^2),$$

where T is the last time period for which data are available. Given that a_t is a
normally distributed random variable, they obtain

$$L(\theta_1, \phi, a_1^*, \sigma_a^2) = \log \prod_{t=1}^{T} p(a_t \mid \theta_1, \phi, a_1^*, \sigma_a^2)$$

$$= \log \prod_{t=1}^{T} \left[\frac{1}{\sqrt{2\pi\sigma_a^2}} \exp\left(-\frac{1}{2}\frac{a_t^2}{\sigma_a^2} \right) \right]$$

$$= k - T \log \sigma_a - \frac{1}{2\sigma_a^2} \sum_t a_t^2 \quad (k \text{ is a constant}). \quad (3.37)$$

In the multivariate case, we need only use the multivariate normal distribution,
Equation (3.6), for $\mathbf{a}_t$, to get an equivalent expression:

$$L(\theta, P, A, \mathbf{a}_1^*) = k - \frac{T}{2} \log \det A - \frac{1}{2} \sum_t \mathbf{a}_t^T A^{-1} \mathbf{a}_t. \quad (3.38)$$

They note, in Equation (3.37), that the term Σa_t^2 is a function only of θ_1, ϕ,
and a_1^*, not of σ_a^2, and that we can go on to minimize this term without consideration of σ_a^2. Also, they have a rather elaborate discussion [1, p. 221 and
502] about finding "good" values for a_1^*, or for estimates of prior data used
to predict a_1^*. My own view is that the "best" empirical value for a_1^* is simply
the value of maximum likelihood for the data given, and that the best procedure
is simply to append a_1^* to the list of parameters to be estimated. See Section

[3]In Hannan [2], see pp. 32–106, pp. 127–136, and the greater part of pp. 245–405.

3.6.5 for more explanation of this. In any case, as Box and Jenkins point out, the choice of procedure here should make little difference for long or moderate time series.

At this point, with two parameters to estimate—θ_1 and ϕ—Box and Jenkins suggest that the parameters be lumped into a coefficient vector, $\mathbf{B}$, to be analyzed by the general method of "nonlinear estimation."[4] The first step of this algorithm is to construct some initial estimate, $\mathbf{B}_0$, of the coefficient vector, $\mathbf{B}$. The second step is to calculate the a_t and L for this value, $\mathbf{B}_0$, by using the dynamic equation, (3.1). With T periods of time t, this implies on the order of T calculations; if we use the multivariate dynamic equation, (3.5), with n variables and Cn terms to be calculated and added per variable, this implies Cn^2T calculations per time period, Cn^2 calculations in all. (C will be used throughout this discussion as an arbitrary proportionality constant.) The third step is to calculate the derivatives,

$$\frac{\partial a_t}{\partial B_k} \quad \text{for all } k \text{ and } t,$$

by differentiating Equation (3.1) to get an iterative equation:

$$\frac{\partial a_t}{\partial B_k} = \theta_1 \frac{\partial a_{t-1}}{\partial B_k} + a_{t-1} \frac{\partial \theta_1}{\partial B_k} - z_{t-1} \frac{\partial \phi}{\partial B_k}. \tag{3.39}$$

(From a formal point of view, their differentiation is straightforward, because the a_t, a_{t-1}, θ_1, and ϕ are all considered here to be functions of $\mathbf{B}$; all the differentiations are carried out with respect to vector $\mathbf{B}$. The set of observed data, $\{z_t\}$, is a constant parameter throughout this entire analysis.)

In the multivariate case, we must recall that any coefficient B_k may affect any component $a_{t,i}$ of the error vector indirectly, and we will see that the iterative equation below for calculating these derivatives does not allow us to limit our attention to, say, $(\partial/\partial B_k) (\mathbf{a}_t^T A^{-1} \mathbf{a}_t)$. Thus the generalization of the Box and Jenkins method requires us to compute

$$\frac{\partial a_{t,i}}{\partial B_k} \quad \text{for all } k, i, \text{ and } t,$$

by using the iterative rule that comes from differentiating Equation (3.5) in the same way as we differentiated Equation (3.1) above:

$$\frac{\partial a_{t,i}}{\partial B_k} = \sum_j \left(\frac{\partial P_{ij}}{\partial B_k}\right) a_{t-1,j} - \sum_j P_{ij} \left(\frac{\partial a_{t-1,j}}{\partial B_k}\right)$$

$$- \sum_j \left(\frac{\partial \theta_{ij}}{\partial B_k}\right) z_{t-1,j}. \tag{3.40}$$

---

[4]This is discussed in Box and Jenkins [1] on p. 231 and defined specifically on p. 504 as the Marquardt algorithm.

For each actual B_k in θ or P or elsewhere, this equation will still require Cn^2 calculations for any period of time t, to handle all the possible combinations of i and j. Thus with Cn^2 coefficients B_k, Cn^2 calculations per time period per coefficient, and T time periods, this leads to a grand total of $Cn^4 T$ calculations. And this is only the beginning.

The next step, in the general nonlinear estimation routine, as discussed by Box and Jenkins [1, p. 232], is to go back to our likelihood function, Equation (3.37) or (33.8), and substitute in a first-order Taylor series for a_t or $\mathbf{a}_t$ in terms of $\mathbf{B}$. In the multivariate case, this gives us the major term

$$\sum_{i,j} \sum_{t} \left(a_{t,i} - \sum_{k} \left(\frac{\partial a_{t,i}}{\partial B_k} (B_k - B_k^{(0)}) \right) \right) A_{ij}^{-1} \left(a_{t,j} - \sum_{m} \frac{\partial a_{t,j}}{\partial B_m} (B_m - B_m^{(0)}) \right),$$

leading to a generalized form of the matrix that Box and Jenkins unfortunately call A:

$$\sum_{i,j,t} \frac{\partial a_{t,i}}{\partial B_k} A_{ij}^{-1} \frac{\partial a_{t,j}}{\partial B_m}.$$

For the Cn^4 combinations of k and m, the calculation of this matrix requires the summation of $n^2 T$ terms per combination, and $Cn^6 T$ calculations in all. By summing the products of the two terms on the right, over j for all i, t, and m, we may reduce the cost down to $Cn^5 T$. But at this point, the simplifications stop; an M of these dimensions and with these properties is clearly central to the algorithm presented in Box and Jenkins. We could go on to discuss further details of the Marquardt algorithm in the multivariate case, but the number of calculations required—$Cn^5 T$—is already large enough to contrast strongly with the new algorithm presented below.

How do we arrive at a less expensive algorithm to accomplish the same objectives?

To begin with, we will build our new algorithm on a well-established foundation, the classic method of steepest ascent. We will maximize $L(\theta, P, \mathbf{a}_1, A)$ by writing

$$B_k^{(n+1)} = B_k^{(n)} + wg_k \frac{\partial L}{\partial B_k}, \tag{3.41}$$

where w is an arbitrary scale factor to be adjusted during maximization, and where g_k is an arbitrary positive "metric factor" to be applied to B_k. We will include θ, P, and $\mathbf{a}_1$ as components of $\mathbf{B}$; however, we will not include A. Starting from the given $\mathbf{B}^{(0)}$, $A^{(0)}$, and w, we will first compute $\partial L/\partial B_k$. Then we will compute $\mathbf{B}$. From $\mathbf{B} = \mathbf{B}'$ alone, Equation (3.5) allows us to compute all the $\{a_t\}$ from times $t = 1$ to $t = T$. It is a well-known fact, for a given set of data, $\{a_t\}$, that the maximum likelihood estimate A of the covariance matrix generating these data, as a random process of zero mean, will simply be the observed covariance of the $\{a_t\}$:

$$A'_{ij} = \frac{1}{T} \sum_t a'_{t,i} a'_{t,j}$$

Thus for a given B', we can maximize the likelihood function (3.38) by finding the $\{a_t\}$ and picking A' accordingly. For this combination, we will immediately be able to estimate $L(A', \mathbf{B}')$ by Equation (3.38). If $L(A', \mathbf{B}')$ is less than $L(A^{(0)}, \mathbf{B}^{(0)})$, we may reduce w in half and try again. Eventually, for w small enough, we may be sure that

$$L(A', \mathbf{B}') > L(A^{(0)}, \mathbf{B}') > L(A^{(0)}, \mathbf{B}^{(0)}), \quad \text{if } \frac{\partial L}{\partial B_k}(A^{(0)}, \mathbf{B}^{(0)}) \neq 0,$$

by the definition of the derivative. We may then set $\mathbf{B}'$ to be the new $\mathbf{B}^{(0)}$, and A' to be the new $A^{(0)}$. As a practical matter, if $L(A', \mathbf{B}') \gg L(A^{(0)}, \mathbf{B}^{(0)})$, we may increase the value of w, to speed convergence. Also, while it would complicate the logic above to change g_k while changing w, it would not hurt to choose a new value for g_k while estimating $\partial L/\partial B_k$.

At any rate, this procedure clearly allows a steady improvement in our choice of A and $\mathbf{B}$, up until a local maximum is attained—that is, until $\partial L/\partial B_k \approx 0$. The steepest ascent method, like other variational algorithms, including the Marquardt algorithm, does not have the capacity to ensure that local maxima are also global maxima. In principle, this means that supplementary routines of varying complexity may be added to the basic algorithm. In practice, we will follow Box and Jenkins by placing emphasis on reasonable initial estimates of $\mathbf{B}_0$; we will discuss this, and the practical problem of speeding up convergence, in Section (3.4)

We face one real theoretical problem in converting the steepest ascent method into a useful algorithm for ARMA estimation: how to calculate the derivatives $\partial L/\partial B_k$ at an acceptable cost. The most elegant way to solve this problem is by the direct application of the ordered derivative concept mentioned in Chapter 2, or at least to apply related concepts. However, in order to avoid the use of unfamiliar mathematics and in order to make our derivation self-contained, we will use a more conservative, algebraic derivation here.

Let us begin by recalling that $a_{t,i}$ in Equation (3.5) can be considered to be a function of $\mathbf{a}_1$, θ, and P, insofar as Equation (3.5) allows us to solve for the $\mathbf{a}_t$ by repeated application. In fact, it is simple for us to write out this solution explicitly, for times $t > 1$:

$$\mathbf{a}_t = \sum_{m=1}^{t} P^{(t-m)}(\mathbf{z}_m + \theta \mathbf{z}_{m-1}) + P^{(t-1)}\mathbf{a}_1. \tag{3.42}$$

The validity and uniqueness of this solution can be proved easily by induction; for $t = 2$, this expression reduces to (3.5) with $t = 2$. For $t + 1$, Equation (3.5) gives us

$$\mathbf{a}_{t+1} = \mathbf{z}_{t+1} + \theta \mathbf{z}_{(t+1)-1} + P\mathbf{a}_t,$$

and, if we substitute in from Equation (3.42) for $\mathbf{a}_t$, as the induction hypothesis allows us to, we get

$$\mathbf{a}_{t+1} = \mathbf{z}_{t+1} + \theta \mathbf{z}_{(t+1)-1} + P \left(\sum_{m=2}^{t} P^{t-m}(\mathbf{z}_m + \theta \mathbf{z}_{m-1}) + P^{t-1}\mathbf{a}_1 \right)$$

$$= \mathbf{z}_{t+1} + \theta \mathbf{z}_{(t+1)-1} + \sum_{m=2}^{t} P^{t+1-m}(\mathbf{z}_m + \theta \mathbf{z}_{m-1}) + P^t \mathbf{a}_1,$$

which reduces to Equation (3.42) for the case $t + 1$. Thus if we think of $\mathbf{a}_t$ as a shorthand for the algebraic expression (3.42), it is clear that we can make use of Equation (3.40) and of the similar equation, which comes from differentiating Equation (3.38):

$$\frac{\partial L}{\partial B_k} = \frac{\partial}{\partial B_k} \left(-\frac{1}{2} \sum_{i,j,t} a_{t,i} A_{ij}^{-1} a_{t,j} \right)$$

$$= -\frac{1}{2} \sum_{i,j,t} \frac{\partial a_{t,i}}{\partial B_k} A_{ij}^{-1} a_{t,j} - \frac{1}{2} \sum_{i,j,t} a_{t,i} A_{ij}^{-1} \left(\frac{\partial a_{t,j}}{\partial B_k} \right),$$

which, by the symmetry of A, equals

$$\frac{\partial L}{\partial B_k} = - \sum_{i,j,t} \frac{\partial a_{t,i}}{\partial B_k} A_{ij}^{-1} a_{t,j}. \tag{3.43}$$

It will also be convenient for us to write out Equation (3.40) explicitly for the cases $B_k = \theta_{rs}$, $B_k = P_{rs}$, and $B_k = a_{1,r}$:

$$\frac{\partial a_{t,i}}{\partial \theta_{rs}} = - \sum_{j} P_{ij} \left(\frac{\partial a_{t-1,j}}{\partial \theta_{rs}} \right) - \delta_{ir} z_{t-1,s}, \tag{3.44}$$

$$\frac{\partial a_{t,i}}{\partial P_{rs}} = - \sum_{j} P_{ij} \left(\frac{\partial a_{t-1,j}}{\partial P_{rs}} \right) - \delta_{ir} a_{t-1,s}, \tag{3.45}$$

$$\frac{\partial a_{t,i}}{\partial a_{1,r}} = - \sum_{j} P_{ij} \left(\frac{\partial a_{t-1,j}}{\partial a_{1,r}} \right). \tag{3.46}$$

Now let us define a new variable, $w_{t,i}$, by induction:

$$w_{T,i} = -\sum_j A_{ij}^{-1} a_{T,j}$$

$$w_{t,i} = -\sum_j A_{ij}^{-1} a_{t,j} - \sum_j w_{t+1,j} P_{ji}. \tag{3.47}$$

(Note that $w_{t,i}$ is really $(\partial^+ L/\partial a_{t,i})$, in the notation of Chapter 2.) We now claim that

$$\frac{\partial L}{\partial \theta_{rs}} = -\sum_{t=2}^{T} w_{t,r} z_{t-1,s}. \tag{3.48}$$

(In Chapter 2, this would follow from a direct application of the chain rule for ordered derivatives, Equation (2.13), without reference to Equation (3.44) or (3.45).) This claim can be proved, by proving the more general proposition that follows and by considering the special case $m = 1$:

$$\frac{\partial}{\partial \theta_{rs}} \left(-\frac{1}{2} \sum_{t=m}^{T} a_t^T A^{-1} a_t \right) = -\sum_{t=m+1}^{T} w_{t,r} z_{t-1,s}$$

$$+ \sum_i w_{m,i} \frac{\partial a_{m,i}}{\partial \theta_{rs}}, \quad 1 \le m \le T.$$

(For $m = 1$, recall that a_1 is an externally supplied parameter not affected by θ. In the case $m = T$, the first sum of the right will be held simply to have zero terms.) Differentiating the term on the left, as we did with Equation (3.43), we can simplify this new proposition:

$$-\sum_{t=m}^{T} \sum_{i,j} \frac{\partial a_{t,i}}{\partial \theta_{rs}} A_{ij}^{-1} a_{t,j}$$

$$= -\sum_{t=m+1}^{T} w_{t,r} z_{t-1,s} + \sum_i w_{m,i} \frac{\partial a_{m,i}}{\partial \theta_{rs}}, \quad 1 \le m \le T. \tag{3.49}$$

We will prove this by induction on m, downward from the case $m = T$. For $m = T$, this expression reduces to

$$-\sum_{i,j} \frac{\partial a_{T,i}}{\partial \theta_{rs}} A_{ij}^{-1} a_{T,j} = \sum_i w_{T,i} \frac{\partial a_{T,i}}{\partial \theta_{rs}}.$$

Substituting in for $w_{T,i}$ from Equation (3.47), this is equivalent to

$$-\sum_i \sum_j \frac{\partial a_{T,i}}{\partial \theta_{rs}} A_{ij}^{-1} a_{T,j} = \sum_i \left(-\sum_j A_{ij}^{-1} a_{T,j} \right) \left(\frac{\partial a_{T,i}}{\partial \theta_{rs}} \right),$$

which clearly holds true. Now we try to prove Equation (3.49) for $T > m \geq 1$, on the assumption, provided by the induction hypothesis, that it is true for $m + 1$. We note, for $m < T$, that

$$
- \sum_{t=m}^{T} \sum_{i,j} \frac{\partial a_{t,i}}{\partial \theta_{rs}} A_{ij}^{-1} a_{t,j} = - \sum_{t=m+1}^{T} \sum_{i,j} \frac{\partial a_{t,i}}{\partial \theta_{rs}} A_{ij}^{-1} a_{t,j} - \sum_{i,j} \frac{\partial a_{m,i}}{\partial \theta_{rs}} A_{ij}^{-1} a_{m,j},
$$

which by the induction hypothesis is equivalent to

$$
- \sum_{t=m}^{T} \sum_{i,j} \frac{\partial a_{t,i}}{\partial \theta_{rs}} A_{ij}^{-1} a_{t,j} = - \sum_{t=m+2}^{T} w_{t,r} z_{t-1,s}
$$

$$
+ \sum_{i} w_{m+1,i} \frac{\partial a_{m+1,i}}{\partial \theta_{rs}} - \sum_{i} \sum_{j} \frac{\partial a_{m,i}}{\partial \theta_{rs}} A_{ij}^{-1} a_{m,j}.
$$

By substitution from Equation (3.44), the above equation equals

$$
- \sum_{t=m+2}^{T} w_{t,r} z_{t-1,s} + \sum_{i} w_{m+1,i} \left(- \delta_{ir} z_{m,s} - \sum_{j} P_{ij} \frac{\partial a_{m,j}}{\partial \theta_{rs}} \right)
$$

$$
- \sum_{i} \sum_{j} \frac{\partial a_{m,i}}{\partial \theta_{rs}} A_{ij}^{-1} a_{m,j}
$$

$$
= - \sum_{t=m+2}^{T} w_{t,r} z_{t-1,s} - w_{m+1,r} z_{m,s} - \sum_{i} \sum_{j} w_{m+1,i} P_{ij} \frac{\partial a_{m,j}}{\partial \theta_{rs}}
$$

$$
- \sum_{i} \sum_{j} \frac{\partial a_{m,i}}{\partial \theta_{rs}} A_{ij}^{-1} a_{m,j}
$$

$$
= - \sum_{t=m+1}^{T} w_{t,r} z_{t-1,s} + \sum_{i} \left(\frac{\partial a_{m,i}}{\partial \theta_{rs}} \right) \sum_{j} \left(- P_{ij} w_{m+1,i} - A_{ij}^{-1} a_{m,j} \right),
$$

which, by Equation (3.47), equals

$$
- \sum_{t=m+1}^{T} w_{t,r} z_{t-1,s} + \sum_{i} \frac{\partial a_{m,i}}{\partial \theta_{rs}} w_{m,i},
$$

proving Equation (3.49), as required in induction, for the case m. With the induction complete, Equation (3.49) is proved and the special case (3.48) follows immediately.

In a similar way, we claim that

$$
\frac{\partial L}{\partial P_{rs}} = - \sum_{t=2}^{T} w_{t,r} a_{t-1,s}. \tag{3.50}
$$

The proof of this claim is exactly the same as that of Equation (3.48), if we replace all instances of θ_{rs} by P_{rs}, of z by a, and of references to Equation (3.44) by references to Equation (3.45).

Our final claim is that

$$\frac{\partial L}{\partial a_{1,i}} = w_{1,i}. \tag{3.51}$$

This comes out as a special case of

$$\frac{\partial}{\partial a_{1,r}} \left(-\frac{1}{2} \sum_{t=m}^{T} \mathbf{a}_t^T A^{-1} \mathbf{a}_t \right) = -\sum_{t=m}^{T} \sum_{i,j} \frac{\partial a_{t,i}}{\partial a_{1,r}} A_{ij}^{-1} a_{t,j} = \sum_{i} w_{m,i} \frac{\partial a_{m,i}}{\partial a_{1,r}},$$

for $m = 1$. This follows from induction too by the exact same proof as used for Equation (3.49), but with θ_{rs} replaced by $a_{1,r}$, with references to Equation (3.44) replaced by references to Equation (3.46), and with references to z_{t-1} replaced by zero—that is, with these terms left out.

In short, Equations (3.49), (3.50), and (3.51) will give us all the derivatives we need to operationalize Equation (3.41), once we have computed the $w_{t,i}$ in Equation (3.47). Equations (3.49), (3.50), and (3.47) each require us to carry out Cn^2 computations for every period of time t, and Equation (3.51) requires us to carry out fewer. Thus the total number of computations required to get all the derivatives is Cn^2T per iteration. *This is substantially less than the Cn^5T per iteration of the Box and Jenkins method.* For an n (number of variables) of about 10, it implies a 1000-fold reduction of cost. Also, we may recall that it requires Cn^2T iterations even to solve for the $\mathbf{a}_t$, given $\{\mathbf{z}_t\}$, $A^{(0)}$, and $\mathbf{B}^{(0)}$; thus the cost of our method here is on the order of the theoretical minimum. Even classical regression costs on the order of Cn^2T operations per analysis.[5]; Thus the technique above brings ARMA (1,1) analysis down into the range of costs acceptable to those who can now afford multiple regression.

3.4 DESCRIPTION OF COMPUTER ROUTINE TO ESTIMATE ARMA PROCESSES

The primary goal in applying the dynamic feedback method to the problem of ARMA estimation was to construct an operating computer program for use with social science data. This program was written as a new command, "ARMA," in the TSP (time-series processor) package for economists, which

---

[5]With n dependent variables and n independent variables, one must compute two n by n covariance matrices, with each term requiring T multiplications and summations, in conventional regression. When the estimation of such a model is carried out by the separate estimation of n simple regression equations, directly from raw data, one computes an $n + 1$ by $n + 1$ matrix n different times, implying an even greater cost.

in turn is a major subsystem of the MIT Cambridge Project Consistent System for social scientists; through TSP, the program has been available for several months to anyone with access to the MIT Multics machine (built by Honeywell), which, as part of the ARPA computer network, can be used directly from all types of computer consoles in a variety of cities from Honolulu, to Washington, DC, to London, England. Donald Sylvan, working with Professor Bobrow at the University of Minnesota, has made extensive use of this routine to evaluate the impact of American aid programs overseas. The usage of this program is documented in the current TSP manual[6]; our concern in this section is with the mathematics behind the program.

In order to convert the algorithm of Section 3.3 into a working computer program, it is necessary to go back and deal with a number of more practical issues.

To begin with, how do we choose the values for w and g_k in Equation (3.41) to give us enough progress *per iteration* to make the reductions in cost described above meaningful? Wasan [5, pp. 151–152] has pointed to this difficulty as the central problem in using steepest ascent in ordinary problems of statistical estimation. This difficulty was encountered in earlier tests but a simple interpretation of the problem and a solution were quickly found.

In essence, the problem is one of scaling. Suppose that we have two variables—say, world population and average births per female—to be called z_1 and z_2, respectively, and to be used in predicting each other's future values. Let us suppose that about 10% of the value of each variable can be explained by the value of the other variable in the preceding year. Then the maximum likelihood value for θ_{12}, for our data, will be a number in the billions; θ_{12}, when multiplied by a z_2 that is much less than 1, must lead to a product, $\theta_{12}z_2$, on the order of billions. θ_{21}, by similar logic, must be on the order of billionths. A change on the order of unity in θ_{12} will have very little effect on L, because it represents such a small fraction of the current value of θ_{12}' or of z_1. Thus $(\partial L/\partial \theta_{12})$ will be extremely small, even if θ_{12} has been misestimated by, say, 10%. On the other hand, a very small change in θ_{21}, much less than unity, could still double the value of θ_{21} and thus lead to a very large effect on L; thus $(\partial L/\partial \theta_{21})$ will be a very large number, if θ_{21} has been misestimated by, say, 10% or so. Looking at Equation (3.41), we can see what the result would be without the g_k terms: θ_{12}, which requires a huge change in absolute terms, would be changed very little, while θ_{21}, which requires a small change, would be changed by a much larger amount. Balanced improvement in the two coefficients would be impossible. One might imagine the possibility of imbalanced growth—that w might be made very small at first, that θ_{21} would converge to its own optimum, where it would generate a zero derivative, and that w could then grow enough to allow θ_{12} to move to *its* optimum. However, in general,

---

[6]The best, most recent description is available in Brode et al.[4]; discussions are underway regarding the publication of this manual through the MIT Press. The command language has been changed to increase flexibility.

the coefficients in a statistical model are not so completely independent of each other. If the optimum of θ_{21} depends at all on the estimate of θ_{12}, then our first small changes in θ_{12} will lead to enormous derivatives from θ_{21} again, destablizing the system again before there is a chance for w to build up enough to allow a large increase in θ_{12}. Thus, at least when the scaling problem is severe, the hope of imbalanced growth is not an answer to the danger of slow convergence.

The solution of this problem was rather straightforward for ARMA estimation; we simply scaled the variables of the problem according to a common scale. More precisely, we achieved the same effect by setting

$$g_k \text{ for } \theta_{rs} = \frac{\sigma_r^2}{\sigma_s^2} \quad \text{and} \quad g_k \text{ for } P_{rs} = \frac{\sigma_r^2}{A_{nn}},$$

where σ refers to the standard deviation. On a more sophisticated level, what we are doing here is trying to maximize the expected progress per iteration, *in light of* our prior probabilistic knowledge about L. We do not expect the units of measurement of the variables to tell us anything about their relative influence on each other; therefore we demand a choice of g_k that ensures that a change of units will have no effect on our algorithms. More generally, these variances give us an idea of the expected order of size of a coefficient, and we set g_k to keep the changes in line with the expected ratios between sizes and derivatives. To handle the case of $B_k = a_{1,r}$ therefore, we write a rough but reasonable expression:

$$g_r = \max \left(T(1 - P_{rr})A_{rr}, A_{rr} \right).$$

By changing $a_{1,r}$ by a certain amount, we are changing $a_{t,r}$ in *units proportional to 1*. Thus our formula for g_r is like our formula for the g_k with θ_{rs}, except that σ_s^2 is replaced by 1. If $P_{rr} = 1$, then this effect will take place on all the $a_{t,r}$, and the analogy is exact. *Otherwise*, if P_{rr} is smaller, the derivative with respect to $a_{1,r}$ of L will be much smaller, even when the optimal size of $a_{1,r}$ is still just as large; thus we propose a large g_r in that case. Note that as $A^{(0)}$ is recalculated in every major iteration, the formulas above encourage us to recalculate the g_k at the same time. In Chapters 4 and 6, I have included a brief discussion of the success of this general procedure with the estimations carried out; in Section 2.13, I have suggested ways of generalizing the procedure for use with general, nonlinear models.

The choice of w requires a similar exercise in prior estimation. At each step, the program looks at three essential pieces of data—$L(A^{(0)}, B^{(0)})$, $L(A', B')$, and $\Sigma_k (B_k' - B_k^{(0)}) \, \partial L/\partial B_k$. Assuming that L is essentially quadratic and that the current choice of w is "right" (i.e., that $L(A', B')$ is the maximum of the quadratic distribution), the program "expects" that $L(A', B')$ will be better than $L(A^{(0)}, B^{(0)})$ by exactly half what the gradient would appear to indicate. If this expectation is correct, then the program concludes that B' is not only acceptable, but also that there probably is little point in exploring further in the same direction; it sets $\mathbf{B}^{(0)} = \mathbf{B}'$, $A^{(0)}$ to A', and begins a new major iteration. If $L(A', \mathbf{B}')$ is worse, then, by the quadratic assumption, we have overshot by at least a factor of 2; w should be cut in half, and a new $\mathbf{B}'$ tried accordingly. In order to be a bit more conservative, the program specifies that w will be reduced by 40%, *if* the actual gain is less than 25% of what is indicated by the gradient. If $L(A', \mathbf{B}')$ is better than 75% of what is indicated by the gradient, the quadratic assumption tells us to double w. In an earlier version, I was more conservative here and required 100%; however, convergence was slow in some cases, and I reduced the requirement to 87%, which has proved adequate. In the intermediate range, when $\mathbf{B}'$ is deemed acceptable for the start of a new major iteration, w is still changed somewhat, for the sake of the next iteration; w is multiplied by twice the actual gain, $L(A', \mathbf{B}') - L(A^{(0)}, \mathbf{B}^{(0)})$, divided by the gain predicted by the gradient. At the other extreme, if w appears to be far off, the program will multiply w by 4 or by 0.3 in each minor iteration; more precisely, if w appears to be too small to let us set $\mathbf{B}^{(0)} = \mathbf{B}'$, even after w has just been doubled within the same major iteration, or if w appears to be too large after having just been cut to 60%, then a larger change will be tried in the next minor iteration. Flags are set in the program, to force it to stop changing w, as soon as it starts changing w in opposite directions within the same major iteration; in such cases, the procedures above ensure that either the last $\mathbf{B}'$ or the one before it gave an $L(A', \mathbf{B}')$ much better than $L(A^{(0)}, \mathbf{B}^{(0)})$, and the program will set $\mathbf{B}^{(0)}$ to this new $\mathbf{B}'$ for the next major iteration. For reasons similar to those mentioned in the previous paragraph, w is initialized at $1/T$.

At each step, the program prints out L, as defined in Equation (3.38), and the direction of change of w. After five major iterations, or after L appears to have stabilized to within 0.01, whichever comes first, the program stops and asks the user if he/she wishes to continue; if not, it prints out the analysis so far and transfers to another program to carry out simulation studies of the user's model. In the current version describe above, five major iterations have usually been enough for a close approximation, for analyses of actual social science data; for safety, however, I have generally used 10 in my own analyses. (Once L is about 0.1 away from its maximum, then the current set of coefficient estimates has almost as high a probability of exact truth—90% as high—as the maximum likelihood set itself; thus 0.1 is a conservative upper limit to how much accuracy it makes sense to request.) Unfortunately, the changes above were made piecemeal over a number of runs on different data, with the final improvements existing only in the basic subroutine incorporated into the MIT version. This routine has a more effective procedure for generating initial estimates than I used with the earliest test data; thus the direct comparison, before and after, would overstate somewhat the relative merits of the current system. Section 3.5 contains a numerical example of convergence results before and after these procedures for convergence were introduced.

The fundamental purpose in using ARMA estimation, as I have described it, is to improve on classical multiple regression. Thus I use multiple regression itself to provide the initial estimates $\mathbf{B}^{(0)}$. Not only are these likely to be reasonable estimates, in terms of their general order of size and in terms of the size of the biggest terms, but they also assure that our ARMA model will either represent an improvement on multiple regression or, in some cases, will confirm multiple regression. The subroutine has been written to allow other initial estimates, but the main program now available at TSP does not make use of this option. Originally, I used the regression coefficients that came from a standard model including regression constants; the results on Norway, in Section 6.5 of Chapter 6, were based on that system. With the constants, one introduces a greater degree of freedom into the regression models, to offer a more interesting (though perhaps artificial) comparison against the ARMA models, which do not include that degree of freedom. However, in order to ensure convergence under all circumstances, the regression constants have been eliminated from the MIT version; users of that system still have the freedom, in any case, to obtain regression constants based on constant terms by using other modules in the same system or even by another run of the ARMA command. Both the MIT version and my private version used on the Norway data print out all the ARMA estimates and regression coefficients, along with the standard deviations of the variables (to assist in interpretation) and the likelihood values for both models. The significance of the various coefficients can be estimated by looking at the likelihood of the models that result when the coefficients are removed from the model.

Several other options have been added, to extend this algorithm somewhat. First, there is now provision for "exogenous variables." In the discussion above, the expression θz_{t-1} could have been replaced systematically by θy_{t-1}, where θ is now a rectangular matrix, and where y_{t-1} includes both z_{t-1} and a few other components; none of the equations above would have had to be changed in form. The program in its current form allows both endogenous and exogenous variables.

Second, there is provision to allow the user to dictate a priori that certain components of θ will be constrained to equal zero. This is done simply enough, by setting their initial values to zero, and constraining Equation (3.41) to apply only to the other components of θ. Thus L is maximized as a function of the other components subject to this constraint. The basic subroutine allows this for any coefficient, but, in the MIT version, we have limited this to those θ_{ij} for which y_j is an exogenous variable.

Third, there is provision to give the user some ability, at least, to handle nonstationary processes. Box and Jenkins [1, pp.85–94] discuss at great length the prominence of nonstationary processes in practical statistics; they point out the value of introducing some kind of careful procedure for dealing with nonstationary processes, even if the procedure must have a less rigorous foundation than the usual statistical processes, in order to give the social scientist confronted with such processes an alternative other than either giving up or using an inappropriate tool. However, the procedures they introduce [1, pp.

87 and 113] involve processes that tend to grow as t^k for some constant k. By contrast, the commonest processes of growth in the social sciences would appear to be those of exponential growth, processes that may come out of a dynamic relation like that of Equation (3.5), but with a choice of θ large enough to allow growth. The concept of maximum likelihood, as discussed in Chapter 2, does not require a θ that generates a stationary process; thus at first glance, the special procedures suggested by Box and Jenkins might appear irrelevant. However, my estimation procedure has depended on Equation (3.6), not just on Equation (3.5) and the likelihood concept. Equation (3.6) implies that the average size of the random component of our process remains the same across time. If we were analyzing a 200-year series of data on the U.S. GNP, for example, this would imply that a $10 billion error in our predictions for 1790 from 1789 should be treated as a smaller matter than an $11 billion error in our predictions of 1973 from 1972; a $10 billion error would always be regarded as less significant than an $11 billion error, *regardless* of the year in which the error occurred. In practice, both the measurement errors and random fluctuations are likelier to be a fixed percentage of the variable itself—GNP—than to be a fixed independent process. To handle this kind of situation, an option called ARMAWT has been introduced to deal with a model of error slightly different from Equation (3.6):

$$p(a_t) = \frac{1}{\sqrt{(2\pi)^n \det A}} \exp\left(-\frac{1}{2} \sum_{i,j} \frac{a_{t,i}}{z_{t,i}} A_{ij}^{-1} \frac{a_{t,j}}{z_{t,j}} \right),$$

which is simply the normal distribution for the n-dimensional vector

$$\begin{Bmatrix} a_{t,i} \\ z_{t,i} \end{Bmatrix}$$

and which requires us to calculate A_{ij} as the covariance of this vector. In practice, however, the simulation studies of Chapter 4 suggest that the ordinary ARMA command generally performs at least as well as ARMAWT, even for most of the nonstationary processes studied.

Finally, provision has been made for the possibility—mentioned in Chapter 2—that the available data would consist not of one string of observations across time for our variables but of a whole set of such strings; a general model of the process of population growth, for example, might encourage us to develop a model for application to data series involving the same variables across many different countries. In order to handle this possibility, we can use Equation (3.41) as before, but we must note the following: (a) $(\partial L/\partial \theta_{rs})$ and $(\partial L/\partial P_{rs})$, across all the data strings, will simply equal their sum across all the individual data strings; (b) each data string, S, will require its own $\mathbf{a}_1^{(S)}$ for initialization; and (c) $(\partial L/\partial a_{1,r}^{(S)})$ will, of course, equal the value of $(\partial L/\partial a_{1,r})$ calculated in string S. (Note that this example might be a good candidate for the use of

ARMAWT to prevent the analysis from being dominated by nations of large population–unless such weighting is actually desired.)

3.5 NUMERICAL EXAMPLE OF THE BEHAVIOR OF DIFFERENT CONVERGENCE PROCEDURES

All the ARMA estimations reported in Chapters 4 and 6 were based on the final form of my algorithm, making use of the special convergence procedures described in Section 3.4. However, before installing these procedures, I carried out a number of tests on the preliminary version of the ARMA routine, on simple made-up data sets, in order to check out the accuracy of the routine. One of these simple test series was used before introducing the possibility of different g_k for different B_k, as in Equation (3.41); thus we can see the effect of adding the new convergence procedures by comparing the old test results against a new analysis of the same series. The data series in question is a simple univariate series of length seven—1.0, 1.2, 1.2, 1.3, 1.5, 1.4, 1.0— fit to the model $z_{t+1} = \theta z_t + a_t + Pa_{t-1}$. This series does not fit well to a simple arithmetic progression; thus the "distance" from the regression model to the ARMA model turns out to be fairly great; the series is a relatively severe test of convergence possibilities. (The cost per iteration is low, because the series is short, but the progress per iteration in log probability, as a percentage of the gap in log probability, is extremely slow.) The initial test output was a string of numbers, which may be arranged in a table (Table 3.1).

TABLE 3.1 Example of Convergence Results with Early Version of the ARMA Estimation Routine

Major Iteration Number	Theta in $\mathbf{B}^{(0)}$	Log P at $(\mathbf{B}^{(0)}, A^{(0)})$	Log P at $(\mathbf{B}, A')$	Change of w
1	0.8204	−0.8925	−0.2017	0
1	0.8204	−0.8925	1.6138	−1
1	0.8204	−0.8925	0.2602	−1
2	1.0049	1.6138	1.5624	0
2	1.0049	1.6138	1.6571	−1
2	1.0049	1.6138	0.0325	−1
3	0.9746	1.6571	1.6773	0
4	0.9843	1.6773	1.6849	0
5	0.9849	1.6849	1.7004	0
5	0.9849	1.6849	1.7162	1
5	0.9849	1.6849	1.8176	2
5	0.9849	1.6849	2.3374	2
5	0.9849	1.6849	−8.8156	2
5	0.9849	1.6849	3.6485	−1

"Change of w" means the value of "$n$test," a number indexing the source of the current $\mathbf{B}'$. If the w used in generating $\mathbf{B}'$ was taken directly from the last major iteration, "0" is used; if w was cut by 40% in the previous minor iteration within the same major iteration, a "-1" is used; and so on, as one might expect from the description in Section 3.4. Note that the calculations implied by this table include five computations of the gradient of likelihood, and 14 computations of likelihood (average errors) for sample coefficient vectors $\mathbf{B}'$.

There follows the script of a TSP session based on the same data series. The ordinary user, to get into TSP, would have to sign in on the MIT Multics, then enter the consistent system, and then issue the command "tsp:x" or "tspr:x"; in my directory, the user only needs to issue the command "tspr" directly (see Table 3.2).

After this, I went on to check out the simulation routine, and other routines in TSP to make sure that all was working correctly. Note that the convergence information would not have been printed out in so much detail if the "output some" flag had been turned on.

The variance of the error with the ARMA model—.0098203—was quite a bit smaller than the variance of the error with regression—.036896. This is a good index of the distance between the two models. It is interesting that the economic cost of using ARMA analysis, measured in iterations, would appear to be less when it turns out to be unnecessary, when the distance is small; the number of iterations can get large, mostly in the case where the benefit from using ARMA analysis is also large. I deliberately used many iterations in this recent run to confirm that convergence was reasonable after 10 major iterations or so, in this difficult special case. An earlier test run was continued for only five major iterations, as shown in Table 3.1; however, in those five iterations, it covered roughly the same distance, in increasing log p, that the new system did in the first two. More significantly, the old routine showed major signs of floundering, and one has the impression that its final breakthrough was partly a matter of luck. The new routine moved systematically towards convergence. Note also that the problem of scaling is not unusually great in this case; the variables P and a_1 need scaling vis-à-vis θ, but with long multivariate time series one expects a far greater scaling problem, and a more dramatic need for the new procedures suggested in Section 3.4 and in Section 2.13.

3.6 ENDNOTES TO CHAPTER 3

3.6.1 Popularity of Multiple Regression

In principle, this statement might call for a statistical survey itself, although for those familiar with the usual procedures in social science it is an understatement. The MIT computing center, which now serves both MIT and Harvard, has put out a brief survey of statistical procedures available to its users on the IBM 370, in its publication AP-77. This survey lists six available sta-

TABLE 3.2 Sample Session with Convergence Results for Final Version of the ARMA Estimation Routine

```
tspr                                                    (me)
T 23:25   4.916   $ .33                                 (tsp)
data$                                                   (me)
T 23:25   .965   $.07                                   (tsp)
smpl 1 7$ load oldtst$ 1 1.2 1.2 1.3 1.5 1.4 1.0$ end$  (me)
smpl vector                                             (tsp)
     1      7                                           (tsp)
T 23:26   .581   $0.05                                  (tsp)
arma oldtst$ end$                                       (me)
it.no. 1, from logp=           1.616           (tsp from here down)
   0;newlogp=    1.709
  -1;newlogp=    2.281
it.no. 2, from logp=           2.281
   0;newlogp=  -12.660
  -1;newlogp=    1.900
  -2;newlogp=    2.864
   1;newlogp=    3.468
   1;/newlogp=  -2.119
   1;newlogp=    3.468
it.no. 3, from logp=           3.468
   0;newlogp=  -47.638
  -1;newlogp=  -30.132
  -2;newlogp=    3.396
  -2;newlogp=    4.032
   1;newlogp=    4.706
   1;newlogp=   -0.044
   1;newlogp=    4.706
it.no. 4, from logp=           4.706
```

```
                0;newlogp=     -22.527
               -1;newlogp=     -11.374
               -2;newlogp=       3.865
               -2;newlogp=       4.895              4.895                    (tsp)
it.no. 5, from logp=
                1;newlogp=       5.114
                1;newlogp=       5.249              5.249                    (tsp)
continue?                                                                    (me)
yes                                                                          (tsp)
it.no. 1, from logp=      -11.615
                0;newlogp=     -11.615
               -1;newlogp=      -3.843
               -2;newlogp=       4.928
               -2;newlogp=       5.381              5.381
it.no. 2, from logp=
                0;newlogp=       5.445
               -1;newlogp=       5.445              5.445
it.no. 3, from logp=
                0;newlogp=       5.542
               -2;newlogp=       5.542              5.542
it.no. 4, from logp=
                0;newlogp=       5.204
               -1;newlogp=       5.537
               -2;newlogp=       5.586              5.586
it.no. 5, from logp=
                0;newlogp=       5.636
                1;newlogp=       5.684
                2;newlogp=       5.846
continue?
yes                                                5.846                     (tsp)
it.no. 1, from logp=      -20.319                                            (me)
                0;newlogp=     -20.319                                       (tsp)
               -1;newlogp=     -12.058
```

TABLE 3.2 Sample Session with Convergence Results (Continued)

```
-2;newlogp=       1.427
-2;newlogp=       5.825
-2;newlogp=       5.968            5.968
it.no. 2, from logp=      6.005
0;newlogp=        6.005            6.005
it.no. 3, from logp=      6.127
0;newlogp=        6.021
1;newlogp=        6.037
2;newlogp=        6.127
2;newlogp=        6.020
2;newlogp=        6.127
it.no. 4, from logp=      6.127            (tsp)
0;newlogp=         .947
-1;newlogp=       4.054
-2;newlogp=       6.046
-2;newlogp=       6.147
it.no. 5, from logp=      6.147
0;newlogp=        6.162                    (tsp)
continue?                                  (me)
yes                                        (tsp)
it.no. 1, from logp=      6.162
0;newlogp=        6.184            6.184
it.no. 2, from logp=      6.184
0;newlogp=        6.197
-1;newlogp=       6.203
it.no. 3, from logp=      6.203
0;newlogp=        6.202
-1;newlogp=       6.219
```

110

```
it.no. 4, from logp=        6.219
    0;newlogp=      6.235        6.205
it.no. 5, from logp=        6.249
    0;newlogp=      6.249
continue?
no
logp=       6.249(    1.610)
predicting oldtst
indep.var.    theta       rho
oldtst     .9722708    1.0000000
reg error = 0.36896e-01
continue?
no
continue with simulation?
yes
```

```
                                        (tsp)
                                        (me)
                                        (tsp)

error       rms
0.98203e-02  1.276715                   (tsp)
reg.coeff.                              (tsp)
.9867076                                (me)
                                        (tsp)
                                        (me)
```

tistical packages—the Statistical Package for the Social Sciences, Data-Text, Econometric Software Package, the (IBM) Scientific Subroutine Package, P-STAT (Princeton statistical package), and the BioMeDical package. Five of the six include "multiple regression"; ESP, the sixth, would appear to contain the same provision under the term "simpler linear regression." Bayesian statistics are not included in any of the listings. Nonlinear least squares is present only in BMD. (We suspect, however, that ESP—a cousin of TSP—might have this capability by now.) Moving average models are not mentioned. Spectral analysis is not mentioned as such; the X Supplement to the BMD manual indicates its presence in the more recent version of that package, but in none of the others. This probably gives as accurate indication of the dominance of regression analysis in actual work in the social sciences.

3.6.2 Why Stationarity Rules Out $M = \theta M \theta^T$

One way of expressing the idea of stationarity is that the norm of θ^n, and thus of $(\theta^T)^n$, will become arbitrarily small for n sufficiently large; in particular, let us choose an n for which these norms are less than 1. If $M = \theta M \theta^T$, then, by substitution and induction, $M = \theta^n M \theta^{T^n}$. If M is nonzero, then there must exist some vector, $\mathbf{v}$, of unit length, for which $M\mathbf{v}$ is of nonzero length; let us pick the unit vector $\mathbf{v}$ for which the length of $M\mathbf{v}$ is a maximum. (Given that the matrix M is of finite dimension, at least one such vector must exist). Then our assumptions clearly tell us that the length of $M\mathbf{v}$ would be greater than the length of $\theta^n M \theta^{T^n}\mathbf{v}$, contradicting our matrix equality.

3.6.3 Why $M \neq \theta M \theta^T$ Is Weaker Than Stationarity

Consider, for example, $\theta = kI$, where k is neither $+1$ nor -1, and where I is the identity matrix. If k is larger than $+1$, this θ would correspond to a highly nonstationary process. Yet this θ still meets our requirements. If $M = \theta M \theta^T$, then, by substitution, $M = k^2 M$; this cannot happen for the k we have mentioned, for a nonzero M. Indeed, it would appear that our assumption could only be violated for that infinitesimally small proportion of matrices θ which have eigenvalues exactly equal to 1 in absolute value. If this were proven, it is conceivable that our reasoning could be extended even to that set of matrices by some sort of limit theorem; however, such possibilities go beyond the scope of the discussion here.

3.6.4 ARMA-Related Work In Engineering

It has been pointed out to me that R. L. Kashyap, in the area of engineering, has suggested a procedure for the "estimation" of models of the form of Equation (3.7). [6] "Estimation" in his article is different from what a statistician would call estimation; the article concerns itself with the *use* of a model of the form (3.7), with coefficients already determined, to predict future values of z and the like. Nevertheless, another article by Kashyap [7] does present a general method of approach that could be extended to yield an algorithm similar to our own for estimating processes of the form (3.5). Kashyap's general algorithm is considerably weaker than our own or Jacobson's, discussed in Chapter 2, insofar as it applies only to linear processes. Kashyap [7, p. 26] discusses the possibility of using a representation for his statistical processes involving a "moving average error"; however, he uses a form of moving average with considerably more degrees of freedom than the form used in statistical theory and comes to the conclusion that such a representation is impossible. A study of the relation between his parameters and ours might yield a solution procedure, like the one discussed in Section 3.2. Alternatively, the same general approach might have been used from the beginning on our own representation. Wasan [5, pp. 151–152] has pointed out the importance of adding a rational procedure for handling w and g_k, an issue that Kashyap does not discuss, before one can claim to have a workable algorithm in the field of statistics. Kashyap also mentions the notion of "constrained derivative," which looks like a precursor of the "ordered derivative" of Chapter 2, but based on notions of variational calculus. The concept, as Kashyap uses it, does not include his "lambdas" as a set of constrained derivatives, while they correspond very clearly to ordered derivatives in our own system.

3.6.5 On the treatment of a_1^*

Strictly speaking, our estimate of $p(a_1)$ should include reference to the general probability of the z_0, which we would deduce. However, as pointed out later in the text, our estimation procedures are not very sensitive to the assumption of stationarity. Accounting for this extra piece of information, z_0, becomes rather doubtful when nonstationarity is involved and when z_0 represents the beginning of a process previously governed by different dynamics. As in Section 2.6 of Chapter 2, we have decided that "perfection" on this point would not be worth the cost, especially in light of Box and Jenkins' similar loose approach to the point.

REFERENCES

1. G. E. P. Box, and G. M. Jenkins, *Time Series Analysis: Forecasting and Control*, Holden-Day, San Francisco, 1970.
2. E. J. Hannan, *Multiple Time-Series*, Wiley, New York, 1970.
3. G. M. Jenkins, and D. G. Watts, *Spectral Analysis*, Holden-Day, San Francisco, 1968.
4. J. Brode, P. Werbos, and E. Dunn, *TSP in the Datatran Language*. Available in draft form from Cambridge Project, 5th Floor, Technology Square, Cambridge, MA 02138.
5. M. T. Wasan, *Parametric Estimation*, McGraw-Hill, New York, 1970.
6. R. L. Kashyap, A new method of recursive estimation in discrete linear systems, *IEEE Transactions*, Vol. AC-15, No. 1, pp. 18–25.
7. R. L. Kashyap, Maximum likelihood identification of stochastic linear systems, *IEEE Transactions*, Vol. AC-15, No. 1.

4

Simulation Studies of Techniques of Time-Series Analysis

4.1 INTRODUCTION

Most of the discussion in this thesis about the disadvantages of multiple regression—the classical mainstay of time-series analysis—has emerged from the study of concrete data in political science. One might ask, however, whether the discussion applies to other sorts of times series, in economics or ecology or elsewhere. The discussions in Section 2.7 of Chapter 2 and in Chapter 5 suggest that the superiority of the ARMA approach and of the robust approach are due to special characteristics of the data studied; in particular, this superiority may be due to the presence of complex measurement noise. While measurement noise may be almost universal in the social sciences, it would still be very interesting to get some kind of tangible idea about *how much* measurement noise, of *what kind* and *where*, leads to *how big* of a failure of ordinary regression. Indeed, in Section 2.7 of Chapter 2, in discussing the trade-off between the maximum likelihood approach, as represented by ARMA estimation, and the robust approach, it was emphasized that some weight should be given to the findings of each approach, and that there is no universal prescription for what these weights should be in all cases. Even if a universal prescription is impossible, however, a number of clear concrete numerical examples may help us greatly in building up an intuitive map of the trade-offs.

Simulation studies can provide us with these examples. Indeed, with simulation studies it is possible to generate hundreds of sample time series, all standardized, all based on known types of statistical processes; time series in the real world rarely offer such tidiness and rarely allow us to feel so secure in our interpretations. Even the possibility of unique, erratic events can be accounted for, if we insert terms for erratic types of random disturbance into the simulation process, as described in Section 4.2. In principle, one could even simulate unique, all-encompassing shifts, in which one is asked to predict

114

the behavior of a time series that will, in the future, obey a different system of dynamic laws form those it has obeyed in the past. However, it is not reasonable to expect *any* statistical routine to pass this last test, in its most general form. Difficulties of this last sort, in the real world, can only be minimized by intelligent human use of statistics, as discussed in Chapter 5.

The goal in this chapter is to begin the process of mapping out the domains in which different techniques of time-series analysis are appropriate, as indicated by the analysis of simulated data. The territory to be mapped out, in principle, is extremely vast; it includes all the statistical processes and models, multivariate and nonlinear and highly complex, which could ever be relevant to the social or natural sciences. Thus there is no choice but to try and pick out a subregion of this territory, small enough to be manageable but large enough to illustrate the qualitative factors most important in the discussion.

The goal, more precisely is to compare the ability of different estimation techniques to fit the coefficients of a simple model, in such a way that it predicts effectively the behavior of an "unknown" process, which may actually be more complex than what the model itself can express completely. In social science, in general, I assume that a true, complete description of the actual processes going on would contain far too many parameters to be estimated from the available data. The discussion here will focus on the problem of estimating the simplest model possible of relevance to social science:

$$Z(t + 1) = cZ(t). \tag{4.1}$$

Sample time series Z, of length 200, have been generated by simulating the results of more complex processes; then, for each sample time series Z, we have compared the ability of each of our basic estimation techniques to come up with a good value for c. It should be noted that ordinary linear multivariate estimation problems are simply the extension of this example to the case where Z is a vector and c is a matrix.

In Section 4.3, we will see that the studies carried out here generally support the conclusions outlined in Chapter 1; however, before describing these results, it is necessary to define in detail precisely what studies were carried out.

4.2 DEFINITION OF STUDIES CARRIED OUT

The main results of these tests are summarized in Table 4.1, while the secondary results are summarized in Table 4.2, and the raw computer output is tabulated at length in Tables 4.3 and 4.4. In order to explain precisely what these tables mean, we must define (1) the 12 more complex processes that are used in simulating sample time series, (2) the six estimation techniques that are used to estimate c from the first 100 observations of each sample time series, and (3) the criteria that are used to evaluate these estimates.

The complex processes used in simulation were all chosen to be "compatible'' with Equation (4.1), in the sense that (4.1) could do an adequate job of prediction if the constant c were chosen appropriately. This implies a constant average rate of growth for the variable Z. Thus I decided to focus attention on 12 processes that generate a single observed time series Z on the basis of homogenous linear equations.

Chapters 2 and 3 have placed great emphasis on the possibility of ''measurement noise'' or ''transient noise,'' as distinct from ''process noise'' or ''objective randomness.'' The simulations here follow up on that emphasis by focusing on processes that generate an ''observed'' (or ''superficial'') variable Z, as the result of two subprocesses: (1) an ''inner,'' or ''objective,'' process, which determines the evolution of the ''true'' or ''underlying'' variable, X, over time; and (2) an ''outer,'' or ''measurement,'' process, in which Z, the ''measured value'' of X (or an ''index of X''), is determined, by superimposing some noise factor over the true value of X. Z, *and only* Z, was later made available to the estimation routines. (Strictly speaking, this situation is merely a special case of the more general situation, where one can observe directly only a subset of the variables of dynamic significance.) The first six of these processes are determined by equations of the form

$$X(t + 1) = (1.03)X(t)[1 + P(t)],$$

$$Z(t) = X(t)[1 + M(t)]. \tag{4.2}$$

$P(t)$ and $M(t)$ are both ''noise processes'' of various sorts; $P(t)$ represents ''objective'' or ''process noise,'' while $M(t)$ represents ''transient'' or ''measurement noise.'' Note that a 3% natural growth rate, per time period, is chosen for X and Z; this would seem rather typical for economic and social science data.

The equations generating $P(t)$ and $M(t)$ are different for each of these six processes. In essence, they were chosen from three different noise processes, A, B, and C. A was a normal random process of mean zero and of variance one:

$$p(A(t)) = \frac{1}{\sqrt{2\pi}} \exp\left\{-\frac{1}{2}[A(t)^2]\right\}. \tag{4.3}$$

Thus A is a simple classical noise process, based on a bell-shaped curve. To generate B, we first generate a random number A as above. Then, with probability .95, we set $B = A$; however, in 5% of the cases, chosen at random, we set $B = 10A$. This implies a probability distribution:

$$p(B(t)) = \frac{.95}{\sqrt{2\pi}} \exp\left\{-\frac{1}{2}[B(t)^2]\right\} + \frac{.05}{10\sqrt{2\pi}} \exp\left[-\frac{1}{2}\left(\frac{B(t)}{10}\right)^2\right]. \tag{4.4}$$

B is generated by a ''distribution with outliers.'' To generate $C(t)$, a more complex noise process, we first generate $B(t)$; then we generate $\theta(t)$, another random variable, by picking $\theta(t) = 1$ with a probability of 20%, or by setting $\theta(t)$ to a number chosen at random from a uniform distribution between 0.0 and 0.2 in all other cases. We then generate $C(t)$ via the equation

$$C(t) = [1 - \theta(t)]C(t - 1) + 4\theta(t)B(t). \qquad (4.5)$$

This procedure for generating $C(t)$ is an attempt to express the idea of noise that "may or may not correlate with itself across time," whose correlation itself, $1 - \theta(t)$, can change randomly with time. Equation (4.5) was further modified by the use of an occasional cutoff, which is described in the next paragraph.

The choices used in Processes 1–6, for insertion into Equation (4.2), may be summarized as follows:

Process 1 (and 7): $P(t) = .05A$; $M(t) = 0$

Process 2 (and 8): $P(t) = .05A$; $M(t) = .15A$

Process 3 (and 9): $P(t) = .05B$; $M(t) = .15A$

Process 4 (and 10): $P(t) = .05A$; $M(t) = .15B$

Process 5 (and 11): $P(t) = .05A$; $M(t) = .05C$

Process 6 (and 12): $P(t) = .05B$; $M(t) = .05C$ (4.6)

Five percent and 15% errors were chosen on grounds that they seem "typical"; computer time was not available to replicate this study for different values of these parameters. It should be noted that the appearance of A twice with Process 2 above does *not* mean that the same random number, $A(t)$, was used in both processes; in general, every time a random number was needed for a new application, a new call was invoked to "random," the random number generator of the Project Cambridge TSP–CSP system. In Equation (4.2), one should also note that an unrealistic change of sign could occur if $P(t)$ should ever equal -1 or less; this would be a very rare event with the systems specified here, but even one such incident would persist throughout an entire simulated time series, making it totally unrealistic as a representative of social science time series. Similarly, while measurement errors are occasionally quite gross for social science variables, it is unrealistic to imagine someone getting the sign wrong for such variables as GNP or population. Thus for both $P(t)$ and $M(t)$ we instituted a cutoff of $-.75$; values less than this were set equal to the cutoff. (No simulations were run without a cutoff; thus it is possible that the cutoff was never actually invoked.) A more elegant procedure, mathematically, might have been to use e^P and e^M instead of $(1 + P)$ and $(1 + M)$ in Equation (4.2). However, major and enduring crashes do sometimes occur in those social science variables subject to erratic behavior; for example, phenomena such as zero or negative population seem to be avoided as a result of extraordinary processes different from those operating on normal populations. Thus on grounds of realism, we decided to use cutoffs instead of a more elegant approach. Also, a cutoff of -15.0 was used for the value of $B(t)$ inserted into Equation (4.5), on the grounds that this would prevent the possibility of invoking a cutoff several times in a row on $M(t)$.

In summary, the choices above allow one to look at the four possibilities of no measurement noise, of simple measurement noise, of medium-complex measurement noise, and of complex measurement noise, all in the presence of simple process noise; they also allow one to look at simple measurement noise and complex measurement noise, in the presence of medium-complex process noise. Processes 1 and 2 closely resemble the processes for which simple regression and ARMA models, respectively, should be ideal, in theory. The extreme case of zero process noise—the case that should be most favorable to the "robust approach"—was not included on the grounds that we are interested in evaluating that approach under more normal, mixed conditions. In order to account for the possibility of more complex processes, without violating homogeneity, Processes 7–12 were introduced based on the following equations, which yield a growth rate of 1.6% (from the linearized difference equation):

$$X(t + 1) = [.38X(t) + .35X(t - 1) + .3X(t - 2)][1 + P(t)],$$
$$Z(t) = X(t)[1 + M(t)]. \tag{4.7}$$

The choices of $P(t)$ and $M(t)$ here were identical to those with Processes 1–6, as indicated in Equations (4.6), and the same cutoffs were used.

For each of the 12 processes defined above, 10 sample time series, $Z1$ through $Z10$, were generated. Then, in order to estimate c in Equation (4.1) for each of those sample time series, I used the three general techniques discussed throughout this thesis—(1) classical regression, (2) the ARMA approach, and (3) the robust approach. The most conventional way of estimating c for model (4.1) is to use a standard regression program to do a maximum likelihood estimation of the related model:

$$Z(t + 1) = cZ(t) + k + a(t), \tag{4.8}$$

where k is a constant to be estimated and $a(t)$ is a normal random noise process. In practice, this amounts to doing a least-squares estimation, as in Section 2.2 of Chapter 2; one hopes that k, which is expected to be zero, will be estimated as something close to zero. This technique, regression with a constant term, is abbreviated as "reg + k" in the tables (see Tables 4.2–4.4).

A better way of using classical regression to estimate c in model (4.1) is to use a simpler model, without the meaningless constant term:

$$Z(t + 1) = cZ(t) + a(t). \tag{4.9}$$

This kind of regression can be performed automatically in the Time-Series Processor system. This technique, regression without a constant term, is abbreviated as "reg" in the tables.

Corresponding to these two simple regression models are two simple ARMA models. According to the result in the beginning of Chapter 3, the correspondence is more than just one of similarity; the ARMA models below are the generalizations of Equations (4.8) and (4.9) to account for the possibility of "white noise" in the process of data measurement. Model (4.8) corresponds to

$$Z(t + 1) = cZ(t) + a(t) + Pa(t - 1) + k, \qquad (4.10)$$

which can be estimated directly in the Project Cambridge Time-Series Processor by use of the command "ARMA," described in the latter part of Chapter 3. This technique for estimating c is abbreviated as "arma + k" in the tables. Model (4.9) corresponds to

$$Z(t + 1) = cZ(t) + a(t) + Pa(t - 1), \qquad (4.11)$$

which can also be estimated by the command "ARMA"; this technique for estimating c is abbreviated as "arma" in the tables. Finally, the estimation algorithm described in Chapter 3 allowed me to write another command, "AR-MAWT," to estimate the model

$$Z(t + 1) = cZ(t)[1 + a(t)] + Pa(t - 1)z(t - 1). \qquad (4.12)$$

This command, mentioned briefly in Chapter 3, is essentially equivalent to estimating Equation (4.11), with the assumption that the noise process $a(t)$ in Equation (4.11) is determined as a *percentage* of the actual variable, as in Equation (4.2), rather than a process of constant mean and variance. This technique for estimating c is abbreviated as "armawt" in the tables.

Finally, a "robust procedure" had to be found for estimating c, drawn from the discussion of Section 2.7 of Chapter 2. In the pure case of zero process noise, these procedures require one to estimate the initial "underlying" values of the variables measured, and the coefficients of the model, by directly minimizing the average errors of long-term predictions made with this model. In other words, for the estimated initial values and a given set of coefficients, one makes a full set of predictions for the variables of interest, *without ever* making use of the measured values of the variables at intermediate times. One uses the average error in *these* predictions, predictions that are generally long-term predictions, as one's criterion of fit; one uses the method of steepest descent or a related procedure in order to pick coefficients and initial estimates to minimize the total error in *these* predictions. (A "relaxed" version of these procedures would permit a little bit of allowance to be made for intermediate measured values, in predicting more distant time periods.)

The full multivariate, nonlinear version of this procedure, based on the dynamic feedback algorithm of Chapter 2, was not available at the time these simulations were carried out. However, for Equation (4.1), there is a measurement-noise-only model, which is much easier to estimate than is usually the case:

$$X(t + 1) = cX(t),$$

$$Z(t) = X(t)e^{a(t)} \approx X(t)[1 + a(t)]. \tag{4.13}$$

If the measurement noise, $a(t)$, is on the order of 10% or less, the approximate equality here will be very good, according to the Taylor expansion of $e^{a(t)}$. In order to estimate $X(0)$ and c in this model, one can transform Equations (4.13) algebraically to deduce

$$Z(t) = X(0)c^t e^{a(t)},$$

$$\log Z(t) = t \log c + \log X(0) + a(t). \tag{4.14}$$

In order to pick the constants, $\log c$ and $\log X(0)$, to maximize the likelihood of this model, according to standard maximum likelihood theory, one need only perform a simple regression of $\log Z(t)$ against the independent variable t and a constant term. A special routine to perform this operation, called GRR (GRowth Rate), was added to the Project Cambridge Time-Series Processor in January 1974. Note that this routine estimates c and $X(0)$ in exactly the same way as the old routine EXTRAP did, in the work reported in Chapter 6.

Finally, after the simulation processes and the estimation techniques are defined, there remains the problem of measuring how well the estimation techniques actually perform. Two different criteria are used here. First, there is the criterion of predictive power, measured explicitly. For each combination of time series (out of $12 \times 10 = 120$ sample time series) and of estimation technique, we used the value of c, as estimated for the *first* 100 time periods, to try to predict the values of the variable Z over the *remaining* 100 periods. For each such set of predictions we calculated four measures of error: (1) rms (root mean square) average percentage error in predicting periods 101 through 110, (2) rms average percentage error in predicting periods 101 through 125, (3) rms average percentage error in predicting periods 101 through 150, and (4) rms average percentage error in predicting periods 101 through 200. (Also, a set of predictions was made, from period 1 to periods 1 through 100.) The exact results of these tests are shown in Table 4.4, for every sample time series.

Let us define in a bit more detail how these predictions were arrived at. For the regression models (4.8) and (4.9), I inserted the *known* value of $Z(100)$, the estimates of c and k, and the most probable value for $a(100)$ (i.e., zero), in order to predict $Z(101)$; this prediction for $Z(101)$ was reinserted, along with $a(101) = 0$, to give a prediction of $Z(102)$, which in turn was reinserted, and so on. For Equation (4.9), this has the same effect as inserting the estimate of c into Equation (4.1), and using (4.1) to make the forecasts. With the ARMA models, Equations (4.10), (4.11), and (4.12), almost the same procedure was used. The measured value of $Z(100)$ was inserted to give the first prediction, the prediction of $Z(101)$; $a(100)$ through $a(199)$ were set to zero. However, the ARMA equations also refer to $a(t - 1)$; thus in the very first round, in predicting $Z(101)$, the value of $a(99)$ has to be accounted for; for $a(99)$, I used the estimated value that was generated by the ARMA estimation procedure, which had been used on periods 1 through 100. With Equation (4.11), as with Equation (4.9), this has the same effect as inserting the estimate of c into Equation (4.1), starting from the *predicted* value of $Z(101)$. "Percentage error" was defined, in general, as a percentage of the average of predicted and actual values, on the grounds that this is a good intelligible approximation to exponential error in the normal range and that it does not place overemphasis on outliers. All these decisions were made, not at the time of simulation, but at the time when the TSP command "ARMA" was written; at the time of simulation, the initial time and the number of periods to predict were specified, and the ARMA (ARMAWT) command carried through the decisions described in this paragraph by itself. (When the full nonlinear algorithm of Chapter 2 is operationalized, however, the user will be able to choose his/her own index of prediction error, according to what he/she considers important to policy-makers in the particular domain of interest. With ARMA, a linear system, it was necessary to make a general choice for all users, based on mathematical rather than substantive considerations.) With the univariate robust approach, there are two reasonable bases for prediction. One is to use Equations (4.14) directly, assuming that $a(101)$ through $a(200)$ equal zero; this method is abbreviated as "ext1." (This corresponds to the old EXTRAP procedure, described in Chapter 6; also, it corresponds to using Equation (4.1), starting from the *estimated* value of $X(0)$ as the initial value of $Z(0)$.) The other is to use the estimated value of c in Equation (4.1), inserting the measured value of $Z(100)$ into this equation; this is abbreviated as "ext2." The rms average errors are computed as with the ARMA model, automatically by command GRR.

Table 4.4 is a bit too complex to be assimilated directly by intuition. Thus the major results of Table 4.4, regarding prediction errors, are summarized in Table 4.2. For each of the 12 simulated processes described in Equations (4.2) through (4.7), for each of the seven prediction techniques described above, and for each of the four prediction intervals, the *average* prediction errors across the 10 sample time series have been calculated. More precisely, to avoid a picture distorted by outliers, I have tabulated the *worst* (biggest) of the errors out of the 10 and the average across the remaining nine. The rows containing the average values, for different prediction techniques, are labeled "av"; the rows containing the maximum errors are labeled "max." Finally, the last column gives the "dispersion" of the errors of the best technique, defined as the average over the nine better sample time series of the absolute value of the difference between the error in each sample series and the average error.

A quick scan of Table 4.2 indicates a general tendency of "ext2" to be superior substantially to regression; in some cases, "ext2" and "arma" are approximately equal, while in other cases "arma" and regression are approximately equal. A more detailed scan reveals three difficulties with these measures of predictive power. At long time intervals, errors get so high that it is hard not to worry about the effects of the percentage-taking procedure, and hard to feel fully comfortable about the significance of the averages; this difficulty may not be as real as it seems, but it is worth noticing. A more serious difficulty is the tendency of *all* prediction techniques to do equally well at very short time intervals, with most of the processes. With short-term predictions, the effects of different estimates of c have not had time to build up; thus all the predictions are close to each other, *relative* to the very large short-term fluctuations that the simulated processes impose. It is the medium and long-term predictions that separate the sheep from the lambs. This reminds me of certain schools of thought in the stock market, who compare the short-term fluctuations of stocks to a roulette game, and who claim that superior analysis makes money only by pointing out longer-term trends. With complex, large-scale multivariate processes in the social sciences, however, one might expect the fluctuations to look a bit smoother through time, even though the measurement noise problem remains. A few of the 12 processes do show significant differences between estimation techniques in the 10-year prediction tests; these processes may be more representative of the social sciences. A third difficulty is the limitation of having only 10 sample time series per analysis.

Table 4.1 uses a second criterion to measure the success of different estimation techniques. To construct this table, I have looked *directly* at the values of c, as estimated by the different models. With simulation studies, *unlike* studies in the real world, one can be sure that the "true" value of c is the same for all the samples of a given process; this is what makes a direct comparison possible. With a direct comparison, one does not worry about having one's conclusions randomized by the effects of random fluctuations in later periods of time, in a limited number of sample time series; the actual prediction errors in Table 4.2 may be interpreted as a noisy measurement of the quality of the estimates of c. Indeed, in most studies of political and economic phenomena, people tend to be interested in the validity of the coefficients c and only vaguely aware of the connection between the validity—*even in the short-term*—and the long-term predictive power of the resulting model. (This attitude would be quite reasonable if it were a choice between focusing on the validity of c and focusing on short-term predictive power. An accurate model of the effects of government policy might reduce prediction error by only 20%, in comparison with a null model, if short-term fluctuations are large enough, in accord with the pattern described in the paragraph above; however, this 20% would include 100% of the effects that the decision-maker can have on the situation.)

For all these reasons, the estimates of c, evaluated directly for accuracy, appear to be the best criterion to use in evaluating the estimation techniques

TABLE 4.1 Average Coefficient Estimates and Dispersion Errors of Estimates for the Six Estimation Routines and Twelve Simulated Processes Defined in Section 4.2

Process	Average or Dispersion	ext	reg + k	arma + k	reg	arma	armawt	(true)
1	av	1.0266	1.0149	1.0151	1.0205	1.0208	1.0211	1.0266
	disp	0.00392	0.00692	0.00690	0.00390	0.00404	0.00370	1.8 : 0
2	av	1.0262	0.9597	1.0160	1.0035	1.0267	1.0064	1.0262
	disp	0.00480	0.01944	0.01720	0.01090	0.00556	0.00580	6.6 : 0
3	av	1.0199	0.9181	0.9851	0.9893	1.0134	0.9374	1.0198
	disp	0.00952	0.04228	0.03626	0.01322	0.01464	0.06372	4.7 : 0
4	av	1.0270	0.9682	1.0203	1.0019	1.0272	0.9913	1.0270
	disp	0.00340	0.04832	0.01556	0.02376	0.00780	0.02638	4.5 : 2
5	av	1.0274	0.9819	0.9919	1.0099	1.0156	0.9698	1.0274
	disp	0.00540	0.04056	0.03256	0.01876	0.01376	0.04408	1.6 : 0
6	av	1.0280	0.9935	0.9969	1.0174	1.0190	0.9714	1.0279
	disp	0.01040	0.04620	0.04332	0.02352	0.02220	0.04212	6.3 : 2
7	av	1.0140	0.9960	1.0028	1.0110	1.0124	1.0122	1.0140
	disp	0.00200	0.00600	0.00504	0.00180	0.00168	0.00184	3.1 : 0
8	av	1.0138	0.8590	0.9503	0.9904	1.0139	1.0042	1.0138
	disp	0.00244	0.04760	0.05098	0.00628	0.00194	0.00364	7.5 : 2
9	av	1.0122	0.7884	0.9198	0.9801	1.0106	0.9811	1.0122
	disp	0.00396	0.08312	0.08428	0.00792	0.00456	0.02608	6.0 : 4
10	av	1.0143	0.8967	0.9638	0.9924	1.0145	0.9843	1.0143
	disp	0.00190	0.06202	0.03932	0.01484	0.00230	0.02218	6.0 : 5
11	av	1.0153	0.9182	0.9361	0.9947	1.0008	0.9399	1.0153
	disp	0.00356	0.06494	0.05808	0.01822	0.01488	0.05294	2.2 : 0
12	av	1.0156	0.9274	0.9547	1.0023	1.0116	0.9658	1.0156
	disp	0.00524	0.06904	0.05542	0.01424	0.00960	0.02808	2.3 : 0

TABLE 4.2 Prediction Errors as Defined in Section 4.2

Timespan	extl	ext2	reg + k	arma + k	reg	arma	armawt	disp
				Process 1				
10 av	11.7	7.8	8.4	8.2	8.0	7.9	7.4	2.4
10 max	29.1	12.2	23.1	23.1	21.6	21.6	21.1	
25 av	13.7	10.2	15.2	15.0	13.4	13.5	12.2	2.5
25 max	33.2	18.7	37.7	38.7	33.4	33.5	31.6	
50 av	23.7	18.1	28.4	28.3	24.9	24.8	22.7	6.1
50 max	38.8	35.3	66.2	66.2	56.9	57.1	53.2	
100 av	32.1	26.3	57.0	56.8	45.7	45.0	41.7	8.6
100 max	53.9	59.4	104.0	104.0	87.0	88.6	82.2	
				Process 2				
10 av	20	21	32	22	27	18	22	3.1
10 max	48	37	58	36	53	31	33	
25 av	22	23	53	33	45	24	32	4.4
25 max	55	44	88	61	80	48	55	
50 av	29	29	80	48	69	33	50	7.6
50 max	76	60	116	102	106	80	97	
100 av	36	36	120	72	103	40	95	14.5
100 max	104	81	149	138	144	105	140	
				Process 3				
10 av	52	25	32	22	34	22	39	5.1
10 max	93	51	77	52	62	46	106	
25 av	77	51	61	50	64	46	90	10.6
25 max	109	96	112	81	103	84	167	

50 av	98	77	76	78	91	73	122	15.4
50 max	139	134	143	114	134	121	184	22.2
100 av	111	97	100	100	116	107	134	
100 max	165	161	165	148	165	146	189	
Process 4								
10 av	30	17	20	17	18	17	24	6.6
10 max	42	113	110	33	145	32	100	
25 av	33	22	33	24	27	22	41	3.9
25 max	56	119	129	35	172	32	150	
50 av	37	28	57	35	43	26	.65	8.7
50 max	63	125	149	63	186	49	176	
100 av	44	44	95	62	77	39	101	15.3
100 max	91	132	170	119	193	100	188	
Process 5								
10 av	26	19	19	20	20	20	34	5.1
10 max	60	57	78	71	89	69	102	
25 av	29	24	29	28	27	28	58	5.8
25 max	61	65	83	82	114	78	141	
50 av	32	29	48	44	38	39	86	9.8
50 max	75	82	124	125	156	128	172	
100 av	51	46	90	82	66	61	126	10.8
100 max	85	87	154	155	179	161	186	
Process 6								
10 av	31	22	24	24	27	28	29	8.3
10 max	109	43	45	47	56	55	73	
25 av	38	32	41	41	44	44	63	8.2

TABLE 4.2 Prediction Errors as Defined in Section 4.2 (Continued)

Timespan	ext1	ext2	reg + k	arma + k	reg	arma	armawt	disp
				Process 6 (Continued)				
25 max	104	55	85	90	112	111	133	
50 av	57	47	66	67	66	65	95	10.3
50 max	119	81	116	123	148	147	166	
100 av	82	70	98	97	93	91	136	13.7
100 max	140	116	157	162	174	174	184	
				Process 7				
10 av	7.2	6.7	7.5	5.5	6.9	5.2	5.1	0.9
10 max	14.7	9.9	15.9	12.5	13.2	10.0	8.4	
25 av	8.0	7.8	12.6	8.8	9.6	6.7	6.6	1.7
25 max	17.2	12.4	26.3	21.3	19.0	14.6	13.9	
50 av	12.9	10.6	23.0	15.7	14.1	11.4	11.2	2.8
50 max	20.0	21.4	46.9	36.0	31.9	21.4	20.9	
100 av	17.1	13.8	51.0	37.4	24.0	18.8	18.4	3.8
100 max	29.8	32.7	83.5	61.4	54.9	31.6	37.3	
				Process 8				
10 av	17	21	37	22	27	17	19	2.1
10 max	31	38	55	43	49	21	27	
25 av	17	22	54	30	40	17	22	2.8
25 max	33	35	74	58	69	30	37	
50 av	21	24	75	44	63	21	31	3.0
50 max	44	41	89	79	93	34	62	
100 av	25	28	106	70	103	26	57	8.8
100 max	62	53	120	113	135	36	101	

Process 9

10 av	28	21	32	19	28	16	25	3.8
10 max	39	45	69	53	60	27	81	5.5
25 av	41	36	52	34	51	28	50	9.0
25 max	62	56	87	75	96	45	128	
50 av	51	46	64	46	76	36	72	14.8
50 max	81	78	110	101	178	69	163	
100 av	58	57	91	76	118	55	93	
100 nax	109	98	139	122	160	85	182	

Process 10

10 av	19	14	24	15	16	14	21	6.7
10 max	29	114	78	53	135	28	80	5.4
25 av	23	17	44	25	26	18	38	3.3
25 max	30	120	90	76	162	26	133	
50 av	24	20	67	39	44	19	60	6.1
50 max	33	123	106	95	180	28	166	
100 av	27	27	101	70	77	25	93	
100 max	52	127	131	124	190	47	183	

Process 11

10 av	21	20	21	21	20	21	39	5.1
10 max	55	57	56	54	86	61	108	4.7
25 av	24	23	33	30	29	27	70	9.1
25 max	66	66	65	68	103	93	158	
50 av	26	26	52	46	39	35	102	8.7
50 max	62	75	92	95	149	140	180	
100 av	36	35	91	84	65	52	143	
100 max	75	74	118	120	175	170	190	

TABLE 4.2 Prediction Errors as Defined in Section 4.2 (Continued)

Timespan	extl	ext2	reg + k	arma + k	reg	arma	armawt	disp
				Process 12				
10 av	22	20	21	20	22	21	24	5.5
10 max	49	34	31	31	33	33	75	
25 av	28	27	39	35	35	34	54	6.4
25 max	44	47	53	60	80	58	134	
50 av	39	35	57	56	55	48	89	7.8
50 max	61	66	94	85	118	74	169	
100 av	51	49	80	81	84	66	124	7.1
100 max	80	75	128	122	116	111	185	

here. The exact estimates of c for each sample time series are shown in Table 4.3. In Table 4.1, this information is summarized for easier interpretation. For each estimation technique and each simulated process, the table provides the *average* values of the estimates of c across all 10 sample time series. It also provides the "dispersion" of these estimates, the average value of the absolute value of the difference between the estimate of c for a given sample time series and the average estimate across all 10 samples. The rows labeled "av" give the average; the rows labeled "disp" give the dispersion. These calculations were made with the help of a hand calculator, directly from Table 4.4. (Note,

TABLE 4.3   Estimates of Growth Factor c

Time Series	ext	reg + k	arma + k	reg	arma	armawt
Z1	1.019	1.016	1.016	1.018	1.018	1.015
Z2	1.026	1.011	1.010	1.019	1.019	1.020
Z3	1.031	1.029	1.031	1.030	1.031	1.031
Z4	1.034	1.002	1.002	1.014	1.014	1.015
Z5	1.023	1.001	1.000	1.012	1.012	1.016
Z6	1.024	1.021	1.021	1.023	1.023	1.021
Z7	1.023	1.016	1.016	1.021	1.021	1.022
Z8	1.029	1.016	1.015	1.022	1.022	1.024
Z9	1.032	1.011	1.014	1.020	1.022	1.023
Z10	1.025	1.026	1.026	1.026	1.026	1.024
			Process 2			
Z1	1.014	0.896	0.984	0.995	1.024	0.994
Z2	1.026	0.967	1.007	1.020	1.022	1.015
Z3	1.025	1.001	1.033	1.020	1.031	1.006
Z4	1.020	0.959	1.026	1.002	1.029	1.002
Z5	1.032	0.957	1.028	0.992	1.033	1.008
Z6	1.032	0.959	1.001	0.994	1.030	1.009
Z7	1.027	0.940	0.998	0.994	1.015	0.998
Z8	1.022	1.000	1.052	1.024	1.037	1.003
Z9	1.034	0.950	1.004	0.990	1.018	1.017
Z10	1.030	0.968	1.027	1.005	1.028	1.012
			Process 3			
Z1	1.006	0.905	0.998	0.986	1.015	0.876
Z2	1.029	0.932	1.017	0.986	1.031	0.988
Z3	1.024	0.926	0.955	0.967	0.982	0.883
Z4	1.030	0.972	1.017	1.008	1.023	1.009
Z5	1.003	0.760	0.841	0.959	0.979	0.783
Z6	1.032	0.928	0.978	0.984	1.006	0.987
Z7	1.027	0.932	0.988	0.994	1.018	0.998

TABLE 4.3   Estimates of Growth Factor c (Continued)

Time Series	ext	reg + k	arma + k	reg	arma	armawt
			Process 3 (Continued)			
Z8	1.014	0.895	0.987	0.988	1.020	0.889
Z9	1.025	0.901	1.020	0.989	1.022	0.997
Z10	1.009	1.030	1.050	1.032	1.038	0.964
			Process 4			
Z1	1.020	1.017	1.037	1.025	1.031	1.011
Z2	1.028	0.766	1.015	0.898	1.034	0.890
Z3	1.022	0.991	1.005	1.010	1.015	1.004
Z4	1.028	0.968	1.030	1.004	1.031	0.990
Z5	1.026	0.929	1.002	0.987	1.022	1.006
Z6	1.028	0.980	0.992	1.006	1.011	0.997
Z7	1.033	0.988	1.019	1.011	1.025	1.020
Z8	1.034	1.036	1.050	1.038	1.045	1.020
Z9	1.028	0.978	1.011	1.010	1.024	1.013
Z10	1.023	1.029	1.042	1.030	1.034	0.962
			Process 5			
Z1	1.023	1.011	1.013	1.020	1.022	0.987
Z2	1.021	0.835	0.905	0.943	0.984	0.908
Z3	1.035	0.993	1.011	1.014	1.021	1.022
Z4	1.026	0.998	1.007	1.025	1.030	0.982
Z5	1.020	0.992	0.994	1.014	1.015	0.984
Z6	1.035	0.926	0.916	0.983	0.979	0.909
Z7	1.020	1.015	1.018	1.023	1.024	1.015
Z8	1.028	1.013	1.013	1.022	1.022	1.008
Z9	1.029	1.005	1.008	1.018	1.020	0.872
Z10	1.037	1.031	1.034	1.037	1.039	1.011
			Process 6			
Z1	1.023	1.016	1.015	1.021	1.021	1.010
Z2	1.020	1.002	1.013	1.024	1.027	0.967
Z3	1.016	0.935	0.950	0.999	1.006	0.887
Z4	1.025	1.022	1.014	1.032	1.029	0.986
Z5	1.045	0.980	0.982	1.002	1.003	0.994
Z6	1.029	1.060	1.066	1.053	1.056	1.020
Z7	1.035	0.890	0.888	0.952	0.953	0.918
Z8	1.053	1.050	1.047	1.053	1.052	1.052
Z9	1.004	0.938	0.951	0.999	1.003	0.903
Z10	1.030	1.042	1.043	1.039	1.040	0.977
			Process 7			
Z1	1.010	0.989	0.994	1.009	1.010	1.008
Z2	1.014	0.998	1.002	1.011	1.012	1.012

TABLE 4.3 (Continued)

Time Series	ext	reg + k	arma + k	reg	arma	armawt
			Process 7 (Continued)			
Z3	1.016	1.002	1.011	1.014	1.016	1.016
Z4	1.018	0.990	0.997	1.009	1.011	1.013
Z5	1.012	0.987	0.993	1.007	1.009	1.009
Z6	1.013	1.001	1.009	1.011	1.012	1.011
Z7	1.012	1.002	1.004	1.012	1.012	1.012
Z8	1.015	0.998	1.006	1.013	1.015	1.014
Z9	1.017	0.988	1.004	1.010	1.014	1.015
Z10	1.013	1.005	1.008	1.014	1.013	1.012
			Process 8			
Z1	1.008	0.673	0.740	0.980	1.011	0.996
Z2	1.013	0.906	0.969	1.002	1.011	1.007
Z3	1.014	0.933	1.017	1.004	1.016	0.999
Z4	1.010	0.834	0.914	0.988	1.014	1.002
Z5	1.016	0.884	0.979	0.985	1.018	1.013
Z6	1.017	0.897	1.012	0.987	1.016	1.004
Z7	1.014	0.847	0.992	0.986	1.010	1.004
Z8	1.012	0.844	0.981	0.994	1.014	1.002
Z9	1.018	0.889	0.957	0.985	1.015	1.006
Z10	1.016	0.883	0.942	0.993	1.014	1.009
			Process 9			
Z1	1.008	0.786	1.003	0.978	1.012	0.966
Z2	1.016	0.834	1.014	0.978	1.017	1.009
Z3	1.015	0.839	0.961	0.967	1.001	0.972
Z4	1.016	0.883	0.951	0.994	1.014	1.005
Z5	1.004	0.475	0.619	0.966	0.999	0.932
Z6	1.018	0.863	0.958	0.981	1.009	1.000
Z7	1.015	0.835	1.000	0.987	1.012	1.006
Z8	1.011	0.734	0.886	0.973	1.012	0.924
Z9	1.013	0.743	0.833	0.979	1.014	1.009
Z10	1.006	0.892	0.973	0.998	1.016	0.988
			Process 10			
Z1	1.011	0.958	0.983	1.008	1.014	1.006
Z2	1.015	0.662	0.791	0.929	1.015	0.914
Z3	1.011	0.936	0.973	1.002	1.010	1.002
Z4	1.015	0.867	0.940	0.988	1.016	0.987
Z5	1.014	0.851	0.987	0.986	1.014	1.011
Z6	1.015	0.937	0.987	1.000	1.009	0.985
Z7	1.018	0.925	0.986	0.997	1.017	0.978
Z8	1.018	0.971	1.005	1.008	1.021	1.007
Z9	1.014	0.903	1.001	0.998	1.014	1.003
Z10	1.012	0.958	0.985	1.008	1.015	0.950

TABLE 4.3   Estimates of Growth Factor c (Continued)

Time Series	ext	reg + k	arma + k	reg	arma	armawt
			Process 11			
Z1	1.013	0.968	0.975	1.007	1.009	0.972
Z2	1.012	0.731	0.849	0.944	0.985	0.888
Z3	1.023	0.967	0.988	1.003	1.012	0.973
Z4	1.014	0.916	0.935	1.004	1.011	0.957
Z5	1.008	0.870	0.879	0.990	0.993	0.953
Z6	1.020	0.831	0.791	0.959	0.950	0.828
Z7	1.012	0.964	0.978	1.009	1.011	0.998
Z8	1.015	0.968	0.991	1.010	1.012	0.994
Z9	1.017	0.971	0.976	1.006	1.008	0.839
Z10	1.019	0.996	0.999	1.015	1.017	0.997
			Process 12			
Z1	1.013	0.980	0.987	1.008	1.010	0.997
Z2	1.012	0.938	0.978	1.008	1.016	0.966
Z3	1.010	0.839	0.874	0.988	1.000	0.867
Z4	1.013	0.943	0.962	1.006	1.015	0.973
Z5	1.024	0.946	0.971	0.993	1.002	0.981
Z6	1.015	1.018	1.028	1.023	1.025	1.001
Z7	1.020	0.834	0.891	0.964	0.990	0.941
Z8	1.029	1.017	1.027	1.027	1.032	1.012
Z9	1.005	0.764	0.822	0.993	1.008	0.971
Z10	1.015	0.995	1.007	1.013	1.018	0.949

TABLE 4.4   Errors in Prediction and Miscellany

Method	Z1	Z2	Z3	Z4	Z5	Z6	Z7	Z8	Z9	Z10
			Process 1: Predicting Z(101)–Z(110) from Z(100)							
ext1	11	14	10	29	22	6	9	5	25	5
ext2	12	8	12	12	8	6	6	6	7	5
reg + k	11	10	12	23	14	6	4	10	6	4
arma + k	10	8	12	23	15	5	4	11	4	4
reg	11	8	12	22	13	6	4	9	5	4
arma	11	7	12	22	13	5	5	9	4	4
armawt	9	8	12	21	11	5	5	8	4	4
			Predicting Z(101)–Z(125) from Z(100)							
ext1	11	23	15	33	16	9	11	9	24	5
ext2	13	11	13	11	19	9	8	14	8	5

TABLE 4.4 *(Continued)*

Method	Z1	Z2	Z3	Z4	Z5	Z6	Z7	Z8	Z9	Z10

Predicting Z(101)–Z(125) from Z(100) (Continued)

Method	Z1	Z2	Z3	Z4	Z5	Z6	Z7	Z8	Z9	Z10
reg + k	11	10	12	38	38	11	5	27	21	4
arma + k	10	9	13	38	39	11	5	28	17	5
reg	12	7	13	33	32	10	6	23	15	4
arma	12	6	13	34	34	11	7	23	12	5
armawt	8	6	13	32	28	12	7	21	11	5

Predicting Z(101)–Z(150) from Z(100)

Method	Z1	Z2	Z3	Z4	Z5	Z6	Z7	Z8	Z9	Z10
ext1	24	19	24	36	23	8	27	30	39	23
ext2	25	10	22	8	20	8	24	35	22	23
reg + k	20	37	19	66	49	9	11	60	30	22
arma + k	20	36	21	66	50	10	12	61	23	21
reg	24	25	20	57	38	8	18	51	18	22
arma	24	24	21	57	40	9	20	52	13	20
armawt	16	21	21	53	30	11	21	48	12	26

Predicting Z(101)–Z(200) from Z(100)

Method	Z1	Z2	Z3	Z4	Z5	Z6	Z7	Z8	Z9	Z10
ext1	23	20	50	53	26	13	24	54	35	44
ext2	24	26	47	24	19	13	21	59	19	44
reg + k	27	84	40	104	83	22	33	102	80	43
arma + k	27	84	46	104	86	22	32	104	70	41
reg	24	63	43	87	61	16	21	87	55	42
arma	24	62	46	87	64	17	21	89	46	39
armawt	31	55	45	80	45	25	20	82	39	36

Predicting Z(1)–Z(100) from Z(1)

Method	Z1	Z2	Z3	Z4	Z5	Z6	Z7	Z8	Z9	Z10
ext1	12	8	12	16	11	9	8	6	11	13
ext2	12	10	39	20	11	16	25	9	20	17
reg + k	16	27	21	51	30	23	14	39	42	14
arma + k	15	30	35	51	31	20	16	40	38	13
reg	12	47	42	103	56	12	37	31	76	16
arma	12	47	39	104	59	12	35	33	68	15
armawt	22	39	41	98	39	12	33	25	61	23

Iterations and Significance of ARMA Versus Regression

Method	Z1	Z2	Z3	Z4	Z5	Z6	Z7	Z8	Z9	Z10
its/ak	0	1	1	0	3	3	3	1	3	1
its/a	0	1	3	0	3	3	3	1	3	1
its/aw	3	2	1	8	6	4	2	1	6	4
p/ak	0.49	0.00	0.05	0.50	0.25	0.01	0.15	0.42	0.02	0.26
p/a	0.49	0.00	0.05	0.50	0.23	0.01	0.14	0.43	0.02	0.26

TABLE 4.4 Errors in Prediction and Miscellany (Continued)

Method	Z1	Z2	Z3	Z4	Z5	Z6	Z7	Z8	Z9	Z10
			Process 2: Predicting Z(101)–Z(110) from Z(100)							
ext1	48	15	8	26	24	22	29	27	18	11
ext2	18	12	22	16	25	37	23	37	18	14
reg + k	40	16	15	28	45	58	44	30	40	33
arma + k	22	17	22	18	26	36	22	35	22	11
reg	20	12	19	20	42	53	39	36	34	25
arma	18	13	21	19	28	19	18	31	19	11
armawt	33	31	11	15	23	33	28	21	15	20
			Predicting Z(101)–Z(125) from Z(100)							
ext1	55	14	21	34	26	22	26	22	15	19
ext2	21	12	37	22	19	37	24	44	19	17
reg + k	76	25	19	62	66	88	73	28	78	53
arma + k	37	22	43	14	27	53	38	61	43	16
reg	39	12	31	43	61	80	65	45	71	35
arma	18	13	41	15	32	20	27	48	33	16
armawt	55	37	14	36	23	50	50	20	28	26
			Predicting Z(101)–Z(150) from Z(100)							
ext1	76	21	20	55	34	25	25	28	22	33
ext2	41	19	36	44	20	30	29	60	18	27
reg + k	116	53	28	105	98	111	107	27	112	80
arma + k	73	42	51	20	32	63	66	102	62	26
reg	81	23	27	83	94	103	101	63	106	50
arma	24	23	47	18	43	23	47	80	43	27
armawt	97	52	34	76	44	60	86	24	39	32
			Predicting Z(101)–Z(200) from Z(100)							
ext1	104	21	23	90	32	24	30	26	50	31
ext2	73	20	30	81	20	25	30	60	39	25
reg + k	149	96	78	148	141	147	142	50	143	131
arma + k	118	76	58	40	28	107	105	138	91	22
reg	129	37	31	131	141	144	140	66	144	104
arma	33	30	48	32	43	22	74	105	55	24
armawt	140	76	86	127	96	103	127	74	52	110
			Predicting Z(1)–Z(100) from Z(1)							
ext1	26	18	18	22	18	20	25	21	18	21
ext2	26	25	19	28	18	21	33	32	18	47
reg + k	47	58	62	54	75	81	61	80	85	67
arma + k	66	50	24	67	44	78	36	180	67	22
reg	91	52	33	76	142	137	142	38	148	134

TABLE 4.4 (Continued)

Method	Z1	Z2	Z3	Z4	Z5	Z6	Z7	Z8	Z9	Z10
			Predicting Z(1)–Z(100) from Z(1) (Continued)							
arma	60	39	33	56	19	21	79	83	75	38
armawt	94	64	95	85	108	101	132	86	78	116
			Iterations and Significance of ARMA Versus Regression							
its/ak	10	3	8	10	10	10	10	8	9	10
its/a	4	1	4	4	10	10	6	6	4	9
its/aw	7	6	7	4	8	9	9	4	5	7
p/ak	0.00	0.20	0.00	0.00	0.00	0.01	0.00	0.00	0.00	0.00
p/a	0.00	0.17	0.00	0.00	0.00	0.00	0.00	0.00	0.00	0.00
			Process 3: Predicting Z(101)–Z(110) from Z(100)							
ext1	90	16	84	34	34	65	48	83	16	93
ext2	17	44	26	30	21	16	38	51	14	23
reg + k	43	66	26	14	18	36	14	77	42	28
arma + k	17	17	29	18	16	17	22	52	23	35
reg	26	62	50	18	42	38	20	62	23	29
arma	12	15	46	20	23	14	27	40	20	31
armawt	84	36	98	14	120	27	18	106	34	29
			Predicting Z(101)–Z(125) from Z(100)							
ext1	107	34	108	98	48	67	91	96	44	109
ext2	43	61	55	96	40	35	83	67	45	28
reg + k	87	106	48	58	40	73	40	112	69	26
arma + k	43	43	49	81	39	55	58	77	43	42
reg	66	103	67	74	73	80	52	93	47	27
arma	31	29	58	84	47	50	69	53	43	33
armawt	115	83	141	70	167	70	50	153	52	80
			Predicting Z(101)–Z(150) from Z(100)							
ext1	137	52	139	120	49	52	139	118	95	122
ext2	92	71	86	118	36	53	134	94	98	42
reg + k	132	132	56	52	40	119	75	143	52	30
arma + k	93	62	55	94	40	103	104	114	83	69
reg	121	134	82	77	110	129	92	131	41	33
arma	73	49	58	101	67	95	121	77	87	48
armawt	173	117	168	74	184	121	92	177	46	126
			Predicting Z(101)–Z(200) from Z(100)							
ext1	165	77	132	122	68	43	164	127	120	142
ext2	141	70	75	119	85	77	161	105	124	79
reg + k	165	142	88	85	77	157	68	163	70	49
arma + k	143	51	88	77	77	148	111	139	102	109

TABLE 4.4   Errors in Prediction and Miscellany (Continued)

Method	Z1	Z2	Z3	Z4	Z5	Z6	Z7	Z8	Z9	Z10
				Predicting Z(101)–Z(200) from Z(100) (Continued)						
reg	161	153	143	64	157	165	84	159	68	54
arma	124	83	126	90	134	141	146	79	109	76
armawt	187	136	185	61	192	161	90	189	58	142
				Predicting Z(1)–Z(100) from Z(1)						
ext1	60	20	43	21	43	31	22	42	18	42
ext2	69	64	95	25	62	43	22	43	30	60
reg + k	68	67	78	71	43	74	67	54	62	129
arma + k	85	34	75	32	43	59	59	54	71	148
reg	85	165	137	113	135	162	135	120	145	130
arma	93	26	115	45	90	132	53	45	24	143
armawt	184	160	178	108	190	160	127	185	129	132
				Iterations and Significance of ARMA Versus Regression						
its/ak	9	10	4	5	7	9	10	10	10	3
its/a	2	9	2	6	3	3	9	4	7	2
its/aw	3	9	6	9	5	8	9	9	10	4
p/ak	0.00	0.00	0.18	0.00	0.24	0.00	0.00	0.00	0.00	0.15
p/a	0.00	0.00	0.12	0.00	0.03	0.00	0.00	0.00	0.00	0.06
				Process 4: Predicting Z(101)–Z(110) from Z(100)						
ext1	34	30	8	29	26	42	42	38	29	32
ext2	7	113	9	31	5	15	29	22	29	10
reg + k	7	110	19	24	30	27	11	20	35	9
arma + k	6	25	15	31	9	18	23	13	33	11
reg	5	145	15	23	24	25	16	19	30	9
arma	5	26	13	32	19	16	25	14	29	9
rrarmawt	12	100	18	27	7	23	18	31	36	40
				Predicting Z(101)–Z(125) from Z(100)						
ext1	43	35	12	23	30	53	56	42	25	38
ext2	18	119	13	26	13	15	42	31	25	17
reg + k	17	129	37	41	61	40	14	28	45	16
arma + k	10	35	28	29	14	29	27	25	31	24
reg	12	172	28	26	54	34	15	28	30	17
arma	9	26	22	31	21	22	32	25	24	19
armawt	31	150	36	48	20	39	21	46	37	87
				Predicting Z(101)–Z(150) from Z(100)						
ext1	60	39	17	31	25	50	63	44	33	38
ext2	35	125	19	35	15	17	49	31	31	21
reg + k	36	149	65	73	100	77	47	26	64	25

TABLE 4.4 (Continued)

Method	Z1	Z2	Z3	Z4	Z5	Z6	Z7	Z8	Z9	Z10
				Predicting Z(101)–Z(150) from Z(100) (Continued)						
arma + k	11	50	47	39	40	63	24	26	28	48
reg	23	186	47	46	100	66	26	23	31	26
arma	9	20	35	43	18	49	30	20	22	34
armawt	60	176	62	82	54	79	19	65	36	130
				Predicting Z(101)–Z(200) from Z(100)						
ext1	90	49	35	25	30	38	91	38	40	55
ext2	70	132	36	27	43	34	79	35	37	33
reg + k	74	170	113	130	145	129	87	41	113	22
arma + k	17	83	90	30	100	119	22	87	55	72
reg	50	193	88	107	149	118	43	47	66	24
arma	19	17	67	34	46	100	40	72	19	41
armawt	105	188	108	138	112	132	17	68	64	161
				Predicting Z(1)–Z(100) from Z(1)						
ext1	16	29	23	18	16	23	18	16	15	17
ext2	16	36	29	28	22	45	19	18	22	18
reg + k	54	76	52	74	66	41	73	57	63	53
arma + k	25	55	47	18	57	33	42	190	31	76
reg	29	186	52	98	135	127	105	22	99	47
arma	58	37	32	23	19	112	50	49	29	66
armawt	53	186	74	130	89	142	70	78	81	162
				Iterations and Significance of ARMA Versus Regression						
its/ak	10	9	7	10	9	7	8	5	10	9
its/a	3	10	3	10	9	2	5	6	7	1
its/aw	4	6	3	3	10	9	9	6	10	6
p/ak	0.00	0.00	0.00	0.00	0.00	0.00	0.00	0.00	0.00	0.00
p/a	0.00	0.00	0.00	0.00	0.00	0.00	0.00	0.00	0.00	0.00
				Process 5: Predicting Z(101)–Z(110) from Z(100)						
ext1	28	33	60	19	41	33	20	21	13	29
ext2	19	57	33	23	23	21	6	17	16	15
reg + k	21	78	17	15	29	48	5	11	14	14
arma + k	20	71	19	16	29	50	6	11	14	15
reg	19	89	21	22	24	42	7	13	14	15
arma	18	69	22	23	24	43	7	13	14	15
armawt	35	102	22	24	40	78	4	6	83	16
				Predicting Z(101)–Z(125) from Z(100)						
ext1	21	61	56	23	36	36	22	19	20	29
ext2	18	65	30	22	19	20	21	16	27	40

TABLE 4.4   Errors in Prediction and Miscellany (Continued)

Method	Z1	Z2	Z3	Z4	Z5	Z6	Z7	Z8	Z9	Z10
\multicolumn{11}{c}{Predicting Z(101)–Z(125) from Z(100) (Continued)}
reg + k	18	83	29	21	33	79	19	15	13	35
arma + k	17	77	20	17	32	82	20	15	13	38
reg	17	114	21	21	22	72	22	13	16	39
arma	18	78	18	25	22	76	23	13	16	42
armawt	48	138	18	61	59	133	18	25	141	18
\multicolumn{11}{c}{Predicting Z(101)–Z(150) from Z(100)}
ext1	17	64	75	32	51	29	23	21	22	29
ext2	16	82	52	20	33	25	20	19	30	44
reg + k	21	124	45	50	70	13	19	34	31	35
arma + k	17	120	26	36	68	125	20	34	29	42
reg	14	156	27	20	45	122	24	23	19	45
arma	15	128	24	25	42	125	26	23	18	50
armawt	86	170	26	109	107	167	21	54	172	36
\multicolumn{11}{c}{Predicting Z(101)–Z(200) from Z(100)}
ext1	48	63	85	55	84	46	66	39	27	32
ext2	43	87	62	32	68	31	54	41	36	50
reg + k	71	153	100	105	122	154	67	90	71	33
arma + k	65	150	59	86	119	155	56	91	65	45
reg	49	179	61	34	89	159	43	68	36	41
arma	46	161	33	26	84	161	39	68	31	60
armawt	139	185	27	154	152	184	75	115	186	106
\multicolumn{11}{c}{Predicting Z(1)–Z(100) from Z(1)}
ext1	28	36	29	24	35	46	27	22	37	20
ext2	28	43	76	25	48	47	54	41	52	20
reg + k	54	63	74	79	59	83	42	57	79	97
arma + k	53	62	58	80	59	83	38	57	79	92
reg	30	176	68	26	67	159	43	29	49	29
arma	28	145	50	30	62	162	40	29	46	24
armawt	135	184	75	151	149	184	76	81	185	111
\multicolumn{11}{c}{Iterations and Significance of ARMA Versus Regression}
its/ak	2	8	8	1	1	1	2	0	1	1
its/a	2	3	4	1	1	1	2	0	1	1
its/aw	8	9	10	10	9	10	7	6	9	6
p/ak	0.40	0.03	0.02	0.41	0.45	0.44	0.20	0.50	0.42	0.38
p/a	0.39	0.01	0.00	0.37	0.43	0.47	0.18	0.50	0.41	0.37
\multicolumn{11}{c}{Process 6: Predicting Z(101)–Z(110) from Z(100)}
ext1	29	42	16	26	50	23	109	22	36	35
ext2	26	21	11	28	7	30	15	17	40	43

TABLE 4.4 (Continued)

Method	Z1	Z2	Z3	Z4	Z5	Z6	Z7	Z8	Z9	Z10

Process 6: Predicting Z(101)–Z(110) from Z(100) (Continued)

Method	Z1	Z2	Z3	Z4	Z5	Z6	Z7	Z8	Z9	Z10
reg + k	26	15	16	27	29	43	21	16	27	45
arma + k	26	17	12	23	28	47	21	14	28	46
reg	25	22	5	30	26	41	56	17	35	45
arma	25	22	7	28	26	43	55	16	37	45
armawt	30	18	67	12	31	23	73	16	41	22

Predicting Z(101)–Z(125) from Z(100)

Method	Z1	Z2	Z3	Z4	Z5	Z6	Z7	Z8	Z9	Z10
ext1	42	36	35	46	58	28	104	28	34	35
ext2	36	25	31	30	17	55	22	30	44	53
reg + k	41	15	56	29	55	85	52	28	26	63
arma + k	42	20	51	30	53	90	52	27	27	65
reg	38	29	38	31	50	80	112	30	38	62
arma	38	30	33	29	48	83	111	29	42	62
armawt	52	58	129	58	59	43	133	29	101	37

Predicting Z(101)–Z(150) from Z(100)

Method	Z1	Z2	Z3	Z4	Z5	Z6	Z7	Z8	Z9	Z10
ext1	57	58	69	81	75	35	119	40	36	63
ext2	50	60	56	52	40	64	33	28	41	81
reg + k	60	56	109	51	89	116	67	28	36	98
arma + k	61	56	105	65	88	123	67	29	34	100
reg	53	63	88	40	82	107	148	28	34	96
arma	54	65	75	43	77	112	147	28	39	96
armawt	78	101	166	118	97	46	165	28	149	69

Predicting Z(101)–Z(200) from Z(100)

Method	Z1	Z2	Z3	Z4	Z5	Z6	Z7	Z8	Z9	Z10
ext1	68	48	66	102	113	92	140	52	92	102
ext2	63	47	51	73	86	114	66	65	69	116
reg + k	85	63	135	74	126	157	101	56	100	139
arma + k	87	45	131	99	125	162	101	47	98	141
reg	70	58	112	42	118	152	174	68	83	135
arma	71	67	87	55	114	155	174	61	72	136
armawt	112	151	184	157	137	86	183	62	176	159

Predicting Z(1)–Z(100) from Z(1)

Method	Z1	Z2	Z3	Z4	Z5	Z6	Z7	Z8	Z9	Z10
ext1	16	32	33	22	31	18	48	40	42	25
ext2	31	54	38	22	57	18	54	46	50	74
reg + k	45	85	51	90	101	190	88	150	50	96
arma + k	46	90	50	87	100	190	88	151	51	90
reg	25	68	99	49	128	108	175	47	45	108
arma	23	80	74	35	126	116	175	44	46	109
armawt	52	146	185	138	139	50	182	44	178	140

TABLE 4.4 Errors in Prediction and Miscellany (Continued)

Method	Z1	Z2	Z3	Z4	Z5	Z6	Z7	Z8	Z9	Z10
Iterations and Significance of ARMA Versus Regression										
its/ak	1	1	2	1	0	1	0	2	2	2
its/a	1	1	1	1	0	1	0	2	2	2
its/aw	8	5	8	10	4	9	9	4	3	10
p/ak	0.40	0.37	0.39	0.43	0.49	0.32	0.50	0.15	0.40	0.04
p/a	0.40	0.35	0.29	0.45	0.49	0.36	0.50	0.15	0.31	0.05
Process 7: Predicting Z(101)–Z(110) from Z(100)										
ext1	7	9	6	15	11	5	6	4	13	4
ext2	10	6	8	9	7	6	7	7	4	6
reg + k	6	4	11	16	12	6	6	11	8	4
arma + k	4	5	9	13	9	6	4	6	3	4
reg	9	5	9	13	9	5	7	8	5	5
arma	6	5	7	10	7	5	5	4	5	4
armawt	5	5	7	8	7	6	5	4	5	4
Predicting Z(101)–Z(125) from Z(100)										
ext1	7	12	8	17	9	6	7	6	13	4
ext2	11	8	7	9	12	6	9	10	6	6
reg + k	6	6	10	26	26	12	5	23	22	5
arma + k	6	6	6	20	21	9	5	14	8	6
reg	9	5	7	19	19	7	8	15	11	6
arma	6	5	7	14	15	7	6	6	5	4
armawt	5	5	8	10	14	8	6	8	5	5
Predicting Z(101)–Z(150) from Z(100)										
ext1	13	10	13	19	12	5	14	17	20	13
ext2	17	7	11	7	12	5	15	21	10	11
reg + k	10	23	16	44	35	18	6	47	35	21
arma + k	8	20	7	36	27	9	5	33	12	20
reg	14	10	8	29	21	7	15	32	14	10
arma	12	9	11	21	15	6	12	18	8	13
armawt	7	8	12	15	14	8	11	21	8	17
Predicting Z(101)–Z(200) from Z(100)										
ext1	13	11	26	28	13	8	12	30	18	24
ext2	14	13	23	12	11	8	13	33	9	21
reg + k	48	58	27	74	62	41	28	84	76	46
arma + k	42	50	7	61	51	20	25	61	40	41
reg	15	27	13	44	34	15	13	55	37	20
arma	13	25	22	30	22	10	11	32	11	24
armawt	20	23	24	18	22	16	11	37	10	23

TABLE 4.4 (Continued)

Method	Z1	Z2	Z3	Z4	Z5	Z6	Z7	Z8	Z9	Z10
				Predicting Z(1)–Z(100) from Z(1)						
ext1	7	5	7	9	6	5	5	5	7	7
ext2	9	6	26	10	7	12	14	7	9	11
reg + k	16	14	12	23	17	19	10	20	23	13
arma + k	13	10	6	20	17	11	6	18	17	7
reg	8	19	35	53	26	8	15	19	44	11
arma	7	16	20	41	16	7	14	5	21	10
armawt	12	14	22	30	16	7	14	7	19	17
				Iterations and Significance of ARMA Versus Regression						
its/ak	9	7	9	7	9	9	7	10	9	8
its/a	3	4	4	3	2	4	3	2	3	3
its/aw	3	2	5	6	3	3	2	5	4	2
p/ak	0.00	0.00	0.00	0.00	0.00	0.00	0.00	0.00	0.00	0.00
p/a	0.00	0.00	0.00	0.00	0.00	0.00	0.00	0.00	0.00	0.00
				Process 8: Predicting Z(101)–Z(110) from Z(100)						
ext1	31	16	9	19	21	21	18	23	18	11
ext2	18	11	22	18	30	38	25	33	19	16
reg + k	47	27	16	38	48	55	42	32	39	40
arma + k	43	24	18	23	22	20	16	21	26	27
reg	23	11	17	24	43	49	39	26	30	26
arma	18	20	18	17	21	18	14	21	15	13
armawt	27	25	11	15	19	25	18	22	16	17
				Predicting Z(101)–Z(125) from Z(100)						
ext1	33	14	17	21	19	18	17	19	15	14
ext2	19	14	32	19	25	35	25	33	19	16
reg + k	62	47	25	61	62	74	58	49	66	59
arma + k	58	33	31	46	24	19	19	18	45	39
reg	46	12	21	46	61	69	60	20	58	39
arma	19	19	30	14	22	16	15	21	14	14
armawt	37	27	14	21	16	31	24	21	24	19
				Predicting Z(101)–Z(150) from Z(100)						
ext1	44	19	17	32	23	20	18	20	18	21
ext2	25	18	32	30	22	29	27	41	16	18
reg + k	83	74	52	86	80	89	78	60	87	75
arma + k	79	55	35	75	39	19	32	20	64	54
reg	87	29	19	82	91	93	92	24	89	58
arma	23	25	34	16	28	19	21	31	14	16
armawt	64	38	27	43	18	37	39	22	34	19

TABLE 4.4   Errors in Prediction and Miscellany (*Continued*)

Method	Z1	Z2	Z3	Z4	Z5	Z6	Z7	Z8	Z9	Z10
				Predicting Z(101)–Z(200) from Z(100)						
ext1	62	19	18	54	21	18	22	19	36	20
ext2	43	18	29	53	23	27	28	41	25	18
reg + k	112	103	92	120	113	119	105	90	110	109
arma + k	109	87	38	113	80	23	57	51	91	93
reg	134	56	41	130	135	134	131	68	129	105
arma	33	30	36	26	28	18	30	34	21	18
armawt	101	55	67	83	22	68	64	50	48	58
				Predicting Z(1)–Z(100) from Z(1)						
ext1	20	16	16	16	16	16	19	19	16	17
ext2	20	19	18	29	16	17	22	28	17	33
reg + k	29	36	36	33	44	45	39	38	48	40
arma + k	30	32	22	33	39	20	30	42	47	41
reg	118	68	46	90	128	122	128	78	134	122
arma	28	20	24	31	17	16	33	25	20	27
armawt	60	42	74	46	24	63	69	54	64	60
				Iterations and Significance of ARMA Versus Regression						
its/ak	10	10	9	10	10	10	10	10	10	10
its/a	9	9	5	4	9	10	8	7	9	10
its/aw	9	10	6	6	9	9	10	10	10	8
p/ak	0.01	0.00	0.00	0.00	0.00	0.00	0.00	0.00	0.00	0.00
p/a	0.00	0.00	0.00	0.00	0.00	0.00	0.00	0.00	0.00	0.00
				Process 9: Predicting Z(101)–Z(110) from Z(100)						
ext1	39	16	29	19	22	34	27	39	16	47
ext2	12	45	15	25	15	18	24	40	15	27
reg + k	44	59	28	21	13	34	22	69	44	26
arma + k	13	15	23	15	13	16	19	53	37	20
reg	23	60	34	15	31	34	14	58	17	23
arma	11	15	20	15	15	9	21	24	14	27
armawt	38	18	34	14	52	12	17	81	19	20
				Predicting Z(101)–Z(125) from Z(100)						
ext1	50	24	51	50	31	37	54	46	30	62
ext2	21	56	34	56	26	29	51	47	32	24
reg + k	72	85	38	31	25	59	34	87	62	62
arma + k	25	24	32	27	25	43	41	75	54	37
reg	57	96	57	32	58	68	28	89	41	28
arma	17	21	30	44	25	27	45	31	30	23
armawt	78	35	53	33	98	37	37	128	31	44

TABLE 4.4 (Continued)

Method	Z1	Z2	Z3	Z4	Z5	Z6	Z7	Z8	Z9	Z10
			Predicting Z(101)–Z(150) from Z(100)							
ext1	73	31	68	59	26	31	81	60	42	70
ext2	46	60	45	66	26	39	78	60	50	24
reg + k	103	103	36	41	28	91	30	110	56	86
arma + k	54	31	30	27	28	77	60	101	47	58
reg	105	127	91	39	102	112	27	178	54	41
arma	34	28	27	49	27	47	69	43	44	22
armawt	126	45	83	29	143	69	52	163	32	72
			Predicting Z(101)–Z(200) from Z(100)							
ext1	109	33	61	58	42	28	101	62	53	86
ext2	87	45	40	65	55	52	98	62	63	40
reg + k	139	114	83	81	67	128	32	128	71	114
arma + k	100	31	78	66	67	119	65	122	63	94
reg	151	155	145	72	151	153	58	160	105	75
arma	68	36	69	43	67	79	85	43	58	31
armawt	164	39	139	37	173	112	54	182	35	86
			Predicting Z(1)–Z(100) from Z(1)							
ext1	33	18	28	18	26	22	18	25	16	27
ext2	44	40	49	18	33	24	25	27	18	31
reg + k	40	42	50	45	28	47	41	37	37	36
arma + k	36	18	44	44	28	36	29	36	38	39
reg	108	153	141	107	134	143	129	137	136	40
arma	56	18	53	21	30	60	24	26	16	72
armawt	134	55	145	68	165	99	61	175	30	79
			Iterations and Significance of ARMA Versus Regression							
its/ak	10	10	10	10	9	10	10	10	10	10
its/a	5	10	5	7	6	8	10	6	10	3
its/aw	6	10	9	9	10	6	10	2	10	4
p/ak	0.00	0.00	0.00	0.00	0.00	0.00	0.00	0.00	0.00	0.00
p/a	0.00	0.00	0.00	0.00	0.00	0.00	0.00	0.00	0.00	0.00
			Process 10: Predicting Z(101)–Z(110) from Z(100)							
ext1	18	28	6	25	15	21	23	21	29	18
ext2	6	114	4	27	6	16	14	17	29	10
reg + k	15	78	18	32	28	26	14	30	37	17
arma + k	10	53	14	27	7	11	9	16	29	12
reg	7	135	8	22	18	22	7	22	28	10
arma	6	26	5	25	16	8	19	11	28	10
armawt	9	80	11	29	9	25	19	21	33	39

TABLE 4.4 Errors in Prediction and Miscellany (Continued)

Method	Z1	Z2	Z3	Z4	Z5	Z6	Z7	Z8	Z9	Z10
				Predicting Z(101)–Z(125) from Z(100)						
ext1	24	30	8	19	18	27	30	30	22	25
ext2	12	120	6	22	12	15	20	28	23	17
reg + k	38	90	38	54	50	38	33	51	52	39
arma + k	25	76	27	41	20	19	10	30	24	25
reg	15	162	17	32	42	31	15	35	27	19
arma	10	26	9	21	19	13	26	24	22	16
armawt	19	133	20	44	12	46	44	36	33	87
				Predicting Z(101)–Z(150) from Z(100)						
ext1	32	28	13	25	15	26	33	28	21	27
ext2	19	123	11	29	11	17	23	25	23	21
reg + k	66	106	62	73	72	61	62	78	67	59
arma + k	47	95	47	60	44	37	25	37	19	37
reg	27	180	33	58	78	52	42	46	35	25
arma	12	21	15	27	16	22	28	18	19	21
armawt	33	166	36	71	12	83	88	48	35	131
				Predicting Z(101)–Z(200) from Z(100)						
ext1	52	31	22	19	18	20	51	23	23	32
ext2	40	127	19	22	25	26	42	22	25	23
reg + k	106	131	97	110	111	100	89	105	97	97
arma + k	88	124	83	102	92	78	44	41	31	72
reg	55	190	66	113	129	92	73	54	71	42
arma	25	20	28	21	18	47	43	30	19	18
armawt	63	183	69	122	34	132	134	58	58	163
				Predicting Z(1)–Z(100) from Z(1)						
ext1	11	28	16	17	13	17	18	14	15	15
ext2	12	31	18	22	17	24	18	14	15	15
reg + k	27	47	33	43	38	30	44	40	38	31
arma + k	30	49	30	40	28	16	43	40	27	36
reg	19	177	48	110	115	88	101	52	88	29
arma	21	28	17	18	14	49	18	19	16	23
armawt	26	182	45	111	19	133	143	59	59	165
				Iterations and Significance of ARMA Versus Regression						
its/ak	10	10	10	10	10	9	10	10	10	10
its/a	5	10	4	10	10	3	10	9	10	9
its/aw	4	10	6	9	10	4	9	3	10	3
p/ak	0.00	0.00	0.00	0.00	0.00	0.00	0.00	0.00	0.00	0.00
p/a	0.00	0.00	0.00	0.00	0.00	0.00	0.00	0.00	0.00	0.00

TABLE 4.4 (*Continued*)

Method	Z1	Z2	Z3	Z4	Z5	Z6	Z7	Z8	Z9	Z10
Process 11: Predicting Z(101)–Z(110) from Z(100)										
ext1	22	28	55	14	28	32	10	18	15	21
ext2	18	57	29	26	21	23	6	23	18	14
reg + k	24	56	13	18	36	45	8	14	18	12
arma + k	23	54	17	16	36	48	6	14	17	11
reg	19	86	18	20	28	46	5	19	16	12
arma	18	61	20	21	26	50	5	19	15	13
armawt	35	108	13	29	47	103	6	9	93	13
Predicting Z(101)–Z(125) from Z(100)										
ext1	18	66	47	16	26	31	17	17	19	28
ext2	18	66	23	26	18	19	19	21	27	38
reg + k	26	63	35	45	48	65	24	16	18	22
arma + k	23	63	24	38	47	68	21	15	17	24
reg	17	103	24	18	38	84	17	17	16	33
arma	17	67	19	20	34	93	18	17	17	35
armawt	53	144	63	73	84	158	20	23	150	17
Predicting Z(101)–Z(150) from Z(100)										
ext1	14	55	62	20	36	27	17	17	22	23
ext2	16	75	40	24	27	18	22	21	32	35
reg + k	43	89	50	75	72	92	39	35	38	23
arma + k	37	87	32	69	72	95	31	32	35	21
reg	16	149	31	24	72	131	18	18	17	27
arma	13	109	24	18	64	140	20	17	16	31
armawt	95	172	99	122	131	180	31	51	176	40
Predicting Z(101)–Z(200) from Z(100)										
ext1	34	44	75	32	64	43	37	23	27	23
ext2	32	74	53	26	55	27	31	22	37	35
reg + k	88	111	90	112	110	118	91	84	77	56
arma + k	82	109	62	108	110	120	83	78	7	48
reg	49	175	59	55	122	165	41	41	34	23
arma	40	144	25	29	112	170	33	35	24	29
armawt	143	187	147	162	167	190	85	106	188	98
Predicting Z(1)–Z(100) from Z(1)										
ext1	23	37	28	25	33	43	21	20	33	16
ext2	23	44	74	25	43	47	41	33	44	16
reg + k	36	47	54	44	40	60	28	37	53	48
arma + k	36	46	51	43	40	61	27	36	52	46
reg	40	172	60	60	111	165	53	25	48	25
arma	30	126	41	31	100	171	43	25	41	18
armawt	143	186	160	162	168	188	97	87	188	103

TABLE 4.4   Errors in Prediction and Miscellany (*Continued*)

Method	Z1	Z2	Z3	Z4	Z5	Z6	Z7	Z8	Z9	Z10

Iterations and Significance of ARMA Versus Regression

Method	Z1	Z2	Z3	Z4	Z5	Z6	Z7	Z8	Z9	Z10
its/ak	2	8	9	3	0	4	5	2	2	1
its/a	1	4	6	1	2	1	2	2	2	1
its/aw	2	3	10	4	4	5	4	3	4	5
p/ak	0.28	0.05	0.00	0.38	0.48	0.24	0.11	0.23	0.39	0.43
p/a	0.22	0.00	0.00	0.23	0.39	0.39	0.08	0.19	0.34	0.40

Process 12: Predicting Z(101)–(110) from Z(100)

Method	Z1	Z2	Z3	Z4	Z5	Z6	Z7	Z8	Z9	Z10
ext1	22	36	10	15	30	20	49	9	27	29
ext2	22	23	12	29	12	23	13	19	29	34
reg + k	26	6	22	13	31	24	25	14	31	28
arma + k	25	8	18	16	24	28	19	19	27	31
reg	23	20	6	24	29	26	33	17	25	32
arma	22	18	7	30	20	28	18	20	27	33
armawt	28	18	75	13	32	14	49	9	31	25

Predicting Z(101)–Z(125) from Z(100)

Method	Z1	Z2	Z3	Z4	Z5	Z6	Z7	Z8	Z9	Z10
ext1	27	29	28	33	33	25	44	19	28	26
ext2	26	30	31	30	13	47	14	28	36	37
reg + k	44	27	45	47	53	52	52	22	36	27
arma + k	41	11	42	40	41	60	44	28	31	33
reg	32	25	34	30	49	55	80	26	28	35
arma	30	27	29	31	33	58	48	31	35	39
armawt	47	50	134	57	61	28	105	21	48	68

Predicting Z(101)–Z(150) from Z(100)

Method	Z1	Z2	Z3	Z4	Z5	Z6	Z7	Z8	Z9	Z10
ext1	35	54	42	59	46	32	61	22	26	33
ext2	33	66	35	40	28	53	28	25	28	48
reg + k	66	62	83	94	80	62	62	25	49	27
arma + k	61	54	81	85	68	77	54	25	43	39
reg	44	60	78	55	80	69	118	23	37	45
arma	41	66	52	34	56	74	67	30	29	53
armawt	71	89	169	114	99	32	145	41	93	118

Predicting Z(101)–Z(200) from Z(100)

Method	Z1	Z2	Z3	Z4	Z5	Z6	Z7	Z8	Z9	Z10
ext1	42	40	37	74	71	49	80	38	61	48
ext2	40	58	29	52	49	75	45	51	50	64
reg + k	101	86	98	128	108	92	86	27	92	33
arma + k	94	64	97	122	96	116	80	47	87	46
reg	64	46	111	82	116	104	157	43	90	59
arma	57	65	63	40	79	111	107	64	44	75
armawt	108	142	185	155	141	29	173	55	144	168

TABLE 4.4 (Continued)

Method	Z1	Z2	Z3	Z4	Z5	Z6	Z7	Z8	Z9	Z10
				Predicting Z(1)–Z(100) from Z(1)						
ext1	14	25	29	20	23	16	33	30	22	24
ext2	26	35	30	20	33	16	39	34	25	34
reg + k	30	45	39	40	60	52	58	82	27	47
arma + k	31	51	38	39	55	48	57	75	29	50
reg	20	28	106	43	117	44	165	31	59	30
arma	18	48	62	24	89	54	134	43	31	43
armawt	69	144	186	143	139	77	173	77	128	164
				Iterations and Significance of ARMA Versus Regression						
its/ak	2	7	7	7	5	1	9	3	10	5
its/a	2	2	2	2	3	1	3	2	4	2
its/aw	3	2	3	2	3	4	3	10	10	3
p/ak	0.14	0.07	0.29	0.26	0.08	0.37	0.02	0.03	0.00	0.07
p/a	0.11	0.03	0.08	0.11	0.06	0.37	0.00	0.03	0.00	0.05

however, that the version of Table 4.4 in this chapter has been rounded off to save space; the calculations were made from the unrounded original.)

Unfortunately, the noise components of the 12 processes, while "unbiased" in the sense of an arithmetic average, do produce a negative shift in the average rate of growth. In order to give some sort of measure of the "true" rate of growth, I have taken the geometric average of the estimates of c by GRR; this appears in the "av" rows, in the last column, of Table 4.1. Following the logic of Section 2.7 of Chapter 2, I would contend that the "true average rate of growth" might even be *defined* as the expected "estimate" or "observation" of the rate of growth, c, based on fitting an exponential curve such as Equations (4.13) imply, over an infinitely long sample of the process in question. (For the last column, the data sample was 10 times as large as that used with any of the specific estimates.) The potential difficulty with the "robust" technique is not with *consistency*—the ability to converge to the value most useful in long-term prediction when unlimited data are available—but with *efficiency*—the ability to make full use of the limited data available as recommended by the maximum likelihood technique. (More precisely, the maximum likelihood method, as sketched out in Section 2.5 of Chapter 2, claims to yield the estimates of maximum probability, conditional *all information* in the observed data.) If simple regression does outperform the robust method, one would expect it to do best for simulated processes that fit a regression model; one would expect the (geometric) *average* of the estimates of c to be equally good for both methods, but one would expect the *dispersion* to be less with regression, because regression, in exploiting more information per sample of data, can converge more quickly to its asymptotic estimates.

4.3 DESCRIPTION OF RESULTS

In short, in examining Table 4.1; one can sort out two *different* sources of error in using the estimation techniques: (1) *systematic bias*, the gap between the average estimate and the "true" estimate, as indicated in column seven and in the estimates of all the better techniques; and (2) *inefficiency*, the inability to converge quickly to the asymptotic estimates, as indicated by the *dispersion* of the estimates across different sample time series. (In all that follows, please note that the "true" estimate is being defined as the estimate that leads to the best predictions.) Classic maximum likelihood theory would claim total efficiency as its prime advantage over the robust approach, as discussed above; thus the dispersion errors are particular interest.

Looking carefully at Table 4.1, one immediately observes a startling fact: in nine out of the 12 simulated processes, the "robust method" outperforms every other method, even in terms of dispersion. Regression without a constant term does better than the robust approach for only two processes in terms of dispersion: Processes 1 and 7, the simple processes with no measurement noise at all, following a regression model almost exactly. Even in these very special cases, the dispersion with the robust method is only slightly larger. Even with Process 1, the ARMAWT technique outperforms regression by a larger margin than that of regression over the robust approach, which comes in third. With Process 7, the simple ARMA technique is best. Process 8 is the only other process for which the robust approach is not superior; in that case, where the measurement noise is "white," the situation discussed in Section 3.1 of Chapter 3, the simple ARMA model does a bit better than the robust approach, but both of these two do substantially better than the others. Even with Process 2, where the process and measurement noises are again both "white," the robust approach is ahead. In seven out of the eight remaining processes (all but Process 3), the robust method outperforms all the other methods, except for the simple ARMA models, by at least a factor of 2 in all cases.

In summary, *even in the domain of statistical efficiency, where the maximum likelihood methods should have their greatest advantage, the robust method enjoys substantial superiority—that is, dispersion errors less than half the size—in all but the simplest cases, where the advantages of the other methods, where they exist, are slight.*

In the domain of systematic bias, where it is expected that the robust approach will enjoy its greatest advantage, the criteria available are unfortunately less objective. The estimated growth factors c are all less than 1.03 and 1.016, the growth factors inserted into the original sets of processes, due to the expected watering-down effect of random noise. With every one of the 12 processes, however, the estimate of the "true" value of c, in column seven of Table 4.3, is either closer to the original growth factor than are any of the six average estimates or else within .0002 of whichever of those estimates is closest; this tends to support the value of the estimate in column seven.

Looking at Table 4.1, one can see very clearly a strong negative bias in all the averaged estimates of c, which are from simple regression. In five out of the 12 processes, regression has estimated a *negative* rate of growth for processes that are known to have at least a *positive* rate of growth; thus the very *sign* of the trends in these processes are reversed. In four of the remaining processes, regression gives a growth rate of less than 1%. *The size of these bias errors is much greater than the average dispersion errors, which were already quite a bit larger than those of the robust method; thus if both sources of error are added together, the overall errors in coefficient estimates are considerably worse than a mere factor of 2 for regression, in comparison with the robust approach.* Looking more closely at the three processes most favorable to regression in terms of bias error, one finds that in two of them the bias error is still larger than the average dispersion error, and that in the third the bias error is still larger than 1%, that is, larger than 35% of the actual growth rate. The estimates of c, with a constant term present, are still worse than those of simple regression as one might expect. The ARMAWT analysis also performs surprisingly poorly, with negative growth rates for all but four of the processes; in this case, it is theoretically possible that a hidden bug in programming was involved, insofar as cross-checks against existing programs were not possible, but a simple lack of robustness would seem to be a more likely explanation.

The contest between the ARMA and the robust methods is closer and more interesting. After doing the analyses of political data reported in Chapter 6, I was frankly surprised at how much better the ARMA method did here. In one process—Process 8—the ARMA model had the *same* average estimate of c as the robust approach did, and a smaller dispersion error; thus for this one process, the robust approach was actually somewhat inferior to the ARMA approach. On the other hand, Process 8 was defined in terms of pure white noise; most social science variables, like the ones studied in Chapter 6, may be more like Processes 11 and 12, or much further in the same direction, in terms of complexity. In four out of the 12 processes, the ARMA and robust approaches gave average estimates of c within .0005 of each other; this tends to reinforce the validity of these estimates as an indication of the "true" growth rate. Only for two of the processes was the bias error of the ARMA estimate larger than 1%, *relative* to the estimate in column seven. In general, the bias errors of the ARMA estimates were less than their dispersion errors. *On balance*, the robust approach did better, only because *the dispersion errors of the ARMA estimates were substantially larger than the errors of the robust approach for the majority of our processes, especially the more complex processes.* (For the 12 simulated processes, in order, the ARMA dispersion errors, as a fraction of the robust method errors in Table 4.1, equaled 1.03, 1.16, 1.54, 2.29, 2.55, 2.13, 0.84, 0.80, 1.15, 1.21, 4.18, and 1.83.)

Table 4.1 includes one other piece of information of relevance to our discussion in Chapter 3. It includes a description of the number of major iterations required before convergence, with our algorithm for ARMA estimation. In the ARMA estimations, we allowed for 10 major iterations before stopping the routine. In the last column, in the "disp" rows, the table first shows the number of iterations actually required, on the average, before the likelihood scores converged to within 0.1 of their final value (i.e., the posterior probability of the estimates was at least 90% of the posterior probability of the "most likely" estimates to which they finally converged.) This average was taken *only* for those sample time series in which such convergence was attained before the last iteration. Second, after a colon, the table shows the number of sample time series, out of the 10, in which the 0.1 level of convergence was achieved only on the last iteration or later. In most cases, convergence was achieved well before the last iteration. In those processes where convergence was slower, such as Processes 8, 2, and 10, the final estimates of c do not appear to have suffered as a result; indeed, the negative bias of the initial estimates obtained from regression was overcome more completely in these processes than in the others. Again, the cost of the ARMA estimation in terms of iterations was highest precisely in those cases where the payoff of the approach was also greatest.

Finally, a little more should be said about Table 4.2. Here again, the competition is mostly between the robust approach—ext2, more exactly—and the simple ARMA approach. The errors in short-term prediction tend to be watered down and randomized, due to the sheer size of the unpredictable short-term fluctuations, as discussed previously. A closer look at Table 4.3 shows that these prediction errors are affected heavily by outlying time series. Otherwise, the ARMA technique appears to do a little better here, relatively, than it does with its estimates of c; also, the differences between all the estimation techniques are watered down, with only a few examples of ratios of 2 in average error. On balance, however, Table 4.2 appears to follow the conclusions for Table 4.1 fairly closely.

5

General Applications of
These Ideas

Practical Hazards and
New Possibilities

5.1 INTRODUCTION AND SUMMARY

Fierce debates continue to rage between those who would study behavior "with mathematics" and those who would study it "by traditional means." These debates, by drawing attention to the extremes, have obscured many of the serious hazards and many of the most important applications of mathematical approaches in government and in psychology. In extending the mathematical approaches further, I have a special responsibility to discuss the new applications and the continuing hazards that may result.

To begin this discussion, Section 5.2 presents the viewpoint of the practical decision-maker, who has not used mathematical methods so far, for good reasons. The entire chapter is organized around the difficulties that decision-makers face; other possible users of these ideas—the social scientist, the psychologist, and the ecologist—are mentioned within more limited contexts. Section 5.2.1 discusses the example of strategic thinking in military history.

In Section 5.3, I will propose a common framework for evaluating both verbal and mathematical tools, based on the common goal of prediction; within this framework, the mathematical methods have a role to play, at least in principle, both for what they tell us directly and for what they tell us about common abuses of verbal methods. Section 5.3.1 discusses some of the classical grand theories of history as verbal predictive models. Section 5.3.2 gives examples of the pitfalls of descriptivism. The last part of this section describes in detail how this framework has motivated the development of new mathematical procedures described in the other chapters of this thesis.

Section 5.4 carries the reader from principle to practice; it discusses specific ways in which statistical methods may be used, *in close relation* with verbal methods, and may be of significant value in real prediction efforts. This discussion is not based on the well-known philosophy of logical positivism, but on the more recent philosophy of Bayesian utilitarianism (see Section 2.5 of Chapter 2), the philosophy that underlies the actual mathematical developments discussed so far; at any rate, the utilitarian approach helps one to focus on the value of these methods to serious policy-makers. In this section, I have also tried to crystallize my own experience with the numerous ways in which statistical research can turn out to be useless and misleading for the policy-maker if it is done in a cavalier manner; the suggestions given are not a definitive answer to all these difficulties, but at least they may help. Section 5.4.1 gives an example from economics: the role of empirical forecasting in the birth of macroeconomics.

Finally, in Section 5.5, there is a discussion on the central role of human psychology in politics and how it seriously limits the possibilities of naive empiricism, both verbal and mathematical. Statistical studies, like verbal research of the purely empirical variety, may be unable to transcend these limits. However, the mathematical ideas discussed in Chapter 2, along with other offshoots of the Bayesian approach, can be applied in a different way to help overcome these limitations in a way that words alone cannot; to illustrate this point, I will mention specific possibilities for using these ideas in the future to cope with and explain the phenomenon of intelligence, whether in human societies or in human brains. Section 5.5.1 specifically discusses cybernetics and neural networks.

5.2 THE LIABILITIES OF MATHEMATICAL METHODS IN PRACTICAL DECISION-MAKING

Let us start out by reconsidering my tacit assumption that mathematical methods do have some use after all in political science and in political decision-making. Many people have questioned this idea in the past few decades, and many more may have felt strong private reservations about the idea. While I clearly can be expected to reaffirm the value of mathematical methods on the whole, I also believe that the traditional complaints against mathematical methods do contain real information that the user of such methods should not ignore.

In particular, let us try to express the reservations about mathematical methods that might be held by the active political actor. Practicing diplomats and politicians have often found that their margin of success depends on their ability to seize on unique twists in the political or psychological environment, twists that allow the individual to escape the seemingly uncontrollable tide of events that one would expect a mathematical model to extrapolate. Sometimes this involves the ability to establish channels of serious communications between different political groups, channels that can grow in importance once they have been established. Sometimes this involves the ability to seize on an economic or military advantage. Caesar's *Gallic Wars* are a classic example of the latter sort of imagination, evading Lanchester's Laws at every turn; Liddell Hart, in his classic text on military strategy [1]), has emphasized that such imaginative approaches have been decisive in wars throughout history. Section 5.2.1 discusses these examples in more detail.

In both cases, one achieves a greater "benefit" within a given "cost constraint," not by being tight and precise about budgeting one's resources but rather by preserving the detachment and the freedom one will need in order to seize upon whole new options, which may open up a whole new frontier of possibilities. Political creativity in this form is difficult enough to encompass within any scholastic context, let alone the context of mathematical models; therefore political scientists who have a strong attachment to this process would naturally tend to be skeptical of mathematical models. More generally, successful political actors, like most successful professionals, would tend to believe that they stretch their minds to the limit in order to arrive at their policy decisions; they may conclude that the sheer complexity of their own decision-making militates against the prediction of its outcome by mathematical systems that account for far less information content. Furthermore, it is also likely that a large part of this information, even when accessible to the political scientist, may be encoded in a verbal form that militates against its being accounted for by mathematical models.

5.2.1 Examples from Military Strategic Thinking

One might take up considerable space discussing the example of military decision making.

Traditional Lanchester's Laws for ancient warfare indicate an equal number of deaths on both sides, regardless of who has a greater concentration of force; thus they tend to imply no possibility of strategy in such warfare. On the other hand, the laws usually have the disclaimer *ceteris paribus* attached, implying equal levels of material and social "technology." If social technology includes superior strategic ability on the part of the commander, like Caesar, then the laws become a poor guide for the would-be superior strategist. Therefore the statement in Sec. 5.2 is limited to the claim that Caesar won his victories by *evading* Lanchester's Laws, by avoiding the necessity for attrition, or perhaps by exploiting the loopholes in the laws, rather than invalidating them. This much, at least, seems fairly clear to us from Caesar's account itself.

Liddell-Hart, in his classic military textbook, *Strategy* [1, p. 338], cites Caesar's Ilerda campaign, Cromwell's Preston campaign, and a few others, as the classic bloodless victories. He goes on to write [1, p. 339]: "While such bloodless victories have been exceptions, their rarity enhances rather than detracts from their value—as an indicator of latent possibilities, in strategy, and grand strategy. Despite many centuries' experience of war, we have hardly begun to explore the field of psychological warfare. From a deep study of war, Clausewitz was led to the conclusion that 'All military action is permeated by intelligent forces and their effects.'"

Liddell-Hart generally prefers to talk about the "indirect approach" and the "unexpected" more than the use of imagination, but clearly the former require the latter. Hart writes [1, p. 342]: "A more profound appreciation of how the psychological permeates and dominates the physical sphere has an indirect value. For it *warns us of the fallacy and shallowness of attempting to analyze and theorize about strategy in terms of mathematics.* To treat it quantitatively, as if the issue turned only on a superior concentration of forces at a selected place, is as faulty as to treat it geometrically." In a section entitled "Conclusions from Twenty-Five Centuries," Liddell-Hart [1, p. 162] discusses the characteristics of the more usual, bloody victories: "Scanning, in turn, the decisive battles of history, we find that in almost all the victor had his opponent at a psychological disadvantage before the clash took place . . . . Most of the examples fall into one of two categories . . . described in the words 'lure' and 'trap'." The full weight of these objections will not be dealt with until Section 5.5.

5.3 PREDICTION: A COMMON GOAL FOR VERBAL AND MATHEMATICAL SOCIAL SCIENCE

These difficulties can be dealt with on several different levels. Let us begin on the simplest level.

The difficulties above point to the impossibility of constructing mathematical models that will predict exactly what will happen in politics, in detail, in the short-term and in the medium-term. However, these difficulties have also been enough to make it impossible for any human being, political actor or otherwise, to predict exactly what will happen in all of politics, in the short-term or medium-term. Traditional political scientists or mathematicians might deduce at this point that "true prediction," in the sense of exact prediction, is impossible in political science. Therefore, in order to assure themselves that they are involved in serious work, they may restrict their attention to propositions that meet an Aristotelian test of "truth," such as statements about historical documents or abstract theorems that can be proved by rigorous deduction. See Section 5.3.2 for examples.

Very few political actors, however, feel that they would want to turn away from the difficult but primary question of predicting the differences in outcome between the different actions they could take. These predictions may always include factors of uncertainty, but the political actors would find it interesting enough to reduce this uncertainty as much as possible, in any possible way.

Thus, insofar as political scientists are concerned with developing objective insights of the maximum possible value to their consumers, the political decision-makers at all levels, their ultimate concern would be the development of effective probabilistic theories to predict political and social systems.

There are five points worth noting about my emphasis on prediction here. First, this emphasis does not restrict itself to the overtly mathematical phases of political science. The development of "predictive models"—mathematical *or* verbal or even analogue for that matter— is a general concept, which can be used to guide historical research as easily as it guides statistics. Many of the "grand theories" of political history, including especially the theories of Spengler, Toynbee, Turner, Hegel, and Marx, were designed to help people "understand" history in terms of a verbal dynamic model that could also be used to predict the future. Section 5.3.1 discusses this in more detail.

Traditional approaches to research in political science, however, might tend to "develop" such theories by adding complex strings of qualifications and by forcing an elaborate, perfect Aristotelian fit of the weaker, more specialized propositions that emerge. The approach taken here would ask that political scientists continually return to the main question, to the ability of their theories, with the disclaimers removed, to predict the broad first-order trends in the major, most obvious variables of political history.

Second, my emphasis on prediction can be justified on deeper grounds than that of satisfying those who pay for the bulk of political research. Following the philosophy of utilitarianism, one might simply regard political science itself as one particular phase of political activity; one might even suggest that its major justification for existence in the long term is its ability to contribute to constructive political activity. This takes us back to the primary need of the decision-maker to predict the results of his or her actions, at least on a probabilistic basis. On the other hand, even if one were willing to accept the ethical principle that truth should be pursued for its own sake, as an ultimate goal equal to or higher than the goal of human welfare, one still faces the problem of defining what this "ultimate truth" would consist of. One might suggest that ultimate truth, if it does exist in political science, lies not in the changeable facts of current happenstance, but rather in the less changeable dynamic laws that lead from one set of circumstances to another; in physics, for example, the dynamic field equations are considered the highest scientific truth, while the codification of the wave-function of the universe is not an object of serious study. Admittedly, our *knowledge* of the dynamic laws, unlike the laws themselves, is likely to be changeable for a long time, in political science as in physics; however, it would be meaningless to speak about the advancement of knowledge as a worthwhile goal, were there not such a possibility for change and expansion in the state of knowledge. There are those who would question, in varying degrees, the primacy of the most abstract dynamical equations even in a field like physics; however, even the "phenomenological approach," in that field, involves the construction of powerful, generalized predictive statements, statements about what to expect after setting up experiments of different types.[1]

Many times in political science, the concepts of "causation" and "explanation" have been cited as forms of truth worth pursuing.[2] The statement that "A caused B" may be translated roughly into the statement that "A occurred before B, and the dynamics of the system were such that B would not have occurred if A had not occurred when it did, *ceteris paribus*." Once again, the critical question to answer is that of the dynamic laws which govern political systems.

Beyond the goals of social utility and "ultimate truth," the political scientist might also pursue the goals of cultural enrichment and entertainment. These goals are often cited as a justification for extreme traditionalism in political science. Whether these goals are now being pursued effectively by all those who cite them is a difficult matter to judge, well beyond the range of the present discussion. However, a large part of the "cultural enrichment" here would appear to involve the learning of lessons about human psychology and about what patterns of thought and behavior one might *predict* on the part of human beings or human groups in unusual circumstances in other cultures.

Third, one should note that my emphasis on prediction as the ultimate goal of political science does not imply that work of a more descriptive nature should simply be abandoned. Using statistical methods, for example, one must first collect a set of data, before one can fit or test a model. After one has fit a verbal or statistical model to a given set of first-order data, one can then go back to the original sources of information to specify the strengths and weaknesses of one's model in more detail, with greater accuracy; even if one cannot modify one's model easily to handle the exceptions, one can try to express the information embodied in the exceptions in a more compact, more abstract form, to make life easier for those who wish to make predictions or to modify the current models in the future.

In brief, I am suggesting that descriptive research be viewed as a means to an end, with the end being prediction. A direct and total assault on the objective of prediction may indeed be a poor strategy for achieving this end. However, success is likely to be even less if we do not keep the basic objective fixed firmly in our minds. Every once in a while, it is important to bring together the various propositions, mathematical and verbal, that one believes to be useful in prediction, and to see how effective (and consistent) they really are in coping with the overall picture. When there are major new defects or possibilities apparent at the general level, it is important to take note of them

[1]The most phenomenological approach in basic physics, the "*S*-matrix" approach, restricts its attention to describing the *S* matrix. This matrix is defined as the matrix that predicts *all* scattering results, for all possible scattering experiments in high-energy physics; these, in turn, constitute the vast majority of high-energy data. See Schwinger's [2] Preface, especially the second paragraph.
[2]In quantitative political science, the obvious reference here is to Blalock [3]. Hayward Alker also recommends Simon [4] and Dahl [5].

at that level, so that they can be used as a guide for more specialized research in different branches of political science.

Descriptive work may not only help provide the basis for evaluating dynamic models of politics; it may also help those who wish to predict politics, by telling them what the current states of the systems are to which they would like to apply the dynamic laws. The longer the policy horizon, however, the more important it is to use more general dynamic models, instead of assuming some sort of simple extension of present trends and conditions as gauged by descriptive studies. Finally, while prediction may be advocated as the primary goal of objective political science, normative political science remains another matter.

One may note, in this connection, that the attempt to maximize accuracy in *description*, by itself, leads naturally to a number of uncoordinated, specialized efforts, focused in depth on different primary sources of information. (See Section 5.3.2). In *predicting* complex dynamic systems, in contrast, one is led to focus first on the *interactions* between the primary subsystems at an aggregate level. Thus in order to make "interdisciplinary research" a reality in the social sciences, it is essential that the ideal of predictive power gain at least as much credence as the ideal of descriptive finesse, in the detailed conduct of actual studies.

Fourth, one should note that my emphasis on prediction does not require a reduction in the rigor of thought, even if it does require that we go beyond the Aristotelian concepts of truth versus falsehood as ascertained by traditional uses of deductive logic. The mathematical theory of probability and the Bayesian theory of inductive logic have long provided a rigorous basis for handling models that do predict the future but that avoid the determinist's pretense of absolute certainty. Aristotelian statements, which tell us that a proposition is simply true (probability one) or false (probability zero), are simply a subset of the statements that can be expressed in rigorous probabilistic fashion. In either case, the statements that we make may well be inaccurate, if they are founded on faulty information; the language of probability, however, at least lets us express precisely how much confidence we do have in a proposition, instead of forcing us to say nothing or to exclude totally a real but less probable contingency. When social trends will depend on long-lasting but uncertain and novel phenomena, the language of probability encourages us to escape the fallacy that definite optimistic or pessimistic predictions are somehow more informative than the truth. (See, for example, the discussion of Turner's theory in Section 5.3.1.)

To the statistician, all these concepts have long been obvious. In verbal research, however, the classical Aristotelian procedures have remained dominant. Only in recent years has the "Bayesian school" begun to educate verbal decision-makers in the use of probability theory as a generalized language of thought. (See Section 5.6.1). In Section 2.5 of Chapter 2, it is emphasized that the Bayesian approach to inductive reasoning can be applied to inductive reasoning as a whole, not merely to reasoning about quantitative variables.

When, in verbal research, one finds oneself dealing with the behavior of quantitative variables, such as the *degree* of popular discontent, one may even go so far as to discuss the "degree of fit," the "degrees of freedom," and the "exogenous variables" of one's verbal model on the understanding that one is expressing one's model in verbal terms only because of the lack of hard data. Even then, one may want to draw together the elements of one's model and express them in increasingly mathematical terms, even if the parameters cannot easily be measured, in order to make its meaning more and more explicit and in order to improve its "coherence," that is, its completeness and consistency.

Finally, and most importantly, *the emphasis on prediction has been the driving force behind both my empirical research and my conclusion that conventional routines for time-series analysis are inadequate.* The empirical work on political science in this thesis was motivated almost entirely by the attempt to convert the Deutsch–Solow equations, mentioned in Chapter 2, into a useful tool for the prediction of national assimilation and political mobilization. I started out years ago by testing the Hopkins routines,[3] which try to estimate the coefficients of the Deutsch–Solow model from only three data points, on the assumption that the Deutsch equations are totally "true" in the Aristotelian sense; it came as no surprise that the resulting predictions were rather poor.

The next step was to try out time-series multiple regression, the mainstay of "econometrics,"[4] of "causal analysis,"[5] of "path analysis" (described in Section 5.6.2), and so on. It was easy enough to measure assimilation and mobilization coefficients that were significantly different from zero, and multiple correlation coefficients larger than 90%. These results were well within the range of what are regarded as "successful conclusions" in most quantitative political research today.[6] However, my emphasis on prediction led me to look a bit more closely at these results; I wrote a new program, SERIES, to estimate the regression models and then to test their ability to predict data across long intervals of time, intervals comparable to those tested with the Hopkins program. The errors, while less than those of the Hopkins programs, were still unacceptably large. A simple curve-fitting procedure, by contrast, was able to make predictions with less than half as much error, averaging to about 4% error over periods of time on the order of a century; this average encompasses a number of cases wherein the model was fitted to data in one period of time and used to predict data in later periods.

---

[3]The programs EVAL, DIFF, and DELTA of Raymond Hopkins were made available by Professor Deutsch, Department of Government, Harvard University. They have been described in Hopkins and Raymond [6].

[4]See Johnston [7, p. ix]: "The purpose of this book is to provide a fairly self-contained development and exploration of econometric methods . . . . It is divided into two parts. Part 1 contains a full exposition of the normal regression model. This serves as an essential basis for the theory of econometrics in Part 2."

[5]See Blalock [3]. Simple correlation was usually used in "causal analysis" based on Blalock; this is the univariate special case of regression analysis.

Walter Isard, in his classical study of methodology in regional science [9, p. 22], has made strong statements against the ability of regression models to predict the future; while his argument is phrased in theoretical terms, the wide coverage of his studies would imply an empirical basis for his conclusions. The Brookings Institute has also reported major difficulties in the use of regression in forecasting; they found that these difficulties could be reduced by the use of an "adjustment" factor not too different in spirit from my simple curve-fitting procedure (See Sec. 5.6.3). Thus the empirical basis of these conclusions goes well beyond my own examples.

In my recent phase of empirical political research, I began with the hope that this weakness of regression, in estimating predictive models, could be understood within the classical and elegant framework of maximum likelihood theory, as described in Section 2.5 of Chapter 2. Instead of questioning the classical procedures of statistics, I hoped to apply these procedures to more sophisticated models. In Chapter 3, I have noted that "white noise" in the process of measuring data can turn an ordinary "autoregressive process" into a "mixed autoregressive moving average process." According to statistical theory, multiple regression is a good way to estimate the former process, but a bad way to study the latter.

A simple diagram can show how bad this problem might become in practice. Given a single variable, z, which has a true correlation of ϕ with itself across time (i.e., $z(t)$ with $z(t + 1)$), and a correlation of r with the measurements, x, that are made for z, we find that the correlation between $x(t)$ and $x(t + 1)$ is due to an indirect path of correlations; see Figure 5.1. If we make the simplifying assumption (a big one) that the process is not any worse—that there is not correlation between $x(t)$ and $x(t + 1)$ independent of this pathway—then classical theory tells us that the correlation between $x(t)$ and $x(t + 1)$ will equal r times ϕ times r, that is, $r^2\phi$. If regression were used to predict $x(t + 1)$ from $x(t)$ (the *observed* data), the regression coefficient would equal the simple correlation coefficient, $r^2\phi$, instead of the number ϕ; yet when predictions are made over longer intervals of time, then ϕ, the coefficient of the underlying process in the real world, is the proper basis for prediction.[7]

This example would also appear to point to the idea that simple "path coefficients," which are not effective in prediction, are not likely to represent the true underlying relations either.

If r—the correlation between the true variable and the measurements of the variable—were about 95%, then the observed regression coefficient ($r^2\phi = (.95)(.95)\phi$) would be about 10% smaller in size than the right regression

---

[6]As an arbitrary example, picked from a good anthology of papers in this field, consider Singer's [8] tables of results (on pp. 278–281, 112, 152–153, 199. 205, 65, and 232). Statistical significance scores (p) here often run to .05, or even to as poor as .10.

[7]From Chapter 3, ϕ is simply the matrix θ in the univariate case; *given* past error levels, $a(t - k)$, it is the best basis even for predicting $x(t + 1)$. However, looking at $x(t + n)$ from $x(t)$ only, we get a long path of correlations multiplying out to $r^2\phi^n$. Thus to get the optimal prediction of $x(t + n)$, one multiplies one's prediction of $x(t + n - 1)$ by ϕ.

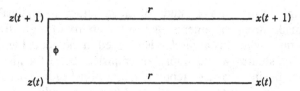

FIGURE 5.1   Pathways of correlation with noisy data.

coefficient (ϕ) for use in long-range prediction. Furthermore, since this 10% error would represent a general shift in the value of a coefficient, one would expect that the use of the regression model would lead to errors that *accumulate* at the rate of 10% per time period; it is easy to see how this phenomenon alone could vitiate the predictive power of regression. In the case of a single variable, this 10% error applies to a single large correlation coefficient; therefore one can hope that regression will at least preserve the sign of this coefficient intact. In the case of many variables, however, the 10% error would apply to a cor- relation *matrix*; small but critical cross-terms, on the order of $\pm 5\%$, might conceivably have their signs reversed due to the spurious effects related to other, larger terms in the same matrix. After all, the importance (and much of the detectability) of such "feedback terms" lies precisely in their ability to accumulate and determine the long-term behavior of the system; it is precisely the long-term behavior that we find poorly accounted for by regression.

In order to account for such effects, within a classical statistical framework, I have devised a new algorithm to estimate mixed autoregressive moving av- erage processes (ARMA processes) at a manageable cost. This new algorithm has been applied to the old Deutsch–Kravitz data on assimilation and mobili- zation in a dozen or so nations and also to new data on linguistic assimilation in Norway. In both cases, statistical theory indicated that the ARMA model was better than the old regression model; it indicated only a small probability, far less than 1% in almost every run, that the improvement was due to coin- cidence. However, *when I went on to apply the test of prediction*, I was quite disappointed. The ARMA model did indeed reduce prediction errors, in com- parison with regression, by about 10% of the original root-mean-square aver- age of the errors, in the case of the largest data sample; yet this is still far less than the 50% reduction achieved earlier with extrapolation.

The success of extrapolation would appear to indicate that the underlying processes are still more deterministic than either the regression *or* the ARMA models were able to discover. Apparently, the measurement noise and transient fluctuations were too complicated for a "white noise" model to cope with. In retrospect, it seems clear that one should have expected precisely such a situ- ation, in the case of both this and most other data in political science. The solution to such difficulties, in the classical philosophy of maximum likeli- hood, is to pose ever more complicated higher-order models of process noise and measurement noise. (With some other data series, however, the ARMA model or even the usual regression model might be adequate.) However, the multivariate ARMA model already contains a large enough number of degrees of freedom; to double or triple the number of coefficients to estimate would put a heavy burden on all but a few very large data sets, while still compensating for only moderate complication in the noise process.

The success of simple extrapolation points to a more practical approach to prediction. It points to the possibility of "robust" estimation, of estimation techniques that can perform well despite any oversimplifications in one's original model [10–17]. A good performance in this context means that the coefficients of the model are estimated in such a way that the model will have maximum predictive power. It is suggested in Section 2.7 of Chapter 2 that simple extrapolation is "robust"—more robust than ARMA estimation, even a priori—because it is based on a simple "measurement-noise-only model," a statistical model built to extract the deterministic underlying trends (if they exist) from a process afflicted by a complex pattern of transient noise and measurement error. Note that the general dynamic feedback procedure of Chapter 2 can be used to estimate more general models of this type, economically, (It is also possible to make *some* allowance for process noise in an ad hoc way,[8] but the best way to make such allowance while preserving robustness is unclear; there might be no general theoretical solution to this problem.) Another new technique is also discussed in Chapter 2—pattern analysis—to draw out more direct measurements of the underlying dynamic variables.

In brief, *an emphasis on prediction has led me to the conclusion that statistical methods based on the concept of maximum likelihood alone are inadequate in practical empirical research. It has led to the theoretical conclusion that predictive power itself needs to be maximized more explicitly in the model estimation techniques available to behavioral scientists.* In Chapter 2, I have suggested ways to build new systems on this principle. These systems are scheduled to be available as part of the Time-Series Processor package, designed for social scientists, in 1974 at Project Cambridge, M.I.T.

5.3.1 Grand Historical Theories as Verbal Predictive Models

This section shows how several of the most important classical theories of history may be understood as predictive models.

Spengler writes [18, pp. 106–107]: "The aim once attained—the idea, the entire content of inner possibilities, fulfilled and made externally actual—the Culture suddenly hardens, it mortifies, its blood congeals . . . . This—the inward and outward fulfillment, the finality, that awaits every living Culture—is the purport of all the historic "declines," amongst them that decline of the Classical which we know so well and fully, and another decline, entirely comparable to it in course and direction, which will occupy the first centuries of

---

[8]See Section 2.11 of Chapter 2 for a way to introduce a kind of "interest rate" or "discount factor" to predictions of more distant times in the future. Such procedures may be unavoidable when a small amount of process noise does exist and does accumulate through time.

the coming millenium but is heralded already and sensible in and around us today—the decline of the West.'' He goes on to write [1, pp. 109–110] ''every Culture, every adolescence and maturing and decay of a Culture, every one of its intrinsically necessary stages and periods, has a definite duration, always the same, always recurring with the emphasis of a symbol.''

Toynbee has written [19, p. 244]: ''The problem of the breakdowns of civilizations is more obvious than the problem of their growths. Indeed it is almost as obvious as the problem of their geneses. The geneses of civilizations call for explanation in view of the mere fact that this species has come into existence and that we are able to enumerate twenty-six representatives of it— including in that number the five arrested civilizations and ignoring the abortive civilizations. We may go on to observe that, of these twenty-six, no less than sixteen are now dead and buried.''

He continues [19, p. 245]: ''If we accept this phenomenon as a universal token of decline, we shall conclude that all the six nonWestern civilizations alive today had broken down internally before they were broken in upon by the impact of Western civilization from outside . . . . For our present purposes it is enough to observe that of the living civilizations every one has already broken down and is in process of disintegration except our own.'' Toynbee then goes on to state that [19, pp. 253–254]: ''The metaphor of the wheel in itself offers an illustration of recurrence being concurrent with progress . . . . Thus the detection of periodic repetitive movements does not imply that the process itself is of the same cyclic order as they are. On the contrary, if any inference can historically be drawn from the periodicity of these minor movements [such as the rise and decline of Graeco-Roman civilization], we may rather infer that the major movement which they bear in mind is not recurrent but progressive.'' Also, in various places, Toynbee emphasizes both scholastic rigidity and corruption as symptoms of decaying civilizations; he hints at a different, less charitable explanation of the common methodological difficulties mentioned in this text. However, even if Toynbee's explanation has some truth in it, a reduction in the cost of adhering to good methodology should still facilitate more worthwhile research.

Frederick Jackson Turner—a famous American historian—appears more optimistic, but provides insights consistent with those of Spengler and Toynbee, of relevance to those policy makers who are truly concerned about our long-term future.

Turner's theory is well-known as an attempt to articulate the factors that caused American progress in the last few centuries. However, it is not only interesting in its own right but is an example of how such ideas can be useful to those trying to decipher more general laws of history, which *in turn* may be useful to present policy-makers. Walter Prescott Webb [20, p. 136], comments on Turner's ideas: ''Assuming that the frontier closed about 1890, it may be said that the boom [in *all* of Western civilization] lasted approximately four hundred years. It lasted so long that it came to be considered the normal state, a fallacious assumption for any boom. It is conceivable that this boom has given the peculiar character to modern history, to what we call Western civilization.''

Webb goes on to suggest that the search for "new frontiers" is essentially an irrational, desperate attempt to preserve a dying enterprise; however, his assumption that new foci of economic development cannot be found does not allow for some of the possibilities of technological progress over the next few decades. Over centuries, the limits of the Earth itself may be expected to prevent unlimited growth; on the other hand, when one speaks in terms of centuries, one cannot entirely rule out the possibility of developing economic activities beyond the planet Earth itself. Certain aspects of economic and technological growth depend on large number of *independent* random disturbances, which on the whole may accumulate and be subject to accurate prediction by statistical procedures or the verbal equivalent. However, the historic development of nuclear power, for example, or the future possibilities of elementary particle physics and nonequilibrium (nonlocal) thermodynamics (see Section 5.5.1) involve a more sweeping form of prior ignorance, which translates into probabilities far from one or zero and whose values may change according to government or even individual decisions. At any rate, it is possible that the ideas mentioned by Webb may have application to other parts of the historical database, beyond the West.

Finally, Hegel states [21, pp. 21–22] that "the Principle of development contains further the notion that an inner destiny or determination, some kind of presupposition, is at the base of it and is brought into existence. This final determination is essential. The spirit which has world history as its stage, its property and its field of actualization is not such as would move carelessly about in a game of external accidents, but is instead the absolute determining factor." He concludes [21, p. 23] that "world history presents therefore the stages in the development of the principle whose memory is the consciousness of freedom." Hegel then lists the stages.

5.3.2 Examples of the Perils of Descriptivism

In writing this and remembering some of the interesting generalizations I had heard from pure verbal political science, it was difficult to overcome my selective memory and face up to the overall methodological views still prominent in the field. But a quick review soon set my memory straight. For example, Heckscher [22, p. 40] writes: "It should be noted that the emphasis here is on deduction, not on induction. In the words of another participant in the seminar, Professor S. E. Finer, we are making an attempt at 'describing the political possibilities.' Considerable emphasis should be put on the word '*describing*': we remain in the humble sphere of description and do not attempt to rise to the more lofty one of speculation.''

In historical research, the problem is more serious, as Morison [23, pp. 44–45] points out: "My principles and methods of research and writing were largely worked out unconsciously, through listening to excellent teachers and following the best models . . . . The historian has both the right and the duty to make moral judgements. He should not attempt to prophesy, but he may offer cautions and issue warnings." One may ask what the warnings are supposed to be based on, if not on probabilities of undesirable events conditional on certain policy decisions; also, one may question whether methodological decisions ought to be based on unconscious factors.

H. R. Trevor-Roper, the noted traditional historian (and antagonist of Toynbee), writes [24, p. vi]: "It is perhaps anachronistic to write of a historian's philosophy. Today most professional historians 'specialize.' They choose a period, sometimes a very brief period, and within that period they strive, in desperate competition with ever-expanding evidence, to know all the facts. Thus armed, they can comfortably shoot down any amateurs who blunder or rivals who stray into their heavily fortified field; and, of course, knowing the strength of modern defensive weapons, they themselves keep prudently within their own frontier. Theirs is a static world, a Maginot Line, and large reserves which they seldom use; but they have no philosophy. For a historical philosophy is incompatible with such narrow frontiers." Section 5.45 in this text considers interdisciplinary effects in somewhat more detail; also, see Section 5.6.6.

5.4 POSSIBILITIES FOR STATISTICS AS AN EMPIRICAL TOOL IN REAL-WORLD PREDICTION

Now let us come back and look more closely at the questions posed in Section 5.2. Let us reconsider the worries of the political actor about the use of mathematical approaches. These worries have been dealt with so far on a very basic level, on the level of defending the concept of predictive theories in the social sciences. It has been emphasized that the *explicit* statistical techniques proposed are merely one tool among many in constructing such theories. It has been implied that the choice between these techniques for constructing theories and the verbal and Bayesian techniques should be decided on a case-by-case and even study-by-study basis, based on the ideal of predictive power, rather than decided by any a priori fiat in favor of one approach or the other. This implies that statistical analyses should merge into other analyses, mathematical and nonmathematical, in such a way that political science is divided up according to interfaces between substantive issues rather than interfaces between methodological schools of thought.

All these comments, while controversial within the domain of political science, would seem rather bland and basic to many real political actors. Most political actors would be quite willing to try any methodology that "works," at any time, without getting too committed to one methodology or another. What worries them is a question on another level: Can we expect statistical methods to "work" very often in practice?

In principle, this question can only be answered after the fact in each case. However, there are a number of reasonable guesses one might make, based on past experience, as to the most likely areas of fruitful future statistical research in political science.

First, we may expect to be surprised in the future by statistical methods having a larger range of application than one might expect a priori. Given that present emotional expectations are built on verbal techniques that have been thoroughly used and thoroughly developed, while statistical techniques are only now being perfected and have barely begun to be used to construct predictive models, we may expect that the development of statistics will demonstrate a much greater value than one's intuition would indicate today.

Second, we may expect statistics to provide the basic "reality testing" for operational political theories of the quantitative type *or* the verbal analytic type. A simple regression analysis may make a poor test of a verbal "hypothesis" if interpreted naively. However, a full statistical analysis of a given set of variables will give a much larger quantity of information, information that the analyst should not gloss over, either in his or her work or in his or her written reports. If, in fact, it is difficult to make a connection between one's verbal theories and the aggregate statistical behavior of the variables that these theories pretend to explain, then one has much to learn in trying to explain the difficulty. Oftentimes, an "obvious" verbal theory will turn out, though true in the abstract, to require major qualification in terms of what it tells us to expect to find in concrete data. When government policy is concerned with the concrete results themselves, these qualifications may turn out to be of central importance.

The classical theory of full-employment equilibrium, for example, depended on the idea that the supply of savings would increase with higher interest rates, just as the supply of any other commodity increases when a higher price is offered. Empirical studies have not refuted this idea; however, they have shown that the predictive power of interest rates in predicting savings is extremely small, while the effect of income variables, cited by Keynes, has turned out to be very large. Keynes himself was able to observe these effects by analytic methods alone, but major governments were very slow to change their established viewpoints despite his arguments; the statistical studies, by confronting people directly with the trends that had persisted up to the current day, may have been a crucial form of "reality testing" on this issue. Section 5.4.1 discusses this history in more detail.

Third, one may hope that statistics will help illuminate the slow and stubborn trends that underlay social phenomena. It has often been suggested that the most visible variables in politics—the turmoil, the yearly ups and downs in economies, alliances and wars—are all superficial ripples riding on a deeper current. Economists have often discussed a "technological" increase in production capacity per capita, an increase that continues during recession and boom at virtually the same rate, an increase that is not fixed but that varies slowly according to uncertain causes over long periods of time. Almost any discussion of the "production function" includes reference to this "autonomous" or "technological" term. (See Section 5.6.4.)

Sociologists like Max Weber,[9] philosophers like Hegel [21] or Marx, and historians like Spengler [18], Toynbee [19], and even McNeil [26], and Eisenstadt [27] have all discussed such trends.[10] Even in the simulation studies in Chapter 4, it is found that errors in short-term predictions were reduced far less by sophisticated analysis than were errors in medium-term and long-term prediction.

Political actors, in the short-term, are compelled to immerse themselves in details too small and too unpredictable to be dealt with effectively by statisticians. But the effectiveness of political actors also depends on their "historical vision," on their ability to judge the results of their life's work on the subsequent tide of events. Long-term trends may be more deterministic and more susceptible to mathematical analysis. In order to sort out these underlying trends, one must somehow adjust for the existence of a great deal of short-term fluctuation. This short-term fluctuation would typically have a very complex and changeable pattern of autocorrelation; thus a complete model of the "measurement noise" process is doubly infeasible, and one must face up to the need for robust procedures, as described in Section 5.3 and in Section 2.7 of Chapter 2.

After a robust analysis, one may find that some variables tend to follow deterministic laws over time, but that others still involve a great deal of apparent randomness. In this case, one might expect that the political actor would have the greatest personal effect on history by trying to change the latter variables—which *can* be changed—and by aiming only indirectly at the former variables. Also, by knowing where events would be headed if he/she acted like the *average* political actor, an informed political actor may judge the importance of taking unusually intense actions to break out of the existing trends. Furthermore, if there should turn out to be a "crossroads" of possibilities ahead ("bifurcation" in mathematical language), such that the choice of possibilities ahead would produce very long-lived effects, while other implications of present policy would be washed out in time by random noise, one might well choose to organize one's entire policy around the goal of moving down the right road, even if this means focusing one's attention on variables that are harder to affect.

[9]Weber's [25] concept of "rationalization," as a trend extending from the "'Concept' of Plato" to the "cage" of modern machine civilization, does amount to a long-term vision of history.
[10]The themes in McNeil's book [26] are a bit too complex to summarize here. Many of them are reminiscent of Turner (Section 5.3.1). Throughout the book, however, McNeil does keep returning to the theme of human societies adapted to the pastoral niche as providing the soil on which new civilizations may develop or to which old civilizations may spread, as the old heartland decays. On the other hand, Eisenstadt [27], in his Chapter 2, attempts to explain the "universal states" of the Toynbee and Spengler theories, almost the same societies.

In practice, there are serious difficulties in using statistics by themselves to deal with this third objective. Statistics might do well in predicting the stress that will pull at the fabric of various societies; it will not do as well in predicting the ability of local political leaders to cope with the stress. Still, to know the causes and the magnitude of the stress would be interesting in any case. But there is a bigger difficulty with using statistics here. *The deeper historical trends can be analyzed best if we make use of the longest possible relevant data series*; yet much of our historical database, as described by Toynbee and McNeil, involves information about civilizations that have not left us a large supply of statistical data series.

In some cases, a large supply of recent data may be enough. It may even seem superior to historical data on the grounds that it reflects exclusively modern phenomena, which one would expect to continue in the future. For example, certain aspects of population dynamics may be dealt with reasonably enough from recent data, especially insofar as the future will depend heavily on the impact of recent phenomena such as large-scale female literacy. On the other hand, if there is any truth at all in the findings of Toynbee [19] and Spengler [18], then the central trends of history may include regular rises and declines, regular curvatures, which would be much harder to observe in short data series—even short representative data series—than in very long data series. Thus the long data series do much more than increase the number of observations and improve the accuracy of our estimates of parameters; they give us the power to deal with important *qualitative* effects, with whole new terms in the model, which might otherwise be missed.

Furthermore, one might expect that the future would represent a dynamic domain just as different from the present as the present is from the past; in order to predict this domain, it may be more rational to look for regularities that have extended from the distant past to the present and extrapolate them, rather than extrapolate models specific to the dynamic domains of the present. If, in some cases, history were dominated by large, infrequent, and apparently irreversible changes, as in technology, then a longer database would be even more essential, to give us an adequate sample to represent the varieties of such changes and configurations in the past; only in this way can we hope to deal with the future changes, which, under this assumption, would dominate the future. (This does *not*, of course, entail building models tailored to shorter, well-delimited periods in ancient history as unrepresentative and restricted as recent history.) Also, to deal with the possibility that the human race might be entering a new domain of experience, totally different from any of its past history, one might simply extend the basic context of one's analysis still further to include the more general history of species on this planet and the patterns of evolution revealed therein. The biological example of the trilobites, which became totally extinct after overspecialization, does not have a full-scale parallel in the human past; this particular example has been mentioned often in the popular press, but there may be other aspects of biological history more general and even more relevant to our own future (for example see Section 5.6.5.)

In general, it would appear futile to try to predict the fine details of a complex, natural system such as human society before we can construct first-order models, which can cope with a general review of the aggregate behavior of this system across the whole of the available database.

All these visions of history emphasize that rapid periods of expansion, lasting for decades or millennia, have existed often enough in the past and have been terminated often enough by the growth of countertrends; they emphasize that an analysis of social dynamics, based only on the data available in recent decades, may lead to a totally false picture of the possibilities that lie ahead. This difficulty certainly applies to verbal theorizing, just as much as to statistics; with verbal theorizing, however, the historical data are far more extensive for those who are willing to examine them. While I would not agree with the exact details of the theories of Spengler and Toynbee, I would consider it all the more important to describe and explain the phenomena they have discussed.

Finally, statistical methods may help on another level—as a paradigm to guide verbal research, both in general and in specific cases. Throughout this chapter, I have emphasized the value of verbal research, *conceived* as an attempt to do with verbal data what statistical research does with mathematical data. Yet even in statistics, where the methods used are spelled out explicitly in advance, I have shown that the popular methods of analysis can be quite unrealistic and deceptive. It would seem unreasonable to expect any more, a priori, from verbal research. Indeed, this thesis has compared the two forms of research in respect to three issues: the emphasis on prediction, the willingness to deal with the longest possible time series, and the willingness to accept noise as part of predictive theories. In all three cases, especially the first and most basic, classic verbal political science—with a handful of notable exceptions—does not appear to have grounds to claim superiority in its attitudes, at least not in the parts of the literature with which I am familiar.[11]

In this situation, the methodological advances in statistics—which are well defined and which can be consolidated—can be of major value in educating the verbally oriented political scientist. The concept of stochastic predictive theories may seem reasonable in the abstract to the verbal political scientist; however, when he/she tries to translate this idea into a strategy for his/her own research, it would not be surprising if the difficulty of doing so brought him/her to withdraw back to Aristotelian procedures. Indeed, the classic attempt to track down the long-term ''causes'' of historical events is very closely linked to the search for dynamic models. However, the concept of ''cause'' is a weak enough paradigm so that historians have often found themselves forced to ad-

---

[11]Aron [28, p. 4] puts it succinctly: ''American sociologists, in my own experience, never talk about laws of history, first of all because they are not acquainted with them, and next because they do not believe in their existence.'' Also, see Sections 5.3.2 and 5.6.7.

mit "multicausality"[12] and then to withdraw into more descriptive, more "objective" questions. Furthermore, historians have often admitted themselves to be intrigued by the great "what if" questions of history, such as, "What would have happened if the Spanish Armada had won in 1588?" Yet such questions—which clearly call for the use of some kind of predictive model—have been dismissed as speculative. (See Section 5.6.6 for an example.)

In short, there would appear to be a need for a more durable paradigm in analytic verbal research. If verbal social scientists can become more and more familiar on an intuitive level with the concrete methods of statistics, in coming to grips with concrete data, then they may be able to develop a clearer picture of what it means to search for robust predictive models, mathematical or verbal. Also, they may be expected to learn to appreciate the value of treating quantitative variables as such , even in verbal discussion, rather than reducing them to such possibilities as "high" and "low." (Discussed in Section 5.6.7.).

The value of statistical methods as a paradigm for verbal research may be especially great in those cases where statistics can deal explicitly with some, but not all, of the historical data of interest. One can imagine two ways in which this value would be felt, as statistics are brought to bear on those data which are available.

First, those people doing the statistical research would have to choose a set of variables to use in developing predictive models. When predicting a system like a missile, made up of five major subsystems or so, one's primary concern in making medium-term predictions is with the "overall system," with the system made up of the interactions between the five major subsystems. Similarly, when asking for long-term prediction of a statistical system, made up of five clusters of heavily intercorrelated systems of variables, one would normally start out by aggregating each of the clusters, by use of factor analysis, pattern analysis, or other procedures, and then studying the relations between the aggregate variables. To try to predict where a missile will go by predicting what each of the subsystems would do in total isolation from each other is to ignore the most important functional relations. Statistical analysis, by drawing us away in concrete cases from a fixation on the internal dynamics of specialized subsystems, may help bring us back to studying the broad structure of interfaces and multiple subsystems, which is crucial to even a first-order prediction of human societies. Then, when researchers go back to look inside the subsystems, we may hope that they will focus more attention on those questions about the interfaces that appeared important at the global level. The "unity of science" may be a debatable proposition when applied to predictive models of, say, biological systems and astronomical systems, However, when one is trying to predict a single, highly integrated system, the need for interdisciplinary unity becomes overwhelming. When small feedback terms from one sub-

---

[12]The "multicausal approach" has appeared in historical research, but the sociologists—who find it harder to retreat into simple narrative—have spoken much more about the idea. See, for example, Vernon [29, pp. 30, 80–81] and MacIver [30].

system to another can have overwhelming effects in determining system behavior, it is essential to try to measure the aggregate behavior directly.

In the next phase, *after* the statistics have pointed to concrete interdisciplinary effects, human verbal knowledge can go on to explain and to qualify these conclusions. One might, on verbal grounds, regard the conclusions as misleading, as oversimplified, or as one-sided in their emphasis. In any case, however, even to discuss these conclusions intelligently, one must try to discuss, on the basis of *verbal* knowledge, why one would expect certain *correlations* and certain *dynamic patterns* to work out as they do. One would have to discuss the "true" dynamic relations between different subsystems in order to express what one feels is wrong with the statistics. One would be tempted to engage in "hypothetical" or "analytic" modeling—to suggest what would have happened to the statistics if one had included, as hard data, certain variables for which hard mathematical data do not happen to exist. One would focus one's attention on the variables of central interest, rather than lose oneself in a morass of unrelated higher-order vicissitudes. In brief, one might acquire the momentum necessary to launch into a full-scale verbal dynamic analysis, without crashing back under the weight of pure classical traditions.

Before closing this discussion of the value of statistics to political analysis, it may be worth noting that important applications may also exist in politics proper. Early in Chapter 2, I mentioned the possibility of a growth in ecological and sociological models, based on the vast accumulation of data by Earth satellites. Many of the difficulties cited above—particularly the dominance of verbal data over quantitative data—would not apply in this case. Also, the emphasis on feedback effects and interdisciplinary research would apply more than ever. Given the importance of world balances of agricultural production and population, given the dangers of ecological catastrophe through high stress and imbalance in such systems, and given the possibilities here for treaties to set up a coordinated global system to monitor and help control these systems from space, the practical political scientist would have good reason to think about these applications. This is doubly true insofar as the development of these applications may be far from automatic.

5.4.1 Empirical Forecasting and the Birth of Macroeconomics

The subject of macroeconomics has evolved considerably over the past few decades, but it clearly owes its birth to the paradigm shift due to the work of Keynes. In describing this work, McCracken [31, p. 51] writes: "Perhaps one of the finest contributions Keynes made to economic theory and economic policy has been on the subject of investment. According to previous classical analysis, savings, investment, and the rate of interest all fitted into the standard pattern of demand, supply, and price. A high rate of interest increased savings and decreased savings and increased investment, so it was a function of price—the rate of interest—to gravitate to the equilibrium point where saving equalled investment. There would be no such thing as over-saving or underinvestment [i.e., depression], as they were continuously being brought into balance by an automatic regulator.''

"For Keynes classical interest theory was in error at two basic points. First, while a priori reasoning leads to the natural conclusion that a high rate of interest stimulates saving and a low rate reduces saving, a posteriori evidence . . .''

Gardner Ackley describes equivalent ideas [32, pp. 154–155]: "Wicksell's analysis [the classical analysis] . . . gave us, as has been stressed, a rudimentary theory of the aggregate demand for goods. This demand consists of two main divisions: consumer demand and investment demand. Each of these demands was conceived to be interest-elastic: the lower the interest-rate, the greater the investment demand; and the greater the consumer demand, too [the later idea is, of course, merely a restatement of the idea that saving depends negatively on the interest rate] . . . . If either type of demand declined, the resulting fall in the rate of interest would stimulate them both, and shift resources to the one which had not declined. If, however, for any reason [particularly expansion or contraction of the money supply by the banks] the rate of interest were prevented from performing this regulatory function, aggregate demand . . . would be altered . . . . But if wages and prices should not decline [enough] . . . workers would become unemployed, and real as well as money income would be cut.''

But then came the empirical studies on the relative impact of income, versus interest rates, on demand. The history of these studies is rather complex. The major initial study, by Simon Kuznets [33], uses technical language difficult to summarize here. Elizabeth W. Gilbey writes [34, p. 25] that "in attempting to test this hypothesis, contradictory results arose from the use of time-series and cross-sectional data. Simon Kuznet's study of data going all the way back to 1870 showed that the percentage of aggregate income saved had in fact remained constant in the United States.'' (The contradiction involved the *distribution* of saving across households.) A more recent survey has been done by Patinkin [35, pp. 651–664]. He discusses largely the "wealth effect" based on the "Pigou effect,'' a more recent attempt to resurrect classical ideas. Patinkin [35, pp. 656–657] cites numerous studies that measure wealth as real assets times interest rates. He describes [35, p. 663] his own results for "beta,'' which he equates with "YL"(income), and "alpha,'' defined [35, p. 659] as beta times interest rate. Thus the latter results explicitly measure the hypothesis that interest rates affect the *percentage* of income saved, while the former do measure something closely related. Also, the studies of Goldsmith cited by Patinkin reaffirmed the idea of a "constant saving-income ratio.'' Patinkin describes his own studies, and some of the previous studies, as showing large and significant effects by variables derived from interest rates; however, the actual regression coefficients of alpha ran to .04–.08, at the most, much smaller than the coefficient of beta, which was already a larger number to begin with.

The slow response of governments to Keynes' ideas may seem surprising, because many would identify the "liberal" Roosevelt with the "liberal"

Keynes. However, U.S. GNP data indicate rather strongly that the main recovery from the Depression coincided with major military spending induced not by economic theory (though Keynes' theory might have recommended it, given no alternative spending options on the same scale) but by World War II. Keynesian theory, in many respects, was not fully accepted in the United States until John Kennedy became president. As Schlesinger [36, p. 1005] points out: "The [tax cut] bill made slow progress through Congress. Public reaction at first was muted. Kennedy used to inquire of the professors of the Council what had happened to the several million college students who had presumably been taught the new economics . . . . Still . . . on September 25, 1963, the worst was over . . . . The Yale speech had not been in vain; and the American government, a generation after *General Theory*, had accepted the Keynesian revolution."

Regarding Keynes and Roosevelt, Schlesinger [37, p. 236] has written: "The First New Deal, in the main, distrusted spending. Its conservatives, like Johnson and Moley, were orthodox in their fiscal views and wanted a balanced budget; and its liberals, like Tugwell and La Follette, disliked spending as a drug which gave the patient a false sense of well-being before surgery could be completed." He goes on [37, p. 403–404]: "Shortly after Roosevelt's inauguration [1933] Keynes spoke once again in a brilliant pamphlet called 'The Means to Prosperity.' Here he argued with new force and detail for public spending as the way out of the depression. Employing the concept of the 'multiplier,' introduced by his student." In April 1933, Keynes wrote, "Unfortunately it seems impossible in the world of today to find anything between a government which does nothing at all and one which goes right off the deep end!" Schlesinger further reports [37, pp. 405–406] that "on May 28, 1934, Keynes came to tea at the White House. The meeting does not seem to have been a success . . . . To Frances Perkins Roosevelt complained strangely, 'He left a whole rigamarole of figures. He must be a mathematician rather than a political economist.'"

5.5 BEYOND NAIVE EMPIRICISM: ADAPTING OUR IDEAS TO FILL THE GAP LEFT BY STATISTICS

Now let us return once more to our starting point, to the worries of the political actor about using mathematics. (See Section 5.2.) The worries were dealt with on two levels: (1) the level of defending the notion of prediction and (2) the level of describing the practical applications of statistical modeling to political prediction. I have emphasized the empirical approach, for both verbal and statistical research.

On another level, however, the political actor might question the idea that empirical approaches are enough, when the subjects of one's investigation are intelligent human beings. In particular, the political actor would have to reconcile the use of objective methods to predict other actors, while preserving the sense of free will in making one's own decisions. On a primitive level, this paradox poses no difficulties at all to the political actor; it is easy to conjure up the image of a fast-dealing political hack, working for a city machine, gleefully pushing people around as if they were buttons on a pin-ball machine. At a more advanced level, politicians find that they can predict people better and influence their actions more constructively by exploiting empathy, by using their own reaction patterns as a kind of analogue model to predict the reactions of others. Thus there are the old, persistent adages: "If you want to predict what a man will do, try to put yourself in his shoes" and "If you were a . . . what would *you* do?" This procedure is particularly effective when the political actors come from the same background as the people they are predicting, when their background is cosmopolitan, or when their reaction patterns are defined at a general enough level to make it easier to imagine how another person would really respond to a situation very different from that of the political actor himself/herself. (Empathy may also be used, of course, as a tool in thinking of approaches one might borrow from others in coping with one's own problems.) When a political actor oscillates between thinking about others "subjectively," in terms of empathy, and thinking about them "objectively," in terms of predictive empiricism, a conflict emerges, long before the use of statistics as such arises. Rationality, and the acknowledgment of others' capacity for rationality, would appear to allow no escape from this conflict; as long as we have two distinct sources of information from which to predict the behavior of people, we must live as best we can with the conflicting predictions, *while trying to reconcile them by concrete improvements in the concepts we use on both sides.*

Predictive statistical models, like empirical verbal models, cannot directly express the insights derived from "empathy." In particular, they cannot express the insights derived from acknowledging the intelligence of other human beings.[13] This limitation may be of enormous importance to the practical political actor. On the other hand, the related mathematical concept of maximizing a cardinal utility function expresses the ideal of human intelligence, more vividly and more precisely than the usual verbal formulations. The arguments of Von Neumann and Morgenstern [38, pp. 15–33] and of Raiffa [39] in favor of this concept require little more than logical consistency on the whole, in the ultimate values that the individual pursues. While the serious political actor would normally admit that he sometimes acts stupid, and sometimes acts at cross-purposes against himself, especially when limitations on time and on knowledge constrain his detailed decision-making, he would rarely consider such mistakes as a matter of *fixed or deliberate policy*. Often, when the polit-

---

[13]Strictly speaking, it would be more accurate to say that verbal or mathematical models derived from external empirical data alone do not incorporate the information, both quantitative and structural, to be derived from accounting for the mutual underlying resemblance of different human brains. Once one's "empathy" has led one to postulate a certain model structure, one can, of course, try to translate this model into a related empirical model for empirical estimation; even then, however, the empirical test would only account for one of *two* sources of validation.

ical analyst would accuse the political actor of indulging in irrationality, the actor would have a counterargument based on the knowledge and concepts available to him/her at the time of the decision.

If we agree with Raiffa, then, that the maximization of cardinal utility is "valid" as a foundation for most political decision-making, we find ourselves led to important conclusions about political analysis too. First, we find ourselves reemphasizing the point that verbal research may be regarded as an attempt to perform valid statistical inference, accounting for data that are less structured and less manageable than the usual statistical time series. Within Raiffa's framework, the basic questions one asks are quantitative in nature: for example, "If we carry out action A, *how much* will it cost, *how much* do we gain, and what are the *probabilities* that we will succeed?" More generally, Raiffa would have us ask: "If we carry out action A, starting from situation B, what is the distribution of *probabilities* attached to the different possible *levels* of cost and to different possible outcomes? *How much* do we expect to gain from each of the possible outcomes, if our subsequent strategy is optimal?"

In each case, we do the best we can to estimate these *quantities* on the basis of the available verbal information; thus the research carried out on that information is carried out for the purpose of extracting the most accurate possible statistical information. We also account for the intelligence of other actors. We also account for more direct quantitative evidence, whenever we can find it. From most sources of information, we expect to get probabilistic indications of various kinds, never certainties. Through practice, we may hope to learn more and more the art of formulating accurately the interrelated patterns of statistical implications of our verbal knowledge, and to reduce the losses in translation that always intervene in going from raw observation to decision.

Second—and more important—the concept of utility maximization offers us an idealized model of intelligent decision-making for use in the prediction of other political actors. At first glance, this concept may sound rather culture-bound. However, the concept of utility function is very generalized in the range of concrete behavior it can include. One can imagine all sorts of different utility functions. One can imagine many different levels of knowledge and aptitude brought to bear in maximizing utility functions. One can even imagine different levels of basic cognitive structure, as suggested by Piaget [40] and by ego psychiatrists,[14] levels that one may hope either to remember or to advance to. One can imagine states of short-term psychological disequilibrium, where a political actor does not yet take the actions best suited to maximizing his/her utility function, because on some level the actor has not yet become aware of the possibilities. (The detection of such disequilibria is particularly

---

[14]The school of ego psychiatrists [41, pp. 111–134] is much larger, but less mapped out, than many other fields for the wandering political scientist; the concept of stages, while often present, often requires digging out. Another reference, less transparent but also influential, is Hartmann [42]. One advantage of these approaches is that they can be more easily compared with cybernetic views, emphasizing human intelligence.

important to political actors whose job is to persuade others to change their course of action.) Thus *starting* from the concept of utility maximization, one can approach empirical reality bit by bit, by using both empathy and empirical data to add qualifications to one's view of other actors as ideal decision-makers. Even as one adds qualifications to this (Section 5.6.8), one can continue to insist that all interpersonal differences in personality be analyzed in terms of the current state parameters of a system that obeys the same general dynamic laws as one's own mind and that is capable of *changing* its state parameters as a result of the general learning capability shared by all humans.

From a theoretical point of view, the choice of starting point is not a matter of mere bookkeeping; it defines one's implicit "prior probability" distribution, as described in Section 2.5 of Chapter 2. From a practical point of view, this procedure can help us avoid rigid stereotypes of other political actors; it can help us remember that they too have a capacity for change, and that the likely directions of change are not entirely random. In any case, this procedure allows us to make use of both major sources of information: information derived from empathy and information derived from more objective data. This procedure also suggests that the procedures mentioned in Section 2.10 of Chapter 2 for utility maximization might be used not just as a technique for analyzing decision-making systems but as the basis for substantive models of such systems.

The use of utility maximization as a model of decision-making has already led to a number of practical applications, notably in game theory and in microeconomics. The concept of ideal utility maximization predicts the behavior of an actor *conditional* on the information that is available to him/her; thus it may lead to an *implicit* model, a model defined in terms of variables that are not directly observable to other actors. In terms of behaviorist attitudes, this is a major liability, insofar as it makes it much more difficult to predict behavior concretely; on the other hand, such implicit models may allow us to infer something about the hidden variables from the overt behavior.

In the case of microeconomics, one does not attempt to predict, say, the actual levels of steel production, at least not in the early stages of research; instead, one defends the proposition that the levels of steel production will be equal to *whatever* level is necessary in order to maximize some kind of utility function, if the decision is made by an economy that enjoys perfect competition.[14] (Strictly speaking, however, economists now tend to avoid the concept of "social utility function" on the grounds that they can deduce similar conclusions from weaker versions of the same criterion.) One might well have attacked this theory, in its early stages, as an unscientific—though mathematical—exercise in propaganda. However, as the theory was developed, it turned out to be a powerful framework for evaluating the *in*efficiencies produced by

[14]The reference from Triffin, in Section 5.6.9, implies quite strongly that "our textbooks" have emphasized these points about perfect competition. Ferguson [43] refers to the "extreme aprioristic" school of microeconomists, "prominent since John Stuart Mill"; much of the rest of that text deals with the classic theory of perfect competition and its later developments.

situations of *im*perfect competition in the real world. (See Section 5.6.9.) The theory has been used to analyze the effects of taxes and labor laws [43, Chapter 14] on economic efficiency; it has led to the development of Lieberman's principles of economic organization [44, p. 441], now a mainstay of the Soviet economy (See Section 5.6.10.)

Microeconomics, initially an isolated and essentially unempirical theory, has turned into a powerful mathematical framework for analysis, a framework allowing the useful bringing together of vast quantities of empirical data, a framework important to both the prediction and the comprehension of economic phenomena.

Yet all this success was based on a static concept of utility maximization, a concept of optimal equilibrium, related to the classic concepts of Lagrange.[15] Since then, Norbert Wiener [46] has discussed the more modern, more powerful dynamic theories of maximization, which he would consider a substudy of "cybernetics." He has suggested that this body of theory be applied to the human brain. Karl Deutsch has gone on to suggest that cybernetics may also be applied to political science. See Section 5.5.1. Considering the power that a primitive, static concept of maximization has had, over decades, in economics, these suggestions would appear to make a great deal of sense.

Unfortunately, these ideas are caught between the "mighty opposites" of modern methodology—the behaviorists, who would demand quantitative empirical proof that the initial model predicts all the variables in detail, and the traditionalists, who would not have patience with the mathematics. Also, in the last few years, the relevant phase of cybernetics has been renamed "control theory." Chapter 2 has discussed the value of control theory (i.e., of optimization techniques) as a tool in analyzing social systems; however, control theory itself may also be used as a normative model of the processes that allow human societies—or even the human brain itself—to function. Section 5.5.1 discusses these possibilities in more detail.

As with microeconomics, one will expect to find that the real systems involve imperfections and approximations to the optimum.[16] However, one may also find it interesting to be able to see where these imperfections are, and to appreciate the capacities that human beings and political societies—like economies—*do* have, to cope with data on a scale far beyond the capacity of present-day computers. Insofar as one agrees with the traditionalist that the human being is still the most relevant unit of analysis in politics, one can try, in the future, to expand the interface between cybernetics in psychology and cybernetics in political science.

In summary, the mathematical methods outlined in Chapter 2 can indeed be applied to political science, but they should always be considered as only one

[15]Lagrange multipliers are used in maximizing a fixed function, subject to static constraints. These multipliers correspond essentially to prices [45].

[16]See the discussion by Herbert Simon on "optimizing" and "satisfaction" in Lazarsfeld [47]. A deeper understanding of Simon's observations would require, of course, a more general framework.

branch of a more complex, integrated system of analysis, oriented towards the goal of prediction. The Bayesian philosophy of utility maximization and conditional probabilities could play a central role in organizing this system of analysis, but the behaviorist philosophy of total empiricism does not have the power to account for major parts of this system, parts that appear essential in the last part of this chapter.

5.5.1 Cybernetics: The Brain, Politics, and a Neural Approach

Before proposing a new approach, I first cite the classical views of Wiener and Deutsch.

In a later article, Wiener [48] emphasizes the statistical subdivision of cybernetics, in particular, as the portion of cybernetics most worth pursuing. This is quite close to the suggestions here, insofar as the mathematics of Chapter 2 tend to be part of the statistical subdivision, but Wiener's specific suggestions are very different from my own in terms of the overall explanations they point to for gross behavior. Wiener emphasizes patterns of resonance among multiple sources of radiation, an idea that would conceivably relate to my technique of pattern analysis, but the connections do not appear simple. Wiener goes on to suggest strongly that the new statistics developed to deal with the analysis of time series (one-dimensional phenomena) for living systems may someday be extended to statistical physics (four-dimensional phenomena, thermodynamics) and provide a revolutionary new understanding of the possibilities for maintaining order in equilibrium.

Karl Deutsch [49, p. xxvi] summarizes his framework as follows: "In the main, these pages offer notions, propositions and models derived from the philosophy of science, and specifically from the theory of communication and control—often called by Norbert Wiener's term 'cybernetics'—in the hope that these may prove relevant to the study of politics, and suggestive and useful in the essential development of political theory that will be more adequate—or less inadequate—to the problems of the later decades of the twentieth century."

My own views of these connections are complex, but a few brief hints may be in order here, to indicate the existence of specific possibilities.

If one presumes that some sort of inborn "reinforcement" mechanism provides the brain with a current measure of a cardinal utility function to maximize, then Section 2.10 of Chapter 2 indicates the optimal way to adapt an elaborate behavior-generating network, to maximize this function, conditional the availability of a network model of the "external" environment. This involves the passing back of "ordered derivatives," a quantitative piece of information represented by some physical information flowing *backward* along the same network, which overtly carries only gross, direct behavior-generating information (electrical impulses). The microtubules, which criss-cross almost all neurons, could well be implementing a hidden network of chemical feedback of this kind, carried back from cell to cell to cell, originating in the hypothalamus and epithalamus (effectively in the pituitary and pineal, whose exact rules of operation I would not pretend to know at this point).

Network models to predict the external environment, as in Chapter 2, could be generated ("estimated") by a similar mechanism, based on measuring predictive accuracy at some sites like the glomeruli of the thalamus. (This hypothesis yields the empirical prediction that certain states of chronic insensitivity and rigidity in behavior governed by the cerebrum would be replaced by normal cerebral learning, if only the inputs could get as far as the glomeruli; this could be accomplished either by nerve growth factors, synthesized to enhance the growth of random connections from the hypothalamus or epithalamus to the glomeruli, or even by learning procedures that take full advantage of the microscopic bootstrap process that develops new connections to the glomeruli under normal conditions. This prediction is not only testable, but also of potential practical value.)

The giant pyramids of the cerebral cortex might be performing pattern analysis, as in Section 2.9 of Chapter 2; the duality of the functions f_i and g_i in generating and predicting the same pattern-description variable may well correspond to the dual poles of these cells. The time factor, of course, requires that all these ideas only be approximations; still, they may have some suggestive value even in experimentation.

5.6   ENDNOTES TO CHAPTER 5

5.6.1   References on Probabilistic Concepts for Decision-Making

Raiffa [39] is clearly intended to communicate to a broader community. The philosophical foundation of this view of probability is described in Kyburg et al [50]. Anatol Rapoport has criticized the abuse of probabilistic concepts by decision-makers who do not fully understand them; see [51], especially Chapter 10. Nevertheless, a false estimate of uncertainty may be less dangerous than a forced choice of absolute certainties; Raiffa, in a memo co-authored with Marc Alpert, has discussed in detail the problem of educating and "calibrating" decisions-makers (i.e., compensating for their overconfidence), to estimate probabilities more realistically. (See "A Progress Report on the Training of Probability Assessors," available in 1971 as an unpublished manuscript from the office of Prof. Raiffa in the Littauer Building, Harvard University.) Still, Rapoport's comments on the hazards of mathematical approaches are well worth noting, for those who would want to use such approaches.

5.6.2   Path Analysis in Political Science

It was surprising to find the phrase "path analysis" so rare in books up to 1973. In 1971, I discussed the subject at length with Professor Alker, at MIT, one of the main exponents of this approach, with Professor Raymond Tanter then of the Center for Research in Conflict Resolution at the University of Michigan, and with students taking path analysis as a subject in the Inter-University Consortium for Political Research. In all cases, it was clear that path analysis was intended as a kind of refined causal analysis, using regression coefficients (or time-series regression coefficients, in the sophisticated versions?) as indices of the size and direction of influence. Simon, Blalock, and Boudon have also been associated with path analysis in discussions at various universities.

5.6.3 The Brookings Model: Example of Focus on Prediction

Duesenberry et al. [52, p. 296–297] describe some experience with the Brookings econometric model.

The full regession model, justified by solid significance indications, did not perform as well as a "condensed"—dramatically reduced—model, at first. Then "adjustments" were applied, which dramatically improved the fit; these adjustments seemed to entail multiplying each coefficient by a constant, suitable to adjust the predictions of each variable to the right level in the first-half test data. Duesenberry et al. [52, p. 298] still caution that "if the model does indeed suffer from omission of important but slowly-changing variables, then it is probably not very useful for long-run analysis or projection." Estimating or adjusting coefficients to maximize predictive power *directly*, over the trial data, is the essence of my proposal in Sections 2.7 and 2.11 of Chapter 2.

5.6.4 Autonomous Term in Production Functions

For example, Solow [53] writes: "Not only is delta A over A [the percentage increase in the autonomous term] uncorrelated with K/L, but one might almost conclude from the graph that delta A over A is essentially a constant in time, exhibiting more or less random fluctuations about a fixed mean." Looking at Figure 3 in Solow, one notes a possible exception to this, which Solow admits is a very tentative conclusion: the growth of this term might have actually been *slightly faster* during the depths of the Depression (actually lagging it by 3 years in the graph) than under normal conditions.

5.6.5 Possible Biological Links to Human History

Konrad Lorenz [54] is already popular among some political scientists. Just as relevant may be George Gaylord Simpson, who writes [55, p. 391]: "The populations making a quantum shift [e.g., evolution of human intelligence] do not lose adaptation altogether; to do so is to become extinct. It is also clear that *the direction of change is adaptive, unless at the very beginning* . . . . Yet the very fact that selection pressure is strong can only be a concomitant of movement from a more poorly to a better adapted status. *Selection is not linear but centripetal when adaptation is perfected.* It is the 'stabilizing selection'

. . . . The quantum change is a break-through from one portion of stabilizing selection to another.'' The Indian caste system and the early Caribbean system of Carib predators and Arawaks are interesting examples of centripetal development among humans in relatively static ecologies/economies.

Simpson continues [55, p. 392]: "Quantum evolution usually is and at some level it may always be involved in the opening or so-called 'explosive' phase of adaptive radiation. The relative rapidity with which a variety of adaptation zones are then occupied seems quite inexplicable except by a series of (?) and also, often, successive quantum shifts into the varied zones. The rates thereafter slow down.'' New frontiers (discussed in Section 5.3.1) are closely related to quantum shifts.

5.6.6   An Example of Historians Opposing Prediction

The noted historian Trevelyan [56, p. 91] has written: "The endlessly attractive game of speculating on the might-have-beens of history can never take us very far with sense or safety. For if one thing had been different, everything would thenceforth have been different—and in what way we cannot tell . . . . *As serious students of history, all we can do is to watch and to investigate how in fact one thing led to another in the course actually taken.* This pursuit is rendered all the more fascinating and romantic because we know how very nearly it was all completely different. Except perhaps in terms of philosophy, no event was 'inevitable.'''

Historians have often discussed the "turning points," times when the subsequent course of events *would* have been very different *if* small events had worked out differently; see, for example, Handlin [57]. However, as the last two chapters of Handlin make clear, it is usually not considered acceptable to imagine just how the subsequent events might have been different concretely.

5.6.7   Disadvantage of "High/Low" Treatment of Continuous Variables

It has been suggested that differences in behavior of "high" and "low" situations may make such a treatment valuable, or that an actual division of the world into "high" and "low" makes it desirable. However, just because our *sample* is weak in the middle range of the spectrum, we do not have to conclude that we have to break our sample into smaller subsamples, capable of supporting less detailed analysis. If there is *some* qualitative difference in behavior in the different zones, this difference in behavior may be tied to a smooth continuum of different behaviors as one moves from one pole to the other. Even if a clear-cut threshold effect does exist, then, in order to *explain* this effect, operating on a set of continuous variables, we would normally study the discontinuous implications of the continuous interactions of the original continuous variables. Exceptions may exist, but in more cases than one might expect a priori, it is better to treat continuous variables as such, even if they have strange properties.

5.6.8 Interpersonal Differences As a Limit on Empathy

One must make allowance for a few state parameters—such as metabolic, respiratory, and hormone levels—which are less often subject to learning. Sex and intelligence may both be affected by such variables. However, to say that learning may proceed faster or slower does not invalidate a person's ability to learn in most cases. On the *behavioral* level, flexibility remains critical, particularly when we are speaking of heads of state and the like, who are rarely literal imbeciles.

5.6.9 Market Competition Theory Explains Imperfections

Triffin [58, p. 5] states that ''for most of Professor Chamberlain's and Mrs. Robinson's readers, this is the basic distinction between monopolistic (or imperfect) and pure (or perfect) competition. If the sales curve of the firm is perfectly elastic, we are concerned with pure competition. If, on the contrary, the curve is tipped, competition is taken to be monopolistic or imperfect . . . . The substitution of the equation of marginal cost and marginal revenue for the less general and less elegant equation of marginal cost and price has been the main contribution of monopolistic competition theory to the 'pure economics' of our textbooks.''

5.6.10 Lieberman Economics As a Mainstay of the USSR

Lindblom [44] provides some evidence on this point. In the fall of 1973, an article appeared in *The New York Times* indicating that more than 90% of Soviet consumer industries, at a minimum, had been converted to the Lieberman system. *The New York Times Index* at this writing was complete up to August 15, 1973; it listed a major article on the front page, June 3, 1973, elaborating on how thoroughly the conversion has been made, and at any rate quoting *Pravda* on Soviet condemnation of those who oppose the new methods. While the same *Pravda* article was discussed briefly on June 6, p. 23, in the *Washington Post*, I was unable to find *The New York Times* article in its indexed location at Harvard or in nearby locations. However, subsequent copies of the *Index* should clarify these points.

REFERENCES

1. B. H. Liddell-Hart, *Strategy*, 2nd ed., Praeger, New York, 1967.
2. J. Schwinger, *Particles, Sources and Fields*, Addison-Wesley, Reading, MA, 1970.
3. H. M. Blalock, Jr., *Causal Inference in Nonexperimental Research*, University of North Carolina Press, Chapel Hill, 1964.
4. H. Simon, *Models of Man, Part I*, Wiley, New York, 1957.
5. R. A. Dahl, Cause and effect in the study of politics and discussion, in D. Lerner (ed.), *Cause and Effect*, Free Press, New York, 1965.
6. R. Hopkins and J. Raymond, Projections of population change by mobilization and assimilation, *Behavioral Science*, p. 254, 1972.

7. J. Johnston, *Econometric Methods*, 2nd ed., McGraw-Hill, New York, 1972.

8. J. D. Singer (ed.), *Quantitative International Politics, Insights and Evidence*, Free Press, New York, 1968.

9. Walter Isard, *Methods of Regional Analysis: An Introduction to Regional Science*, 3rd printing, MIT Press, Cambridge, MA, 1963.

10. W. L. Hays, *Statistics for the Social Sciences*, 2nd ed., Holt, Rinehart and Winston, New York, 1973.

11. D. V. Lindley, Professor Hogben's crisis—a survey of the foundations of statistics, *Applied Statistics*, Vol. 7, No. 3, pp. 186–198. 1958.

12. H. Raiffa and R. Schlaifer, *Applied Statistical Decision Theory*, Harvard Business School, 1961.

13. R. Hogg and A. Craig, *Introduction to Mathematical Statistics*, 3rd ed., Macmillan, London, 1970.

14. M. T. Wasan, *Parametric Estimation*, McGraw-Hill, New York, 1970.

15. G. E. Box and G. Tiao, *Bayesian Inference in Statistical Analysis*, Wiley.

16. J. Brode, *Time-Series-Processor—TSP*. Available from Project Cambridge, MIT, 5th floor, 575 Technology Square, Cambridge, MA 02139.

17. R. Schlaifer, *User's Guide to the AQD Programs*, Part III, p. 18. Available from the Harvard Business School.

18. O. Spengler, *The Decline of the West*, Knopf, New York, 1926. (Translated by Charles Atkinson from the 1918 original version.)

19. A. J. Toynbee, *A Study of History*, abridgement of Vols. I–VI, 1st American edition, 4th printing, Oxford University Press, New York, 1947.

20. W. P. Webb, The frontier and the 400-year boom, in G. R. Taylor (ed.), *The Turner Thesis: Concerning the Role of the Frontier in American History*, 3rd ed., Heath, Lexington, MA, 1972.

21. G. Hegel, The philosophy of history, in C. Friedrich (ed.), *The Philosophy of Hegel*, Modern Library, New York, 1954.

22. G. Heckscher, General methodological problems, in H. Eckstein, and D. E. Apter (eds.), *Comparative Politics*, Free Press, Glencoe, IL, 1963.

23. S. E. Morison, *Vistas of History*, Knopf, New York, 1964.

24. H. R. Trevor-Roper, *Historical Essays*, Harper & Row, New York, 1966.

25. M. Weber, *From Max Weber: Essays in Sociology*, H. Gerth and C. Millstr., Oxford U. Press, New York, 1958.

26. W. H. McNeil, *The Rise of the West*, Mentor, New York, 1965.

27. S. N. Eisenstadt, *The Political Systems of Empires*, Free Press, Glencoe, IL, 1963.

28. R. Aron, *Main Currents in Sociological Thought*, Vol. I, Basic Books, New York, 1965, translated by H. Weaver.

29. G. M. Vernon, *Human Interaction: An Introduction to Sociology*, Ronald Press, New York, 1965.

30. R. M. MacIver, *Social Causation*, Ginn and Co., Boston, 1942.

31. H. L. McCracken, *Keynesian Economics in the Stream of Economic Thought*, Louisiana State University Press, Baton Rouge, 1961.

32. G. Ackley, *Macroeconomic Theory*, Macmillan, New York 1961 (12th printing, 1967).

33. S. Kuznets, *National Income: A Survey of Findings*, NBER, New York, 1946.

34. E. W. Gilbey, *The Economics of Consumption*, Random House, New York, 1968.

35. D. Patinkin, *Money, Interest and Prices*, 2nd ed., Harper & Row, New York, 1965.

36. A. Schlesinger, *A Thousand Days*, Houghton Mifflin, Boston, 1965.

37. A. Schlesinger, *The Age of Roosevelt*, Vol. III, Houghton Mifflin, Boston, 1966.

38. J. Von Neumann and O. Morgenstern, *The Theory of Games and Economic Behavior*, Princeton University Press, Princeton, NJ, 1953.

39. H. Raiffa, *Decision Analysis: Introductory Lectures on Making Choices Under Uncertainty*, Addison-Wesley, Reading, MA, 1968.

40. John H. Flavell, *The Developmental Psychology of Piaget* (including Foreword by Piaget), Van Nostrand, Princeton, NJ, 1963.

41. E. H. Erikson, *Insight and Responsibility*, Norton, New York, 1964.

42. H. Hartman, *Ego Psychology and the Problem of Adaptation*, International Universities Press, New York, 1958, translated by D. Rapoport.

43. C. E. Ferguson, *Microeconomic Theory*, rev. ed., Irwin, Homewood, IL, 1969, 3rd printing.

44. C. E. Lindblom, The rediscovery of the market, in P. A. Samuelson (ed.), *Readings in Economics*, 6th ed., McGraw-Hill, New York, 1970.

45. P. A. Samuelson, *Foundations of Economic Analysis*, Harvard University Press, Cambridge, MA, 1947.

46. N. Wiener, *Cybernetics, or Control and Communications in the Animal and the Machine*, 2nd ed., MIT Press, Cambridge, MA, 1961.

47. P. F. Larzarsfeld (ed.), *Mathematical Thinking in the Social Sciences*, Free Press, Glencoe, IL, 1954.

48. N. Wiener, Perspectives in cybernetics, in N. Wiener and J. P. Schade (eds.), *Cybernetics of the Nervous System*, Elsevier, Amsterdam, 1965.

49. K. W. Deutsch, *The Nerves of Government*, Free Press, Glencoe, IL, 1966.

50. H. E. Kyburg, Jr., and H. E. Smokler (eds.), *Studies in Subjective Probability*, Wiley, New York, 1964.

51. A. Rapoport, *Strategy and Conscience*, Harper & Row, New York, 1964.

52. J. S. Duesenberry, G. Fromm, L. R. Klein, and E. H. Kuh, (eds.), *The Brookings Model: Some Further Results*, Rand McNally, Chicago, 1969.

53. R. M. Solow, Technical change and the aggregate production function, *Review of Economic Statistics*, pp. 312–320, 1957.

54. K. Lorenz, *On Aggression*, Harcourt, Brace and World, New York, 1966, translated by M. Wilson.

55. G. G. Simpson, *The Major Features of Evolution*, Columbia University Press, New York, 1953.

56. G. M. Trevelyan, *An Autobiography and Other Essays*, Longman, Green, and Co., London, 1949.

57. O. Handlin, *Choice or Destiny: Turning Points in American History*, Atlantic Monthly Press, Boston, 1954.

58. R. Triffin, *Monopolistic Competition and General Equilibrium Theory*, Harvard University Press, Cambridge, MA, 1956.

6

Nationalism and Social Communications

A Test Case for Mathematical Approaches

6.1 INTRODUCTION AND SUMMARY

The previous Chapter has emphasized the importance of carrying out statistical research within the context of a broader analytic effort. The substantive goal of this thesis, however, in political science was to carry through an analytic point of view, already developed by Karl Deutsch and formulated mathematically with the assistance of Robert Solow.[1] In the first phase of this research, carried out in 1971, I attempted to develop the original Deutsch–Solow model as a predictive model of national assimilation and political mobilization; more precisely, I attempted to predict such indicators of national assimilation as language or ethnicity (see Table 6.24), and such indicators of social mobilization as urbanization or literacy (see Table 6.23). (Note that these indicators were suggested originally by Karl Deutsch, not as operational definitions of nationalism but as usable series of numerical data with some sort of correlation, albeit noisy, with the underlying concepts he has discussed.)

Even though the Deutsch–Solow model seems very simple from the mathematician's point of view, the existing statistical routines turned out to be unable to cope effectively with even this level of complexity. Because of this result, which I found rather surprising at first, it was necessary to postpone the more ambitious goal of predicting long-term political trends by way of more interesting, complex models. I have, instead, developed two distinct strands of thought—one methodological and the other substantive—which may be pre-

---

[1]See Deutsch [1]. Chapter 6 contains the main argument leading up to the mathematical model; Appendix V contains the mathematical model and a verbal description of it.

requisites to success in the more ambitious undertakings of the future. Even in their present form, however, these two strands do offer predictions and insights, respectively, of some relevance to the decision-maker concerned with nationalism.

First, a new methodology was developed for statistical analysis, the *robust method* of Section 2.11 of Chapter 2, able to deal effectively with prediction over time. This method emerged from the study of the Deutsch–Solow model and of similar simple models. Sections 6.2 and 6.3 of this chapter will describe the empirical results, based on the Deutsch–Kravitz data from more than a dozen nations, that led to this new approach. These results appear to indicate that prediction errors are cut in half, for prediction over about five or six "units" of time, following whatever units—years, decades, or 5-year intervals—were used in the original data collection. (Note that *all* nations were studied for which sufficient data were available from Deutsch and Kravitz, who, in turn, limited their collection effort only by the requirements that a nation must have a significant problem of national assimilation and that the data must be easily available in the Harvard libraries.) Although these indications have been rather strong, one should still be warned that strict statistical generality and uniformity have not been possible in this case, due to the limited supply of data per nation and due to limitations of existing computer software routines; thus the use of judgment is required to interpret these results. Chapter 4, by contrast, has been written to provide a test of the various methods, which avoids such real-world difficulties. (See Table 4.1.) Figures 6.1–6.4 graph the distributions of prediction errors for the three methods tested by comparable procedures over the Deutsch–Kravitz data: (1) classical regression, (2) the ARMA technique of Chapter 3, and (3) the robust method.

Figures 6.1–6.4 describe the average percentage errors found when making long-term predictions of four variables—the sizes of the mobilized, underlying assimilated, and differentiated populations—in a variety of different cases, by use of different estimation techniques. In each "case" (i.e., a nation and a choice of data to study in that nation), I calculated the root-mean-square (rms) *average* of the errors in the predictions made for all different years for which data were available; this may be thought of as taking an average across different intervals of prediction. For each of the three basic techniques—regression, ARMA, and the robust method (GRR or EXTRAP)—and for each variable, a curve was drawn that represents the *distribution* of average error size from case to case. These distribution curves are like the distribution curves for college board scores; to find out how bad the errors were for the 20th percentile down from the top, we look at 20% on the horizontal axis, and then look up at the curves to see how high the prediction errors go in the vertical direction. Note that the vertical axis is spread out at the bottom and compressed at the top to allow us to fit the whole curve on one page; it is still correct, however, when a curve is exactly halfway between, say, 50% and 70%, to conclude that the error was exactly 60%. Thus in comparing the area under different curves, it is important to note that the horizontal line at 5% should be thought of as

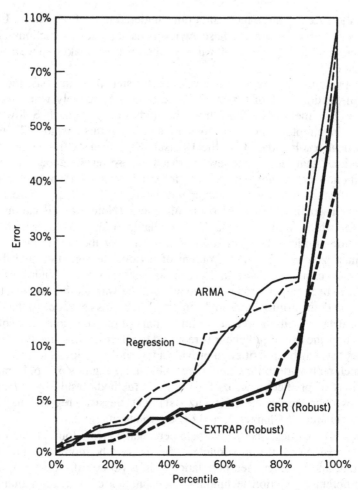

FIGURE 6.1 The rms average errors in long-term predictions of assimilated populations, in percentages. Distributions are based on 21 or 22 cases each. Error is over 30–
40 years.

the base of the graph, in regions where the error percentages are between 10%
and 50%, in order to compensate for the spreading out at the bottom.

The distributions for regression, ARMA, and GRR were drawn from Tables
6.15–6.20, from the columns labeled "Uni." and "extl." They all represent
predictions based on the reduced form of the Deutsch–Solow model, Equations
(6.1) and (6.2), with the bD and fU terms removed, for the same cases defined
in Tables 6.23 and 6.24. The definitions of these procedures may be found in
Section 6.3. The distributions for EXTRAP, described in Section 6.2, were
based on the same model but a slightly different set of sample cases (i.e., data
were not interpolated, because it was not necessary to do so with this program);
see Tables 6.8 and 6.9 for the original data.

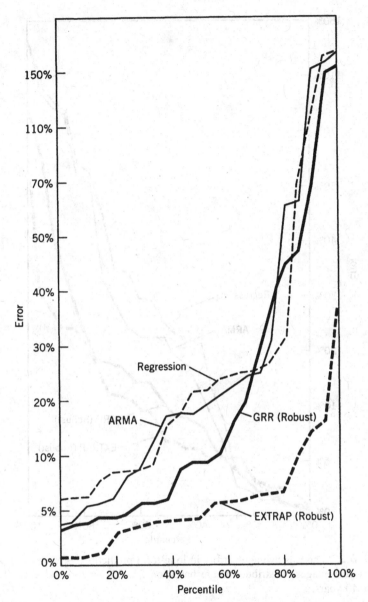

FIGURE 6.2 The rms average errors in long-term predictions of differentiated populations, in percentages. Distributions are based on 21 or 22 cases each. Error is over 30–40 years.

In Figure 6.1, which gives the curves for predicting the assimilated population—for which the comparison between methods is exact—one can see that the robust method yields errors distributed uniformly between 0% and 7%, except for three or four (i.e., probability 20%) "fluke" cases. In predicting the *percentage* of populations assimilated—which is not directly affected by

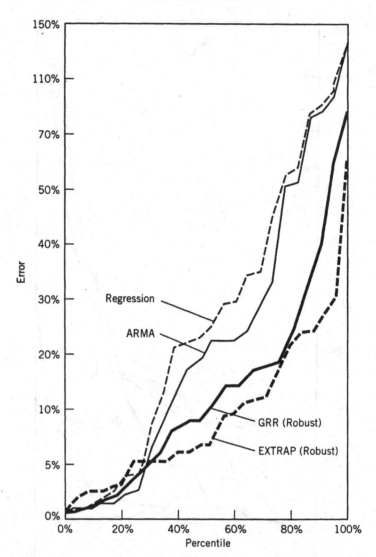

FIGURE 6.3 The rms averages errors in long-term predictions of mobilized populations, in percentages. Distributions are based on 22, 24, or 26 cases each. Error is over 30–40 years.

random population loss in war or the like—Table 6.9 shows a uniform error distribution with the robust method between 0% and 2%, with four "flukes" at 2.68%, 3.08%, 3.09%, and 6.21% errors. Insofar as much of the data here have been encoded in terms of decades, these prediction errors refer to periods of time on the order of 30 or 40 years for the most part.

Tables 6.21 and 6.22 tabulate the predictions of the robust method for assimilation and mobilization in the countries studied, for the years 1980, 1990,

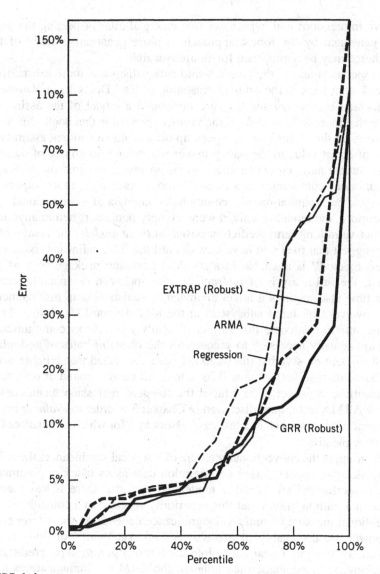

FIGURE 6.4 The rms average errors in long-term predictions of underlying populations. Distributions are based on 22, 24, or 26 cases each. Error is over 30–40 years.

and 2000. It must be emphasized, however, that the model used in generating these predictions—unlike the more complex models discussed later—is not suitable for evaluating the effects of policy in *changing* what the numbers will equal in those years; furthermore, these predictions require care in their interpretation, as discussed in Section 6.3. Sections 6.2 and 6.3 contain the details of the statistical methods that led to these tables and graphs. Also, in keeping with the general philosophy expressed in Chapter 5, I will mention some substantive impressions and hypotheses that emerged after inspecting the predictions generated by the robust approach; a more quantitative study of these hypotheses may be appropriate for future research.

The second strand of the research into nationalism was more substantive in nature. I went back to the original reasoning of Karl Deutsch, in *Nationalism and Social Communications* [1] and formulated a model of the assimilation process that more fully articulates the vision expressed in that book; this model, by describing the forces that can speed up or slow down national assimilation, can be of direct value to the policy-maker who wishes to do one of these two things. Such a more complete articulation, however, required the addition of *intranational* "communications terms," whose evaluation in turn required detailed data on assimilation and communications data at a subnational level. Furthermore, the models involved were strongly nonlinear; before anyone can carry out valid long-term prediction *based on these models*, the results of this thesis suggest that they will have to wait until the full nonlinear version of the "robust method" is available in a standard computer package such as TSP. (Indeed, the full analysis of *interaction terms* between comparable subunits across time also requires a novel approach to statistical data management as well; however, the Janus subsystem at the MIT–Harvard Cambridge Project may be able to overcome this further difficulty.) Insofar as communications terms are actually necessary to account for the *changing* rates of assimilation crucial to Deutsch's verbal discussion, I have concluded that reliable *predictions* based on that discussion will have to await another round of research. In the meantime, however, I have used the standard regression techniques and the new ARMA techniques discussed in Chapter 3 in order to *evaluate* my new communications approach in a test case—Norway—for which intranational data were very plentiful.

According to the conventional measure of statistical significance, the ARMA communications model, based on migration data as an index of communications, outperformed all the other models so well that there is less than one chance in a million billion that this superiority was due to a coincidence. The conventional measure of statistical significance depends on *short-term* predictive power, on the quality of predictions over one "unit" of time. (In this case, one unit means 1 year ahead into the future.) In *long-term* prediction of the percentage of population assimilated, the ARMA communications model made errors that were only about 10% less than the errors with the best competing models. (In this case, long-term errors are the average errors over all possible intervals of prediction from 1 to 30 years into the future; the averages are based on the root-mean-square (rms) averaging procedure, which places greater weight on the largest errors and thus on the longest prediction intervals.) However, given the large, diverse database available, this 10% reduction would appear to be just as significant as the reduction in error in short-term prediction.

In Section 6.5, by looking at the final two studies of the Norway data and also by *comparing* them with my earlier, less perfect studies of the same data, it was possible to extend further the discussion of the regression method and the ARMA method as such. In particular, the significance scores of ARMA models do indeed seem to be more sensitive to the quality of the substantive part of the model and to the quality of the data involved (i.e., flukes) than are those of regression models. On the other hand, the ARMA method shows only a modest improvement over regression in reducing the size of errors in long-term prediction (again, about a 10% reduction in error size), particularly if one's model and data are good to start with; this reinforces the conclusion, from Sections 6.2 and 6.3, that the estimation of model parameters for use in the long-term prediction of real social data is better done by way of the robust approach.

Finally, in the study of the Norway data, I have looked into the possibility of using "gravity models" to reconstruct the networks of interregional communication for years in which no data were available. These models, in standard form, do not allow one to express or explain the changes in communications patterns that underlie the effects of modernization, as discussed by Deutsch and interpreted in Section 6.4. Thus the simple gravity model of internal migration has been generalized in order to remedy this defect, and the validity of this generalization has been established.

6.2 INITIAL STUDIES OF THE DEUTSCH-SOLOW MODEL

Before plunging into the mathematical details of the work on the Deutsch–Kravitz data, let us begin with a general description of the studies carried out. These studies fall into two subcategories. This section will discuss my initial studies in 1971, in which my sole objective was to make use of existing methods and existing models—primarily the Deutsch–Solow model—in order to make concrete predictions of national assimilation and political mobilization. Given that I did not expect to generate or evaluate any new methods as such, and given that the software packages available then did *not* allow long-term forecasting for a linear model structured like the Deutsch–Solow model, I set up special purpose computer programs of my own, tailored to this particular problem alone. Each of these programs included an *estimation* part, to estimate the constants of the Deutsch–Solow model for each nation individually, and a *prediction* portion, to make long-range predictions. Three programs were used, based on three methods of estimation, in the order (1) the Hopkins [2] programs[2], (2) standard regression, and (3) the robust method.

With each of the first two programs, it required no more than a glance at the computer outputs of predicted versus actual values, and of the estimated values of the constants, in order to see that something was not working according to plan. (See Tables 6.1 and 6.4–6.7. The latter group of tables seem

---

[2]These programs were made available by Professor Deutsch at the Harvard Department of Government.

to imply that assimilation was much easier for SERIES to predict than was mobilization. However, in the actual year-by-year printouts, the difference was less; the use of "median error" appears to exaggerate the difference.) It looked as if the main objective of these early studies—the construction of reasonable predictions—was not going to be possible. A more detailed examination of the regression statistics convinced me that *bad estimates* of the constants of the Deutsch–Solow model were at fault, not the model itself, for the large size of the errors; the statistics also hinted very strongly that the bad estimates might be due to the random inaccuracies—"measurement noise"—that afflict all normal sources of data in the social sciences.

At this point, I was very lucky to be unable to do what I wanted to do and to be restricted to a method that recent work has shown to be much better. I wanted to carry out estimation based on the Deutsch–Solow model, with terms added to reflect the presence of "white noise" in data collection, *in addition to* terms reflecting randomness in the process itself; however, I was able to account for white noise in data collection only by *dropping* one substantive term in the Deutsch–Solow equations and by dropping the terms that allow for randomness in the assimilation and mobilization processes themselves. Thus I was unintentionally using a special case of the "measurement-noise-only" method, the "robust method" discussed in Sections 2.7 and 2.11 in Chapter 2. This special case is essentially equivalent to an advanced form of curve-fitting and extrapolation. The predictions of this method were quite good, as discussed in the introduction and illustrated in Figures 6.1–6.4; the graphs for this method are based on Tables 6.8 and 6.9. Having found a method suitable for the purpose, I then modified the computer program to calculate root-mean-square average percentage errors for the predictions of this model.

Now let us look more closely at the mathematics of these three sets of studies. All three studies were based on variations of the revised version of the Deutsch–Solow model.[3] This model includes two equations for the process of national assimilation:

$$\frac{dA}{dt} = aA + bD, \tag{6.1a}$$

$$\frac{dD}{dt} = cD, \tag{6.1b}$$

where A represents the assimilated population and D represents the differentiated population. The first of these equations states that the rate of growth of

---

[3]See Deutsch [1], Appendix V. Several versions of this model have appeared in print. The version here, in all fairness, was actually taken directly from Hopkins, Raymond and Carol, A Difference Equation Model for Mobilization and Assimilation Processes (1969, unpublished); a copy of this paper was provided by Professor Deutsch and described by him as containing the final revision of the model. This revision appears, in difference equation form, in Hopkins [2]. The reasons for the revisions to earlier versions are described in Hopkins [3, p. 381].

the assimilated population A with time is equal to the sum of two different terms. The first of these terms, aA, refers to the natural growth of the assimilated population through births and deaths. It is assumed that a is effectively constant for our purposes; in other words, it is assumed that births and deaths average out to a fixed percentage of the population itself. The second of these terms refers to increases in the assimilated population, due to unassimilated people being assimilated. It is assumed that b is effectively constant; in other words, it is assumed that the number of people assimilated per unit of time averages out to be a fixed percentage of the number of unassimilated people still available. Finally, in the bottom equation, a single term—cD—is enough, mathematically, to express the total effect of both such assumptions on the growth rate of the differentiated population. Also, the "uniqueness" of different countries is acknowledged by acknowledging that a, b, and c will be different in different countries. The Deutsch–Solow model for political mobilization is virtually identical:

$$\frac{dM}{dt} = eM + fU, \tag{6.2a}$$

$$\frac{dU}{dt} = gU, \tag{6.2b}$$

where M is the mobilized population, U the underlying population, e the natural growth rate of the mobilized population, f the rate of mobilization as a fraction of the underlying population, and g a constant analogous to c above. Deutsch [1] and Hopkins [3, p. 381] have discussed in great detail the ability of the model to capture the essence of certain portions of the history of nationalism. Section 6.4 of this chapter will suggest ways in which larger aspects of this history may be captured by extending this model; that section and Chapter 2 also discuss ways in which one can go beyond the initial simplifying assumption that a, b, and c are constant.

Mathematically, Equations (6.1) imply that there exist constants a_1, b_1, and c_1 such that

$$A(t + 1) = a_1 A(t) + b_1 D(t), \tag{6.3a}$$

$$D(t + 1) = c_1 D(t). \tag{6.3b}$$

This time, instead of talking about the *instantaneous* rates of growth of population, we are talking about the total growth over one unit of time, from time t to time $t + 1$. The actual unit could be a year, 5 years, a decade, or anything else we choose. a_1 represents the natural factor of increase of the assimilated population over one unit of time; thus an annual population growth of 3% per year would imply $a_1 = 1.03$. b_1 represents the fraction of the differentiated population that is assimilated *per unit of time*, adjusted slightly for their own natural increase during the period in which they are assimilated. c_1 represents the natural growth factor of the differentiated population *minus* the fraction of the people assimilated. In a similar manner, Equations (6.2) imply that

$$M(t + 1) = e_1 M(t) + f_1 U(t), \tag{6.4a}$$

$$U(t + 1) = g_1 U(t). \tag{6.4b}$$

In order to make actual predictions of assimilation and mobilization data by use of equations (6.3) and (6.4), the major substantive problem is to estimate the values of the "constants" a_1, b_1, c_1, d_1, e_1, and f_1. (In order to be more precise, instead of calling these things "constants," they are referred to hereafter by the mathematical term "parameters"; a parameter is assumed to be fixed *within* a given process (e.g., assimilation in one nation) but may vary from process to process and may also be treated as a kind of unknown variable.) In my initial work in 1971, I used three different methods to estimate these parameters.

First, I tried to use the Hopkins [2] methods.[4] The Hopkins method is based on the assumption that Equations (6.3) and (6.4) are *exactly* true for the measured values of the variables in every country, for the right values of the parameters. Thus if we know $D(t + 1)$ and $D(t)$ for some time t, then we can *solve* for c_1 as an unknown in Equation (6.3b). In a similar way, we can solve for all the other parameters, by use of simple algebraic equations, if we know the values of A, D, M, and U at three consecutive times. In order to solve for these parameters and to carry out predictions on the basis of the resulting estimates, we simply make use of the original Hopkins programs, DELTA and ESTIMATES. Fourteen runs were made, on data from 11 nations, selected from the Deutsch–Kravitz data. The results are shown in Table 6.1. These predictions appear to be extremely poor; a quick examination of the table will make it clear why further effort was not invested in this approach. Indeed, from the point of view of a statistician, as discussed early in Chapter 2, one would not expect to achieve much success with the false assumption that Equations (6.3) or (6.4) are exactly true. Even more emphatically, one would expect that the use of all the data available would give better estimates of the parameters than would a series of only three time points, *given that* the model may be "true" only in a statistical sense.

The next step was to estimate the parameters a_1, b_1, c_1, e_1, f_1, and g_1, by use of the classic statistical method, by multiple regression. More precisely, I fit a regression model of the form

$$A(t + 1) = a_2 A(t) + b_2 D(t) + k_1 + n(t), \tag{6.5a}$$

$$D(t + 1) = c_2 D(t) + k_2 + m(t), \tag{6.5b}$$

---

[4]More precisely, I used the Hopkins routines directly, on sample cases suggested by Professor Hopkins and on a few others.

TABLE 6.1 Sample of Results from DELTA

Nation and Base Years	Predicted Values			Actual Values			% Error	
	Year	Mobil.	Assim.	Year	Mobil.	Assim.	Mobil.	Assim.
Ceylon	1921	1,471	2,791	1921	1,537	2,770	4.29	0.76
1981, 1901, 1911	1951	3,444	4,166	1953	4,509	5,209	23.6	20.0
Thailand 1925*, 1936, 1947	1958	19,926	—	1960	18,381	—	8.4	—
Malaysia	1951	891	3,045	1947	835	2,428	6.7	25.4
1911, 1921, 1931	1961	1,258	4,064	1957	1,425	3,126	11.7	30.0
Ceylon	1885	602	1,302	1881	394	1,698	52.8	23.3
1919*, 1936*, 1953	1902	885	1,815	1901	773	2,141	14.5	15.2
Scotland 1881, 1914*, 1947	1815	0	—	1821	697	—	100.	—
USSR	1970	101,331	—	1965	121,600	—	16.7	—
1928, 1942*, 1956	1914	0	—	1914	25,800	—	100.	—
Malaysia	1905	188	994	1911	193	1,368	2.59	27.3
1931, 1944*, 1957	1918	269	1,316	1921	292	1,569	7.88	16.1
Canada	1901	3,138	2,653	1901	2,014	3,711	55.8	28.5
1941, 1951, 1961	1931	4,838	5,670	1931	5,572	7,000	13.2	19.0
Philippines	1900	870	1,205	1903	1,003	3,219	13.3	62.6
1936*, 1948, 1960	1924	2,960	3,287	1918	3,139	3,977	5.7	17.4
Quebec	1901	1,972	746	1901	645	1,212	206.	38.5
1941, 1951, 1961	1931	2,058	1,903	1931	1,814	2,292	13.5	17.0
Argentina	1915	5,863	5,012	1914	4,157	5,511	41.0	9.05
1930*, 1945*, 1960	1900	5,575	1,857	1892*	1,857	2,733	200.	32.1
Czechoslovakia	1930	5,396	5,960	1930	7,850	7,340	31.3	18.8
1900, 1910, 1920*	1940	4,828	5,588	1937	8,020	7,500	39.8	25.5
India	1911	30,210	294,756	1911	28,482	217,197	6.07	35.7
1881, 1891, 1901	1941	0	0	1941	49,792	270,187	100.	100.
Argentina	1936	17,743	10,879	1930*	6,914	8,625	157.	26.1
1870*, 1892*, 1914	1958	79,683	24,650	1960	14,758	17,440	440.	41.3

All data measured in thousands of people. The asterisk represents estimates from ESTIMATES. Mobil., mobilized population; Assim., assimilated; exact definitions are given in Table 6.10. % Error is a crude percentage from figures listed.

where $n(t)$ and $m(t)$ are error terms to be minimized, and where the parameters a_2, b_2, and c_2 have the same interpretations as a_1, b_1, and c_1. The "constant terms", k_1 and k_2, were added because they tend to be standard in regression studies; otherwise, this model is essentially just another way of interpreting the Deutsch–Solow model, Equations (6.1) or (6.3). In like manner, I fit a regression model of mobilization:

$$M(t + 1) = e_2 M(t) + f_2 U(t) + k_3 + n(t), \qquad (6.6a)$$

$$U(t + 1) = g_2 U(t) + k_4 + m(t). \qquad (6.6b)$$

In addition, a number of standard regression statistics were computed to go with these models. These included the autocorrelations of A, D, M, and U (e.g., the correlation coefficient of $A(t)$ against $A(t + 1)$); they included the *probability* of the proposition that b_2 and f_2—the rates of assimilation and mobilization—might be zero, as measured by standard statistical significance tests; they included the correlations ("multiple R") between the actual and predicted values of $A(t + 1)$; and so on. Statistics of this sort are usually reported as the final results of studies on quantitative political science, as if they themselves were conclusive. Thirty-one runs were made, on 12 nations, again on the Deutsch–Kravitz data. The results are summarized in Tables 6.2 and 6.3.

Looking at these tables, we can see that the values of R, the correlations between the predictions of our model for $A(t + 1)$ or $M(t + 1)$ and the actual values of $A(t + 1)$ or $M(t)$, tend to be very close to 100%. Thus one would expect these regression models to have unusually great predictive power. Also, b_2 and e_2, the rates of assimilation and mobilization in Equations (6.5) and (6.6), tend to be very large; this hints that all terms of the Deutsch–Solow model are justified and measurable quantitatively. However, the autocorrelations, r_M and r_A, also tend to be very large. Given the short length of the data series, this would imply that there is not much information (residual variation) here about those components of $A(t + 1)$ and $M(t + 1)$ that cannot be predicted from knowledge of $A(t)$ and $M(t)$ alone; indeed, the standard errors of b_2 and f_2 turned out to be very large, implying large expected errors in the estimation of these parameters. Even so, in a number of cases, b_2 and f_2 were significantly different from zero, despite the large standard errors, enough to validate the importance of the cross-terms, $b_2 D(t)$ and $f_2 U(t)$. (Note that "significantly different from zero" means that there was a low *probability* that they could actually be zero, according to the usual significance measure. When b_2 is estimated to be large, but the estimation error appears to be larger yet, then the true value of b_2 might just as well equal zero.) When b_2 or f_2 is not significantly different from zero, but still apparently large, and when both R_M and r_M or R_A and r_A are near to 100%, one would expect *both* the regression model *and* the autocorrelation model (i.e., Equations (6.5) with the bD term removed, or Equations (6.6) with the fU term removed) to have unusually great predictive power.

TABLE 6.2 Regression Statistics for Mobilized and Underlying Populations

Nation	Database	r_M	g	R_M	f	SE of f	P of f
Ceylon	1811–1921	.999	.834	1.000	−0.26	0.241	.3
Cyprus	1881–1931	.999	.996	.999	−0.082	0.095	.4
Taiwan	1960–1966	.999	.999	.999	0.051	0.146	.7
USSR	1950–1965	.999	.703	.999	0.484	0.206	.02
Finland	1800–1960	.996	.988	.996	0.002	0.030	.9
USA	1790–1960	.995	.998	.995	0.168	0.112	.15
Japan	1920–1940	.440	.307	.995	2.73	0.310	.01
Finland	1958–1967	.993	.976	.994	0.581	0.532	.3
Quebec	1851–1961	.992	.917	.994	1.13	0.745	.15
Quebec	1901–1961	.981	.885	.993	3.03	1.27	.05
Finland	1880–1960	.992	.965	.992	0.036	0.128	.75
Canada	1851–1961	.989	.983	.991	−0.85	0.632	.2
USSR	1922–1931	.986	.991	.990	0.281	0.167	.1
USA	1880–1960	.986	.989	.987	1.03	1.24	.45
Canada	1901–1961	.974	.992	.983	−1.96	1.56	.2
Belgium	1880–1930	.952	.318	.972	−4.54	3.85	.3
India	1881–1941	.969	.902	.970	−0.1	0.2	.7
Japan	1920–1960	.923	.519	.948	0.874	0.576	.15

f is the estimate of f_2, the rate of mobilization, in the regression model (6.6a). The SE of f is the standard error of f, the conventional measure of the likely size of errors in the estimate of f. P of f is the probability that an estimate of f this large or larger (of *either* sign) would have happened by coincidence for an f that is zero, *according* to conventional theory. g is the estimate of g_2, the natural growth factor for the underlying population, *minus* the rate of mobilization, in Equations (6.6b); it is also a close approximation to the autocorrelation of the size of the underlying population. R_M is the multiple correlation coefficient between the predictions of Equations (6.6) for mobilization and the actual values; r_M is the autocorrelation of mobilization. Data definitions are given in Table 6.10; cases are listed in order of R_M here.

TABLE 6.3 Regression Statistics for Assimilated and Differentiated Populations

Nation	Database	r_A	c	R_A	b	SE of b	P of b
Taiwan	1956–1965	1.000	.997	1.000	−0.031	0.065	.6
Quebec	1901–1961	.998	.938	1.000	−1.7	0.406	.01
Cyprus	1881–1931	.999	.991	.999	−1.91	1.41	.2
USA	1790–1960	.998	.971	.999	3.489	0.927	.01
Israel	1951–1967	.998	.969	.998	−1.29	1.20	.3
USA	1880–1960	.994	.934	.998	9.939	3.11	.01
Finland	1880–1960	.996	.464	.996	−0.57	0.69	.45
Taiwan	1946–1965	.994	.999	.996	0.104	0.049	.05
Israel	1951–1960	.994	.999	.994	0.795	3.90	.85
Canada	1901–1961	.972	.981	.991	0.815	0.326	.05
Belgium	1880–1930	.915	.915	.942	0.391	0.421	.4
India	1881–1941	.863	.976	.922	2.44	1.67	.15
Ceylon	1881–1921	.814	.994	.847	0.376	0.862	.7

b is the estimate of b_2, the assimilation rate, in the regression model (6.5). The SE of b is the standard error of b, the usual measure of the likely size of errors in the estimate of b. P of b is the probability that an estimate of b this large or larger (of *either* sign) would have happened by coincidence if b is actually zero, *according* to conventional theory. c is the estimate of c_2, the natural growth factor of the differentiated population *minus* the assimilation rate as in Equation (6.5b). R_A is the multiple correlation coefficient, between the predictions of Equations (6.5) for assimilation and the actual values; r_A is the autocorrelation of assimilation. Data definitions are given in Table 6.10; cases are listed in order of R_A here.

For our purposes, however, it was not enough simply to look at the regression statistics. The multiple correlation coefficient, R_A, is a reasonable measure of the ability to predict $A(t + 1)$ from knowledge of $A(t)$ and $D(t)$, with the help of Equations (6.5); however, true long-range prediction entails the ability to predict $A(t + T)$ from $A(t)$ and $D(t)$, *without* knowledge of intermediate values of A and D, for time differences, T, which may be very large. In order to carry out and test such predictions, based on Equations (6.5) or (6.6), for all possible values of T, I wrote a special-purpose program, SERIES, in FORTRAN. In each test case, for assimilation or mobilization in one country, SERIES computed the standard regression statistics, shown in Table 6.2 or 6.3, and estimated the parameters of model (6.5) or (6.6). Model (6.5), with the error terms removed, corresponds to a unique real differential equation of the form

$$\frac{dA}{dt} = a_3 A + b_3 D + k_5, \tag{6.7a}$$

$$\frac{dD}{dt} = C_3 D + k_6. \tag{6.7b}$$

Note that these equations are essentially the same as the original Deutsch–Solow equations for assimilation, (6.1), with only a couple of constant terms added. SERIES would begin by using regression to estimate a_2, b_2, c_2, k_1, and k_2 in Equations (6.5); then, by solving the corresponding equations, (6.7), it could calculate the values of a_3, b_3, c_3, k_5, and k_6 corresponding to those estimates; finally, by using its solution of Equations (6.7), it could then predict $A(t + T)$ and $D(t + T)$, for *any* T, even T values that are not whole numbers, from the initial data, $A(t)$ and $D(t)$, at any time period t. For comparison purposes, SERIES also carried out a parallel set of estimations and predictions, based on Equations (6.5) and (6.7) with the bD terms removed. This corresponds, in effect, to assuming that assimilation is proportional to the population *already assimilated*, when we try to predict the assimilated population. The procedures to predict $M(t + T)$ and $U(t + T)$, based on Equations (6.6), were essentially identical to those described earlier for $A(t + T)$ and $D(t + T)$.

Thirty-one runs were carried out with SERIES, based on data from 12 countries, selected from the Deutsch–Kravitz data. In each country, SERIES actually printed out the prediction and error for every individual year; however, it would be impossible to reproduce all that output here. Thus Tables 6.4–6.7 contain a list of the median errors, in numerical and percentage form, for each run. From a formal statistical point of view, Tables 6.15 and 6.18, to be discussed in Section 6.3, give a more standard measure of the validity of the regression methods as such. However, these earlier results do retain some interest.

TABLE 6.4 Long-Term Prediction Errors with SERIES in Predicting Mobilization

Nation	Database	Base Year	Median Error Model	Median Error Uni.	Median Size	% Error Model	% Error Uni.
Taiwan	1960–1966	1960	4	5	3,340	0.120	0.150
Cyprus	1881–1931	1901	0.18	0.12	48	0.375	0.250
Ceylon	1881–1921	1901	19	9	773	2.46	1.16
India	1881–1941	1901	792	697	28,500	2.78	2.45
Belgium	1880–1930	1900	171	53	3,846	4.45	1.38
Finland	1880–1960	1880	31	40	642	4.83	6.23
Canada	1901–1961	1911	149	524	5,572	2.67	9.40
Japan	1920–1960	1930	3,739	2,680	20,022	18.7	13.4
USA	1790–1960	1830	1,550	1,780	12,000	12.9	23.2
Finland	1800–1960	1800	193	123	642	30.1	19.2
USSR	1950–1965	1965	64,000	1,000	78,500	81.5	1.28
Canada	1851–1961	1871	2,609	347	2,644	98.7	13.1
Japan	1920–1940	1930	10,336	5,482	20,022	51.6	27.4
Quebec	1901–1961	1911	703	211	710	99.0	29.7
USA	1880–1960	1880	9,850	4,610	12,000	82.1	38.4
USSR	1922–1931	1924	19,000	Huge	78,500	24.2	Huge
Finland	1958–1967	1958	824	607	642	128.	94.5

In each case, that is, a row in this table, the coefficients of Equations (6.6), the full Deutsch–Solow model, and of the univariate (Uni.) form of this model (i.e., with the fU term removed) were estimated by regression over the database. Then, starting from real data in the base year, predictions were made to *all* years for which data were available in that case. (See Table 6.10 for data definitions.) The median of the prediction errors, across the years, is shown in thousands in the two columns on the left, first for the full model, then the univariate; from the median mobilization, a rough median percentage error was calculated whose limitations and downward bias are mentioned in the text.

TABLE 6.5 Long-Term Prediction Errors with SERIES in Predicting the Underlying Population

Nation	Database	Base Year	Median Error	Median Size	% Error
Taiwan	1960–1966	1960	4	8,562	0.047
Canada	1901–1961	1911	11	4,805	0.229
Belgium	1880–1930	1900	40	3,184	1.26
Finland	1880–1960	1880	35	2,529	1.38
Ceylon	1881–1921	1901	39	2,793	1.40
Cyprus	1881–1931	1901	3.9	208	1.88
India	1881–1941	1901	5,785	274,518	2.11
Canada	1851–1961	1871	102	3,645	2.80
Finland	1958–1967	1958	81	2,529	3.20
USA	1880–1960	1880	1,760	33,000	5.33
Finland	1800–1960	1800	150	2,529	5.93
Quebec	1901–1961	1911	75	1,017	7.37
Japan	1920–1940	1930	3,906	46,358	8.43
USA	1790–1960	1830	4,970	33,000	15.1
Japan	1920–1960	1930	7,220	46,358	15.6
USSR	1950–1965	1965	39,000	109,200	35.7
USSR	1922–1931	1924	45,560	109,200	41.7

In each case (i.e., a row in the table), the constants of Equations (6.6), the Deutsch–Solow model, were estimated by regression over the database. (Note that the univariate version is the same as the full Deutsch–Solow model in predicting the underlying population.) Then, from real data in the base year, predictions were made to *all* years for which data were available in that case. (See Table 6.10 for data definitions.) The median of the prediction errors across the years is tabulated in thousands; from the median size of the underlying population, a rough median percentage error was calculated whose downward bias is mentioned in the text.

Looking at Tables 6.4–6.7, we can see that SERIES did at least a plausible job of prediction. The median errors run to 10 to 15 percentage points for prediction periods on the order of a half-century. The contrast with Table 6.1 is quite clear. In only one case—the case of mobilization in th USSR—do the Hopkins programs appear to outperform SERIES in predicting one test year (1920). However, in that case, the model used by SERIES was fitted to a database much further away from the test year, relative to the *length* of the database itself, than was the database used with the Hopkins routines; furthermore, the database used with the Hopkins routines, in this case, included only one time point on the early side of World War II, a war that appears to have had a major effect in perturbing the population of the USSR. A perfect comparison, of course, is impossible, since the Hopkins routines by nature require a more limited database than that of SERIES; however, the *overall* performance of the Hopkins routines, over the cases tested, was clearly inferior to the overall performance of SERIES. With both regression models—the full model and the model with b_2 or f_2 removed—the predictions made from a

TABLE 6.6 Long-Term Prediction Errors with SERIES in Predicting Assimilation

Nation	Database	Base Year	Median Error Model	Median Error Uni.	Median Size	% Error Model	% Error Uni.
Taiwan	1956–1965	1955	9	9	899	1.00	1.00
Cyprus	1881–1931	1901	2	3	199	1.01	1.51
Israel	1951–1967	1960	21	25	1,859	1.13	1.34
Israel	1951–1960	1953	25	37	1,859	1.34	1.99
Quebec	1901–1961	1911	41	52	2,270	1.81	2.29
Finland	1880–1960	1880	51	61	2,754	1.85	2.21
Taiwan	1946–1965	1955	14	22	899	1.56	2.45
Belgium	1880–1930	1900	56	76	2,705	2.07	2.81
India	1881–1941	1901	3,531	9,170	216,249	1.63	4.24
Ceylon	1881–1921	1901	56	32	827	6.78	3.87
Canada	1901–1961	1911	582	205	5,381	10.8	3.81
USA	1790–1960	1830	7,960	5,338	38,496	20.7	13.9
USA	1880–1960	1880	253,207	3,660	38,496	658.	9.51

In each case (i.e., a row in this table), the coefficients of Equations (6.5), the full Deutsch–Solow model, and of the univariate form of this model (i.e., Equation (6.5a) with the bD term removed) were estimated by regression over the database. Then, starting from real data in the base year, predictions were made to *all* years for which data were available in that case. (See Table 6.10 for data definitions.) The median of the errors in prediction, across the years, is shown in the two columns on the left, in thousands, first for the full model and then for the univariate; from the median values of assimilation, a rough median percentage error was calculated whose downward bias is discussed in the text.

TABLE 6.7 Long-Term Prediction Errors with SERIES in Predicting the Differentiated Population

Nation	Database	Base Year	Median Error	Median Size	% Error
Israel	1951–1960	1953	1	230	0.434
Ceylon	1881–1921	1901	29	2,739	1.06
Taiwan	1946–1965	1955	87	8,175	1.06
Taiwan	1956–1965	1955	101	8,175	1.24
Cyprus	1881–1931	1901	1	57	1.75
India	1881–1941	1901	1,542	85,803	1.80
Belgium	1880–1930	1900	83	4,336	1.91
Israel	1951–1967	1960	5	230	2.17
Finland	1880–1960	1880	11	393	2.80
Quebec	1901–1961	1911	19	605	3.14
Canada	1901–1961	1911	403	4,996	8.07
USA	1790–1960	1830	920	6,491	14.2
USA	1880–1960	1880	5,563	6,491	85.7

In each case (i.e., a row in the table), the constants of the Deutsch–Solow model (6.5) were estimated by regression over the database. Then, from real data in the base year, predictions were made for *all* years for which data were available in that case. (See Table 6.10 for data definitions.) The median of the prediction errors, across the years, is tabulated in thousands (here, univariate predictions are the same as full model predictions); from the median size of the differentiated population, a rough median percentage error was calculated whose downward bias is mentioned in the text.

smaller database held up fairly well over a later test range, in comparison with predictions made from a longer database.

On the other hand, the full model (*including b_2 or f_2*) performed worse, not better, than the reduced model. If a better estimate of b_2 or f_2 would improve the predictions of model (6.5) or (6.6), then one must conclude that the estimates produced by regression are worse than the estimates produced by arbitrarily setting b_2 and f_2 to zero; if we believe, from a priori knowledge and from Tables 6.2 and 6.3, that b_2 and f_2 are substantially different from zero and that the data do give us some knowledge about this difference, then we must conclude that regression does a poor job of accounting for the existing evidence regarding the values of these parameters. Insofar as a simple model, like (6.5) or (6.6), is too difficult and complex for classical regression to handle, then the development of more complex and more realistic models would indeed require new techniques. Furthermore, *the predictions of both the simple and complex models, while reasonable, were not nearly as good as the high values of R and r seemed to portend.* Therefore, in attempting to generate good predictions, I decided to waste no more effort on this fruitless approach.

Finally, in the third initial study, I considered the possibility that the deficiencies of the regression models were due to measurement noise problems, as discussed in Chapter 5. Indeed, in Tables 6.2 and 6.3, one can see that the autocorrelations—r—do not seem to be much higher for data measured by years than for data measured by decades; this implies that the *predictability* of the underlying process is not much less over longer time intervals, and that the gap between the observed correlations and a perfect correlation of 100% may be largely due to data measurement error.[5] If the ARMA techniques discussed in Chapter 3 had been available at this time to fit all the parameters in the full model, (6.3) and (6.4), they would have been used; fortunately, however, there was no choice but to use a different method, which has turned out to be superior.

In order to make *some* allowance for measurement error, I found myself forced to eliminate the cross-terms in the original Deutsch–Solow model, Equations (6.1), to get

$$\frac{dA}{dt} = a_4 A, \tag{6.8a}$$

$$\frac{dD}{dt} = c_4 D. \tag{6.8b}$$

In predicting the differentiated population, this is equivalent to the original model; in predicting the assimilated population, this is equivalent to assuming that the number of people assimilated per unit of time is proportional to the number *already assimilated* and that a_4 incorporates the sum of the effects of natural growth *and* assimilation. It was necessary to assume that these equations are *exactly* true for the true underlying values of D and A. By making these strong assumptions, I was able to cope with the possibility that the *recorded values* of $A(t)$ and $D(t)$, which may be called $A'(t)$ and $D'(t)$, are different from the *true* values, $A(t)$ and $D(t)$. This possibility can be expressed by writing

$$A'(t) = A(t) + m(t)A(t), \tag{6.9a}$$

$$D'(t) = D(t) + n(t)D(t), \tag{6.9b}$$

where $m(t)$ and $n(t)$ are random error terms that one tries to minimize. Note that I decided to minimize the measurement errors as a *percentage* of the true values, rather than minimizing their absolute values; when the population values grow by a large factor, it seems reasonable to expect that the absolute size of the measurement errors will grow along with them. This model, which makes allowance for *measurement* noise only, is a simple application of the measure-

---

[5]Chapter 5 noted that the correlation across n intervals of time, when both process noise and measurement noise might be present, would equal $\phi^2 r^n$, where ϕ is the correlation involved with measurement noise, and r is the true correlation across time of the process underneath. When this figure changes very little with increases in n but is substantially different from 1 for various values of n, then it would seem that r is very close to 1 and that ϕ is not.

ment-noise-only approach—the robust approach discussed in Section 2.7 of Chapter 2. In this simple case, for $m(t)$ and $n(t)$ much less than 1 (e.g., about 10%), the use of this model reduces to the use of sophisticated curve-fitting. More exactly, Equations (6.8) and (6.9) imply a close approximation[6] to the simple regression models

$$\log A'(t) = k_7 + a_4 t + m(t), \tag{6.10a}$$

$$\log D'(t) = k_8 + c_4 t + n(t), \tag{6.10b}$$

where k_7 and k_8, like a_4 and c_4, are parameters to be estimated and are defined as

$$k_7 = \log A(0), \tag{6.11a}$$

$$k_8 = \log D(0). \tag{6.11b}$$

After using simple regression to estimate these parameters, one may go on to use Equations (6.10) to predict A and D at other times:

$$A(t) = e^{k_7 + a_4 t}, \tag{6.12a}$$

$$D(t) = e^{k_8 + c_4 t}. \tag{6.12b}$$

The procedure used in predicting mobilization by this method is exactly analogous. For the third initial study, I wrote a FORTRAN program, EXTRAP, to fit such a model to the Deutsch–Kravitz data; 47 runs were carried out over 17 nations, as shown in Tables 6.8 and 6.9. The large number of runs were possible because EXTRAP, unlike SERIES or DELTA, *did not require* that the database used in fitting the model involve measurements at regular intervals only; Equations (6.10) do *not* refer to a standard interval of time separation between t and $t + 1$.

The results from using EXTRAP are shown in Tables 6.8 and 6.9. (Table 6.10 gives the definitions for the indices.) The root-mean-square (rms) average percentage errors in predicting the various *populations*—assimilated, mobilized, underlying, and differentiated—have been graphed and are shown in Figures 6.1–6.4.

From these graphs, it is clear that EXTRAP performs surprisingly well. In the case of assimilation, the prediction errors were uniformly distributed between 0% and 7% in 80% of the cases; in 20% (four) of the cases, they were much larger. A case-by-case reexamination of the outlying 20% suggested to us that unusual factors—war or chronic depopulation for economic reasons—

---

[6]The approximation here is that $\exp(1 + a)$ is approximately equal to $1 + a$, with only about 0.5% error when a is about 10%. More precisely, if we take the exponential function of both sides of Equations (6.10), and substitute in from (6.12), the approximation rule cited here brings us back to Equations (6.9).

TABLE 6.8   The rms Average Errors of Predictions of Mobilized and Underlying Populations, by EXTRAP

Nation	Database	Mobil. Error	Under. Error	% Mobil. Error
Taiwan	1960–1966	0.4%	0.4%	0.17%
India	1881–1941	9.5%	3.4%	0.57%
Ceylon	1881–1953	2.8%	3.4%	0.57%
USSR	All[a]	2.5%	4.1%	0.80%
Malaysia	1911–1957	5.1%	3.3%	0.81%
CSSR	1900–1937	2.5%	2.9%	0.83%
Belgium	1880–1931	5.3%	0.9%	1.09%
Israel	1952–1967	1.8%	4.4%	1.18%
Finland[b]	1880–1960	6.1%	6.1%	1.86%
Canada	1901–1961	6.6%	4.6%	2.01%
Quebec	1851–1961	6.8%	5.1%	2.18%
USSR	1950–1965	3.2%	6.5%	2.23%
Argentina	1869–1960	12.2%	17.8%	2.28%
Quebec	1901–1961	5.1%	4.1%	2.36%
Canada	1851–1961	11.0%	4.9%	2.38%
USA	1790–1960	61.7%	28.8%	2.72%
Cyprus[c]	1881–1960	21.8%	8.3%	3.73%
Philippines	1903–1960	6.1%	3.9%	3.77%
Finland	All[a]	9.3%	11.8%	3.79%
USA	1880–1960	11.5%	25.6%	3.98%
Finland	1958–1967	5.2%	340.3%	5.08%
Japan	1920–1960	16.6%	12.2%	6.38%
USSR	1922–1931	30.2%	72.7%	8.03%
Finland	1800–1960	23.8%	24.0%	8.18%
Scotland	1821–1961	24.0%	40.6%	10.05%
Japan	1920–1940	27.3%	22.2%	10.24%

In each case (except Finland), we have given the average of the percentage errors as averaged across predictions to *every year* for which data were available. (See Table 6.10 for data definitions.) The three columns, in order, give (1) the average of the percentage errors in predicting mobilized population, (2) the average of percentage errors in predicting underlying population, and (3) the average of the *absolute* errors in predicting the *percentage* of population that is mobilized. Cases are listed in order of the latter.
[a]Union of all data bases shown in this table.
[b]Test years *only* include database proper.
[c]Errors less than 2% uniformly for runs made over early data, used by SERIES.

were at work on *all* components of the population in these cases; for example, the USSR, Japan, and Cyprus, when predicted from before World War II to after, were prominent among the outliers. Thus one suspects that the *percentage* of assimilation given by the model might be substantially more reliable in such cases. Indeed, when the error in predicting the *percentage* assimilated or mobilized is tabulated (shown in the rightmost columns of Tables 6.8 and 6.9),

TABLE 6.9 The rms Average Errors of Predictions of Assimilated and Differentiated Populations, by EXTRAP

Nation	Database	Assim. Error	Diff. Error	% Assim. Error
Japan	1948–1965	0.9%	4.3%	0.03%
Scotland	1891–1963	4.4%	4.0%	0.14%
Israel	1951–1966	1.0%	1.1%	0.16%
India	1881–1941	4.0%	4.1%	0.37%
Israel	1951–1959	1.4%	3.6%	0.39%
Canada (B)	1931–1961	4.6%	0.9%	0.57%
Cyprus	1881–1960	2.0%	6.4%	0.61%
Quebec (A)	1901–1961	2.9%	6.6%	0.75%
Belgium	1880–1947	4.6%	3.3%	0.80%
Finland	1880–1960	1.9%	10.5%	1.04%
Canada (A)	1901–1961	5.2%	2.8%	1.10%
USA	1790–1960	27.3%	16.4%	1.11%
Ceylon	1881–1963	8.8%	6.3%	1.12%
Quebec (B)	1931–1961	0.8%	5.8%	1.22%
CSSR	1900–1937	1.1%	5.8%	1.41%
Philippines	1903–1961	5.7%	4.0%	1.68%
Malaysia	1911–1957	3.3%	5.5%	2.05%
Taiwan	1956–1965	18.1%	0.7%	2.68%
Taiwan	1946–1965	38.3%	0.7%	3.08%
USA	1880–1960	10.7%	14.5%	3.09%
Argentina	1869–1960	5.0%	37.2%	6.21%

In each case, we give the average of the percentage errors, averaged across predictions to *every year* for which data were available. (See Table 6.10 for data definitions.) The three columns, in order, give (1) the average of the percentage errors in predicting assimilated population, (2) the average of the percentage errors in predicting the differentiated population, and (3) the average of the *absolute* errors in predicting the *percentage* of population that is assimulated. Cases are listed in order of the latter.

the performance of the model looks still better. In the case of assimilation, there was a uniform distribution of error between 0% and 2% in 80% of the cases; in the remaining four outliers, the percentages of error were 2.68%, 3.08%, 3.09%, and 6.21%. Looking at the choices of database and base year indicated in these tables, we can see that these predictions were made over fairly long intervals of time; in 25 out of 47 cases, the total interval, from the earliest database year to the last test year, was at least 60 years. It strikes me as significant, however, that the mobilization process is less predictable than the assimilation process by these methods; one might suspect that mobilization is more easily influenced by the fluctuations of variables not accounted for in any of these simple models—variables such as economic development—and that it is less rigidly governed by inertia.

The performance of EXTRAP was not only good, it was substantially superior to the performances of the regression method and of the ARMA method.

TABLE 6.10   Indices of Mobilization and Assimilation from the Deutsch-Kravitz Data Used for Runs Reported in Tables 6.1-6.9

Argentina   M = Urban. (b); A = Ethnicity (average of series).
Canada   M = Urban.; A = English-Speaking Only (DELTA);
                             = Ethnicity British Isles (SERIES);
                             = Not French Ethnicity (EXTRAP A);
                             = Not French-Speaking Only (EXTRAP B).
Ceylon   M = Literacy; A = Buddhist, except in SERIES, where A = Hindu.
     (Comparison of univariate models still possible by symmetry.)
Cyprus   M = Urban.; A = Greek Orthodox (SERIES);
                            = Not Moslem (civilian) (EXTRAP)
CSSR = Czechoslovakia   M = Urban.; A = Ethnicity Czech. (Deutsch
                   estimates; Bohemia, Moravia, Silesia only.)
Belgium   M = Urban.; A = French-Speaking Only
Finland   M = Urban.; A = Finnish-Speaking
India   M = Urban.; A = Hindu. Deutsch population estimations.
Israel   M = Urban.; A = Total Jews
Japan   M = Urban.; A = Not Korean. Five-year data interval.
Malaysia   M = Urban., A = Malayan Ethnicity
Philippines   M = Literacy; A = Visayan Ethnicity.
Scotland   M = Urban.; A = Speaks No Gaelic
Taiwan   M = Urban.; A = Mainland Chinese
Thailand   M = Literacy
USA   M = Urban.; A = White
USSR   M = Urban.

Urban. means urbanization.

In Figures 6.1–6.4, the error distribution of EXTRAP is substantially lower than the distributions of all other routines, except for GRR. GRR is a slightly altered form of EXTRAP, written to allow an exact comparison of the robust method against the other two methods—regression and ARMA— in the more recent phase of research. The curves for the ARMA and regression method, shown in these graphs, are based on the same reduced form of the Deutsch–Solow model, Equations (6.8), that were used with EXTRAP; the details are mentioned in the next section. (Section 6.6.1 discusses and dismisses another possible source of bias.) The curves for the robust method—EXTRAP and GRR—are lower or equal to the other curves essentially across *all* the probability distributions, from the worst 10% to the best 10%. On the whole, they look about one-half the size of the other curves in true area; they are particularly low in the critical region, from the 40th to the 80th worst percentiles, in which prediction errors are large enough to cost the decision-maker heavily, but normal enough that they can be reduced.

In comparing Tables 6.8 and 6.9 against Tables 6.3–6.7, one can also see that EXTRAP was superior to the old regression procedure, SERIES, which was based on the full Deutsch–Solow model. The contrast is particularly graphic when one inspects the computer outputs of predicted versus actual values for individual years. Unfortunately, these outputs are far too lengthy to be included here; thus we must content ourselves to note that the comparison between EXTRAP and SERIES was *consistent* with the pattern that has been established more objectively by the more recent studies of Section 6.3. Tables 6.8 and 6.9 use a "high" measurement of error, which tends to place greater weight on the largest errors in one's sample; Tables 6.4–6.7 use a "low" measurement of error, median error. Thus the superiority of EXTRAP is greater than indicated by a direct comparison of the tables. (SERIES would have been expanded to include a printout of rms average error if its predictions had been competitive enough to justify further work.) Still, Tables 6.4 and 6.6 do allow us to see that the *reduced* form of the Deutsch–Solow model, Equations (6.5) and (6.6) with the *bD* and *fU* terms removed, performs better than the original form of these equations, with regression, when the *same* measure of error is used; thus the inferiority of the former to the robust method, as shown in Section 6.3, implies an even greater inferiority of the latter. Also, a direct comparison of the printouts indicated a similar or worse performance by this early regression procedure, relative to that of the newer regression procedure, which was described in the graphs; it indicated an inferiority to EXTRAP by at least a factor of 2. For example, in Table 6.9, EXTRAP looks especially bad in predicting the U.S. differentiated population; however, looking at the printout from EXTRAP, for 1790–1960, a *median* error of 230 shows up, versus 920 for SERIES. As percentages of the median size of the differentiated population, these numbers correspond to 3.5% and 14.2%, respectively. In Table 6.7, SERIES looks especially good in predicting the differentiated population of Finland; in the printouts, however, EXTRAP shows a median error of 8.0, versus 11 for SERIES (i.e., 2.0% and 2.8% errors, respectively.) Thus Tables 6.8 and 6.9 provide a stiff test of the ability of EXTRAP to predict the future over long time intervals. They include several tests of prediction from a model fit to one database, to later and earlier sets of data.

From the substantive point of view, it is especially interesting to note what sort of situations have been hardest for EXTRAP to deal with. Japan, Cyprus, and the USSR have the largest recorded errors. An inspection of the actual printouts suggests that they all fit the growth patterns predicted by EXTRAP quite well, except for a breakpoint in World War II. At World War II, the curves shifted by a constant factor, but, except for the resulting change in scale, they seemed to continue on as before the war. This situation is reminiscent of a linear system, affected by a "delta function impulse" (i.e., a transient shock) in the mathematics of engineering and physics; the effect of the shock is to move the system abruptly from one configuration to another, but the *same* dynamic equations continue to govern the system after the shock as before it. Professor George E. Box, in a brief visit to Harvard, mentioned that his group is working on a form of "intervention analysis," which would be suitable for the statistical study of such discontinuities.

The errors in Scottish "mobilization" appear related to the much-discussed "rural depopulation" of Britain, an issue comparable to the issue of Appalachia in the United States. The errors in Scotland appear to depend on the inclusion of data from a full century and a half, a period encompassing different economic trends. Errors were also large, on occasion, when a short database was used to develop a model for predicting over much larger intervals of time (e.g., in Finland); this observation reinforces the emphasis on using a database that is large in actual time, as discussed in Chapter 5. Looking at these two extreme cases—Finland and Scotland—one would be tempted to suggest that the ideal length of the database, per case of data, is somewhere in the middle, somewhere on the order of only twice the interval of time over which one is trying to predict. However, as in Section 2.7 of Chapter 2, one must distinguish between *qualitative* improvements in one's models and *quantitative* estimation of the coefficients of a model, which has already been specified and which one knows to be oversimplified. Here one is dealing with the latter problem; with the former problem, I suspect that the longest possible database would be desirable.

In two other cases—the United States and Argentina—moderately large errors may be related to changes in both birth rates and death rates in different ethnic groups during the periods studied; as with Scotland, one might consider these errors symptomatic of too long a database for the simple model under consideration.

6.3 LATER STUDIES OF THE DEUTSCH-SOLOW MODEL

Let us begin our discussion here from a general point of view, as in the previous section, and hold back the mathematical details until after the overall pattern is clear.

After the work discussed in the previous section, it was clear that I had run up against a *general* methodological problem, which goes well beyond the requirements of the Deutsch–Solow model itself. Therefore, in order to cope with this problem, I wrote a new computer routine, ARMA—discussed at length in Chapter 3, for inclusion in a standard computer statistical package for the social scientist (i.e., the Cambridge Project Time Series Processor, TSP). According to classical maximum likelihood theory, the basis of the arguments in Chapter 3, this routine should have been the answer to the problem of simple "measurement noise." Included in this routine was a provision to test the long-term predictive power *both* of a regression model and of the corresponding ARMA model. Generality, however, required that I *remove* the special-purpose differential equation solver used in SERIES and in EXTRAP, a tool that had allowed me to cope more exactly with the Deutsch–Solow model and the Deutsch–Kravitz data (Tables 6.11–6.24).

When the ARMA routine was applied to the Deutsch–Kravitz data, using several different versions of the Deutsch–Solow model, I found consistently that: (1) according to the usual measure of statistical significance, the ARMA models were indeed superior to the corresponding regression models, with p — the probability that this was a mere coincidence—less than .01 in most cases (see Tables 6.11 and 6.12); (2) in terms of *long-term predictive power*, the ARMA models did *not* do very much better than the regression models; they led consistently to a reduction in the size of prediction errors, but only by about

TABLE 6.11 Statistics Concerning Regression for Mobilized and Underlying Populations

Nation and Database	f_1	Log P $f \neq 0$	Log P ARMA Max.	Log P ARMA Uni.
USSR (1)	0.006	2.4	11.4	11.8
USSR (3)	0.030	4.2	8.7	9.8
Argentina (2)	0.612	6.1	8.2	9.0
CSSR	0.316	0.6	10.2	9.0
Malaysia	−0.046	6.8	5.7	8.3
USA (2)	0.083	0.5	7.9	8.3
Cyprus	0.315	2.9	12.6	8.1
India	−0.142	3.8	7.4	7.0
Philippines	0.087	0.2	6.7	6.6
USA (1)	0.027	1.0	7.0	6.5
Ceylon	−0.013	0.3	6.2	6.1
Taiwan	−0.044	1.7	10.6	6.0
Canada	−0.035	0.1	4.8	4.8
Israel (2)	0.292	7.8	4.0	4.6
USSR (2)	−0.047	1.6	4.2	4.5
Finland (1)	−0.157	0.3	4.5	4.4
Quebec	0.005	0.0	4.5	3.8
Argentina (1)	0.860	1.9	7.3	3.5
Finland (2)	−0.008	0.4	8.0	3.5
*** Log P (ARMA Uni.) Significant Above This Line ***				
Israel (1)	0.493	5.6	6.3	1.8
Finland (3)	−0.037	1.2	4.9	0.4
Japan	0.419	0.1	3.2	0.4
Belgium	0.164	3.1	4.6	0.07

f_1 is the value of the rate of mobilization in Equation (6.4a) as estimated by ordinary regression. Log P is the standard, classical statistical measure of the relative likelihood of one model in comparison with another; it represents the natural logarithm of the odds in favor of the truth of the model we are interested in, compared with some other model, if we assume that both models had an equal chance of being true a priori. (See Section 5.5 in Chapter 5.) Thus if log P is 4.6 or more, the odds are better than 100 to 1 that our model is better. In the first of these columns, Equations (6.4) are compared against (6.14), to get the *probability* that f is not zero; in the second column, the ARMA "maximum" model is compared (i.e., Equations (6.18) adapted to mobilization) against the regression version of the model, to see if ARMA is better; in the third column, the ARMA version of Equations (6.14) ("univariate") is compared against regression. For log P of 6.9 or more, odds are 1000 to 1 or better; for log P of 3, odds are 20 to 1.

Table 6.12 Statistics Concerning Regression for the Assimilated and Differentiated Populations

Nation and Database	b_6	Log P $b \neq 0$	Log P ARMA Max.	Log P ARMA Uni.
Ceylon	−1.853	6.8	8.4	11.6
Argentina	0.977	1.9	9.2	7.8
CSSR	0.137	0.4	10.7	7.1
Malaysia	0.311	1.5	7.9	6.9
USA (2)	2.698	9.0	9.6	6.3
Finland	0.038	0.0	6.2	5.9
Canada	1.945	3.1	8.3	5.7
USA (1)	2.054	3.1	3.4	5.3
Israel (1)	4.215	14.3	7.5	5.3
Scotland (2)	8.343	1.9	4.4	4.8
Scotland (1)	1.471	1.1	4.3	4.7
Quebec	0.365	2.4	7.2	4.3
Israel (2)	3.963	13.1	3.9	3.7
India	1.466	1.5	5.9	3.3
*** Log P (ARMA Univ.) Significant Above This Line ***				
Philippines	−0.627	0.9	4.4	2.6
Taiwan (4)	−0.077	1.7	2.2	2.1
Taiwan (3)	0.021	2.1	1.9	1.8
Cyprus	−0.507	3.2	0.5	1.3
Taiwan (2)	−0.136	1.4	4.4	0.8
Taiwan (1)	−0.107	1.1	0.8	0.8
Belgium	−0.220	2.8	5.7	0.5

b_6 is the value of b_6 the rate of assimilation in Equation (6.15) as estimated by ordinary regression. Log P is the standard, classical statistical measure of the relative likelihood of one model in comparison with another; it represents the natural logarithm of the odds in favor of the truth of the model we are interested in, compared with some other model, if we assume that both models had an equal chance of being true a priori. (See Section 5.5 of Chapter 5.) Thus if log P is 4.6 or more, the odds are better than 100 to 1 that our model is better. In the first of these columns, Equation (6.15) is compared against (6.17) to get the *probability* that b is not zero; in the second column, the ARMA "maximum" model is compared against the regression version (6.18) to see if ARMA is better; in the third column, the ARMA version of Equations (6.16) and (6.17) ("univariate") is compared against regression. For log P of 6.9 or more, odds are 1000 to 1 or better; for log P of 3, odds are 20 to 1.

10% of the error sizes at best. (The slight differences in error distributions between the two methods are visible in Figures 6.1–6.4.) The second of these two results was also corroborated by the results in Norway, to be discussed in Section 6.5.

There are two immediate corollaries to these results. First, the usual significance measure is *not* a good index of long-term predictive power, at least not for models that correspond to the same choices of variables. Second, the robust

TABLE 6.13 ARMA Models for Mobilization Processes

Nation and Database	f	Log P $f \neq 0$	Rho Mobil.	Rho Under.
Israel (1)	0.499	10.1	1.63	0.182
Belgium	0.164	7.7	−1.13	0.03
Cyprus	0.232	7.4	−1.19	−1.424
Israel (2)	0.325	7.2	0.746	0.204
Finland (3)	−0.037	6.7	−1.517	0.317
Taiwan	−0.044	6.3	−1.641	1.710
Malaysia	−0.046	6.2	−1.518	−1.440
Argentina (1)	0.852	5.8	−1.329	1.819
Argentina (2)	0.613	5.3	−1.72	1.780
Finland (2)	−0.012	4.9	−1.009	0.733
India	−0.142	4.2	−1.687	−1.447
Japan	0.089	3.1	0.325	0.064
USSR (3)	0.030	3.1	0.565	1.296
*** Log P Significant Above This Line ***				
USSR (1)	0.007	2.0	0.650	0.712
CSSR	0.316	1.8	−2.204	−2.257
USA (1)	0.030	1.7	0.629	1.529
USSR (2)	−0.047	1.3	0.530	−1.085
Ceylon	−0.012	0.6	−1.096	−1.230
Quebec	0.000	0.6	−1.25	−0.201
Philippines	0.083	0.4	−1.517	−1.643
Finland (1)	−0.158	0.4	−1.27	−0.162
USA (2)	0.08	0.2	0.64	1.196
Canada	−0.036	0.1	0.360	1.229

f_1 is the rate of mobilization in Equations (6.4) as estimated by the ARMA method. Log P, as in Table 6.11, is the classical measure of the *probability* that f is actually nonzero, despite the uncertainty of estimation; in this table, the ARMA models are used to calculate log P. Log P here is the natural logarithm of the odds in favor of the proposition that f is not zero. When log P is 4.6 or more, the odds are 100 to 1 or better that f is nonzero; when log P is 3 or more, the odds are 20 to 1. Rho is a coefficient, discussed in the text, which tends to be nonzero when *data collection* or other measurement errors are large (rho = 1 is very large); when rho is zero, the ARMA model reduces to a regression model.

method, which performed *much* better than regression in the initial research, is superior to the ARMA method as well, in terms of long-term prediction. (See Figures 6.1–6.4.)

In order to document the second corollary more concretely, I also used GRR (GRowth Rate)— a revised form of EXTRAP for robust estimation in the univariate linear case—to establish an exact correspondence between the three methods for the assimilation and differentiation data. Figures 6.1 and 6.2 show the error distributions for all three methods, as methods of making predictions based on the same substantive model, Equations (6.8), and as tested over the

TABLE 6.14 ARMA Models of the Assimilation Process

Nation and Database	b_6	Log P $b \neq 0$	Rho Assim.	Rho Diff.
Israel (1)	4.215	19.7	−0.006	−1.15
Israel (2)	3.959	13.3	0.583	0.441
USA (2)	2.673	12.1	−1.09	1.155
Belgium	−0.219	8.1	−1.35	−0.323
Canada	1.946	5.7	1.926	1.205
Quebec	0.348	5.4	−1.09	1.383
CSSR	0.139	4.1	−1.310	−1.399
India	1.453	4.1	−1.150	1.416
Ceylon	−1.855	3.6	−1.148	1.620
Malaysia	0.309	3.5	−2.142	−1.326
Argentina	0.977	3.4	3.14	1.761
*** Log P Significant Above This Line ***				
Philippines	−0.632	2.7	−1.02	−1.292
Cyprus	−0.507	2.3	0.043	0.336
Taiwan (3)	0.021	2.2	0.017	0.373
Taiwan (4)	−0.076	1.7	−0.079	0.402
Scotland (2)	8.351	1.3	−1.634	−0.324
USA (1)	2.042	1.2	−0.141	−1.15
Taiwan (1)	−0.107	1.1	0.799	0.339
Scotland (1)	1.597	0.7	1.686	0.025
Finland	0.055	0.3	1.407	0.057
Taiwan (2)	−0.137	0.0	5.0	0.360

b_6 is the rate of assimilation in Equation (6.15) as estimated by the ARMA method. Log P, as in Table 6.12, is the classical measure of the *probability* that b is actually nonzero, despite the uncertainty of estimation; in this table, the ARMA models are used to calculate log P. Log P is the natural logarithm of the odds in favor of the proposition that b is nonzero. When log P is 4.6 or more, the odds are 100 to 1 or better that b is nonzero; when log P is 3 or more, the odds are 20 to 1. Rho is a coefficient, discussed in the text, which tends to be nonzero when *data collection* or other measurement errors are large (rho = 1 is very large); when rho is zero, the ARMA model reduces to a regression model.

same sample cases of data drawn from the Deutsch-Kravitz data. *In these graphs, the superiority of the robust method is clear*, for both the GRR and EXTRAP versions. From the simulation studies of Chapter 4, one might suspect that this superiority is due in part to the overlaps between the databases over which the models are fit and the years over which they are tested. However, I have included a few examples of a time series split in half, with the model fitted to the first half and the predictions made to the second half. (See Tables 6.23 and 6.24. Israel, Taiwan, the United States and Finland are the prime examples, because they are the cases where adequate data were available for such a splitting.) These examples do not seem markedly different from the other cases studied; unfortunately, these examples are too few to allow a de-

TABLE 6.15 The rms Average of Percentage Errors with Long-Term Predictions of Mobilized and Underlying Populations, Based on Regression

Nation and Database	Mobil. (6.18) Max.	Mobil. (6.15) Model	Mobil. (6.17) Uni.	Under. (6.18) Max.	Under. (6.16) Uni.
Taiwan	0.26	0.23	0.73	0.19	0.84
USSR (3)	1.24	1.28	0.85	1.32	1.32
USSR (1B)	0.84	0.83	0.95	0.82	4.44
USSR (2)	8.40	7.54	• 1.88	1.08	0.44
Finland (3)	0.99	0.95	2.58	0.70	2.37
Ceylon	5.08	5.27	3.86	3.42	3.73
CSSR	2.52	2.65	3.91	3.89	3.65
USSR (1A)	1.58	1.58	8.39	0.65	4.46
Quebec	8.60	8.22	12.88	8.52	7.42
India `	17.45	241.48	21.02	8.09	5.10
Malaysia	8.29	11.66	22.20	5.80	4.43
Japan	33.09	34.64	22.86	29.74	18.98
Israel (1)	7.18	10.28	24.90	24.55	8.31
Belgium	4.29	4.31	28.94	0.85	3.99
Canada	93.73	99.59	29.11	10.07	19.43
Philippines	14.60	14.67	34.11	5.69	12.18
Israel (2)	31.56	5.60	34.82	52.89	49.91
Finland (1)	10.02	8.57	44.95	508.77	16.98
Cyprus	17.49	18.00	54.67	6.66	17.62
Argentina (1)	11.61	11.45	57.01	7.23	54.93
Finland (2)	59.99	51.32	83.91	100.64	45.94
USA (1)	63.83	67.97	89.00	388.89	64.05
Argentina (2)	14.09	13.02	100.25	16.86	42.58
USA (2)	47.04	45.85	133.14	91.21	116.66

In each case, the four models used were fitted to the database defined in Table 6.23, and predictions were made from the base year to all later years for which data were available. The errors listed here are *averages*, in each case, across all such test years. The five columns give errors with four different models; these models are the equivalents (i.e., have the same structure, with mobilization switched for assimilation, etc.) of the equations whose numbers are listed in the column headings. Mobil. , mobilized; under., underlying; rms, root-mean-square (i.e., averages taken as the square root of the arithmetic average of the squares).

finitive conclusion. We will see, however, that the ARMA model for Equations (6.8) has more free parameters to estimate than do either the regression or the robust methods. When the supply of data is very limited, an overlap between the data samples used for fitting and testing would tend to overstate the relative performance of the model with more parameters. (It is standard practice, for example, to try to correct for "degrees of freedom" in one's model, when the data are quite limited; this subject, however, is a Pandora's Box, which will not be opened here.) In short, the strong superiority of the

TABLE 6.16 The rms Averages of Percentage Errors with Long-Term Predictions of Mobilized and Underlying Populations, Based on the ARMA Method

Nation and Database	Mobil. (6.18) Max.	Mobil. (6.15) Model	Mobil. (6.17) Uni.	Under. (6.18) Max.	Under. (6.16) Uni.
Taiwan	0.43	0.22	0.72	0.10	0.49
USSR (3)	1.19	1.18	0.86	1.31	1.40
USSR (1B)	0.85	0.85	1.00	0.85	3.64
USSR (2)	8.52	-6.82	1.38	1.11	0.47
Ceylon	5.22	2.27	1.48	3.43	2.81
CSSR	2.77	2.63	2.38	3.36	3.77
Finland (3)	0.97	0.79	2.55	0.66	2.41
Quebec	6.72	5.59	6.41	5.22	6.92
USSR (1A)	1.78	1.47	8.92	0.48	3.90
Philippines	14.96	11.53	12.60	4.81	2.83
Cyprus	17.53	16.35	17.01	6.66	6.47
Japan	33.37	38.07	18.91	33.74	19.23
India	16.22	55.83	22.22	6.60	3.21
Canada	57.82	93.74	22.42	12.24	8.82
Malaysia	5.70	1.29	22.70	6.50	2.69
Israel (1)	9.34	8.57	24.04	24.09	7.33
Belgium	4.32	3.44	29.05	0.87	3.98
Israel (2)	29.24	6.05	33.65	54.85	47.94
Argentina (1)	11.69	8.84	51.11	11.64	46.74
Finland (1)	9.65	11.43	53.63	241.79	16.62
USA (1)	63.76	61.76	81.05	481.04	53.27
Finland (2)	14.29	16.59	84.78	7.04	55.10
Argentina (2)	12.86	7.65	96.40	8.18	42.75
USA (2)	53.79	46.19	135.70	110.62	113.57

In each case, the four models used were fitted to the database defined in Table 6.23, and predictions were made from the base year to all later years for which data were available. The errors listed here are *averages*, in each case, across all such test years. The five columns give errors from four different models; these models are the equivalents (i.e., have the same structure, with mobilization switched for assimilation, etc.) of the equations whose numbers are listed in the column headings. Mobil., mobilized; under, underlying. The acronym rms means that root mean-square averaging was used.

robust method over the ARMA method, in these studies, is probably not due to any bias in the details of the procedure.

Before going more deeply into the mathematical details of these studies, the political scientist might be curious about the projections of the future by the models given here, for some of the countries where they have worked well in the past. Tables 6.21 and 6.22 show the predictions of the robust method (GRR) for the future in the countries studied here. The uses of these numbers are for you to decide for yourself; my authorship of the numbers in no way implies

TABLE 6.17 The rms Averages of Percentage Errors with Long-Term Predictions of Mobilized and Underlying Populations, Based on the Robust Method (GRR)

Nation and Database	Mobil. ext1	Mobil. ext2	Under. ext1	Under. ext2
Taiwan	0.59	0.78	0.99	1.49
USSR (3)	0.99	1.76	0.75	1.49
Finland (3)	1.17	2.42	1.33	2.69
Ceylon	1.82	2.08	3.11	4.01
USSR (2)	2.34	3.42	0.77	0.96
CSSR	3.50	4.14	3.83	4.26
Malaysia	4.69	6.61	3.31	4.74
Quebec	5.83	11.47	5.06	9.83
Israel (2)	8.06	29.19	8.46	50.83
India	8.72	10.31	3.64	3.68
Belgium	8.84	15.63	1.83	4.52
Canada	10.42	24.16	4.78	13.40
Finland (2)	13.99	34.76	10.65	21.36
Philippines	14.35	29.90	4.94	9.40
Argentina (1)	16.91	23.10	15.26	24.63
Cyprus	17.95	18.77	7.35	7.39
Japan	18.63	18.96	12.89	17.54
Argentina (2)	24.16	42.12	13.21	21.22
USA (2)	32.25	46.03	24.96	52.04
Israel (1)	39.94	33.84	21.54	12.57
Finland (1)	57.22	53.28	28.20	24.48
USA (1)	85.23	89.70	89.65	84.45

In each case, Equations (6.2) with the fU term removed were fitted to the database defined in Table 6.23, and predictions were made from the base year to all later years for which data were available. The errors listed here are *averages*, in each case, across all such test years. Mobil., mobilized; under., underlying. ext1 is the variety of robust method used by EXTRAP, described in section 6.2; ext2 is another variety mentioned in Section 6.3 and tabulated only for the sake of formal completeness. The acronym rms means that root-mean-square averaging was used.

that my opinions about their use are any better than anyone else's. However, these opinions are probably worth recording here, at least to provide the reader with a starting point.

When one first glances at these tables, a few wild numbers immediately grab the eye. How, for example, could the Republic of China (Taiwan) be expected to have 1,800,000,000 inhabitants in the year 2000? (See Table 6.22.) Then, if one has a little serendipity, one will note that only a few million of these are to be "Taiwanese," that about 450 million are to be mainland Chinese, and that the rest would appear to be neither. Visions spring to mind of a collapse of the People's Republic, of a return to the mainland by Chiang's son, and of the expansion throughout the weak nations of Southern Asia by

TABLE 6.18 The rms Averages of Percentage Errors with Long-Term Predictions of Assimilated and Differentiated Populations, Based on Regression

Nation and Database	Assim. (6.18) Max.	Assim. (6.15) Model	Assim. (6.17) Uni.	Diff. (6.18) Max.	Diff. (6.16) Uni.
Taiwan (3B)	0.36	2.98	0.73	2.89	7.62
Taiwan (2)	2.96	3.80	1.36	13.35	27.13
CSSR	1.67	1.35	1.79	6.87	5.92
Taiwan (1)	3.81	5.37	2.48	17.66	25.81
Taiwan (4)	0.95	0.90	2.85	23.90	161.45
Taiwan (3A)	1.18	25.29	3.23	25.20	166.70
Finland	4.60	4.49	4.82	14.17	17.41
India	6.12	3.91	5.82	7.25	8.80
Scotland (2)	2.97	2.93	6.29	6.89	21.34
Cyprus	1.43	2.14	6.59	4.51	21.94
Scotland (1)	3.34	3.24	6.72	3.26	6.27
Canada	12.59	5.97	12.28	13.84	24.86
Malaysia	3.72	3.81	12.50	3.72	9.18
Belgium	6.47	9.80	12.98	3.58	6.08
Quebec	2.68	2.39	15.64	12.07	31.2
Argentina	41.78	13.64	16.91	145.39	122.23
Ceylon	11.15	192.41	17.49	7.31	15.07
Philippines	27.55	36.40	20.91	22.40	8.47
Israel (1)	1.95	1.95	21.69	8.06	8.37
USA (1)	44.11	5.11	44.40	71.54	69.92
Israel (2)	30.00	3.48	46.56	33.47	23.70
USA (2)	39.04	7.99	97.61	45.61	24.41

In each case, the four models used were fitted to the database defined in Table 6.24, and pre dictions were made from the base year to all later years for which data existed. The errors listed here are *averages*, in each case, across all such test years. The five columns give errors from four different models used in predictions; these models correspond to the equations whose numbers are listed in the column headings. Assim., assimilated; Diff., differentiated. The acronym rms means that root-mean-square averaging was used.

this new, fascistic nationalistic regime. It would be amusing to study the pros and cons of the possibility of such a scenario. However, the simple models used here do not "know" about (do not account for) the complex factors that might make such a scenario possible; while it is possible for a model to "know" about such factors *implicitly*, it is suspected that these models are too simple even for that, in the example at hand. A simpler interpretation of these wild numbers is that the predictions of this model, in the future, will be very much like the predictions in the past; they will contain a handful of wild outliers and a larger number of surprisingly-accurate predictions of the percentage of assim- ilation. It is fortunate that we can spot some of the outliers so easily in advance, simply by using our general knowledge that some of the predictions are absurd.

TABLE 6.19 The rms Averages of Percentage Errors with Long-Term Predictions of Assimilated and Differentiated Populations, Based on ARMA Methods

Nation and Database	Assim. (6.18) Max.	Assim. (6.15) Model	Assim. (6.17) Uni.	Diff. (6.18) Max.	Diff. (6.16) Uni.
Taiwan (3B)	0.37	2.99	0.76	2.97	8.04
Taiwan (2)	3.72	4.81	1.31	13.68	22.64
CSSR	1.41	1.24	1.78	6.92	5.59
Taiwan (1)	3.52	5.48	2.50	17.61	21.08
Finland	2.91	2.86	2.66	17.65	17.51
Taiwan (4)	0.95	0.90	2.84	23.93	157.16
Taiwan (3A)	1.18	25.84	3.15	25.24	167.19
Scotland (1)	3.31	4.64	5.08	3.50	6.03
Scotland (2)	2.69	4.09	5.11	15.49	17.05
India	3.47	2.82	5.77	2.72	12.48
Cyprus	1.34	2.11	6.96	4.69	24.37
Malaysia	3.28	3.56	8.24	3.66	3.55
Canada	14.20	5.63	10.32	14.72	17.54
Belgium	4.65	1.99	13.22	2.97	5.48
Quebec	2.31	1.79	14.87	11.97	25.87
Ceylon	10.37	2.78	19.95	8.01	19.61
Philippines	28.01	14.39	21.60	21.81	3.98
Israel (1)	1.76	1.76	22.43	8.30	8.79
Argentina	41.89	13.83	22.67	145.30	151.99
Israel (2)	30.12	3.55	37.86	33.77	31.25
USA (1)	44.03	5.72	55.80	71.45	61.96
USA (2)	40.80	11.05	96.40	46.28	62.30

In each case, the four models used were fitted to the database defined in Table 6.24, and predictions were made from the base year to all later years for which data were available. The errors listed here are *averages*, in each case, across all such test years. The five columns give errors from four different models used in prediction; these models correspond to the equations whose numbers are listed in the column headings. Assim., assimilated; Diff., differentiated. The acronym rms means that root-mean-square averaging was used.

In the other cases, we would tend to follow the procedures suggested in Chapter 5. We would place greater faith in predictions based on a model estimated over a *long* database—as in Finland—as opposed to predictions based on a *lot* of data restricted to a shorter period of time (e.g., Taiwan or Israel). Indeed, the absurdity of the latter predictions offers some tangible evidence for this point of view. We would try to ask in each case: "What does the model really 'know' about? At what dynamic level could one observe the effects of the forces that will be important in the future? Given those factors that *I* know about, and given the *subset* of those that cannot be subsumed under something for which the model accounts, how would I adjust these predictions?" Questions of this sort lead one to a different approach to applied political science, as discussed in Chapter 5.

TABLE 6.20 The rms Averages of Percentage Errors with Long-Term Predictions of Assimilated and Differentiated Populations, Based on the Robust Method (GRR)

Nation and Database	Assim. ext1	Assim. ext2	Diff. ext1	Diff. ext2
Taiwan (3B)	0.37	0.66	29.71	53.74
Taiwan (3A)	0.75	3.54	47.03	134.42
Taiwan (4)	1.65	3.71	45.04	130.92
CSSR	1.75	1.79	5.73	7.54
Cyprus	2.03	3.01	6.01	9.85
Taiwan (1)	2.25	1.94	154.54	130.61
Finland (2)	2.27	6.03	9.48	15.89
Scotland (2)	3.30	8.67	10.33	15.48
Scotland (1)	3.42	9.01	3.12	7.74
Malaysia	4.05	6.20	4.71	8.13
Taiwan (2)	4.12	3.69	149.89	125.87
India	4.19	4.25	3.78	4.80
Quebec	4.67	12.15	20.12	31.83
Argentina	4.95	4.96	38.74	66.85
Belgium	5.23	6.67	3.70	3.72
Philippines	5.74	11.44	4.26	4.47
Canada	6.21	14.80	8.61	15.26
Israel (2)	6.92	41.69	4.34	5.82
Ceylon	7.43	7.29	5.63	7.73
USA (2)	18.38	34.22	15.91	35.95
Israel (1)	37.56	29.76	9.41	9.17
USA (1)	62.82	59.97	68.33	69.10

In each case, Equations (6.8) were fitted to the database defined in Table 6.24, and predictions were made from the base year to all later years for which data were available. The errors listed here are *averages*, in each case, across all such test years. Assim., assimilated; Diff., differentiated. ext1 is the variety of robust method used by EXTRAP, described in Section 6.2; ext2 is another variety mentioned in Section 6.3 and tabulated only for the sake of formal completeness. The acronym rms means that root-mean-square averaging was used.

In some sense, the predictions of these simple models are based on the continuation of the trends that have existed for a long time in the past. It is often comforting for a decision-maker to assume that one's own administration will somehow be free, at little cost, from the momentum of such trends; indeed, when one is harassed, as most decision-makers are, it is easy to "miss the forest for the trees" and to overestimate the implication of short-term reverse fluctuations. *The predictions of this model, in some sense, show the decision-maker what the forest looks like.* It is still up to him/her to use personal judgement, to decide whether his/her administration is truly and objectively likely to perform much differently from those that have dealt with the same problems in the past. Even in concrete terms, these predictions imply no dra-

TABLE 6.21 Predictions of Future Mobilized and Underlying Populations, by the Robust Method (GRR).

Nation and Database	Mobilization			Underlying Population		
	1980	1990	2000	1980	1990	2000
USA (2)	275.	407.	602.	80.6	95.1	112.
Israel (2)	4.98	9.08	16.6	0.572	0.638	0.713
Finland (2)	3.02	3.80	4.78	2.71	2.94	3.18
Cyprus	0.145	0.171	0.202	0.615	0.703	0.803
CSSR[a]	11.4	12.3	13.3	2.24	2.11	1.99
Malaysia	3.89	6.01	9.30	7.28	8.70	10.4
Japan	136.	207.	313.	31.1	29.7	28.3
Ceylon	11.2	15.6	21.8	4.15	4.39	4.63
India (+ Pakistan)[a]	75.4	84.0	93.4	419.	442.	467.
Taiwan	7.24	11.3	17.8	13.4	17.7	23.2
USSR (3)	255.	419.	687.	141.	170.	204.
Argentina (1)	30.6	44.1	63.6	7.28	8.58	10.1
Argentina (2)	31.5	49.1	76.5	9.86	11.7	13.8
Philippines	30.4	46.4	70.7	18.7	21.6	24.9
Canada	23.5	32.4	44.8	6.49	7.05	7.66
Quebec	6.90	9.31	12.6	1.47	1.54	1.61
Belgium	7.80	8.88	10.1	3.10	3.11	3.12

ext2 used; see discussion in text. All figures are in millions; definitions are given in Table 6.23. Note that 1974 populations for India, Pakistan and Bangladesh total more than 650 million.

[a]Base year for predictions was before 1950.

221

TABLE 6.22 Predictions for Future Assimilated and Differentiated Populations, by the ext2 Version of the Robust Method (GRR)

Nation and Database	Assimilation			Differentiated		
	1980	1990	2000	1980	1990	2000
USA (2)	254.	321.	405.	35.5	42.8	51.6
Israel (2)	4.43	7.12	11.5	0.699	1.01	1.53
Taiwan (3B)	14.4	18.5	23.9	45.2	286.	1815
Taiwan (4)	17.5	24.0	32.9	18.5	90.1	439.
Canada	21.7	26.6	32.6	4.53	5.19	5.96
Quebec	7.20	9.16	11.7	0.701	0.697	0.694
Ceylon	9.25	10.9	12.8	4.54	5.22	6.01
Finland	5.02	5.55	6.13	0.347	0.352	0.356
Malaysia	4.67	5.56	6.62	5.64	7.28	9.40
CSSR[a]	10.1	10.8	11.6	3.08	3.01	2.94
India (+ Pakistan)[a]	329.	346.	364.	165.	179.	195.
Cyprus	0.638	0.742	0.863	0.128	0.142	0.157
Scotland (1)	5.43	5.61	5.80	0.055	0.046	0.039
Scotland (2)	5.45	5.61	5.76	402p	239p	142p
Argentina	30.1	39.5	52.0	4.22	5.41	6.94
Philippines	9.87	25.2	32.0	24.1	30.0	37.1
Belgium	3.44	3.61	3.80	7.43	8.09	8.82

All figures in millions, except in Scotland. Definitions of "assimilated" in Table 6.24.
[a]Base year for predictions was before 1950.
[b]Letter p is used to mean people; too few for millions.

matic shift in the percentages of assimilation in the countries studied; a strong upsurge of the Visayans is predicted in the Philippines, and Chinese with recent roots in the mainland are projected to become a majority of the population of Taiwan, but these are the only exceptions.

A few of our readers might also be interested in the predictions of the regression and ARMA models, in some of the countries where they have worked well in the past. These projections are too voluminous to be duplicated here[7], but their fine details are probably unreliable in any case.

In Canada and Quebec, as a whole, the model predicts little change in the relative balance of French and English speakers, to the year 2000. (This would appear to contradict the separatist claim that the French language would die away without special political measures to bolster it. On the other hand, it implies that French Canadians will remain a political force to be reckoned with. In Canada and Quebec, the models did better in predicting the *longer*

[7]The computer printout here was left in the custody of Professor Karl Deutsch, Harvard Department of Government. The computer printouts from Section 6.2 were also left in his custody, in 1971. These two groups of output are approximately 1 foot thick, put together. For every run reported here, they include predictions and reality for every year, past and future, for which predictions were made.

TABLE 6.23 Definition of Mobilization Variables and Spans of Years Used for Runs Described in Tables 6.11-6.22

Nation and Database	Mobilization Definition	Year to Which Model Is Fitted	Gap in Years	Base Year
USA (1)	Urbanization	1790-1870	10	1870
(2)	Urbanization	1790-1960	10	1790
Israel (1)	Urbanization	1948-1957[a]	1	1957
(2)	Urbanization	1948-1967[a]	1	1948
Finland (1)	Urbanization	1800-1880	10	1880
(2)	Urbanization	1800-1960	10	1800
(3)	Urbanization	1958-1967	1	1958
Cyprus	Urbanization	1881-1961[b]	10	1901
CSSR	Urbanization	1900-1940[b]	10	1900
Malaysia	Urbanization	1911-1961[b]	10	1911
Japan	Urbanization	1920-1960	5	1920
Ceylon	Literacy	1881-1951	10	1881
India (+ Pakistan)	Urbanization	1881-1941	10	1881
Taiwan	Urbanization	1960-1966	1	1960
USSR (1A)	Urbanization	All below	1	1924
(1B)	Urbanization	All below	1	1953
(2)	Urbanization	1922-1931	1	1924
(3)	Urbanization	1950-1965	1	1953
Argentina (1)	(Table 6.10)	1869-1960[b]	22.75	1869
(2)	Literacy (b)	1869-1960[b]	22.75	1869
Philippines	Literacy	1903-1961[b]	14.5	1903
Canada	Urbanization	1851-1961	10	1851
Quebec	Urbanization	1851-1961	10	1851
Belgium	Urbanization	1860-1960[b]	10	1860

All long-term predictions were made *from* data in the base year, up to the end of the continuous string of observations of which it is a part, in the Deutsch-Kravitz data. Gap in years is the interval between observations.

[b] Heavily interpolated (8 years of actual data spaced out into 20-year string).

Interpolated data; *N* not artificially enlarged.

periods of time, rather than the shorter; the "10% errors" listed in the tables are mostly from transient deviations from the trend predicted by the models.) A large increase in urbanization is predicted for Quebec, which, in practice, might shift the assimilation trend more to the advantage of French speakers. In Ceylon, a large increase in literacy is projected. In Scotland, a further large decrease in the knowledge of Gaelic is predicted. (If knowledge of Gaelic were a good indicator of political behavior, this would imply that recent signs of revival of Scottish nationalism are misleading and transient; however, the connection between linguistic nationalism and political nationalism may not be simple in this case, any more than in the case of Ireland.) In Japan, a huge urban population—200-odd million—was forecast; however, from the limitations cited in Section 6.2, it should be emphasized that political and economic

TABLE 6.24 Definition of Assimilation Variables and Spans of Years Used For Runs Described in Tables 6.11-6.22

Nation and Database	Assimilation Definition	Year to Which Model Is Fitted	Gap in Years	Base Year
USA (1)	White	1790–1870	10	1870
(2)	White	1790–1960	10	1790
Israel (1)	Jewish	1948–1957	1	1957
(2)	Jewish	1948–1967	1	1948
Taiwan (1)	Taiwanese	1946–1955	1	1955
(2)	Not Mainlanders	1946–1955	1	1955
(3A)	Taiwanese	1946–1965	1	1946
(3B)	Taiwanese	1946–1965	1	1955
(4)	Not Mainlanders	1946–1965	1	1946
Canada	Not French-Only	1901–1961[a]	10	1901
Quebec	Not English-Only	1901–1961[a]	10	1901
Ceylon	Buddhist	1881–1961[a]	10	1901
Finland	Speak Finnish	1880–1960	10	1880
Malaysia	(No choice)	1911–1961[a]	10	1911
CSSR	Ethnicity	1900–1940[a]	10	1900
India (+ Pakistan)	Hindu	1881–1941	10	1881
Cyprus	Not Moslem	1881–1961[a]	10	1881
Scotland (1)	Speak No Gaelic	1891–1961[a]	10	1891
(2)	Speak English	1891–1961[a]	10	1891
Argentina	Ethnicity	1869–1960[a]	22.75	1869
Philippines	Visayan	1903–1961[a]	14.5	1903
Belgium	Speak French	1850–1950[a]	10	1850

All long-term predictions were made *from* data in the base year, up to the end of the continuous string of observations of which it is a part, in the Deutsch–Kravitz data. Gap in years is the interval between observations.

[a]Interpolated data; length of data sample not artificially enlarged.

factors may cross the threshold of being able to upset this prediction. (In Japan, as in Canada, the errors reported in Tables 6.16 and 6.19 were essentially transient.) In Cyprus and Taiwan, the ARMA models predict little change in the balances between the different factions.

Now let us look more closely at the mathematical details. My primary interest was in the original Deutsch–Solow model—Equations (6.1) and (6.2)—and in the reduced form of this model, with the bD and fU terms eliminated (e.g., Equations (6.8)). Instead of working with the Deutsch–Solow model directly, in terms of differential equations, I worked with the finite-difference equations that the model implies, Equations (6.3) and (6.4); to refresh the reader's memory, let us recall what Equations (6.3) looked like:

$$A(t + 1) = a_1 A(t) + b_1 D(t),$$

$$D(t + 1) = c_1 D(t),$$

where a_1 is the natural factor of growth of the assimilated population, b_1 is the rate of assimilation per unassimilated person per unit of time, and c_1 is the natural factor of growth of the differentiated population *minus* b_1. In like manner, the reduced form of the Deutsch–Solow model, with the bD and fU terms removed, leads to a reduced form of the finite-difference equations:

$$A(t + 1) = a_5 A(t), \tag{6.13a}$$

$$D(t + 1) = c_5 D(t), \tag{6.13b}$$

and

$$M(t + 1) = e_5 M(t), \tag{6.14a}$$

$$U(t + 1) = g_5 U(t), \tag{6.14b}$$

In predicting the differentiated population, Equation (6.13b) is equivalent to (6.3b); in predicting the assimilated population, Equation (6.13a) is equivalent to assuming that the number of people assimilated per unit of time is proportional to the number *already assimilated*. It should be emphasized that this reduced form of the Deutsch–Solow model was studied for the sake of its mathematical simplicity, not for the sake of any hope that it would be superior to the original model on substantive grounds. (Section 6.5 will discuss regression models based on what appears to be an intermediate assumption, that the number assimilated can be explained partly as a constant percentage of the *overall* population; however, the ARMA models to be discussed in that section achieved greater empirical success than these regression models, even though they lacked such a constant term.)

Section 6.2 has already described how the robust method was applied to the reduced form of the Deutsch–Solow model. The new routine, GRR, estimates the parameters of that model in exactly the same way, except that it works only on a continuous series of data spaced at regular intervals. In order to use classical regression on Equations (6.3) and (6.13), I added an "error term", $n(t)$, to each, and attempted to fit the regression equations:

$$A(t + 1) = a_6 A(t) + b_6 D(t) + n(t), \tag{6.15}$$

$$D(t + 1) = c_6 D(t) + n(t), \tag{6.16}$$

$$A(t + 1) = a_7 A(t) + n(t). \tag{6.17}$$

The terms $n(t)$ represent the various random disturbances invoked to explain the actual errors experienced in predicting $A(t + 1)$ and $D(t + 1)$ from the known values of $A(t)$ and $D(t)$, by use of these models. The equations for mobilization were exactly parallel in their structure. For each of the 45 cases of assimilation and mobilization studied, taken from 17 nations, each of these three equations was estimated separately by use of the TSP command ARMA. (More precisely, the three equations, in order, were analyzed by issuing the commands: ''arma assimilated on differentiatedend,'' ''arma differentiatedend,'' and ''arma assimilated$end.'' Note that variables named after the keyword ''on'' are treated as exogenous, that is, as variables to be used in making predictions but not themselves to be predicted by use of the equations at hand.) In *addition*, since it was impossible to *simulate* more than one set of equations at the same time, I estimated the set of equations:

$$A(t + 1) = a_8 A(t) + b_8 D(t) + n(t), \qquad (6.18a)$$

$$D(t + 1) = c_8 D(t) + d_8 A(t) + m(t). \qquad (6.18b)$$

where $m(t)$ is also a random disturbance; this *set* of equations represents the combination of Equations (6.15) and (6.16), with an extra term added solely for the purpose of creating a ''complete set'' of equations that fits the ''vector ARMA'' framework discussed in Chapter 3. (This set of equations was estimated by the command ''arma assimilated differentiated$end'' or, in the case of mobilization, by ''arma mobilized underlyingend.'')

In Chapter 3, it was emphasized that there is a correspondence from any regression model to an ARMA model that says the same thing but that also allows for the possibility of measurement error; for example, Equation (6.15) is equivalent to

$$A(t + 1) = a_9 A(t) + b_9 D(t) + n(t) + Pn(t - 1), \qquad (6.19)$$

where P may be called a ''rho coefficient.'' Note that the rho coefficient does *not* multiply a substantive variable in this problem; rather, it multiplies the *previous* value of the *same* disturbance. (Elsewhere, of course, I have used the same letter, n, to refer to *different* random processes.) From an intuitive point of view, it is simply a measure of the presence of ''measurement noise,'' of collection errors in the available numerical data vis-à-vis the original underlying concepts, as discussed in Chapter 3. When rho is small, this implies that the regression model (i.e., the same model *without* the rho term) is fairly close to the ''truth''; more precisely, it implies that tractable aspects of measurement noise will have little effect on one's estimation. When rho is large, this implies that measurement noise is substantial. The four computer commands mentioned above were sufficient not only to estimate the four sets of regression equations above but *also* to estimate automatically the equivalent ARMA equation in every case. For each model estimated, log P significance scores were printed out; the *differences* between these log P scores, for two models being compared with each other, gave the log P scores reported in Tables 6.11–6.14. The ''rhos'' reported in these tables for the ''maximum'' model (i.e., Equation (6.18) or the equivalent for mobilization) were actually the diagonal terms of the rho matrix, P, of Chapter 3.

As part of the ARMA command, an automatic simulation facility was also available. After the regression and ARMA models were estimated over a given set of years (a database), simulations could be made from any given year (base year) into the future.

Actual data for endogenous variables, for variables which the model can predict, are taken *only* from the base year; predictions are made, further and further into the future, by being compounded on other predictions. *After* the predictions are done, they are checked against real data. Thus the predictions are true long-term predictions. (The percentage errors are calculated as a percentage of the average of the absolute values of the predicted and actual values, and are averaged together by root-mean-square averaging.) *However*, in Equation (6.15), the differentiated population is *not* internal to the equation; thus the predictions made in that case are not true long-term predictions, for our purposes.

In using GRR, to make and evaluate predictions similar to those made by ARMA, we used two different techniques. One of these techniques, exactly parallel to EXTRAP (and thus to ext1 discussed in Chapter 4), has been used in Figures 6.1–6.4; the other, the same as ext2 in Chapter 4, starts from the *real* data in the base year, and uses its estimates of a, c, e, and g in Equations (6.13) and (6.14) to compound predictions of the future. Error percentages were calculated by the same formula as with ARMA.

In brief, with *all* of these techniques—ARMA and GRR—data were used, spaced at regular intervals, for fitting the model; then, from a base year, predictions were made to later periods of time, also by regular intervals, with the same formula used to measure percentage error. Given that the original data were *not* available at regular time intervals, an interpolation routine, INTS, in TSP was used to create equivalent data at regular intervals, by geometric interpolation; except in the case of Israel, however, the data periods interpolated to were quite close to the original data periods. (In Israel, data were collected annually, but missing data occurred rather randomly, and interpolation was to an annual series.)

The results from these runs are shown in Tables 6.15–6.20. We have already discussed the broader implications of these results. A more detailed inspection of the statistics in these tables tends to reinforce those implications, particularly the implications of weakness on the part of the classic maximum likelihood methods (regression or ARMA). Note, for example, that the usual measure of statistical significance gives greater emphasis to the superiority of the ARMA models over the regression models than it does to the values of the cross-coefficients—b and f—which represent the rates of assimilation and mobilization. This would seem almost to imply that it is more probable that assimilation and mobilization are not happening, than that the regression model is as good as the ARMA model, if we accept the classical measure at face value.

In terms of minimizing long-term prediction errors, however, the complex, expanded form of the Deutsch–Solow model, Equations (6.18), which includes the cross-coefficients, did better than the univariate models, (6.16) and (6.17); this applies to *both* the ARMA and regression forms of these models, in whatever combination, implying that the cross-terms really were more important in terms of actual prediction errors than the difference between ARMA and regression.

Admittedly, however, our prediction tests may have been biased in favor of models with more parameters in them. Still, in acknowledging this bias, one must go on to observe that the univariate robust method—based on far fewer parameters than the ARMA variation of Equation (6.18)—still did better in long-term prediction than either form of Equation (6.18); given that our tests were biased in favor of the latter, the superiority of the robust method is clear.

Also, if we look at the values of the rho coefficients, P, in Tables 6.13 and 6.14, we again see that the standard statistical analyses here come out strongly in favor of the ARMA method. As mentioned earlier, the estimated value of rho is a good measure of how different the ARMA model is from the corresponding regression model; the regression model corresponds to the special case where the "rho" coefficients are all set to zero. The rho coefficients do indeed seem to be very different from zero; this would seem to indicate that the processes here strongly require the additional terms provided by the ARMA model. This phenomenon would hint that the mediocre predictive power of the ARMA models may be due to a lack of the quantity of data needed, in each case, to estimate the ARMA coefficients precisely enough. However, the Norway results of Section 6.5 will show that more data per case are not enough to overcome the problem. Also, if we look at both the regression *and* ARMA estimates of the constants b and f in these models (Tables 6.11–6.14), we find many values that look unrealistically high, especially when we stick to the intuitive interpretations of them as "assimilation rates" (e.g., United States, with 267% of all blacks turning white per decade); we know that such assimilation rates are unrealistic, largely because we know that they would lead to absurd predictions if extended *over a few time periods*. If we suspect that the *true* values of these rates would be far smaller, then, according to the usual significance measure, we must admit that the measured values are "significantly different" from zero to about the same extent that they are "significantly different" from their true values. In other words, the error is quite significant; it is not likely to be a coincidence, due to a small quantity of data. Rather, we would say that the error is due to a conventional criterion for likelihood estimation, which emphasizes, in practice, *only short-term* predictive power. If we admit that huge, bad estimates of the cross-coefficients lead to unrealistic predictions when extended *over enough time intervals*, then we imply that a different approach to estimation, based on the direct maximization of long-term predictive power, would give us smaller and more realistic estimates. Insofar as the estimates of these coefficients are artificially inflated by the maximum likelihood approach, it is quite possible that the same process affects the rho coefficients.

Also, the variability of the signs of the rho coefficients tends to imply, from the mathematics at the beginning of Chapter 3, that many of these large values for the rho coefficients are due to something else besides pure measurement noise. In quantitative political science, one often reads statements such as, "measurement noise with these data would tend to invalidate the regression coefficients; however, such noise would tend to understate the strength of the real connections; therefore, the effects demonstrated here are, if anything, more valid than regression would indicate." If there is a strong possibility of effects that move rho coefficients in the *opposite* direction from what measurement noise would indicate, then regression may just as easily be overstating the strength of major coefficients. Thus we find, empirically, yet another weakness in the conventional approach to evaluating models.

Finally, from a technical point of view, one may note that almost all the results in these tables were achieved after 10 "major iterations" of the algorithm of Chapter 3. In most cases, convergence proceeded rather steadily, starting out with large movements of coefficient estimates, but proceeding to smaller movements systematically and quickly; convergence was good, most often, after five iterations. In a few cases, however, the total gain in log likelihood relative to regression looked suspiciously low, when the computer output was reviewed. Ten of the assimilation runs were carried out over again, through many iterations. In all cases but two, it was verified that the routine had indeed converged within 10 iteration; indeed, the convergence was generally better than expected (subsequent progress in log likelihood on the order of 0.01), probably because these were cases where the original regression models required little improvement.

On the other hand, there were two exceptions: (1) the application of Equation (6.4a) to data on urbanization in Cyprus and (2) the application of Equations (6.18) to data from 1790 to 1870 on white and nonwhite populations in the United States. In both cases, the computer printout from the first 10 iterations gave a very clear picture of "imbalance," a convergence problem described in Section 3.4 of Chapter 3. (Very crudely, this problem results form the danger that an estimation system based on first derivatives will be too responsive to some parameters, in comparison with others, and will therefore oscillate so much in response to the former that it makes little headway in dealing with the latter.) In these cases, the general multiplicative factor, used to determine the size of adjustments in each minor iteration, was decreased, then increased, then decreased, then increased, by very large factors, in a suspiciously regular wave-like pattern. In the other cases of small initial movement, by contrast, the multiplicative factor changed very little after the first few iterations and changed almost entirely in the downward direction when it did change. (The adjusted data from Cyprus show up in the tables. However, the adjusted data for this run in the United States do not.) The convergence algorithm used has avoided "imbalance" in almost all cases; however, the cases that remain do point up the value of further improvements in convergence procedures, as part of the effort to operationalize the algorithms of Chapter 2. Also, they are worth noting for those who would wish to actually use the command "ARMA" in TSP-CSP.

6.4 NATIONALISM, CONFORMITY, AND COMMUNICATIONS TERMS: AN EXTENSION OF THE DEUTSCH MODEL

The original goal of this research was to follow up on the suggestion of Karl Deutsch, in *Nationalism and Social Communications*, to begin the development. of a predictive, quantitative theory of nationalism. These suggestions included a specific mathematical model—the Deutsch–Solow model—which provided the major focus of the work described so far. They included the suggestion that the use of the dominant national language be used as an index of national assimilation. They also included a number of verbal propositions, presented as "suggestions for future research." These propositions represent an effort to draw together known verbal relations, bit by bit, into a more coherent dynamic theory, capable of making predictions if only the data were available. By the reasoning of Chapter 5, this makes them of great substantive interest in their own right. Hoping to exhaust the possibilities of the simple Deutsch–Solow model at an early stage of this research, I have gone back to these earlier propositions, in order to draw them together into a mathematical expression both more complete and more capable of significant generalization to other problems in political science.

In Chapter 6 of *Nationalism and Social Communication*, Karl Deutsch presents his main argument that the birth of nationalism may depend on the *relative rates* of national assimilation and political mobilization, particularly on the latter, more volatile variable. He points out that a moderate-to-slow rate of mobilization will tend to keep the unassimilated groups in the minority, in the cities and in the schools; therefore those who do move to the cities may be assimilated more quickly. A rapid, sudden mobilization, on the other hand, may make the unassimilated groups close to half of the population; they may therefore become more self-conscious as a group, and far less likely to feel the need to assimilate themselves to the old status quo. Conflict may result. The Solow model, which assumes that the rate of assimilation (per unassimilated person) is *constant*, cannot account for this kind of variation. Thus the Solow model does not articulate Deutsch's critical insight into the origins of nationalism.

In order to express the idea that the rate of assimilation in any area (urban or rural) depends on how much the differentiated are outnumbered by the assimilated, we may form a model like the following:

$$A(t + 1) = A(t) + k(A(t) - D(t))D(t), \quad \text{for } A(t) > D(t), \quad (6.20)$$

where $A(t)$ is the *percentage* of population assimilated at time t, $D(t)$ is the percentage of population differentiated (i.e., unassimilated) at time t, and k is a constant. In essence, this model states that the *percentage* of the differentiated who are assimilated in any year will not be *constant*, as in the Solow model, but will be proportional to the numerical percentage dominance, $A(t) - D(t)$, of the assimilated population over the differentiated population. In the first half of Chapter 2, a number of refinements were discussed that could be made to this simple model. Stanley Lieberson's [4] study of bilingualism in Canada has shown that the effects of local *percentage dominance* are of overwhelming importance in predicting rates of bilingualism and linguistic assimilation; he has shown that fairly smooth curves[8] result when one plots local percentage dominance against language change, implicitly *holding constant* the overall national linguistic and cultural environment. Even in its simple form, however, Equation (6.20) does express the idea of percentage dominance as a determinant of the rate of assimilation.

In order to improve further on Equation (6.20), let us consider two other *qualitative* factors that also need to be accounted for. First, let us look at demographic factors. Lieberson [4] has emphasized two competing forces that can affect the fate of a minority language: (1) the economic and percentage dominance of the majority language (English), which encourages people to assimilate away from the minority language (French); and (2) the "revenge of the cradle," the high birth rate of the rural, provincial people who speak the minority language. (See Section 6.6.2 for details.) In this study, I have tried to avoid dealing with the demographic factors directly. *By applying Equation (6.20)*, not to the nation as a whole but *to the urban or rural part of one provincial area at a time*, we can expect less difference between the birth rates of the two language groups. If the model is expressed in terms of *percentages* of people speaking different languages, then the overall birth rates need not be estimated. In order to go on to predict the *nationwide* percentages of language use, we would have to predict population, first, in each region, and then convert the predictions of *percentages* of language use in each region to predictions of *numbers* of language speakers in each region. In brief, *this model treats population growth in each region as an exogenous variable*. The primary reason for doing so is simply that this variable has been studied in enormous detail elsewhere, and it would take enormous work merely to duplicate a portion of those studies here; I have looked at the variable briefly, but I have tried to keep it a different issue for the limited purposes here.

Second, the model, as written, defines *percentage dominance* merely as "$A(t) - D(t)$," the percentage by which the majority language dominates the minority language. In reality, percentage dominance consists of two different variables—percentage dominance *within each locality of region* and percentage dominance *nationwide*. The first variable encourages regionalism. For example, it encourages people in Quebec to speak French only, while it encourages people in the rest of Canada to speak English only; it makes the regions more

---

[8]See Lieberson [4], pp. 47, 48 and 183–187, for relatively smooth graphs emerging from scatter plots.

and more distinct from each other, and it reinforces the conflict between them. On the other hand, the second variable encourages people in all regions to conform to a national norm.

6.4.1 Local Versus Regional Language Dominance as a Dynamic Factor

How could we predict which of these two processes will become dominant, the regional or the national? One way to deal with this question is by trying to formulate an abstract theory of language-dominance pressure. We can try to formulate a theory that does not rely on (arbitrary) political abstractions, like the boundary lines between administrative regions. In the spirit of *Nationalism and Social Communications*, we can focus instead on the nationwide network of communication flows. For any given individual inside such a network, the language pressure he or she experiences depends simply on the balance between the two languages *as a percentage of the person's communications*, past and future [5]. (These communications should be weighed, in principle, by their psychological salience. Also, the "natural" level of communication between two people of two regions may sometimes be a more accurate measure of language pressure than the actual level, if the latter differs from the former due to a mutual inability to communicate; a desire to communicate, unfulfilled, can sometimes provide an incentive to learn the other person's language.)

Translating this to the level of regional variables, we may write the model as

$$P_i(t) = \sum_j C_{ji}(A_j(t) - D_j(t)), \qquad (6.21a)$$

$$A_i(t + 1) = A_i(t) + D_i(t) * f(P_i(t)), \qquad (6.21b)$$

where $P_i(t)$ represents the percentage dominance of the majority language as experienced in region i at time t, C_{ji} represents the flow of communications between region i and region j (actually, to region number i, from region j, as a percentage of the total communications to region i), the summation in Equation (6.21a) is to be taken over all regions j if possible, and the asterisk (from computer terminology) is used as a sign of multiplication. In Equation (6.21b) $f(P_i(t))$ is used instead of just $P_i(t)$ to reflect the observation above that, in Equation (6.20), one could have replaced the expression $A(t) - D(t)$ by a more complicated *function* of the percentage dominance.

Let us look briefly at the implications of this model, for a "typical" nation passing through the stages of political development. Let us suppose that the nation starts out as a "traditional" country, mostly rural, heavily dependent on sedentary agriculture. In such a country, one would expect that the vast peasant majority would have few communications, if any, outside their own region; the economics of such a region would provide little incentive and little opportunity for the average person to communicate with other regions. On the other hand, the urban and literate subsections of such a country would still have many communications outside their own area, particularly with the merchants and literati of other cities. The model would therefore predict that *regional* language pressure would be overwhelmingly dominant over national language pressure, for the illiterate majority. Therefore the spoken language will sustain a fragmentation into a host of regional dialects. (Section 6.6.3 elaborates on this effect.) On the other hand, the written language of the elite will experience heavy *long-distance* language pressure, at a national or even international level; it will tend to coalesce into a uniform national or even continental language. All this assumes a fairly stable and well-divided class structure.

However, as economic growth begins, and rural people become mobilized, a conflict will develop between their original dialects and the national language of the cities to which they move *to*. The written language will come into a head-on collision with the spoken system of languages. As the communications network grows more and more integrated, and more extensive for the average person within each nation, national pressures will grow more important for the average person; thus there is likely to be a growth in national assimilation and uniformity at the level of the spoken language. On the other hand, if any of the regional dialects "capture" a cohesive center of mobilized population, such as a city, before they are assimilated to the national language (i.e., extremely rapid mobilization occurs), then this city may exert its *own* language pressure on the surrounding rural population and towns. The widespread, modern communications links acting on this city will *strengthen* the hold of its dialect and perhaps lead to a political separatism, which then outlaws extensive communications between this region and other regions. If there were one dominant city, such as a London or a Paris, in a large area, then this city, once "captured," may set a new national linguistic norm. If there were a number of competing cities, however, one might expect a greater persistence of local dialects, converging perhaps by a process of mutual adjustment of the language norms themselves, if the norms were close to each other, but not by assimilation as such, until one of the cities does succeed in dominating the network of communications; thus a greater level of fragmentation would be predicted. Note that the *average distance* of communications in the new modern network may actually be less than that of the old elite network; thus the new written language may indeed be more restricted, geographically, than the language of the old elite. All these predictions seem broadly consistent with the phenomena discussed in Deutsch [1, Chapter 6].

Finally, one may note that the use of communications terms, as in Equations (6.21), can be generalized to other aspects of the problem of nationalism, and even to social psychology on a wider scale. *It would be inappropriate, in this context, to discuss all these future possibilities.* However, from a practical point of view, these models are only a small beginning in the quantitative theory of nationalism; much of their value lies in the possibilities that they lead to for future research. In order to realize this value, let us sketch out some of these possibilities explicitly.

6.4.2 Some Operational Dimensions of Nationalism: Narcissism, Stereotyping, and Aggression

The Deutsch–Solow model and the models discussed above involve the *origin* of nationalism, the origin of systems of national identification. However, it is also interesting to ask how nationalism, once born, can grow to become a motive force behind militarism, chauvinism, and the like. Indeed, one may regard "nationalism" as consisting of seven clusters of variables, only one of which concerns identification directly:

1. Affiliation with a "nationality"; concretely, this would entail a clustering at the national level of language norms, cultural symbols, and so on.
2. The sharing of "tacit norms" [6] that make cooperation possible in situations of mixed conflict and cooperation (as described in Section 6.6.4). When these norms tend to be close or identical among people of the same nationality, but very different for those of different nationality, then "community," by Deutsch's definition,[9] exists precisely at the national level.
3. The overestimation of the power level of one's own nation ("narcissism" in the language of the psychiatrist).
4. The underestimation of the power levels of other nations (stereotyping).
5. The intensity of positive emotional commitment to one's own nation (utility attributed to the "success" of one's nation; this may be the resultant of both "rational" and "irrational" (narcissistic or neurotic) attachments).
6. The intensity of emotional commitment, positive or negative, to other nations (utility attributed to their "success").
7. The glorification of militaristic, nationalistic behavior for its own sake.

"Nationalism," by this definition, would appear to be a crucial cause of international violence. The likelihood of international violence would appear to depend on the ability to compromise in any given perceived game—which we would associate with cluster 2 above [6]—and in the perception by the participants that compromise is desirable. Insofar as war involves a massive destruction of resources, at least when modern nation-states are involved, one would normally expect it to be far away from what an economist would call "Pareto optimal." One would expect that a compromise would exist, far superior for *both* sides than the actual outcome of the war. If the participants overestimate the gains they would achieve by war, however, they may not be able to appreciate beforehand that any particular compromise would be more

[9]See Deutsch [1, pp. 96–97]. In another book by Deutsch [7, pp. 17], the concept of "community" is defined in terms of an ongoing *ability* to communicate and respond in decision-making processes of a continuous sort.

desirable. Also, if they attach a positive value to hurting their adversary, then they may feel that their own material losses in war would be balanced out by the losses of their adversary. These misperceptions, which may lead to war, are associated with clusters 3–6 above. In practice, the breakdown of bargaining between nations will often depend on some "spark," like the assassination of an Austrian archduke or the sinking of the *Maine*; however, long before the spark appears, there may be a prolonged period of cold war, in which the ability to compromise gradually decreases and peace becomes ever more precarious. Students of conflict, who dismiss the sticky, "irrational" factor of nationalism and focus solely on objective conflicts and capacities, may be helpful in encouraging more objective, less nationalistic, and more peaceful policies by the major powers today; however, by neglecting a primary cause of past conflicts, they may reduce the applicability of their historical studies.

One may note, furthermore, that the concept of nationalism above is important, not only to the simple variable of war-versus-peace, but also to the possibility of bargains on a higher level, to maximize joint production in ways that would have been impossible without cooperation. Trade agreements are only one part of this picture. In the limit, if nations were fully adept at such negotiation, they could achieve the same joint efficiency and productivity that a unified world government could, if they do not place a strong negative intrinsic value on each other's basic welfare. On a lower level, such a gradual improvement in coordination has been crucial, in the past, in the fusing of subnationalities into larger nations [1, 7].

6.4.3 Toward More General Models

In order to predict the variables that make up nationalism, one may try to extend Equation (6.20) to deal with *continuous* psychological variables. Even in dealing with language, it was necessary at times to talk about changes in the language norms themselves, as *continuous* variables, rather than simple adherence to one norm or another. (See Section 6.6.3.) Given a continuous variable, X, which represents some arbitrary cultural norm, such as the pronunciation of a certain vowel, we may try to express the idea that people will change their own norms in response to the norms of those they communicate with. As a first approximation, we get an equation analogous to (6.20):

$$\frac{dX_i}{dt} = k\sum_j C_{ji}(X_j - X_i). \tag{6.22}$$

where X_i is the value of the variable X (a norm) for person i, and where C_{ji} represents the strength of communication between person i and person j. In a sense, the term on the right is a "reinforcement" term impinging on person i.

In practice, however, when we deal with questions like nationalism and fundamental personal values, it is unrealistic to imagine conformity as the only mechanism at work. Somehow, a more general approach must be formulated.

One might hope, at this point, that social psychologists, while neglecting nationalism per se [1, p. 26], would have formulated more satisfactory models for the flow of ordinary psychological variables, models that would predict the seven variable-clusters of nationalism as one special case. In the conflict literature, however, the concepts one normally sees from social psychology tend to involve very specific variables, such as frustration, aggression, and status inconsistency. A fascinating exception to this generalization is the article by Schwartz on prerevolutionary society, in the Feierabend anthology [8]. Schwartz's approach involves the heavy use of approach–avoidance diagrams, with nodes representing clusters of psychological variables and with signs attributed to connecting lines that represent associations between clusters.

Approach-avoidance theory allows Schwartz to predict the likely trends in the level of association—plus or minus—between two clusters of variables, and also in the "distance" between them. The same rules for determining these trends could be applied when more objects of thought are brought into the model; also, they might be applied to other phases of social psychology, such as the variables making up nationalism. Beyond its capacity for being generalized, Schwartz's approach has one other virtue: it evokes a detailed picture of the human, psychological feeling of the societies he describes, a picture that he validates in detail from verbal descriptions, yet a picture both sharper and clearer than the usual verbal summaries.

More generally, following up on Schwartz's approach, one might hope to work toward *open-ended* mathematical models of human behavioral psychology, models capable of achieving greater and greater accuracy as one accounts for more and more variables, within the *same* mathematical structure, a structure that nonetheless makes substantive predictions. This possibility may be compared with the possibility of predicting weather, by using a set of differential equations rewritten into the form of difference equations, so that predictions may be made based on knowledge of the initial conditions only at a fixed set of weather stations on a national grid. As one expands the number of weather stations and makes the grid ever finer, one can make better and better predictions, using the *same* differential equations that one started with. If one described the "initial conditions" of a human mind in terms of some sort of network structure, and if one's equations specified how to predict the future of any mental network from its present state, then a similar flexibility should be possible in social psychology.

In the limit, as one allows the hypothetical possibility of knowing the initial values of *all* the psychological variables in someone's mind, one would hope that one's model would approach equivalence to a general cybernetic model of human intelligence and motivation. On the other hand, if one allowed only for very limited knowledge, one would hope that one's social–psychological model would help one choose the aggregate variables of greatest predictive power in making concrete predictions. In the middle range, one may have to encompass the studies by political scientists such as Sheldon Kravitz [9] on larger-scale psychological structures, as revealed in the voluminous data of public political statements. Any of these constraints is difficult enough to satisfy by itself; the combination goes well beyond the range of the present discussion.

Given that it may take a long time for anyone to construct such high-level models, and a long time to learn how to deal with them, a lower-level generalization of the simple communications model may have some value as an intermediate step. Instead of starting from a full-fledged model of individual psychology, let us consider a simple equation, drawn essentially from Minsky and Selfridge [10, p. 339], to describe the changes of a psychological variable, X, under the influence of a "reinforcement" variable, E:[10]

$$X(t + 1) = (1 - \theta)X(t) + \theta E(t). \tag{6.23}$$

In essence, E measures the individual's feeling, after the fact, of what X "should" have been, vis-à-vis his/her experience at time t. If experiences of E occur at a certain frequency, F, we may approximate this by a differential equation:

$$\frac{dX}{dt} = kF(E - X). \tag{6.24}$$

This model of individual psychology would leave out the crucial fact of *interaction* between different psychological variables; in practice, for example, a strong irrational narcissism on the psychiatric level may provide a pressure toward greater overestimation of the potency of one's nation as well. Again, a thorough description of such interactions would be very complex. However, one may make a simplification based on the idea of cognitive dissonance. If X_e is the value of X one would "expect," or at least find most plausible, based on one's current psychological state with regard to *other* variables, and if C is the level of confidence with which one feels this expectation, then one might generalize Equation (6.24) as follows:

$$\frac{dX}{dt} = k_1 F(E - X) + k_2 C(X_e - X). \tag{6.25}$$

In a sense, we have added a new source of "reinforcement" to X, or a new "pressure" on the individual's psychological state.

---

[10]In discussing this formula, Minsky and Selfridge consider only the cases $E = 1$ or $E = 0$ per episode, but the generalization does not appear very difficult. These authors, in turn, refer to Bush and Mosteller [11] as a basic source.

Finally, it is easy to synthesize this simplified model of individual psychology with Equation (6.22):

$$\frac{dX_i}{dt} = k_1 F_i(E_i - X_i) + k_2 C_i(X_{e,i} - X_i)$$

$$+ k_3 \sum_j C_{ji}(X_j - X_i). \qquad (6.26)$$

With the help of a moderately complex model of *individual* psychology, one might predict C_i and $X_{e,i}$ in a very complex way from one's knowledge of the other psychological variables applying to person i; however, this by itself would not require us to change the final coupling terms, on the far right of the equation. Thus the model here can be extended in a fairly straightforward way, *building on* the work of personal (versus social) psychologists.

Also, one could develop the model further by learning which measures of C_{ji} are most appropriate, and when. For example, one might explore the hypothesis that C_{ji} includes only close family communications, for X_i that represent basic emotional attachments, in communities that have adapted to a combination of intense conflict and extensive ordinary communications for centuries. Or one might explore the hypothesis that tacit norms for cooperation depend most heavily on C_{ji} measured in terms of constructive bargaining (or other mutual coordination of effort) rather than simple trade or general communications; this hypothesis, if validated, would imply that the reduction of nationalism and the stabilization of peace depends critically on efforts by nations to achieve joint benefits from concrete joint activities going beyond simple trade and ordinary cultural exchanges.

Given that the model above is highly linear, it does *not* require us to fall back on the even worse approximation of predicting the "average person," as if all people in a given nation were the same; it would allow us to deal with the flow of psychological variables by mathematics quite similar to those well established for problems such as heat flow. For example, if national narcissism led to uniform values for C and X_e (e.g., a *high* estimate, X_e, of relative national strength) in a nation, and if there were many levels of communication separating the decision-makers and the people who experience the raw data directly (i.e., realistic E, with a high level of F), one would expect a simple geometric decline in the level of $X_e - X$ with increasing distance of communication; with a deep enough hierarchy, the perceived variable, X, may reflect only the prejudices of the nation, the X_e, and have no reality content at all. Thus one would predict a form of "groupthink",[11] based on *large-scale* communications effects.

In other cases, however, it may be more appropriate to treat a national communications system as a conglomerate of distinct subsystems (e.g., elite,

[11]"Groupthink" as a small-group phenomenon has been widely discussed as a result of Janis [12].

burghers, and masses in 19th-century Germany, or workers and industrialists in modern Japan); this is especially important when one considers domestic conflicts, which may lead in turn to revolution and to messianic nationalism as part of a common pattern. *Given* a description of a communications system, conglomerate or continuous or a mixture of the two, and given the exogenous data, Equation (6.26) would be fairly manageable in providing predictions of the continuous psychological variables of one's choice. Panel survey studies would be possible, to refine the model or provide the data for future predictions, when aggregate national data are inadequate. Classical models of history and of conflict may fit in, by helping us to predict the variables left exogenous in Equation (6.26).

In brief, the concept of communications terms has led us to a generalization—equations (6.21)—of the Deutsch–Solow model of assimilation and political mobilization. In Section 6.5 empirical tests of this model in Norway are discussed. This generalization of the Deutsch model, while limited in the present context, offers numerous possibilities for important extensions in the future.

6.5 ASSIMILATION AND COMMUNICATION: THE CASE OF NORWAY

Broadly speaking, the investigation of variants of Equations (6.21), by use of the approaches discussed in Chapter 3, has led to results similar to those of Sections 6.2 and 6.3. The power of communications terms and of ARMA models, vis-à-vis simpler regression models, has been validated, both in terms of statistical likelihood and in terms of long-term predictive power. The validation has been more significant here, due to the larger quantity of data, but the actual improvements range about 10% in terms of reducing the size of errors. Also, when "outliers" are present, the ARMA models appear much worse in terms of their formal likelihood than do the regression models, though they retain a superior capacity for long-term prediction. Erratic noise, in the form of "ratchet effects" that occur erratically like simple outliers but then *persist*, does not appear to reduce the modest superiority of the ARMA techniques. In this research, a substantive explanation has also been verified for some of the inconsistent results reported with "gravity models" to predict communications intensities; gravity models were used to allow us to construct three extra indices of communications within Norway.

In order to test out Equations (6.21) statistically, it was necessary to find a case history with the following characteristics: (1) extensive data on language preference, region by region, distinguishing between urban (mobilized) subregions and rural subregions; (2) data on the matrix of communications between *one* region and *another* region, *not* aggregated in the form of "total communications entering" or the like; and (3) significant variation across time in a large number of regions in the percentage of language use. Four countries were considered as interesting possible case histories early in this study—Canada,

Belgium, Finland, and Norway. (Various parts of the British Isles and Africa also seemed promising but not on the basis of data available at Harvard libraries.) All four have extensive data, commonly available, on language usage. In Canada, however, the data commonly available are aggregated at the level of provinces; except for New Brunswick, most of the provinces of Canada have been consistently close to the extremes of 100% French or no French. In Belgium, the censuses of language were separated by long intervals of time, and the geographical divisions appeared to be just as sharp, on the whole, as in Canada; the slight variations in Brussels and in Brabant were not enough to change this picture. Of the two remaining countries, Norway had much better data on communications variables.

The data from Norway turned out to be quite good for statistical purposes. Einar Haugen, in his book on language problems in Norway, has shown a map [13, p. 229], giving the percentage use of the minority language, Nynorsk, in schools in Norway, in the three years 1931, 1945, and 1957, in each of the 18 provinces of Norway. The data for Oslo (consistent avoidance of Nynorsk) do not appear on the map but can be reconstructed from the Norwegian Official Statistics, which constitute my own source of data; thus we can add in Oslo, to arrive at 19 major regions in Norway. If we ask how great the gap was, in each region, between the maximum percentage of Nynorsk taught in these three years, and the minimum percentage, we find that these variations across time have been quite substantial. In only six of the 19 has there been no variation; in the six with the highest variation, the average variation was by 28.5%; in the middle seven, the average was $12\frac{1}{7}\%$. (For example, in Oppland, one of the largest provinces on the map, the percentage use of Nynorsk was 15% in 1931, 44% in 1945, and 40% in 1957, yielding a maximum variation of 29%.) Thus in predicting the variations of language use across time, we are not predicting a dummy variable. Given that the equations in these models all attempt to predict language use at the time $t + 1$, *controlling* for the independent variable of language use at time t, the different averages of language use in different provinces do not water down the effective size of the data sample. In Haugen's map, it also seems clear that the greatest reductions in the use of Nynorsk were concentrated in "intermediate" provinces, or, more generally, provinces that have a significant Nynorsk population but that have a high percentage of communications with non-Nynorsk regions. (Some of the northern provinces, which are far from *all* the populated parts of Norway, have very strong communications with Oslo, on a *relative* basis, according to the migration data.) In this study, the use of percentage variables instead of numerical totals helped ensure that the results are not dominated by a handful of large subregions.

Data were available in Norway from 36 regions (urban and rural parts of each province, considering Oslo as the urban part of Akershus and the city of Bergen as the urban part of Hordaland), for every year from 1938 to 1969. Section 6.6.5 provides the sources. If we treat all 36 strings of data as sample *strings*, each with $N = 31$, each generated by the same *general* process (i.e., governed by the same equations and coefficients), the effective N of the overall sample was $36 \times 30 = 1080$ (30, not 31, because of the time lags; each string contains 30 *pairs* of data of language use at time t and language use at time $t + 1$.) Data were also available on (1) migration *from* each subregion *to* each other subregion in the three years 1966, 1967, and 1968; (2) total outgoing long-distance telephone calls, from 1938 to 1957, by year and by subregion; (3) total letters posted, in 1938–1940 and 1944–1968; (4) births, deaths, and marriages from 1938 to 1968; (5) real income, from 1938 to 1968; and (6) other information on population, crime rate, and rate of welfare payments not used in this study.

Initially, in coding the data, I was confronted with two interesting choices: (1) whether to define the subregions of each province as "urban" versus "rural," or to define them as the collections of townships that happened to be defined as urban or rural, in an arbitrary base year, such as 1958; and (2) what to do about the one case of zero data, the case of Finnmark (the northernmost part of the entire mainland of Scandinavia), where no languages at all were used in schools during World War II, apparently because schools were shut down. In a normal statistical study, one would tend to account for the limitations of multiple regression and choose definitions for one's variables in order to make them as manageable and as predictable as possible. The moving of townships from the rural to the urban category often had a "ratchet" effect, producing an appearance of change by jerky movements instead of just continuous *observable* movements. In this case, however, the original concepts of Karl Deutsch clearly called for *urban* versus *rural* percentages, not for geographical subregions; also, it was important to the evaluation of the statistical technique to see if it was as sensitive to ratchet effects—which would appear to be quite common in politics—as multiple regression is; finally, the data on urban versus rural language use were relatively accessible, while the consistent use of a fixed group of townships would have required approximately 15 additions and checks for each of 1110 subregion-years, for each of 10 variables or so. With Norwegian postal data, an aggregation of this sort was unavoidable, given that the data were available on a township basis but not on an urban versus rural basis for most years. In the case of Finnmark, it was decided implicitly to set the assimilated-percentage variable to zero, in the war years, in the first runs, partly as a test of the statistical method. (Finnmark has consistently used *no* Nynorsk; that is, it has been 100% assimilated.) This had the effect of introducing a few substantial outliers into the data; this fact turned out to be quite interesting in the runs that followed.

Nine good runs were carried out to predict Norwegian language data, after the prototype version of the ARMA program was fully checked out, and the data in the computer checked for consistency with the original data sheets. The years 1939–1967 were chosen as the main focus of study to avoid calibration problems with different variables. The first seven runs were carried out on the original data, with outliers existing in Finnmark. By and large, these runs were rather disappointing.

In the first run, ARMA tried out two simple models to predict the percentage, A, of language assimilation in Norway. The first model was

$$A(t + 1) = bA(t) + c + a(t),\qquad (6.27)$$

where $a(t)$ is a random noise term to be minimized, and the second model was

$$A(t + 1) = \theta A(t) + a(t) + Pa(t - 1).\qquad (6.28)$$

where *both* terms on the right are noise terms, indicating the presence of more complicated noise. Note that with the regression model (6.27), I have included a constant term, c, while the ARMA model (6.28), described in the notation of Chapter 3, does not include a constant term. Thus both models have the same number of coefficients to estimate. With the prototype version of ARMA, the constant term was consistently included in the regression model and deleted from the ARMA model to ensure that models of the same general level of complexity were being compared.

The results of the first run were relatively disappointing. The regression model received a likelihood score log P larger than that of the ARMA model, based on the standard normal distribution test described in Chapter 3. The gap in scores was equal to 7, indicating odds of $e^7 = 1100$ to 1 against the ARMA model being better than the regression model empirically. (See Section 2.5 of Chapter 2 for a more thorough discussion of the traditional concepts here.) Given the large data set, this meant that the percentage of variance explained— R^2—was 99.49% for the regression model versus 99.48% for the ARMA model. In a test of long-term prediction, however, the ARMA model did better, as the reasoning in Chapter 5 might have indicated. The regression model had average percentage errors of 14.9%, versus 14.1% for the ARMA errors. Note that the "percentage error," in any year, is defined as the gap between the prediction and reality, expressed as a percentage of the averages of the prediction and reality; note also that these errors were averaged by the root-mean-square (rms) method. The "absolute errors" in predicting the percentage of assimilation averaged out to 28% for the ARMA model and 39% for the regression model; the huge figures are due to occasional wild predictions, building up geometrically from 1939 to 1968.

Note that a 2% reduction in square error, from $1 - .9948$ to $1 - .9949$, is considered highly confirmed by the usual likelihood test with a simple this large; *the larger reductions in long-term prediction errors by the ARMA routine would appear to be even more certain in their validity.* Indeed, it seems much more suspicious in some ways to discuss the reduction of very small errors—about 0.50%—than to discuss the reduction of more substantial errors. In theory, the classical likelihood measure is enough to account for such "multicollinearity," but even so such situations have often turned out to cause problems for statisticians. Note that the presence of multicollinearity would presumably be much worse than here, for processes that one would hope to find more predictable in the long-term; the inability of classical approaches to perform well under such circumstances is one more reason to favor a new approach. An approach that attempts directly to minimize the more substantial errors in long-term prediction would appear to be much safer. Also, as in Section 6.3, it is critical that *formal statistical likelihood and predictive power have not gone hand-in-hand in their evaluations of the different models available.*

In later runs, I hoped that the ARMA models would do better in terms of statistical likelihood. After all, the constant term in the regression model could reflect a trend away from Nynorsk, a trend that could be *explained* by communications terms and other terms, so that the value of a constant term as a surrogate variable would disappear when they are accounted for. Also, for reasons described in Sections 2.5 and 2.6 of Chapter 2, I hoped that the ARMA model would be more sensitive to terms of realistic importance, increasing in likelihood by more than the regression model does when such terms are included.

In the second run, I decided to introduce a communications term. In Norway, there was only one *explicit* measure of communications *from* each province *to* each other province available—average migration from 1966 to 1968. Given that population data were not fully available from 1939 to 1967, and given that *intraprovincial* communications are presumably *not* well measured by internal migration data directly, the following simplified model was used:

$$A_i(t + 1) = c_1 A_i(t) + c_2 \sum_j M_{ji}(A_j(t) - D_j(t))$$

$$+ c_3(S_i(A_i(t) - D_i(t)) + S_i^*(A_i^*(t) - D_i^*(t)))S_i, \quad (6.29)$$

where M_{ji} represents migration from region j to region i, S_i represents the sum over j of M_{ji}, and the asterisk refers to variables in the region complementary to region i. (That is, A_i^* is the percentage of assimilation, measured in the same province as region i, but in the rural part, if region i is urban, or in the urban part, if region i is rural.) In principle, M_{ji} should have been divided by the population of region i, but this was not only impossible, it was of limited potential importance in a nation with provinces of comparable population. In retrospect, it might have been better to start out with the full, more complex model, Equations (6.21), even in these early investigations; however, due to the difficulties and potential controversy in estimating the shape of $f(D_i)$, it was decided that priority should be given to the simpler formulation at this stage.

At any rate, the model written out above—Equation (6.29)—did not perform especially well, with the initial Norway data, according to the usual statistical tests based on short-term prediction. In terms of statistical likelihood, the regression model in this run did no better than the regression model of the earlier run, without communications terms. (Gaps in likelihood less than one point, as discussed in the footnotes to Table 6.11, were not recorded, due to the implication of no significance in such differences in apparent performance.) In other words, the extra terms did not appear to add anything. The estimate of c_3 here, as in all the other runs carried out on this model and its analogues, was too small for the computer output formats to cope with. c_2, however, was on the order of 1%. Again, the regression model was superior to the ARMA model, with a gap of likelihood scores of 5.65, indicating odds of 280 to 1 favoring the regression model. The ARMA communications model had a slightly higher likelihood—by 1.5—than the simple model (6.28), indicating odds of 4.5 to 1 in its favor; however, these are not exactly overwhelming odds. The R of the ARMA model was .9948, versus .9949 for the regression model, just as before.

In long-term prediction, however, from 1939 to 1967, the ARMA model did increase its margin of superiority; its rms average percentage errors were 13.4%, versus 14.7% for regression, while its absolute errors were 27% versus 39%. *The communications term, even if poorly estimated, clearly added something to long-term prediction.* With a different estimation approach, oriented toward predictive power instead of maximum likelihood, the gain provided by the communication terms might have been considerably larger. Also, with the original model (6.21), the intermediate provinces of Norway, instead of the minimum-Nynorsk provinces, might have been singled out more effectively as likely areas of large-scale assimilation; again, the predictive power of the model might have been enhanced.

In the third run, as an alternative hypothesis, I considered the possibility of using real income as a variable to predict language:

$$A(t + 1) = c_1 A(t) + c_2 Y(t), \tag{6.30}$$

where $Y(t)$ represents the real income in a region, and where we have not written out the noise terms. In terms of likelihood theory, the performance of this model was *exactly* the same as that of Equation (6.29), as described above. In long-term prediction, however, it did not do quite as well. The ARMA rms average percentage errors were 14.1%, while the absolute errors were 28%; the regression percentage errors were 14.9%, absolute errors 39%. These results are closer to those of the univariate models (6.27) and (6.28) in quality, than to the results with Equation (6.29). In principle, however, the relative potential of the two models in long-term prediction will not be clear until a new type of estimation system is available.

In the remaining runs on the original data, I decided to explore communications indices other than that of simple migration. Two other measures of communication—telephone calls and volume of mail—were available; *however*, these were only available on a province-by-province basis. I faced the problem of how to reconstruct the matrix of communications *from* each province *to* each other province. This problem has often been faced elsewhere in regional science[12] and in sociology and has been resolved by way of a "gravity" model. The original gravity model, proposed by Stewart, would estimate province-to-province telephone communications, for example, as follows:

$$c_{ij} = c_0 \frac{T_i T_j}{r_{ij}}, \tag{6.31}$$

where T_i and T_j are the total volumes of telephone communications (or *other* communications variables, such as migration) in each province, and where r_{ij} is the distance between provinces. A modified version, studied by Galle and Taueber [16] and discovered to have a multiple correlation[13] of between 89% and 93% between prediction and reality, is as follows:

$$c_{ij} = c_0 \frac{T_i T_j}{r_{ij}^k}, \tag{6.32}$$

where k is an unknown exponent to be estimated. (Note that the correlation here, with a *cross-sectional* model, is stronger in its implications than a 90% would be in a predictive-time-series model, *insofar* as a cross-sectional study makes sense here.) Curiously enough, while Equation (6.32) has been successful in empirical tests, the parameter k has varied a great deal in its estimated value; Galle and Taueber report that k was equal to .62 for interurban migration in the United States in 1935–1940, but only .42 for the same data as measured in 1955–1960.

In order to estimate the likeliest value of k for interregional communications in the case of Norway, it was necessary to fit model (6.32) to the only region-to-region communications data available—again, the migration data. A direct fit of Equation (6.32) would have required the use of nonlinear regression; however, Equation (6.32) can be transformed as follows:

$$\log C_{ij} - \log T_i - \log T_j = a - k \log r_{ij}. \tag{6.33}$$

where the entire left side of the equation forms the dependent variable, and where a and k can be estimated by multiple regression.

As long as we were carrying out such a regression, however, it seemed appropriate to test out a new explanation for the reduction in k from .62 and .42 as measured in the United States by Galle and Taueber. It is fundamental

---

[12]See Isard [14], Chapter 11. On p. 500, reference is made to Stewart and Zipf, the two fathers of the idea; on p. 506, a concept of social distance is mentioned, similar in spirit to U_{ij}; on pp. 507–510, empirical results are discussed. See also Deutsch and Isard [15].
[13]See table on p. 8 of [16]. Galle and Taueber are essentially critics of the gravity model; thus their results are particularly interesting. For other work in this area, see Isard [14] and Deutsch and Isard [15].

to the communications theory of nationalism, as described in Section 6.4, that there has been a historic rise in the strength of long-distance communications, *relative* to shorter-distance communications, at least for the average person. Using Equation (6.32), we may compute the *ratio* of communication across a long distance, R_1, to the communications across a shorter distance, R_0, between regions of equal size (T_i the same for all regions):

$$\frac{c_1}{c_0} = \frac{\dfrac{1}{(R_1)^k}}{\dfrac{1}{(R_0)^k}} = \left(\frac{R_0}{R_1}\right)^k \qquad (6.34)$$

For given distances, R_0 and R_1, the terms involving c_0, T_i, and so on cancel out; *thus the only way this ratio can get larger*, for a given comparison of distances, *is if k gets smaller*. (For example, a small variable to the zeroth power will equal 1, which is the maximum this ratio can approach under the stated conditions.) Thus it is critical to our communications theory that k should tend to decrease in time, as the result of some aspect of "modernization;" the most obvious aspect of modernization to consider is the economic factor, the increasing income of people relative to the cost of communication. Thus it was decided to test the model:

$$k(t) = c_1 - c_2 Y(t), \qquad (6.35)$$

where Y represents the real income of a region. Also, I decided to consider the possibility that a term representing social proximity (urban versus rural similarity of regions) should be accounted for. Thus, in the final regression equation, I decided to test

$$\log M'_{ij} = \log M_{ij} - \log S_i - \log S_j$$
$$= c_0 - c_1 \log r_{ij} + c_2 Y \log r_{ij} + c_3 U_{ij}. \qquad (6.36)$$

where U_{ij} is defined to equal one if both regions are rural or both urban, but zero if they differ; a measure of distance was obtained from the *World Atlas*[14]; S_i is defined as with Equation (6.29). Note that $Y(t)$—real income in the sub-

---

[14]A large map of Norway, with major roads indicated, was used [17, p. 57]. Distance was measured with a centimeter ruler, for the most direct major route by road; however, if this should exceed the absolute distance by 40% or more, then the direct distance plus 40% was used. For distances from an urban area, either there was one major city or several that could be averaged. For rural distances, it was assumed that population density was even throughout each region; averages were estimated on that basis. All the data here were punched on cards and read into the MIT Multics machine; the punched cards and code sheets may be made available to future users through the office of Professor Karl Deutsch.

region from which migration occurs—was *not* a surrogate for time in this regression, since the regression was based on a combination of two 36×36 matrices of total migration in the close-by years 1967 and 1968; the primary variation in real income was between subregions. The covariance matrix produced is shown in Table 6.25. Inverting the three-by-three matrix in the upper left of this table, and multiplying the inverse by the vector formed by the three upper numbers of the rightmost column, we can compute the standard regression coefficients for Equation (6.36):

$$c_3 = .24$$

$$c_2 = .26$$

$$c_1 = .70$$

all with the expected signs, and all clearly very significant for the large N we have considered and for the variances displayed in Table 6.25. Thus the income hypothesis appears to have been validated rather strongly. This same regression analysis was also used to construct an approximate measure of communications for one of the other communications variables available in Norway, telephone communications; however, c_2 was deleted from the regression equation, and c_1 thereby reduced to .67, due to the computational difficulty of calculating the full index, as based on different values of the income variable across time.

In the fourth run on Norwegian language data, Equation (6.31) was used to reconstruct the matrix of telephone communications, C_{ij}, to replace M_{ij} in Equation (6.29). The years 1930–1957 were used as a database. Once again, the regression model did better than the ARMA model in terms of log likelihood, with a gap of 3 points, implying odds of 20 to 1 in favor of the regression model. The R^2 of the regression model was .9941, versus .9940 for the ARMA model; this was substantially worse than the earlier runs. On the other hand, this was substantially worse than the earlier *univariate* runs, encompassing a subset of the independent variables here; this signals that the data in the period 1939–1957 average out to be more difficult to predict than the previous database, 1939–1967. Indeed, these years contain all of the wartime "outliers"

TABLE 6.25 Gravity Model Correlations

	U_{ij}	$Y \log r_{ij}$	$\log r_{ij}$	$\log M'_{ij}$
U_{ij}	0.251	0.017	−0.012	0.072
$Y \log r_{ij}$	0.017	1.299	0.286	0.135
$\log r_{ij}$	−0.012	0.286	0.875	−0.549
$\log M'_{ij}$	0.072	0.135	−0.549	1.062

mentioned above, in Finnmark. In light of these difficulties, the model did relatively well in long-term prediction. The rms average percentage errors were 13.7% and 14.1% for the ARMA and regression models, respectively; the rms average absolute errors were 35% and 40% for the two models, respectively. Perhaps a later run without outliers would have given a much better picture.

In the fifth run on Norwegian language data, I studied the same model as in the fourth run; however, this time Equation (6.36) was used, adapted to predict telephone communications, to reconstruct a matrix of telephone communications. The R^2 and the likelihood scores turned out to be the same as in the fourth run, except that the ARMA model gained very slightly in likelihood—by one point; the odds against this being a coincidence are only 3 to 1, according to likelihood theory—not a substantial confirmation. The results of this run seemed sufficiently bad, with R^2 still low, that simulations were not carried out.

In the next run on Norwegian language data, postal data were used, with Equation (6.36), to construct an index of communications, to replace M_{ij} in Equation (6.29). The regression model performed better than the ARMA model, with a gap in likelihood of 9, implying odds of $e^9 = 8100$ to 1 in favor of regression. The R^2 of the ARMA model was .9958, versus, .9959 for the regression model. At first, these high values of R^2 seemed rather encouraging. However, the data period used for this analysis was 1945–1967, due to the absence of postal data in three of the war years; this implied that the outliers in Finnmark were avoided. In the seventh run, as a corrective, I reevaluated the simple univariate models, Equations (6.27) and (6.28), over the same time period; the results were the same as with the postal model—implying that nothing was gained by adding these communications terms—except for an insignificant one-point decrease in the likelihood of the ARMA model.

After these seven runs were completed, a careful review was carried out, first of the ARMA models and then of the communications models. Another run was carried out on a different set of data—on births, deaths, and marriages as a single set of variables. In that case, the ARMA model outperformed the regression model by 339 points, by the usual likelihood measures, implying an astronomically high probability of its superiority. In conventional language, this gap of 339 points implies that "the ARMA model was confirmed with a p less than 10^{-100}." Concretely, the ARMA model had an R^2 of .975 in predicting the marriage rate, versus .85 for regression; also, the variance of the errors in predicting the death rate was reduced by 10%. Unfortunately, the computer refused to calculate a full table of predictions for this case, because the table was too long; however, the ARMA model did not seem notably superior to the regression model in that portion of the predictions which the computer did print out.

In order to explain the mediocre performance of the communications models, one must look very closely, province by province, at the direction and shape of the errors made by the ARMA communication models (from run number 2) in long-term prediction. There did not seem to be a notable tendency for errors to be biased in one direction in any special group of provinces, except for the "intermediate province" group, which the communications terms should have been able to distinguish; however, there *did* seem to be a very strong tendency for the predictions to be systematically low everywhere. With constant terms, of course, this would not have been expected. Still, the independent variables in Equation (6.29) were close enough to being able to represent constant trends, upward, that it seemed very strange that such a bias would develop. A series of intuitive arguments convinced me that the outliers in Finnmark, *extending* for a handful of years in both urban and rural Finnmark, could add a degree of apparent randomness, enough to bias the coefficients substantially. Given that Nynorsk had never been used at all in schools in Finnmark, it was decided to change the data, so that in *all* years the variable A (percentage assimilated) would equal 100% in Finnmark.

After these changes, two runs were carried out, both highly successful. The first run duplicated the original first run, based on Equations (6.27) and (6.28). This time, the R^2 for the ARMA model was .9988, versus .9987 for the regression model. The ARMA model had a likelihood score of 35.46 points higher than the regression model, implying odds of 2.5 million billion to 1 against its superiority being a coincidence. Both models, of course, were doing astronomically better than any of the models discussed above. In simulation, however, the picture was a bit mixed, though still improved on the whole. The rms average percentage errors were 9.9% for the ARMA model and 9.4% for the regression model; the absolute errors averaged to 20% and 27%, respectively.

The second new run duplicated the second old run, in using Equation (6.29) as a model. The superiority of the ARMA model grew larger, when a more complete substantive model was used, just as we had hoped earlier; the gap in likelihood grew to 42.51, implying odds of 3×10^{19} to 1 in favor of the ARMA model. With the regression models, the addition of communications terms produced only a slight gain in likelihood—2 points—but with the ARMA model, the gain in likelihood was 9.03 points, implying a very significant improvement (significant at the level of "$p = .00011$" in conventional terminology). One may note that the coefficient of the main communications term was .0067 for the ARMA model, versus .0054 for the regression model, both about right for a recurrent feedback term. With a better substantive model, the ARMA model also improved much more in its long-term predictive power than the regression model did. The average percentage errors were 8.6% for the ARMA model, versus 9.0% for regression; the absolute errors averaged to 17% for the ARMA model, versus 25% for regression. Between the two measures, it is reasonable to say that the ARMA model here, as elsewhere, displays on the order of 10–15% less error in long-term prediction than the regression model does. Also, as pointed out at the beginning of this section, when *outliers* are removed, the ARMA models are very much superior to the regression models in terms of formal statistical likelihood. These statements remain true despite the "ratchet" effects—similar to outliers, but persistent—which were mentioned earlier in this section.

6.6 ENDNOTES TO CHAPTER 6

6.6.1 Evaluating a Possible Source of Bias

Strictly speaking, one major qualification might be made to this statement [of clear superiority of EXTRAP]. When making a prediction, one usually starts from a given base year and applies the differential equations to that year as an initial condition. This would correspond to *adjusting* k_7 and k_8 here, to fit a given year exactly. One can expect to do better, if one somehow averages different base years to get an estimate of the underlying reality and uses that estimate as the base for predictions. Admittedly, part of the advantage in "ext1" (EXTRAP) extrapolation probably lies in doing just that. If there were a consistent change in the rate of growth of these variables, through time, and if one were using extrapolation models to predict the same period of time as the one they were fitted to, this would lead to an *unfair* advantage for the extrapolation models; the extrapolation models would be centered at the middle of the process, but the ordinary models would be centered at the initial extreme. However, every one of the extrapolation runs here was accompanied by a run testing the predictive power of the hypothesis of a t^2 term in Equations (6.10); these runs gave no support to the idea that factors involving a simple second derivative could be responsible for the advantages of extrapolation. The ability of extrapolation to average out extreme values measured in the *same*, early periods of time is not "unfair," insofar as it reflects an advantage available to those trying to predict the future from an extensive databank from the present and past.

6.6.2 Lieberson Views of Language Shifts

Lieberson focuses strongly on the issues of language "retention" by those brought up in one language, as opposed to "demographic factors." He states [4, p. 35]: "It is far more correct to describe the Canadian scene as an equilibrium based on counterbalancing forces." He emphasizes [4, pp. 50–51], first, that English has been dominant in terms of "retention" or assimilation, but then, that the "revenge of the cradle" has been central to French language maintenance. Lieberson [4, p. 225] defines a variable, "communications advantage," quite similar in spirit to the "language pressure in communications" discussed here; in the subsequent verbal discussion, he implies that this variable is central to "retention" phenomena.

6.6.3 Language Fragmentation Effects

Strictly speaking, one must also try to explain the *origins* and *convergences* of such dialects, instead of merely the decision by individuals to jump from one dialect to another. Equation (6.26), which can deal with the ideal of dialects getting closer or further away as a result of communication, is conceptually quite close to the model here. Yet one is still faced with the problem of explaining how divergence in dialect can come about. If the speech in each region were subject to random drift, or to systematic pressures based on interregional differences in speech equipment, then a *low* level of interregional communications, in our model, would imply little damping of such drift. An increase in communications would imply a greater pressure for convergence, and a damping out of future drift. Note that such phenomena would also apply if there were a dramatic increase in communications between two regions with enough internal communications to resist assimilation as such; the growth of "franglais" is an interesting example.

6.6.4 Tacit Norms, Game Theory and Cooperation

Schelling [6, p. 104] comments: "But where do the patterns [of potential compromise] come from? They are not very visibly provided by the mathematical structure of the game, particularly since we have purposely made each player's value system too uncertain to the other to make considerations of symmetry, equality, and so forth, of any great help [i.e., of help in analyzing Shelling's paradigms for games of mixed conflict and common interest]. Presumably, they find their patterns in such things as natural boundaries, familiar political groupings, the characteristics of states that might enter their value systems, gestalt psychology, and any cliches or traditions that they can work out for themselves in the process of play." He goes on to state [6, p. 151]: "the introduction of uninhibited speech may not greatly alter the character of the game, even though the particular outcome is different." In short, tacit norms, before the introduction of explicit bargaining, are crucial to the existence of possible "patterns of convergence." Schelling hammers home the point [6, pp. 113–114] that mathematical "solutions" to nonzero-sum games do not provide a realistic alternative to his own theory of tacit norms [6, pp. 99–111]. In a sense, one might argue that the idea of "solving" for a unique or optimal static equilibrium may apply only to games similar to those originally discussed in such terms by Von Neumann and Morgenstern [18]; as in economics, there may be situations where dynamic factors cannot easily be encompassed within such a static description. At any rate, Schelling's discussion, applied elsewhere by him to real political analysis, strikes me as fairly convincing.

6.6.5 Sources of Norwegian Data

This section first discusses the data sources in general and the language data.

The primary source for these data, as with the data reported later, was the *Norwegian Official Statistics* (N.O.S.) series, commonly available in U.S. libraries. The Norwegian name is *Norges Offisielle Statistikk*; when author designations are required, the Central Bureau of Statistics or Sentral . . . is usually appropriate. School data for January 1970 may be found in the 1972 *Arbok* (Yearbook), which also appears as Rekke-XII, Number 274. Data on the use of languages in elementary education were used (as on p. 335 of that copy of the *Arbok*). The language use data for earlier years were taken from the earlier *Arboks*, back to 1939. In some years, when the urban/rural breakdown was not available, the *Skolestatistik* issues of the N.O.S. were used. Every number (issue) in the N.O.S. series includes a list of the numbers and topics of other recent issues; also, on the front or back cover are listed the numbers of previous issues on the same topic. (Thus in the 1972 *Arbok* are listed the Rekke and number of all previous *Arboks*.) Language use in elementary schools is essentially a matter of local choice; Haugen [14] gives a few details of the process of language choice. In the computer runs used here, the time periods of the data were recalibrated. Thus language use in force in schools in January 1950 was taken to be an index of actual language use in 1949, given the lags involved in changing policy in the schools.

Sources for other variables were as follows:

For migration from subregion to subregion: N.O.S., Rekke XII, No. 233; Rekke A, No. 244; and Rekke A, No. 292. Original statistics were further broken down by sex but aggregated for this study.

For outgoing telephone calls: N.O.S., Rekke XI, No. 298, for the most recent data and previous items in the same topic series. Note that Rekke XII, No. 232, while not containing the appropriate breakdowns by urban and rural, does provide definitions in English.

For letters posted: N.O.S. backwards from Rekke XII, No. 198. Aggregated according to the urban/rural definitions of townships spelled out in the *Skolestatistikk* series.

For births, deaths and marriages: N.O.S. backward from Rekke XII, No. 220. Some aggregation required in earlier years over sex, and so on. In 1967, Rekke XII, No. 244 was used.

For real income: N.O.S., Rekke A, No. 363, used for 1968 on back. ("Municipal Total Income," from Table IA. In early years, some aggregation was required; however, the column names were uniform enough that it was not too difficult to reconstruct the same aggregations as used by the N.O.S. authors in later years.) In Rekke XII, Nos. 245 and 252, an index of consumer prices was found, for the entire period (i.e., an historical table was available). The average size of the ratio, normalized to units appropriate for statistics, was on the order of unity.

For population, crime, and welfare: These data include data on criminal convictions—easily available in this period, starting back from the Arbok; data on heads of households on welfare, continued back in the *Statistical Monthly* over the entire period; data on population, *not* generally available in recent years with the desired breakdown, but in the *Arbok* when available.

REFERENCES

1. K. W. Deutsch, *Nationalism and Social Communications*, 2nd rev. ed., MIT Press, Cambridge, MA, 1966.
2. R. Hopkins, Projections of population change by mobilization and assimilation, *Behavioral Science*, p. 254, 1972.
3. R. Hopkins, Mathematical modelling of mobilization and assimilation processes, in H. Alker, K. Deutsch, and A. Stoetzel (eds.), *Mathematical Approaches to Politics*, Elsevier, New York, 1973.
4. S. Lieberson, *Language and Ethnic Relations in Canada*, Wiley, New York, 1970.
5. K. W. Deutsch, Mathematics of the Tower of Babel, in *Contemporary Political Science: Toward Empirical Theory*, McGraw-Hill, New York, 1967.
6. T. C. Schelling, *The Strategy of Conflict*, Oxford University Press, New York, 1963.
7. K. W. Deutsch et al., Political community and the North Atlantic area, in *International Political Communities*, Anchor Books, New York, 1966.
8. I. K. Feierabend, L. Rosalind, and T. R. Gurr, (eds.), *Anger, Violence and Politics: Theories and Research*, Prentice-Hall, Englewood Cliffs, NJ, 1972.
9. S. Kravitz, *A Theoretical Model For the Analysis and Comparison of Ideologies*, Ph.D. dissertation, May 1972. Available c/o Widener Library, Harvard University, Cambridge, MA 02138.
10. M. Minsky and O. G. Selfridge, Learning in neural nets, in *Information Theory*, Fourth London Symposium, C. Cherry, ed., Academic Press, NY, 1961.
11. R. R. Bush and F. Mosteller, *Stochastic Models for Learning*, Wiley, New York, 1955.
12. I. Janis, *Victims of Groupthink*, Houghton Mifflin, New York, 1973.
13. E. Haugen, *Language Conflict and Language Planning: The Case of Modern Norwegian*, Harvard University Press, Cambridge, MA, 1966.
14. W. Isard, *Methods of Regional Analysis: An Introduction to Regional Science*, MIT Press, Cambridge, MA, 1966.
15. K. W. Deutsch and W. Isard, Toward a generalized concept of distance, *Behavioral Science*, Nov. 1961.
16. O. R. Galle and K. E. Taueber, Metropolitan migration and intervening opportunities, *American Sociological Review*, No. 31, Feb. 1966.
17. *World Atlas*, Moscow, 1965.
18. J. Von Neumann and O. Morgenstern, *The Theory of Games and Economic Behavior*, Princeton University Press, Princeton, NJ, 1953.

PART 2

APPLICATIONS AND EXTENSIONS

7

Forms of Backpropagation for Sensitivity Analysis, Optimization, and Neural Networks

This Chapter summarizes the major properties and applications of a collection of algorithms involving differentiation and optimization at minimum computational cost. The area of application include the sensitivity analysis of models, new work in statistical or econometric estimation, optimization, artificial intelligence, and neuron modeling. The details, references, and derivations are given in [1].

7.1 CONTEXT OF THE WORK

The Energy Information Administration (EIA) provides data and analysis on all aspects of energy supply and demand. It uses dozens of models, including econometric (statistical, empirical) models, linear programming models based on technological data, a nonlinear microequilibrium model solving for thousands of variables simultaneously across a 50-year span, hybrids, and combinations of these.

Many users of EIA's analyses do not accept EIA's conclusions at face value, especially when reports from other sources disagree. Thus the Forecast Evaluation and Analysis Team of EIA and its predecessors have carried out a broad program to evaluate and explain the qualitative assumptions of EIA models and forecasts. This program includes the development of tools to characterize the properties of large models, studies of estimation methods that are robust

Aside from very minor copy editing, this chapter first appeared under the title "Applications of Advances in Nonlinear Sensitivity Analysis" in R. Drenick & F. Kozin, eds., *System Modeling and Optimization: Proc. of the 10th IFIP Conference* (1981), Springer New York, 1982.

against outliers or model misspecification (i.e., correlated errors), proofs of convergence and existence properties, and many other projects. The first part of this chapter describes how a small part of this work—the minimum cost calculation of first- and second-order derivatives of nonlinear systems—makes an essential contribution to the rest. The second part elaborates on another application, a method for stochastic optimization, which becomes feasible only with the help of low-cost derivatives. This method opens up a wholly new approach to the field of artificial intelligence and neuron modeling; it is especially efficient with the new generation of "parallel" computers.

7.2 WHAT IS AN ORDERED DERIVATIVE?

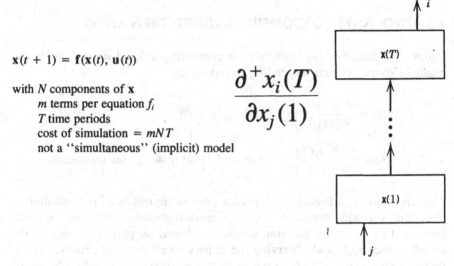

$$\mathbf{x}(t + 1) = \mathbf{f}(\mathbf{x}(t), \mathbf{u}(t))$$

with N components of $\mathbf{x}$
    m terms per equation f_i
    T time periods
    cost of simulation $= mNT$
    not a "simultaneous" (implicit) model

$$\frac{\partial^+ x_i(T)}{\partial x_j(1)}$$

FIGURE 7.1 A simple example.

Figure 7.1 shows a simple example of the kind of "derivative" we are trying to compute. Suppose that we have a nonlinear system, with a vector $\mathbf{x}$ of N endogenous variables and a vector $\mathbf{u}$ of exogenous variables. Suppose that the system is governed by the equation shown in Figure 7.1. The cost of simulating the model over the whole time range is mNT, because in each of the T time periods we compute a forecast for each of the N variables in $\mathbf{x}$, and each such forecast involves m terms. Please note that N is often much larger than m. Given a small change in the variable x_i in time period 1, we want to know how large the resulting change in x_i is in the final time period T.

The change in $x_i(T)$ per change in $x_j(1)$, holding the rest of $\mathbf{x}(1)$ constant, is a fundamental quantity of the system. It goes by many different names. In modeling, it is often called a "sensitivity coefficient." In economics, it is traditionally called an "impact multiplier." Electrical engineers often call it a "transient response" or "constrained derivative." Here it is called an "ordered derivative," using the notation shown in Figure 7.1, for two reasons: (1) the notation is somewhat more explicit than what is usually used; and (2) the concept of ordered derivative is somewhat more general and rigorous, as will be seen.

Well-known applications that require the use of such first-order derivatives are sensitivity analysis, maximization of a system result (i.e., "deterministic optimization"), and statistical estimation. In the last two cases, one actually is concerned with the derivatives of a function of $\mathbf{x}(T)$ or of $\mathbf{x}(t < T)$ rather than the derivatives of $x_j(T)$ for some j, but it is easy to make this extension of the methods; for example, the function to be differentiated or a running total for it may be added to the list of system variables.

7.3 TWO WAYS TO COMPUTE ORDERED DERIVATIVES

Figure 7.2 describes two methods for computing ordered derivatives in the example above. The corresponding equations are

$$\uparrow \quad \mathbf{z}(t) = \frac{\partial^+ \mathbf{x}(t)}{\partial x_j(1)}, \quad \mathbf{z}(t + 1) = f'(t)\mathbf{z}(t);$$

$$\downarrow \quad \mathbf{z}^*(t) = \frac{\partial^+ x_i(T)}{\partial \mathbf{x}(t + 1)}, \quad \mathbf{z}^*(t) = f'^T(t)\mathbf{z}^*(t + 1) \quad \text{(or transpose)}.$$

The large square in Figure 7.2 represents the entire matrix of ordered derivatives of all $x_i(t)$ with respect to all $x_j(1)$. The conventional or "forward" method (indicated by an arrow pointing upward) is based on perturbing one of the initials values $x_j(1)$ and observing the impact on all the final results, that is, on the vector $\mathbf{x}(T)$. Each time we apply this method, we perturb only one of the initial values; thus we obtain only one row of the matrix of ordered deriv-

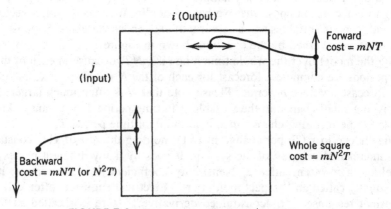

FIGURE 7.2 Two ways to obtain $\partial^+ x_i(T)/\partial x_j(1)$.

atives, as shown in Figure 7.2. This costs us mNT calculations, as shown. Often the initial value $x_j(1)$ is actually changed and the model resimulated. (This costs mNT operations, as did the original run of the model.) However, this leads to problems with the numerical accuracy of the results, because one computes each derivative by subtracting two numbers very close to each other in size. MIT's Troll System uses a special case of the forward closed-form Jacobian formula, shown at the bottom of Figure 7.2, which has the same cost but is more accurate.

The backward method, shown with a downward pointing arrow in Figure 7.2, computes an entire column of the matrix, using only mNT calculations. In engineering, this sort of method has been used for many years with "constrained derivatives" but has not been applied more generally.

The key point about these methods is that the forward method is often used when the backward method would be more appropriate. This can multiply costs (by a factor of N) to the point where it becomes infeasible to do what one wants to do. For example, it has long been known that economic data, like engineering measurements, are fraught with many errors, and that these errors invalidate conventional estimation methods. Statisticians like Hannan observed years ago that white noise converts a simple econometric model (like our example, but linear) into a "vector mixed autoregressive moving average process." In other words, one can account for such errors in data by estimating the corresponding vector ARMA process. However, because of the sheer cost of such estimation, it has rarely been done in economics. Instead, an approximation suggested by Hibbs has become popular of late: a conventional model is estimated by regression, and then simple univariate ARMA ("Box–Jenkins") modeling is used on the residuals, and the process may be iterated. Yet in statistical estimation, one only needs a single column of the derivative matrix (i.e., the derivatives of error), not the whole matrix; using the backward method, one can compute all the derivatives needed in an iteration at the cost of only mNT, which is what it takes to exercise the model. This method was applied to vector ARMA estimation in the early 1970s but has yet to receive wide application in economics. It now appears that vector ARMA estimation (and thus Kalman filtering estimation, which is formally equivalent to it) may have less value in social science than other more robust methods based on a generalization of Hartley's simulation path approach; however, those methods too require a set of derivatives, as part of minimizing a complicated loss function.

Likewise, in sensitivity analysis, a user often wants to know the sensitivity of a few key results to all the initial values, or to be sure he/she knows the largest of these sensitivity coefficients. Again, only a few columns of the matrix are required; it is wasteful to pay for the whole matrix.

With large models or network systems, N may range from the hundreds to the millions or more. Thus cutting the cost of computing derivatives by a factor of N is often crucial to feasibility. One may be sure that the cost of exercising the system (mNT) is affordable, or the system would be of no interest; more than this, by a multiple of N, may be unacceptably expensive.

7.4 ORDERED DERIVATIVES FOR NETWORKS AND PARALLEL PROCESSING

"Chain rule" (dynamic feedback):

$$\frac{\partial^+ x_i}{\partial x_j} = \sum_{k=j+1}^{i} \frac{\partial^+ x_i}{\partial x_k} \cdot \frac{\partial f_k}{\partial x_j}, \quad i > j$$

Conventional perturbation:

$$\frac{\partial^+ x_i}{\partial x_j} = \sum_{k=j}^{i-1} \frac{\partial f_i}{\partial x_k} \cdot \frac{\partial^+ x_k}{\partial x_j}, \quad i > j$$

Now let us consider the more general model shown in Figure 7.3. All non-negative lags—including zero—are permitted in the endogenous variables. However, we still assume here that the model has been reduced to "explicit" form. (In economics, one would call this a recursive model; in mathematics, one calls it a nonrecursive system). We assume that the functions f_i, which make up $\mathbf{f}$, can be ordered in such a way that we can use them one by one to calculate the vector $\mathbf{x}(t + 1)$. The dynamic feedback "chain rule" has not been published before (1981).

Figure 7.3 illustrates an example where $\mathbf{x}(t + 1)$ has 11 components, each represented by a circle; the arrows flowing into a circle represent inputs required to compute that component of $\mathbf{x}$.

The forward and backward methods are generalized as shown in Figure 7.3. The subscripts here refer to an ordered index of all time/variable-number combinations. The key thing to note is that there are only m calculations per time/variable combination. Thus we still only need to make mNT calculations to get a complete row or column of ordered derivatives, as in our earlier example. This has not previously been published. With conventional *matrix* methods for

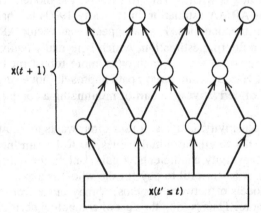

FIGURE 7.3 A more general example: $x(t + 1) = f(x(\text{all } t' \leq t + 1), u(\text{all } t'))$.

constrained derivatives, based on our earlier example, one would have to use N by N matrices f', which would not usually be sparse; thus the generalization here makes it feasible to differentiate large *network* systems, which would have been too expensive to differentiate with conventional methods.

The methods shown in Figure 7.3 remain efficient even if one uses "parallel" computers. Parallel computers—based on many processors operating in parallel rather than one CPU—are becoming increasingly common. With a conventional computer, it would take roughly 11 calculation times to compute $\mathbf{x}(t + 1)$ in our example (one for each component of $\mathbf{x}$). With a parallel computer, it need only take three: in the first period, four processors would calculate the lower tier in parallel, since none of the four lower components depends on the others; in the second period, the middle tier would be calculated; and soon. The backward method shown here allows similar economies: one can calculate ordered derivatives of a model result with respect to the top tier in the first period of calculation, then to the middle tier, and then to the bottom tier. The forward method is similar.

Large-scale models or systems typically can be represented as relatively sparse networks, as in this example. Actual physical networks, made up of units operating in parallel, have a similar structure. To optimize such as system (except in unusual special cases) it is essential to know the derivatives of the desired performance measure with respect to all parameters in the system; for this to be feasible, it is essential to use a method such as the generalized backward method, which does not multiply the cost of getting the derivatives far beyond the cost of exercising the system.

In this chapter, we have discussed derivatives with respect to initial values of the variables only; however, the EIA report [1] does consider parameters, and the case of exogenous variables is a trivial extension of the endogenous variable case. To avoid making a complicated discussion even more complicated, the EIA report only mentions our earlier example when discussing second derivatives; however, it is trivial to substitute the general formulas in Figure 7.3 for those in Figure 7.2, whenever they apply in the second derivative calculation, to arrive at more general methods. Section 7.2 provides a partial example of the possibilities.

Figure 7.4 provides a summary of the properties of the four variable–variable second derivative calculation methods provided in the EIA report. The set of ordered derivatives of $x_i(T)$ to $x_j(1)$ and $x_k(1)$ form an N by N by N cube, as shown; each method computes a subset of the cube, at approximate costs shown. Again, in practice, the key point is to compute only the subset required and not pay for the entire cube. The five methods for computing variable–parameter second derivatives offer the same subsets (except that an upward column and a row pointing backward count as two separate cases) for the same rough costs.

The EIA report notes that variable–parameter second derivatives provide meaningful information about a model, essentially equivalent to what MIT

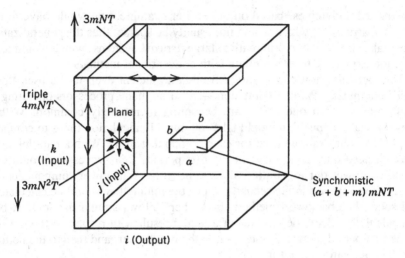

Cube above represents

$$\frac{\partial^{2+}x_i(T)}{\partial x_j(1)\partial x_k(1)}$$

EIA report also spells out   Full cube costs $3mN^3T$

$$\frac{\partial^{z+}x_i(T)}{\partial\theta\ \partial x_j(1)}$$

and linear combinations etc.

FIGURE 7.4   Costs of obtaining various sets of second derivatives.

provides for linear systems by looking at changes in eigenvalues. In effect, they tell us, for a change in a parameter of the system, how its dominant dynamics (revealed in the matrix of ordered derivatives to variables) change.

Among the possible applications is the use of Newton's method in estimation and optimization. It is straightforward to use the full backward approach here for parameter–parameter derivatives; this allows computation of all the second derivatives one needs in order to use Newton's method, for a rough cost of only $3mN^2T$, about the same as what people have paid to get only first derivatives when using forward methods.

7.5   APPLICATIONS OF STOCHASTIC OPTIMIZATION OVER TIME: POLICY MODELS, AI AND NEURON MODELING

The remainder of this chapter discusses a way to implement GDHP, a previously published approach to stochastic optimization over time. The methods discussed earlier make GDHP cheap enough to be feasible with very large-scale models or systems. This open up many possible applications.

GDHP provides an approximate solution to Howard's problem:

```
GIVEN THAT x(t + 1) = F(x(t), u(t), e(t))
  where e(t) is random, u(t) a control,
MAXIMIZE ⟨U(x)⟩, the expectation across all
  future times
```

Applications include (1) use of large stochastic policy models in decision-making (2) devising distributed/decentralized systems to output optimal policy, (3) general adaptive artificial intelligence, and (4) modeling of learning in the brain ("neural plasticity").

The first of these applications is straightforward. Let F be the policy model, and let U represent the values to be served by the decisions. How to formulate U is an old and unavoidable issue, beyond the scope of this chapter.

The second application is an extension of the fields of microeconomics and hierarchical control theory. Economists have proved many theorems about how a large deterministic optimization problem (devising an efficient pattern of production) may be decentralized; however, these theorems typically assume no uncertainty or fundamental structural "change" (nonlinearity). If the actual problem is general and stochastic (beset by uncertainty), one needs a method of solution to the stochastic problem, which can be implemented efficiently in a decentralized (i.e., parallel processor) system. The EIA report [1] describes how GDHP may be implemented in this way.

In artificial intelligence, if one does not impose severe constraints on the range of models F or of action strategies to be considered (which would be inappropriate in an adaptive system), one must develop a generalized approach to optimization in order to find the optimal action strategy. However, numerical analysts have found, even with the much simpler task of maximizing a function of a few variables, that first derivatives at a minimum are essential to finding a maximum in a reliable, efficient manner. Until the failure of the Minsky–Selfridge "jitters" machine, there was widespread recognition of the fact that generalized optimization and adaptive intelligence are almost inseparable concepts [2]. The "jitters" failure does not invalidate the original concept, however; it merely shows that one needs a full set of valid derivatives in each iteration (as is well known to numerical analysts) and that one cannot make do with a factor of N less information (i.e., one derivative per time period, as in "jitters"). Likewise, a system needs to have an explicit model of its environment in order to properly optimize actions over time as in dynamic programming.

There is an additional reason why artificial intelligence research abandoned the idea of explicit optimization in the 1960s. Much of the work at that time was inspired by an early description of the neuron (brain cell) developed by McCulloch and Pitts [3]. In that description, the variables x_j computed by the brain could take on only two values, 0 or 1 ("all" or "none"); thus the functions $\mathbf{F}$, J, and $\mathbf{u}$ in this chapter could not be differentiable. However, more recent work has shown that neurons in the human brain use a "code" based on "volleys," such that the variables vary over a continuous range; thus optimization of a network of model neurons is not intrinsically different from conventional optimization based on a specified functional form.

Similar concepts apply to the field of actual neuron modeling. Like objects in solid state physics, neurons are very complicated and will never be totally encompassed by theory; as with solid state physics, however, a general theory of neuron networks as intelligent systems may help increase the range of important phenomena, which can be understood. This is a far cry from the ad hoc approach to brain modeling, in which a given set of equations is derived by appeals to simplification and common sense only. When the actual functional ability of a model to reproduce intelligence is considered, many otherwise credible models can quickly be ruled out; for example, many theorems have been proved about the Grossberg neuron model, but in statistical terms, this model uses simple correlation coefficients as the parameters of multivariate forecasting equations [4]. Some neurologists have compared themselves to a person who studies a radio as follows: he/she pulls out a transistor, notices that the radio whines, and calls the transistor the "whine center;" a deeper understanding of brain functioning requires more consideration of the mathematical elements that are necessary in order to produce generalized intelligence, defined as the ability to learn and adapt to totally new problems.

The method discussed here—GDHP—does not address all aspects of stochastic optimization. The theory needs further development. However, there is a very close parallel between GDHP and conventional statistical estimation methods. As with statistics, specific examples of problems will be important to improving our understanding of stochastic optimization. However, as with statistics, examples alone will not be enough; the underlying theory needs explicit development at a generalized level, if we are ever to cope with very complex problems and improve the general methods.

7.5.1 General Approach Used in GDHP

The exact solution to Howard's problem, as described in Howard's book on dynamic programming [5], requires the calculation of a scalar function $J(x)$ and a vector function $\mathbf{u}(\mathbf{x})$. $\mathbf{u}(\mathbf{x})$ yields the optimal action (or motor output or policy variables) as a function of the state of the environment, $\mathbf{x}$. $J(\mathbf{x})$ is a measure of how good the results of the actions are in terms of their total long-term impact. Howard proves that one can normally converge on a choice for $\mathbf{u}(\mathbf{x})$ that maximizes the future expected value of utility ($U(\mathbf{x})$) by alternately (1) finding the unique function J that solves a certain equation for the current guess for $\mathbf{u}(\mathbf{x})$; and (2) picking a new guess for $\mathbf{u}(\mathbf{x}(t))$ so as to maximize the expected value of J at time $t + 1$.

In GDHP, one does not find the exact theoretical J and $\mathbf{u}$, because this tends to be infeasible with large systems. Instead, one assumes that the user or a higher-level system has proposed functional forms, J^* and $\mathbf{u}^*$, for J and $\mathbf{u}$. GDHP attempts to adjust the parameters of J^* and $\mathbf{u}^*$ to make them fit the conditions for optimality as closely as possible, over a finite (not necessarily fixed) set of possible scenarios, $\mathbf{x}$. This involves two steps, to be carried out alternately or in parallel until convergence:

1. Maximize $\langle J^*(\mathbf{F}(\mathbf{x}, \mathbf{e}, \mathbf{u}^*(\mathbf{x}, \mathbf{b})))\rangle$ over parameters $\mathbf{b}$, scenarios $\mathbf{x}$, random $\mathbf{e}$.
2. Pick $\mathbf{a}$ in $J^*(\mathbf{x}, \mathbf{a})$ to minimize the sum over scenarios $\mathbf{x}$ of

$$E \triangleq \sum_i W_i \left(\frac{\partial}{\partial x_i} \langle J^*(\mathbf{F}(\mathbf{x}, \mathbf{e})) \rangle - \mathbf{u}^*(\mathbf{x}) - J^*(\mathbf{x}) \rangle \right)^2,$$

where $\mathbf{f}(\mathbf{x}, \mathbf{e})$ is defined as $\mathbf{F}(\mathbf{x}, \mathbf{e}, \mathbf{u}(\mathbf{x}))$ and where the W_i are a set of weights. If J^* can solve Howard's equation exactly with $\mathbf{u}^*$, for some $\mathbf{a}$, then E will always equal zero for that $\mathbf{a}$.

GDHP can be implemented as part of a procedure to optimize the choices of actions over time, in a situation where the dynamics of the environment and

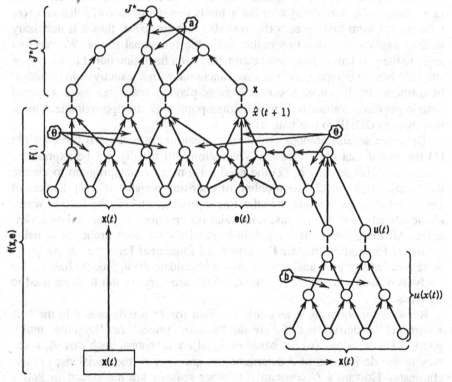

FIGURE 7.5 Realization of GDHP as a triple network to make decisions.

the optimal actions are both to be learned from empirical observation rather than specified a priori. This requires updating the parameters of three functions: J^*, $\mathbf{u}^*$, and $\mathbf{F}^*$. (Updating $\mathbf{F}^*$ is a well-studied problem in statistics.) Such a system can be implemented as a three-level network as shown in Figure 7.5; each level contains a network realization of one of the three functions. GDHP and statistics would be used to adopt the parameters; the network needs no external guidance except for data input and functional forms.

Figure 7.5 has an interesting analogy to the mammalian brain, which is essentially made up of three interlocking networks of brain cells: (1) the "limbic" network, which, like J, calculates system values ("values" as in "values we cherish") that are the basis for reinforcing actions; (2) the corticothalamic system, which, like $\mathbf{F}$, embodies a model of the external environment; and (3) the brain stem, which, like $\mathbf{u}$, directly controls actions in response to what is known about the external environment. There are further correspondences and features to improve performances of this system far beyond the scope of this chapter.

7.5.2 Rationale of the Approximations Used in GDHP

The approximations used by GDHP require some explanation.

First, consider the use of specific functional forms instead of general functions J and $\mathbf{u}$. No realistic system can actually use an estimate of J that involves a functional form that exceeds the available storage space; thus it is necessary to limit explicit attention to specific realizable functional forms. We can first analyze the problem of parameter estimation for a fixed functional form, before studying how to compare and improve functional forms, exactly as in statistics. In artificial intelligence, successful game-playing machines have required "static position evaluators," which correspond with the approximate J function used in GDHP to evaluate $\mathbf{u}(\mathbf{x})$.

There are several obvious problems in assuming a functional form for J^*: (1) the true J that obeys Howard's equation will usually not be expressible exactly as $J^*(\mathbf{a})$ for any $\mathbf{a}$; (2) the need for a user or metaprogram to choose the functional form; (3) the problem of choosing weights W_i; (4) dangers of autocorrelation invalidating the adjustment process; and (5) the need to worry about robustness of the results, influential observations, and unobserved variables. All these problems are precisely parallel to known problems in using statistical forecasting models $\mathbf{F}^*$ with fixed functional forms; as in statistics, these problems require analysis but do not invalidate the approach. Indeed, the methods of analysis needed to extend GHDP are very similar to those used in statistics.

Reasons for choosing E as a loss function for J^* are discussed in the EIA report: (1) the derivatives of J are the "shadow prices" or "Lagrange multipliers;" (2) decisions ($\mathbf{u}$) are based on local comparisons, such that the accuracy of the derivatives of J determine the accuracy of the decisions; (3) this eliminates Howard's $\overline{U}$ constant; (4) other reasons are mentioned in Policy Analysis and Information Systems (Elsevier) [6].

7.5.3 Implementation of GDHP

The major difficulty in implementing GDHP is the difficulty of performing the minimization and maximization described earlier. In the general case, where no strong special assumptions are made about J and F and u, and where there are many parameters in these functions, this requires that we get the derivatives of the quantities to be minimized or maximized. Here, however, E already involves first derivatives; the derivatives of E involve second derivatives. The EIA report derives in detail the calculations that yield the required derivatives. These calculations only cost about three or four times what it costs to compute $J(F, (x, u(x)))$ itself. If the functional forms for J, F and u are "realizable," this means that the cost of calculating $J(F(x, u(x))$ is bearable; the cost of obtaining derivatives, then, is also bearable for all realizable J, F, and u. The EIA report explicitly spells out the details in the case where multiple processors can be used to reduce the cost of calculating J, F, and u; it demonstrates that the cost of getting derivatives can be kept in line with that of getting J, F, and u even in that case.

Minimization and maximization are nontrivial problems, even with the derivatives available. "Sparse quasi-Newtonian" methods are being developed, however, which show promise in handling large systems. EIA has a crude but adequate method, which it now uses to solve 100,000 nonlinear simultaneous equations [7].

In a real-time system, one would want to carry out all the iteration processes above in parallel rather than wait, for example, to complete a minimization before getting new data. For analytical purposes, however, it is convenient for now to consider decision problems focused at one moment in time.

7.5.4 Implications of GDHP Feasibility

This approach makes it possible to develop generalized, adaptive artificial intelligence, capable of achieving results comparable to what is discussed in science fiction, by a rational development of statistics, optimization theory and numerical analysis in the directions indicated above. The implications for psychology and economics raise issue too complex to permit adequate discussion here.

REFERENCES (UPDATED)

1. P. Werbos, *Sensitivity Analysis Methods for Nonlinear Systems*, 1980, originally available from Forecast Evaluation and Analysis Team, Quality Assurance Division, OSS/EIA, Room 7413, Department of Energy (DOE), Washington D.C. Due to reorganizations of DOE and policies regarding model validation reports, this document is no longer available from the government. See Introduction.
2. M. Minsky and O. Selfridge, *Jitters* (approximate title), MIT AI Lab Technical Report, obtained directly from the authors.

3. M. Minsky and S. Papert, *Perceptrons*, Expanded Editions, MIT Press, Cambridge, 1990.

4. Unpublished early manuscripts obtained from Grossberg, using designs now called Hopfield networks with simple Hebbian learning. Grossberg has since developed far more complex designs.

5. R. Howard, *Dynamic Programming and Markhov Processes*, MIT Press, Cambridge, 1960.

6. P. Werbos, "Changes in global policy analysis procedures suggested by new methods of optimization," *Policy Analysis and Information Systems*, vol. 3, no. 1, June 1979.

7. P. Werbos, "Solving and optimizing complex systems: lessons from the EIA long-term model," in B. Lev ed. *Energy Models and Studies*, North Holland, New York, 1983.

8

Backpropagation Through Time

What It Does and How to Do It

Backpropagation is now the most widely used tool in the field of artificial neural networks. At the core of backpropagation is a method for calculating derivatives exactly and efficiently in any large system made up of elementary subsystems or calculations which are represented by known, differentiable functions; thus, backpropagation has many applications which do not involve neural networks as such.

This chapter first reviews basic backpropagation, a simple method which is now being widely used in areas like pattern recognition and fault diagnosis. Next, it presents the basic equations for backpropagation through time, and discusses applications to areas like pattern recognition involving dynamic systems, systems identification, and control. Finally, it describes further extensions of this method, to deal with systems other than neural networks, systems involving simultaneous equations or true recurrent networks, and other practical issues which arise with this method. Pseudocode is provided to clarify the algorithms. The chain rule for ordered derivatives—the theorem which underlies backpropagation—is briefly discussed.

8.1 INTRODUCTION

Backpropagation through time is a very powerful tool, with applications to pattern recognition, dynamic modeling, sensitivity analysis, and the control of systems over time, among others. It can be applied to neural networks, to econometric models, to fuzzy logic structures, to fluid dynamics models, and to almost any system built up from elementary subsystems or calculations. The one serious constraint is that the elementary subsystems must be represented by functions known to the user, functions that are both continuous and differentiable (i.e., possess derivatives). For example, the first practical application of backpropagation was for estimating a dynamic model to predict nationalism and social communications in 1974 [1].

Unfortunately, the most general formulation of backpropagation can only be used by those who are willing to work out the mathematics of their particular application. This chapter mainly describes a simpler version of backpropagation, which can be translated into computer code and applied directly by neural network users.

Section 8.2 reviews the simplest and most widely used form of backpropagation, which may be called "basic backpropagation." The concepts here will already be familiar to those who have read the paper by Rumelhart, Hinton, and Williams [2] in the seminal book *Parallel Distributed Processing*, which played a pivotal role in the development of the field. (That book also acknowledged the prior work of Parker [3] and Le Cun [4], and the pivotal role of Charles Smith of the Systems Development Foundation.) This section uses new notation, which adds a bit of generality and makes it easier to go on to complex applications in a rigorous manner. (The need for new notation may seem unnecessary to some, but for those who have to apply backpropagation to complex systems, it is essential).

Section 8.3 uses the same notation to describe backpropagation through time. Backpropagation through time has been applied to concrete problems by a number of authors, including, at least, Watrous and Shastri [5], Sawai et al. [6], Nguyen and Widrow [7], Jordan [8], Kawato [9], Elman and Zipser, Narendra [10], and myself [1, 11, 12, 15]. Section 8.4 discusses what is missing in this simplified discussion, and how to do better.

At its core, backpropagation is simply an efficient and exact method for calculating all the derivatives of a single target quantity (such as pattern classification error) with respect to a large set of input quantities (such as the parameters or weights in a classification rule). Backpropagation through time extends this method so that it applies to dynamic systems. This allows one to calculate the derivatives needed when optimizing an iterative analysis procedure, a neural network with memory, or a control system that maximizes performance over time.

8.2 BASIC BACKPROPAGATION

8.2.1 The Supervised Learning Problem

Basic backpropagation is currently the most popular method for performing the supervised learning task, which is symbolized in Figure 8.1.

In supervised learning, we try to adapt an artificial neural network so that its actual outputs ($\hat{Y}$) come close to some target outputs (Y) for a training set that contains T patterns. The goal is to adapt the parameters of the network so that it performs well for patterns from outside the training set.

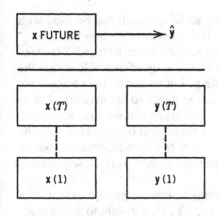

FIGURE 8.1 Schematic of the supervised learning task.

The main use of supervised learning today lies in pattern recognition work. For example, suppose that we are trying to build a neural network that can learn to recognize handwritten ZIP codes. (AT&T has actually done this [13], although the details are beyond the scope of this chapter.) We assume that we already have a camera and preprocessor that can digitize the image, locate the five digits, and provide a 19 × 20 grid of ones and zeros representing the image of each digit. We want the neural network to input the 19 × 20 image and output a classification; for example, we might ask the network to output four binary digits, which, taken together, identify which decimal digit is being observed.

Before adapting the parameters of the neural network, one must first obtain a training database of actual handwritten digits and correct classifications. Suppose, for example, that this database contains 2000 examples of handwritten digits. In that case, $T = 2000$. We may give each example a label t between 1 and 2000. For each sample t, we have a record of the input pattern and the correct classification. Each input pattern consists of 380 numbers, which may be viewed as a vector with 380 components; we may call this vector $X(t)$. The desired classification consists of four numbers, which may be treated as a vector $Y(t)$. The actual output of the network will be $\hat{Y}(t)$, which may differ from the desired output $Y(t)$, especially in the period before the network has been adapted. To solve the supervised learning problem, there are two steps:

1. We must specify the "topology" (connections and equations) for a network that inputs $X(t)$ and outputs a four-component vector $\hat{Y}(t)$, an approximation to $Y(t)$. The relation between the inputs and outputs must depend on a set of weights (parameters) W, which can be adjusted.

2. We must specify a "learning rule"—a procedure for adjusting the weights W so as to make the actual outputs $\hat{Y}(t)$ approximate the desired outputs $Y(t)$.

Basic backpropagation is currently the most popular learning rule used in supervised learning. It is generally used with a very simple network design—

to be described in the next section—but the same approach can be used with any network of differentiable functions, as is discussed in Section 8.4.

Even when we use a simple network design, the vectors $\mathbf{X}(t)$ and $\mathbf{Y}(t)$ need not be made of ones and zeros. They can be made up of any values that the network is capable of inputting and outputting. Let us denote the components of $\mathbf{X}(t)$ as $X_1(t), \ldots, X_m(t)$ so that there are m inputs to the network. Let us denote the components of $\mathbf{Y}(t)$ as $Y_1(t), \ldots, Y_n(t)$ so that we have n outputs. Throughout this chapter, the components of a vector will be represented by the same letter as the vector itself, in the same case; this convention turns out be convenient because $\mathbf{x}(t)$ will represent a different vector, very closely related to $\mathbf{X}(t)$.

Figure 8.1 illustrates the supervised learning task in the general case. Given a history of $\mathbf{X}(1), \ldots, \mathbf{X}(T)$ and $\mathbf{Y}(1), \ldots, \mathbf{Y}(T)$, we want to find a mapping from $\mathbf{X}$ to $\mathbf{Y}$, that will perform well when we encounter new vectors $\mathbf{X}$ outside the training set. The index t may be interpreted either as a time index or as a pattern number index; however, this section does not assume that the order of patterns is meaningful.

8.2.2 Simple Feedforward Networks (MLPs)

Before we specify a learning rule, we have to define exactly how the outputs of a neural net depend on its inputs and weights. In basic backpropagation, we assume the following logic:

$$x_i = X_i, \qquad 1 \le i \le m \tag{8.1}$$

$$\text{net}_i = \sum_{j=1}^{i-1} W_{ij}x_j, \quad m < i \le N + n \tag{8.2}$$

$$x_j = s(\text{net}_j), \qquad m < j \le N + n \tag{8.3}$$

$$Y_i = x_{i+N}, \qquad 1 \le i \le n \tag{8.4}$$

where the function s in Equation (8.3) is usually the following sigmoidal function:

$$s(z) = 1/(1 + e^{-z}), \tag{8.5}$$

and where N is a constant that can be any integer you choose as long as it is no less than m. The value of $N + n$ decides how many neurons are in the network (if we include inputs as neurons). Intuitively, net_i represents the total level of voltage exciting a neuron, and x_i represents the intensity of the resulting output from the neuron. (x_i is sometimes called the "activation level" of the neuron.) It is conventional to assume that there is a threshold or constant weight W_{i0} added to the right side of Equation (8.2); however, we can achieve

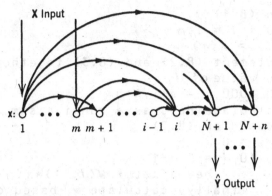

X Input

x:
1   m m+1   i-1 i   N+1 N+n

$\hat{Y}$ Output

FIGURE 8.2   Network design for basic backpropagation.

the same effect by assuming that one of the inputs (such as X_m or X_0) is always 1. Equations (8.1) through (8.5) define what is called a generalized Multilayer Perceptron (MLP).

The significance of these equations is illustrated in Figure 8.2. There are $N + n$ circles, representing all of the neurons in the network, including the input neurons. The first m circles are really just copies of the inputs $X_1, \ldots, X_m$; they are included as part of the vector x only as a way of simplifying the notation. Every other neuron in the network—such as neuron number i, which calculates net_i and x_i—takes input from every cell that precedes it in the network. Even the last output cell, which generates $\hat{Y}_n$, takes input from other output cells, such as the one which outputs $\hat{Y}_{n-1}$.

In neural network terminology, this network is "fully connected" in the extreme. As a practical matter, it is usually desirable to limit the connections between neurons. This can be done by simply fixing some of the weights W_{ij} to zero so that they drop out of all calculations. For example, most researchers prefer to use "layered" networks, in which all connection weights W_{ij} are zeroed out, except for those going from one "layer" (subset of neurons) to the next layer. In general, one may zero out as many or as few of the weights as one likes, based on one's understanding of individual applications. For those who first begin this work, it is conventional to define only three layers—an input layer, a "hidden" layer, and an output layer. This section assumes the full range of allowed connections, simply for the sake of generality.

In computer code, we could represent this network as a FORTRAN subroutine (assuming a FORTRAN that distinguishes uppercase from lowercase):

```
       SUBROUTINE NET(X, W, x, Yhat)
       REAL X(m),W(N+n,N+n),x(N+n),
          Yhat(n), net
       INTEGER, i,j,m,n,N
C First insert the inputs, as per
```

```
C Equation (8.1)
        DO 1 i = 1,m
     1 x(i) = X(i)
C Next implement (8.2) and (8.3) together
C for each value of i
        DO 1000 i = m+1,N+n
C         calculate net, as a running sum,
C           based on (8.2)
        net = 0
        DO 10 j = 1,i-1
     10          net = net + W(i, j)*x(j)
C             finally, calculate x_i based on
C               (8.3) and (8.5)
   1000       x(i) = 1/(1+exp(-net))
C Finally, copy over the outputs, as per
C  (8.4)
        DO 2000 i = 1,n
   2000       Yhat(i) = x(i+N);
```

In the pseudocode, note that X and W are technically the inputs to the subroutine, while x and Yhat are the outputs. Yhat is usually regarded as "the" output of the network, but x may also have its uses outside the subroutine proper, as will be seen in the next section.

8.2.3 Adapting the Network: Approach

In basic backpropagation, we choose the weights W_{ij} so as to minimize square error over the training set:

$$E = \sum_{t=1}^{T} E(t) = \sum_{t=1}^{T} \sum_{i=1}^{n} \tfrac{1}{2}[\hat{Y}_i(t) - Y_i(t)]^2. \tag{8.6}$$

This is simply a special case of the well-known method of least squares, used very often in statistics, econometrics, and engineering; the uniqueness of backpropagation lies in how this expression is minimized. The approach used here is illustrated in Figure 8.3.

In basic backpropagation, we start with arbitrary values for the weights **W**. (It is usual to choose random numbers in the range from -0.1 to 0.1, but it may be better to guess the weights based on prior information, in cases where prior information is available.) Next, we calculate the outputs $\hat{Y}(t)$ and the errors $E(t)$ for that set of weights. Then we calculate the derivatives of E with respect to all the weights; this is indicated by the dotted lines in Figure 8.3. If increasing a given weight would lead to more error, we adjust that weight downward. If increasing a weight leads to less error, we adjust it

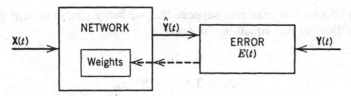

FIGURE 8.3 Basic backpropagation (in pattern learning).

upward. After adjusting all the weights up or down, we start all over, and keep on going through this process until the weights and the error settle down. (Some researchers iterate until the error is close to zero; however, if the number of training patterns exceeds the number of weights in the network—as recommended by studies on generalization—it may not be possible for the error to reach zero.) The uniqueness of backpropagation lies in the method used to calculate the derivatives exactly for all the weights in only one pass through the system.

8.2.4 Calculating Derivatives: Theoretical Background

Many papers on backpropagation suggest that we only use the conventional chain rule for partial derivatives to calculate the derivatives of E with respect to all the weights. Under certain conditions, this can be a rigorous approach, but its generality is limited, and it requires great care with the side conditions (which are rarely spelled out); calculations of this sort can easily become confused and erroneous when networks and applications grow complex. Even when using Equation (8.7) below, it is a good idea to test one's gradient calculations using explicit perturbations in order to be sure that there is no bug in one's code.

When the idea of backpropagation was first presented to the Harvard faculty in 1972, they expressed legitimate concern about the validity of the rather complex calculations involved. To deal with this problem, I proved a new chain rule for ordered derivatives:

$$\frac{\partial^+ \text{TARGET}}{\partial z_i} = \frac{\partial \text{TARGET}}{\partial z_i} + \sum_{j>i} \frac{\partial^+ \text{TARGET}}{\partial z_j} * \frac{\partial z_j}{\partial z_i} \qquad (8.7)$$

where the derivatives with the superscript represent *ordered* derivatives, and the derivatives without superscripts represent ordinary partial derivatives. This chain rule is valid only for *ordered* systems where the values to be calculated can be calculated one by one (if necessary) in the order $z_1, z_2, \ldots, z_n$, TARGET. The simple partial derivatives represent the direct impact of z_i on z_j through the systems equation which determines z_j. The ordered derivative represents the total impact of z_j on TARGET, accounting for both the *direct* and *indirect* effects. For example, suppose that we had a simple system governed by the following two equations, in order:

$$z_2 = 4 * z_1,$$

$$z_3 = 3 * z_1 + 5 * z_2.$$

The "simple" partial derivative of z_1 with respect to z_1 (the direct effect) is 3; to calculate the simple effect, we only look at the equation that determines z_3. However, the ordered derivative of z_3 with respect to z_1 is 23 because of the indirect impact by way of z_2. The simple partial derivative measures what happens when we increase z_1 (e.g., by 1, in this example) and assume that everything else (like z_2) in the equation that determines z_3 remains constant. The ordered derivative measures what happens when we increase z_1, and also recalculate all other quantities—like z_2—which are later than z_1 in the causal ordering we impose on the system.

This chain rule provides a straightforward, plodding, "linear" recipe for how to calculate the derivatives of a given TARGET variable with respect to all the inputs (and parameters) of an ordered differentiable system in only one pass through the system. This chapter does not explain this chain rule in detail since lengthy tutorials have been published elsewhere [1, 11]. But there is one point worth noting: because we are calculating ordered derivatives of one target variable, we can use a simpler notation, a notation that works out to be easier to use in complex practical examples [11]. We can write the ordered derivative of the TARGET with respect to z_j as F_z_i, which may be described as "the feedback to z_i." In basic backpropagation, the TARGET variable of interest is the error E. This changes the appearance of our chain rule in that case to

$$F\_z_i = \frac{\partial E}{\partial z_i} + \sum_{j > i} F\_z_i * \frac{\partial z_j}{\partial z_i} \qquad (8.8)$$

For purposes of debugging, one can calculate the true value of any ordered derivative simply by perturbing z_i at the point in the program where z_i is calculated; this is particularly useful when applying backpropagation to a complex network of functions other than neural networks..

8.2.5 Adapting the Network: Equations

For a given set of weights **W**, it is easy to use Equations (8.1)–(8.6) to calculate **Y**(t) and $E(t)$ for each pattern t. The trick is in how we then calculate the derivatives.

Let us use the prefix $F\_$ to indicate the ordered derivative of E with respect to whatever variable the $F\_$ precedes. Thus, for example,

$$F\_\hat{Y}(t) = \frac{\partial E}{\partial \hat{Y}_i(t)} = \hat{Y}_i(t) - Y_i(t) \qquad (8.9)$$

which follows simply by differentiating Equation (8.6). By the chain rule for ordered derivatives as expressed in Equation (8.8),

$$F\_x_i(t) = F\_\hat{Y}_{i-N}(t) + \sum_{j=i+1}^{N+n} W_{ji} * F\_net_j(t),$$

$$i = N + n, \ldots, m + 1 \tag{8.10}$$

$$F\_net_i(t) = s'(net_i) * F\_x_i(t), \quad i = N + n, \ldots, m + 1 \tag{8.11}$$

$$F\_W_{ij} = \sum_{t=1}^{T} F\_net_i(t) * x_j(t) \tag{8.12}$$

where s' is the derivative of $s(z)$ as defined in Equation (8.5) and F_Y_k is assumed to be zero for $k \le 0$. Note how Equation (8.10) requires us to run backward through the network in order to calculate the derivatives, as illustrated in Figure 8.4; this backward propagation of information is what gives backpropagation its name. A little calculus and algebra, starting from Equation (8.5) shows us that

$$s'(z) = s(z) * (1 - s(z)), \tag{8.13}$$

which we can use when we implement Equation (8.11). Finally, to adapt the weights, the usual method is to set

$$\text{New } W_{ij} = W_{ij} - \text{learning\_rate} * F\_W_{ij} \tag{8.14}$$

where the learning_rate is some small constant chosen on an ad hoc basis. (The usual procedure is to make it as large as possible, up to 1, until the error starts to diverge; however, there are more analytic procedures available [11].)

8.2.6 Adapting the Network: Code

The key part of basic backpropagation—Equations (8.10)–(8.13)—may be coded up into a "dual" subroutine, as follows.

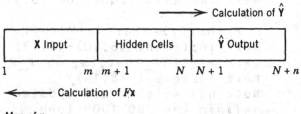

Map of x

FIGURE 8.4 Backward flow of derivative calculation.

```
          SUBROUTINE F_NET(F_Yhat, W, x, F_W)
          REAL F_Yhat(n),W(N+n,N+n),x(N+n),
          F_W(N+n,N+n),F_net(N+n),F_x(N+n)
          INTEGER i,j,n,m,N
C Initialize Equation (8.10)
          DO 1 i = 1,N
     1        F_x(i) = 0
          DO 2 i = 1,n
     2        F_x(i+N)=F_Yhat(i)
C RUN THROUGH (8.10)-(8.12) AS A SET,
C     FOR i RUNNING BACKWARD
          DO 1000 i=N+n,m+1,-1
C             complete (8.10) for the current
C              value of i*j
          DO 10 j = i+1,N+n
C             modify "DO 10" if needed, to be
C              sure nothing is done if i=N+n
    10            F_x(i) = F_x(i)+W(j,i)*F_net(j)
C             next implement (8.11), exploiting (8.13)
              F_net(i) = F_x(i)*x(i)*(1.-x(i))
C             then implement (8.12) for the
C              current value of i
          DO 12 j = 1,i-1
    12            F_W(i,j)=F_net(i)*x(j)
  1000        CONTINUE
```

Note that the array F_W is the only output of this subroutine.

Equation (8.14) represented "batch learning," in which weights are adjusted only after all T patterns are processed. It is more common to use pattern learning, in which the weights are continually updated after each observation. Pattern learning may be represented as follows:

```
C PATTERN LEARNING
          DO 1000 pass_number=1,maximum_passes
          DO 100 t=1,T
              CALL NET(X(t), W, x, Yhat)
C             Next Implement Equation (8.9)
          DO 9 i = 1,n
     9        F_Yhat(i)=Yhat(i)-Y(t,i)
C             Next Implement (8.10)-(8.12)
              CALL F_NET(F_Yhat, W, x, F_W)
C             Next Implement (8.14)
C             Note how weights are updated
C              within the "DO 100" loop.
          DO 14 i = m+1,N+n
          DO 14 j = 1,i-1
```

```
  14                    W(i,j)=W(i,j)-
                        learning_rate*F_W(i,j)
 100       CONTINUE
1000       CONTINUE
```

The key point here is that the weights W are adjusted in response to the *current* vector F_W, which only depends on the current pattern t; the weights are adjusted after each pattern is processed. (In batch learning, by contrast, the weights are adjusted only after the "DO 100" loop is completed.)

In practice, maximum_passes is usually set to an enormous number; the loop is exited only when a test of convergence is passed, a test of error size or weight change that can be injected easily into the loop. True real-time learning is like pattern learning, but with only one pass through the data and no memory of earlier times t. (The equations above could be implemented easily enough as a real-time learning scheme; however, this will not be true for backpropagation through time). The term "on-line learning" is sometimes used to represent a situation that could be pattern learning or could be real-time learning. Most people using basic backpropagation now use pattern learning rather than real-time learning because, with their data sets, many passes through the data are needed to ensure convergence of the weights.

The reader should be warned that I have not actually tested the code here. It is presented simply as a way of explaining more precisely the preceding ideas. The C implementations that I have worked with have been less transparent and harder to debug, in part because of the absence of range checking in that language. It is often argued that people "who know what they are doing" do not need range checking and the like; however, people who think they never make mistakes should probably not be writing this kind of code. With neural network code, especially, good diagnostics and tests are very important because bugs can lead to slow convergence and oscillation—problems that are hard to track down and are easily misattributed to the algorithm in use. If one must use a language without range checking, it is extremely important to maintain a version of the code that is highly transparent and safe, however inefficient it may be, for diagnostic purposes.

8.3 BACKPROPAGATION THROUGH TIME

8.1.3. Background

Backpropagation through time—like basic backpropagation—is used most often in pattern recognition today. Therefore this section focuses on such applications, using notation like that of the previous section. See Section 8.4 for other applications.

In some applications—such as speech recognition or submarine detection—our classification at time t will be more accurate if we can account for what we saw at earlier times. *Even though* the training set still fits the same format as above, we want to use a more powerful class of networks to do the classi-

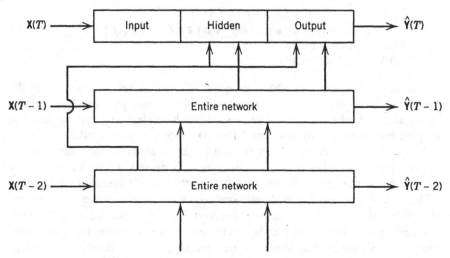

FIGURE 8.5 Generalized network design with time lags.

fication; we want the output of the network at time t to account for variables at earlier times (as in Figure 8.5).

The Introduction cited a number of examples where such "memory" of previous time periods is very important. For example, it is easier to recognize moving objects if our network accounts for changes in the scene from the time $t - 1$ to time t, which requires memory of time $t - 1$. Many of the best pattern recognition algorithms involve a kind of "relaxation" approach where the representation of the world at time t is based on an adjustment of the representation at time $t - 1$; this requires memory of the internal network variables for time $t - 1$. (Even Kalman filtering requires such a representation.)

8.3.2 Example of a Recurrent Network

Backpropagation can be applied to any system with a well-defined order of calculations, even if those calculations depend on past calculations within the network itself. For the sake of generality, I will show how this works for the network design shown in Figure 8.5, where every neuron is potentially allowed to input values from any of the neurons at the two previous time periods (including, of course, the input neurons). To avoid excess clutter, Figure 8.5 shows the hidden and output sections of the network (parallel to Figure 8.2) only for time T, but they are present at other times as well. To translate this network into a mathematical system, we can simply replace Equation (8.2) by

$$\text{net}_i(t) = \sum_{j=1}^{i-1} W_{ij}x_j(t) + \sum_{j=1}^{N+n} W'_{ij}x_j(t-1) + \sum_{j=1}^{N+n} W''_{ij}x_j(t-2) \quad (8.15)$$

Again, we can simply fix some of the weights to be zero, if we so choose, in order to simplify the network. In most applications today, the W'' weights are fixed to zero (i.e., erased from all formulas), and all the W' weights are fixed to zero as well, except for W'_{ii}. This is done in part for the sake of parsimony, and in part for historical reasons. (The "time-delay neural networks" of Watrous and Shastri [5] assumed that special case; however, the term TDNN now refers to networks with *no* internal memory.) Here, I deliberately include extra terms for the sake of generality. I allow for the fact that all active neurons (neurons other than input neurons) can be allowed to input the outputs of any other neurons if there is a time lag in the connection. The weights W' and W'' are the weights on those time-lagged connections between neurons. (Lags of more than two periods are also easy to manage; they are treated just as one would expect from seeing how we handle lag-two terms, as a special case of Equation (8.7).) This general type of network design is now referred to as a Time-Lagged Recurrent Network (TLRN).

These equations could be embodied in a subroutine:

```
SUBROUTINE NET2(X(t), W', W", x(t - 2),
    x(t - 1), x(t), Yhat),
```

which is programmed just like the subroutine NET, with the modifications one would expect from Equation (8.15). The output arrays are $x(t)$ and $Yhat$.

When we call this subroutine for the first time, at $t = 1$, we face a minor technical problem: there is no value for $x(-1)$ or $x(0)$, both of which we need as inputs. In principle, we can use any values we wish to choose; the choice of $x(-1)$ and $x(0)$ is essentially part of the definition of our network. Most people simply set these vectors to zero and argue that their networks will start out with a blank slate in classifying whatever dynamic pattern is at hand, both in the training set and in later applications. (Statisticians have been known to treat these vectors as weights, in effect, to be adapted along with the other weights in the network. This works fine in the training set but opens up questions of what to do when one applies the network to new data.)

In this section, I assume that the data run from an initial time $t = 1$ through to a final time $t = T$, which plays a crucial role in the derivative calculations. Section 8.4 shows how this assumption can be relaxed somewhat.

8.3.3 Adapting the Network: Equations

To calculate the derivatives of F_W_{ij}, we use the same equations as before, except that Equation (8.10) is replaced by

$$F\_x_i(t) = F\_\hat{Y}_{i-N}(t) + \sum_{j=i+1}^{N+n} W_{ji} * F\_net_j(t)$$

$$+ \sum_{j=m+1}^{N+n} W'_{ji} * F\_net_j(t + 1)$$

$$+ \sum_{j=m+1}^{N+n} W''_{ji} * F\_net_j(t + 2). \qquad (8.16)$$

Once again, if one wants to fix the W'' terms to zero, one can simply delete the rightmost term.

Note that this equation makes it impossible for us to calculate $F\_x_i(t)$ and $F\_net_i(t)$ until after $F\_net_j(t + 1)$ and $F\_net_j(t + 2)$ are already known; therefore we can only use this equation by proceeding backward in time, calculating F_net for time T, and then working our way backward to time 1.

To adapt this network, of course, we need to calculate $F\_W'_{ij}$ and $F\_W''_{ij}$ as well as F_W_{ij}:

$$F\_W'_{ij} = \sum_{t=1}^{T} F\_net_i(t + 1) * x_j(t), \qquad (8.17)$$

$$F\_W''_{ij} = \sum_{t=1}^{T} F\_net_i(t + 2) * x_j(t). \qquad (8.18)$$

In all these calculations, $F\_net(T + 1)$ and $F\_net(T + 2)$ should be treated as zero. For programming convenience, I will later define quantities like $F\_net'_i(t) = F\_net_i(t + 1)$, but this is purely a convenience; the subscript i and the time argument are enough to identify which derivative is being represented. (In other words, $net_i(t)$ represents a specific quantity z_j as in Equation (8.8), and $F\_net_i(t)$ represents the ordered derivative of E with respect to that quantity.)

8.3.4 Adapting the Network: Code

To fully understand the meaning and implications of these equations, it may help to run through a simple (hypothetical) implementation.

First, to calculate the derivatives, we need a new subroutine, dual to NET2.

```
      SUBROUTINE F_NET2(F_Yhat, W, W', W", x,
      F_net, F_net', F_net", F_W, F_W', F_W")
            REAL F_Yhat(n),W(N+n,N+n),
               W'(N+n,N+n),W"(N+n,N+n)
            REAL x(N+n),F_net(N+n),F_net'(N+n),
               F_net"(N+n)
            REAL F_W(N+n,N+n),F_W'(N+n,N+n),
               F_W"(N+n,N+n),F_x(N+n)
            INTEGER i,j,n,m,N
C Initialize Equation (8.16)
            DO 1 i = 1,N
      1        F_x(i)=0.
            DO 2 i = 1,n
      2        F_x(i+N)=F_Yhat(i)
C RUN THROUGH (8.16), (8.11), AND (8.12) AS
C A SET, RUNNING BACKWARD
            DO 1000 i=N+n,m+1,-1
```

```
C                   first complete (8.16)
                    DO 161 j = i+1,N+n
      161               F_x(i)=F_x(i)+W(j,i)*F_net(j)
                    DO 162 j = m+1,N+n
      162               F_x(i)=F_x(i)+W'(j,i)*F_net"(j)
                          +W"(j,i)*F_net"(j)
C                   next implement (8.11)
                    F_net(i)=F_x(i)*x(i)*(1 - x(i))
C                   implement (8.12), (8.17), and
C                   (8.18) (as running sums)
                    DO 12 j = 1,i-1
      12                F_W(i,j)=F_W(i,j)+F_net(i)*x(j)
                    DO 1718 j = 1,N+n
                        F_W'(i,j)=F_W'(i,j)
                          +F_net'(i)*x(j)
      1718             F_W"(i,j)=F_W"(i,j)
                          +F_net"(i)*x(j)
      1000        CONTINUE
```

Note that the last two DO loops have been set up to perform running sums, to simplify what follows.

Finally, we may adapt the weights as follows, by batch learning, where I use the abbreviation $x(i,)$, to represent the vector formed by $x(i, j)$ across all j.

```
                    REAL x(-1:T,N+n),Yhat(T,n)
                    DATA x(0,),x(-1,)/(2(N+n)) * 0.0/
                    DO 1000 pass_number=1, maximum_passes
C                       First calculate outputs and
C                       errors in a forward pass
                        DO 100 t=1,T
      100                   CALL NET2(X(t),W,W',W", x(t-2),
                              x(t-1),x(t,),Yhat(t,))
C                       Initialize the running sums to 0
C                       and set F_net(T), F_net(T+1) to 0
                        DO 200 i = m+1,N+n
                            F_net'(i)=0.
                            F_net"(i)=0.
                            DO 199 j = 1,N+n
                                F_W(i,j)=0.
                                F_W'(i,j)=0.
      199                       F_W"(i,j)=0.
      200           CONTINUE
C NEXT CALCULATE THE DERIVATIVES IN A SWEEP
C BACKWARD THROUGH TIME
                        DO 500 t = T,1,-1
```

```
C                   First, calculate the errors at
C                   the current time t
                    DO 410 i = 1,n
    410                 F_Yhat(i)=Yhat(t,i)-Y(t,i)
C             Next, calculate F_net(t) for time
C             t and update the F_W running sums
                    call F_NET2(F_Yhat,W,W',W''', x(t,),
                       F_net,F_net',F_net'',F_W, F_W',F_W''')
C             Move F_net(t+1) to F_net(t), in
C             effect, to prepare for a new t value
                    DO 420 i = m+1,N+n
                       F_net''(i)=F_net'(i)
    420                F_net'(i)=F_net(i)
    500             CONTINUE
C FINALLY, UPDATE THE WEIGHTS BY
C STEEPEST DESCENT
                    DO 999 i = m+1,N+n
                    DO 998 j = 1,N+n
                       W(i,j)=W(i,j)-
                       learning_rate*F_W(i,j)
                       W'(i,j)=W'(i,j)-
                       learning_rate*F_W'(i,j)
    998                W''(i,j)=learning_rate*
                       F_W''(i,j);
    999             CONTINUE
   1000             CONTINUE
```

Once again, note that we have to go backward in time in order to get the required derivatives. (There are ways to do these calculations in forward time, but exact results require the calculation of an entire Jacobian matrix, which is far more expensive with large networks.) For backpropagation through time, the natural way to adapt the network is in one big batch. Also note that we need to store a lot of intermediate information (which is inconsistent with real-time adaptation). This storage can be reduced by clever programming if W' and W'' are sparse, but it cannot be eliminated altogether.

In using backpropagation through time, we usually need to use much smaller learning rates than we do in basic backpropagation if we use steepest descent at all. In my experience [20], it may also help to start out by fixing the W' weights to zero (or to 1 when we want to force memory) in an initial phase of adaptation, and slowly free them up.

In some applications, we may not really care about errors in classification at all times t. In speech recognition, for example, we may only care about errors at the end of a word or phoneme; we usually do output a preliminary classification before the phoneme has been finished, but we usually do not care about the accuracy of that preliminary classification. In such cases, we may simply set $F\_Y$hat to zero in the times we do not care about. To be more sophisticated, we may replace Equation (8.6) by a more precise model of what we do care about; whatever we choose, it should be simple to replace Equation (8.9) and the $F\_Y$hat loop accordingly.

8.4 EXTENSIONS OF THE METHOD

Backpropagation through time is a very general method, with many extensions. This section tries to describe the most important of these extensions.

8.4.1 Use of Other Networks

The network shown in Equations (8.1)–(8.5) is a very simple, basic network. Backpropagation can be used to adapt a wide variety of other networks, including networks representing econometric models and systems of simultaneous equations. Naturally, when one writes computer programs to implement a different kind of network, one must either describe which alternative network one chooses or else put options into the program to give the user this choice.

In the neural network field, users are often given a choice of network "topology." This simply means that they are asked to declare which subset of the possible weights/connections will actually be used. Every weight removed from Equation (8.15) should be removed from (8.16) as well, along with (8.12) and (8.14) (or whichever apply to that weight); therefore simplifying the network by removing weights simplifies all the other calculations as well. (Mathematically, this is the same as fixing these weights to zero.) Typically, people will remove an entire block of weights, such that the limits of the sums in our equations are all shrunk.

In a truly brain-like network, each neuron (in Equation (8.15)) will only receive input from a small number of other cells. Neuroscientists do not agree on how many inputs are typical; some cite numbers on the order of 100 inputs per cell, while others quote 10,000. In any case, all these estimates are small compared to the billions of cells present. To implement this kind of network efficiently on a conventional computer, one would use a linked list or a list of offsets to represent the connections actually implemented for each cell; the same strategy can be used to implement the backward calculations and keep the connection costs low. Similar tricks are possible in parallel computers of all types. Many researchers are interested in devising ways to automatically make and break connections so that users will not have to specify all this information in advance [20]. The research on topology is hard to summarize since it is a mixture of normal science, sophisticated epistemology, and extensive ad hoc experimentation; however, the paper by Guyon et al. [13] is an excellent example of what works in practice. (See also [25], Chapter 10).

Even in the neural network field, many programmers try to avoid the calculation of the exponential in Equation (8.5). Depending on what kind of processor one has available, this calculation can multiply run times by a significant factor.

In the first published paper that discussed backpropagation at length as a way to adapt neural networks [14], I proposed the use of an artificial neuron ("continuous logic unit," CLU) based on

$$s(z) = 0, \quad z < 0,$$

$$s(z) = z, \quad 0 < z < 1,$$

$$s(z) = 1, \quad z > 1.$$

This leads to a very simple derivative as well. Unfortunately, the second derivatives of this function are not well behaved, which can affect the efficiency of some applications. Still, many programmers are now using piecewise linear approximations to Equation (8.5), along with lookup tables, which can work relatively well in some applications. In earlier experiments, I have also found good uses for a Taylor series approximation:

$$s(z) = 1/(1 - z + 0.5 * z^2), \quad z < 0,$$

$$s(z) = 1 - 1/(1 + z + 0.5 * z^2), \quad z > 0.$$

In a similar spirit, it is common to speed up learning by "stretching out" $s(z)$ so that it goes from -1 to 1 instead of 0 to 1.

Backpropagation can also be used without using neural networks at all. For example, it can be used to adapt a network consisting entirely of user-specified functions, representing something like an economic model. In that case, the way one proceeds depends on who one is programming for and what kind of model one has.

If one is programming for oneself and the model consists of a sequence of equations that can be invoked one after the other, then one should consider the tutorial paper [11], which also contains a more rigorous definition of what these F_x_i derivatives really mean and a proof of the chain rule for ordered derivatives. If one is developing a tool for others, then one might set it up to look like a standard econometric package (like SAS or Troll) where the user of the system types in the equations of his/her model; the backpropagation would go inside the package as a way to speed up these calculations and would mostly be transparent to the user. If one's model consists of a set of simultaneous equations that need to be solved at each time, then one must use more complicated procedures [15]; in neural network terms, one would call this a "doubly recurrent network." (The methods of Pineda [16] and Almeida [17] are special cases of this situation. See [25], Chapter 3, and [26], for more information.)

Pearlmutter [18] and Williams [19] have described alternative methods, designed to achieve results similar to those of backpropagation through time, using a different computational strategy. For example, the Williams–Zipser method is a special case of the "conventional perturbation" equation cited in [14], which rejected this as a neural network method on the grounds that its computational costs scale as the square of the network size; however, the method does yield exact derivatives with a time-forward calculation.

Supervised learning problems or forecasting problems that involve memory can also be translated into control problems [15, p. 352; 20], which allows the use of adaptive critic methods, to be discussed in the next section. Normally, this would yield only an approximate solution (or approximate derivatives), but it would also allow time-forward real-time learning. If the network itself contains calculation noise (due to hardware limitations), the adaptive critic approach might even be more robust than backpropagation through time because it is based on mathematics that allow for the presence of noise.

8.4.2 Applications Other Than Supervised Learning

Backpropagation through time can also be used in two other major applications: neuroidentification and neurocontrol. (For applications to sensitivity analysis, see [14] and [15].)

In neuroidentification, we try to do with neural nets what econometricians do with forecasting models. (Engineers would call this the identification problem or the problem of identifying dynamic systems. Statisticians refer to it as the problem of estimating stochastic time-series models.) Our training set consists of vectors $X(t)$ and $u(t)$, not $X(t)$ and $Y(t)$. Usually, $X(t)$ represents a set of observations of the external world, and $u(t)$ represents a set of actions that we have control over (such as the settings of motors or actuators). The combination of $x(t)$ and $u(t)$ is input to the network at each time t. Our target, at time t, is the vector $X(t + 1)$.

We could easily build a network to input these inputs and aim at these targets. We could simply collect the inputs and targets into the format of Section 8.2, and then use basic backpropagation. But basic backpropagation contains no "memory." The forecast of $X(t + 1)$ would depend on $X(t)$, but not on previous time periods. If human beings worked like this, then they would be unable to predict that a ball might roll out the far side of a table after rolling down under the near side; as soon as the ball disappeared from sight [from the current vector $X(t)$], they would have no way of accounting for its existence. (Harold Szu has presented a more interesting example of this same effect: if a tiger chased after such a memoryless person, the person would forget about the tiger after first turning to run away. Natural selection has eliminated such people.) Backpropagation through time permits more powerful networks, which do have a "memory," for use in the same setup.

Even this approach to the neuroidentification problem has its limitations. Like the usual methods of econometrics [15], it may lead to forecasts that hold up poorly over multiple time periods. It does not properly identify where the noise comes from. It does not permit real-time adaptation. In an earlier paper

[20], I described some ideas for overcoming these limitations, but more research is needed. The first phase of Kawato's cascade method [9] for controlling a robot over time, and which uses backpropagation through time in a different way; it is a special case of the "pure robust method," which also worked well in the earliest applications that I studied [1, 20]. See [25], Chapter 10, for recent results.

After we have solved the problem of identifying a dynamic system, we are then ready to move on to controlling that system.

In neurocontrol, we often *start out* with a model or network that describes the system or plant we are trying to control. Our problem is to adapt a *second* network, the action network, which inputs $X(t)$ and outputs the control $u(t)$. (In actuality, we can allow the action network to "see" or input the *entire* vector $x(t)$ calculated by the model network; this allows it to account for memories such as the recent appearance of a tiger.) Usually, we want to adapt the action network so as to maximize some measure of performance or utility $U(X, t)$ summed over time. Performance measures used in past applications have included everything from the energy used to move a robot arm [8, 9] through to net profits received by the gas industry [11]. Typically, we are given a set of possible initial states $x(1)$, and asked to train the action network so as to maximize the sum of utility from time 1 to a final time T.

To solve this problem using backpropagation through time, we simply calculate the derivatives of our performance measure with respect to all the weights in the action network. "Backpropagation" refers to how we calculate the derivatives, not to anything involving pattern recognition or error. We then adapt the weights according to these derivatives, as in Equation (8.12) except that the sign of the adjustment term is now positive (because we are maximizing rather than minimizing).

The easiest way to implement this approach is to merge the utility function, the model network, and the action network into one big network. We can then construct the dual to this entire network, as described in 1974 [1] and illustrated in my recent tutorial [11]. However, if we wish to keep the three component networks distinct, then the bookkeeping becomes more complicated. The basic idea is illustrated in Figure 8.6, which maps exactly into the approach used by Nguyen and Windrow [7] and by Jordan [8].

Instead of working with a single subroutine, NET, we now need three subroutines:

```
UTILITY(X; t; X"; U)
MODEL(X(t), u(t); x(t); X(t + 1))
ACTION(x(t); W; x'(t); u(t)).
```

In each of these subroutines, the two arguments on the right are technically outputs, and the argument on the far right is what we usually think of as the output of the network. We need to know the full vector x produced inside the model network so that the action network can "see" important memories. The

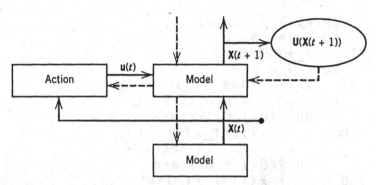

FIGURE 8.6 Backpropagating utility through time. (Dashed lines represent derivative calculations.)

action network does not need to have its own internal memory, but we need to save its internal state (x') so that we can later calculate derivatives. For simplicity, I assume that MODEL does not contain any lag-two memory terms (i.e., W'' weights). The primes after the x's indicate that we are looking at the internal states of different networks; they are unrelated to the primes representing lagged values, discussed in Section 8.3, which we also need in what follows.

To use backpropagation through time, we need to construct dual subroutines for all three of these subroutines:

```
F_UTILITY(x"; t; F_X)
F_MODEL(F_net', F_X(t + 1);x(t); F_net, F_u)
F_ACTION(F_u; x'(t); F_W).
```

The outputs of these subroutines are the arguments on the far right (including F_net), which are represented by the broken lines in Figure 8.6. The subroutine $F\_UTILITY$ simply reports out the derivatives of $U(\mathbf{x}, t)$ with respect to the variables X_i. The subroutine F_MODEL is like the earlier subroutine F_NET2, except that we need to output F_u instead of derivatives to weights. (Again, we are adapting only the action network here.) The subroutine F_AC-TION is virtually identical to the old subroutine F_NET, except that we need to calculate F_W as a running sum (as we did in F_NET2).

Of these three subroutines, F_MODEL is by far the most complex. Therefore it may help to consider some possible code.

```
SUBROUTINE F_MODEL(F_net',F_X',x,F_net,F_u)
C The weights inside this subroutine are
C those used in MODEL, analogous to those in NET2,
C  and are
C unrelated to the weights in ACTION
        REAL F_net'(N+n),F_X'(n),x(N+n),
           F_net(N+n),F_u(p),F_x(N+n)
```

```
       INTEGER i,j,n,m,N,p
       DO 1 i=1,N
1          F_x(i)=0.
       DO 2 i = 1,n
2          F_x(i+N)=F_X(i)
       DO 1000 i = N+n,1,-1
          DO 910 j = i+1,N+n
910           F_x(i)=F_x(i)+W(j,i)
                      *F_net (j)
          DO 920 j = m+1,N=n
920           F_x(i)=F_x(i)+W'(j,i)
                      *F_net' (j)
1000      F_net(i)=F_x(i)*x(i)*(1 - x(i))
       DO 2000 i = 1,p
2000      F_u(i)=F_x(n+i)
```

The last small DO loop here assumes that **u**(*t*) was part of the input vector to the original subroutine MODEL, inserted into the slots between **x**(*n* + 1) and **x**(*m*). Again, a good programmer could easily compress all this; my goal here is only to illustrate the mathematics.

Finally, in order to adapt the action network, we go through multiple passes, each starting from one of the starting values of **x**(1). In each pass, we call ACTION and then MODEL, one after the other, until we have built up a stream of forecasts from time 1 up to time *T*. Then, for each time *t* going backward from *T* to 1, we call the UTILITY subroutine, then F_UTILITY, then F_MODEL, and then F_ACTION. At the end of the pass, we have the correct array of derivatives F_W, which we can then use to adjust the weights of the action network.

In general, backpropagation through time has the advantage of being relatively quick and exact. That is why I chose it for my natural gas application [11]. However, it cannot account for noise in the process to be controlled. To account for noise in maximizing an arbitrary utility function, we must rely on adaptive critic methods [21]. Adaptive critic methods do not require backpropagation through time in any form and are therefore suitable for true real-time learning. There are other forms of neurocontrol as well (Chapter 9), which are not based on maximizing a utility function.

8.4.3 Handling Strings of Data

In most of the examples above, I assumed that the training data form one lone time series, from *t* = 1 to *t* = *T*. Thus, in adapting the weights, I always assumed batch learning (except in the code in Section 8.2); the weights were always adapted after a complete set of derivatives was calculated, based on a complete pass through all the data. Mechanically, one could use pattern learning in the backward pass through time; however, this would lead to a host of problems, and it is difficult to see what it would gain.

Data in the real world are often somewhere between the two extremes represented by Sections 8.2 and 8.3. Instead of having a set of unrelated patterns or one continuous time series, we often have a set of time series or strings. For example, in speech recognition, our training set may consist of a set of strings, each consisting of one word or one sentence. In robotics, our training set may consist of a set of strings, where each string represents one experiment with a robot.

In these situations, we can apply backpropagation through time to a *single string* of data at a time. For each string, we can calculate complete derivatives and update the weights. Then we can go on to the next string. This is like pattern learning, in that the weights are updated incrementally before the entire data set is studied. It requires intermediate storage for only one string at a time. To speed things up even further, we might adapt the net in stages, initially fixing certain weights (like W_{ii}) to zero or one.

Nevertheless, string learning is not the same thing as real-time learning. To solve problems in neuroidentification and supervised learning, the only consistent way to have internal memory terms and to avoid backpropagation through time is to use adaptive critics in a supporting role [25, Chapter 13]. That alternative is complex, inexact, and relatively expensive for these applications; it may be unavoidable for true real-time systems like the human brain, but it would probably be better to live with string learning and focus on other challenges in neuroidentification for the time being.

8.4.4 Speeding Up Convergence

For those who are familiar with numerical analysis and optimization, it goes without saying that steepest descent—as in Equation (8.12)—is a very inefficient method.

There is a huge literature in the neural network field on how to speed up backpropagation. For example, Fahlman and Touretzky of Carnegie–Mellon have compiled and tested a variety of intuitive insights that can speed up convergence a hundredfold. Their benchmark problems may be very useful in evaluating other methods that claim to do the same. A few authors have copied simple methods from the field of numerical analysis, such as quasi-Newton methods (BFGS) and Polak–Ribiere conjugate gradients; however, the former works only on small problems (a hundred or so weights) [22], while the latter works well only with batch learning and very careful line searches. The need for careful line searches is discussed in the literature [23], but I have found it to be unusually important when working with large problems, including simulated linear mappings.

In my own work, I have used Shanno's more recent conjugate gradient method with batch learning; for a dense training set—made up of distinctly different patterns—this method worked better than anything else I tried, including pattern learning methods [12]. Many researchers have used approximate Newton's methods, without saying that they are using an approximation; however an exact Newton's method can also be implemented in $O(N)$ storage and has worked reasonably well in early tests [12]. Shanno has reported new breakthroughs in function minimization, which may perform still better [24-26]. Still, there is clearly a lot of room for improvement through further research.

Needless to say, it can be much easier to converge to a set of weights that do not minimize error or that assume a simpler network; methods of that sort are also popular but are useful only when they clearly fit the application at hand for identifiable reasons.

8.4.5 Miscellaneous Issues

Minimizing square error and maximizing likelihood are often taken for granted as fundamental principles in large parts of engineering; however, there is a large literature on alternative approaches [12], both in neural network theory and in robust statistics.

This literature is beyond the scope of this chapter, but a few related points may be worth noting. For example, instead of minimizing square error, we could minimize the 1.5 power of error; all the operations above still go through. We can minimize E of Equation (8.5) plus some constant k times the sum of squares of the weights; as k goes to infinity and the network is made linear, this converges to Kohonen's pseudoinverse method, a common form of associative memory. Statisticians like Dempster and Efron have argued that the linear form of this approach can be better than the usual least-squares methods; their arguments capture the essential insight that people can forecast by analogy to historical precedent, instead of forecasting by a comprehensive model or network. Presumably, an ideal network would bring together both kinds of forecasting [12, 20, 26].

Many authors worry a lot about local minima. In using backpropagation through time in robust estimation, I found it important to keep the "memory" weights near zero at first, and free them up gradually in order to minimize problems. When T is much larger than m—as statisticians recommend for good generalization—local minima are probably a lot less serious than rumor has it. Still, with T larger than m, it is very easy to construct local minima. Consider the example with $m = 2$ shown in Table 8.1.

The error for each of the patterns can be plotted as a contour map as a function of the two weights w_1 and w_2. (For this simple example, no threshold term is assumed.) Each map is made up of straight contours, defining a fairly sharp trough about a central line. The three central lines for the three patterns form a triangle, the vertices of which correspond roughly to the local minima. Even when T is much larger than m, conflicts like this can exist within the

TABLE 8.1 Training Set for Local Minima

t	$X(t)$		$Y(t)$
1	0	1	.1
2	1	0	.1
3	1	1	.9

training set. Again, however, this may not be an overwhelming problem in practical applications [19].

8.5 SUMMARY

Backpropagation through time can be applied to many different categories of dynamical systems—neural networks, feedforward systems of equations, systems with time lags, systems with instantaneous feedback between variables (as in ordinary differential equations or simultaneous equation models), and so on. The derivatives that it calculates can be used in pattern recognition, in systems identification, and in stochastic and deterministic control. This chapter has presented the key equations of backpropagation, as applied to neural networks of varying degrees of complexity. It has also discussed papers that elaborate on the extensions of this method to more general applications and some of the trade-offs involved.

REFERENCES

1. P. Werbos, *Beyond regression: new tools for predictions and analysis in the behavioral sciences*, Ph.D. dissertation, Committee on Applied Mathematics, Harvard University, Cambridge, MA, Nov. 1974. (Chapters 1–6 here.)

2. D. Rumelhart, D. Hinton, and G. Williams, Learning internal representations by error propagation, in D. Rumelhart and F. McClelland (eds.), *Parallel Distributed Processing*, *Vol. 1*, MIT Press, Cambridge, MA, 1986.

3. D. B. Parker, Learning-logic, MIT Cen. Computational Res. Economics Management Sci., Cambridge, MA, TR-47, 1985.

4. Y. Le Cun, Une procedure d'apprentissage pour reseau a seuil assymetrique, in *Proceedings Cognitiva '85*, Paris, June 1985, pp. 599–604.

5. R. Watrous and L. Shastri, Learning phonetic features using connectionist networks: an experiment in speech recognition, in *Proceedings of the 1st IEEE International Conference on Neural Networks*, June 1987.

6. H. Sawai, A. Waibel, P. Haffner, M. Miyatake, and K. Shikano, Parallelism, hierarchy, scaling in time-delay neural networks for spotting Japanese phonemes/CV-syllables, in *Proceedings of the IEEE International Joint Conference on Neural Networks*, June 1989.

7. D. Nguyen and B. Widrow, The truck backer-upper: an example of self-learning in neural networks, in W. T. Miller, R. Sutton, and P. Werbos (eds.), *Neural Networks for Robotics and Control*, MIT Press, Cambridge, MA, 1990.

8. M. Jordan, Generic constraints on underspecified target trajectories, in *Proceedings of the IEEE International Joint Conference on Neural Networks*, June 1989.

9. M. Kawato, Computational schemes and neural network models for formation and control of multijoint arm trajectory in W. T. Miller, R. Sutton, and P. Werbos (eds.), *Neural Networks for Robotics and Control*. MIT Press, Cambridge, MA, 1990.

10. R. Narendra, Adaptive control using neural networks, in W. T. Miller, R. Sutton, and P. Werbos (eds.), *Neural Networks for Robotics and Control*. MIT Press, Cambridge, MA, 1990.

11. P. Werbos, Maximizing long-term gas industry profits in two minutes in Lotus using neural network methods, *IEEE Transactions on Systems, Man, and Cybernetics, Mar./Apr. 1989.*

12. P. Werbos, Backpropagation: past and future. in *Proceedings of the 2nd IEEE International Conference on Neural Networks*, June 1988. The transcript of the talk and slides, available from the author, are more introductory in nature and more comprehensive in some respects.

13. I. Guyon, I. Poujaud, L. Personnaz, G. Dreyfus, J. Denker, and Y. Le Cun, Comparing different neural network architectures for classifying handwritten digits, in *Proceedings of the IEEE International Joint Conference on Neural Networks*, June 1989.

14. P. Werbos, Applications of advances in nonlinear sensitivity analysis in R. Drenick and F. Kozin (eds.), *Systems Modeling and Optimization: Proceedings of the 10th IFIP Conference (1981).* Springer-Verlag, New York, 1982. (Chapter 7).

15. P. Werbos, Generalization of backpropagation with application to a recurrent gas market model, *Neural Networks*, Oct. 1988.

16. F. J. Pineda, Generalization of backpropagation to recurrent and higher order networks in *Proceedings of the IEEE International Conference on Neural Information Processing Systems*, 1987.

17. L. B. Almeida, A learning rule for asynchronous perceptrons with feedback in a combinatorial environment, in *Proceedings of the IEEE International Conference on Neural Networks*, 1987.

18. B. A. Pearlmutter, Learning state space trajectories in recurrent neural networks, in *Proceedings of the International Joint Conference on Neural Networks*, June 1989.

19. R. Williams, Adaptive state representation and estimation using recurrent connectionist networks, in W. T. Miller, R. Sutton, and P. Werbos (eds.), *Neural Networks for Robotics and Control*, MIT Press, Cambridge, MA, 1990.

20. P. Werbos, Learning how the world words: specifications for predictive networks in robots and brains, in *Proceedings of the 1987 IEEE International Conference on Systems, Man, and Cybernetics*, 1987.

21. P. Werbos, Consistency of HDP applied to a simple reinforcement learning problem, *Neural Networks*, Mar. 1990.

22. J. Dennis and R. Schnabel, *Numerical Methods for Unconstrained Optimization and Nonlinear Equations*. Prentice-Hall, Englewood Cliffs, NJ, 1983.

23. D. Shanno, Conjugate-gradient methods with inexact searches, *Mathematics Operations Research*, Vol. 3, Aug. 1978.

24. D. Shanno, Recent advances in numerical techniques for large-scale optimization, in W. T. Miller, R. Sutton, and P. Werbos, (eds.), *Neural Networks for Robotics and Control*, MIT Press, Cambridge, MA, 1990.

25. D. White and S. Sofge, eds., *Handbook of Intelligent Control*, Van Nostrand, 1992.

26. P. Werbos, Supervised learning: can it escape its local minimum, in *WCNN 93 Proceedings*, Erlbaum, 1993.

[1]This chapter is reprinted from *Proceedings of the IEEE*, Vol. 78, No. 10, October 1990, from manuscript received in 1989, with minor updating.

9

Neurocontrol

Where It Is Going and Why It Is Crucial

In the past few years, enormous progress has been made by a relatively small group of researchers in developing and understanding new kinds of neural network designs which show real promise in explaining and replicating "intelligence" as we see it in biological organisms. These new designs come from the emerging field of *neurocontrol*. Already, there has been substantial real-world success in the control of robot arms (including the main arm of the space shuttle), in chemical process control, and in the continuous production of high-quality composite parts. New benchmark problems and early successes suggest that neurocontrol may become crucial to the National Aerospace Plane (NASP), which in turn may be crucial to the cost-effective settlement of outer space and to the use of hydrogen instead of oil in aviation. (NASP will try to reach orbit *as an airplane*, at low cost). On the other hand, there have been many failures and many reinventions of the wheel, due to inadequate appreciation of what has already been done and how it relates to control theory. This chapter will discuss the goals of neurocontrol, and then describe some applications in the *context* of a roadmap stretching from the past through to new opportunities to build truly intelligent systems in the future.

9.1 BASIC DEFINITIONS

Neurocontrol is the use of neural networks—artificial *or* natural—to directly control *actions* intended to produce a physical result in a world that changes over time.

Aside from minor copy editing and reference [4], this chapter first appeared in I. Aleksander and J. Taylor, eds., *Artificial Neural Networks II*, (ICANN-92), North Holland, Amsterdam, 1992.

295

Many people think of neural networks entirely as artificial neural networks (ANNs) designed to perform *supervised learning*. They think of them as systems that are always given a *database* of *input vectors*, $X(t)$, and target vectors, $Y(t)$, for $t = 1$ to T. They think of neural networks as systems that implement a nonlinear mapping, $\hat{Y}(t) = f(X(t), W)$, which is "learned" by adapting the weights W either in real-time (t) or in batch mode, offline. They think of "basic research" as the development of new supervised learning designs or the analysis of such designs. They think of control as one of many applications areas. However, neurocontrol is an area of research in its own right. It calls for new *types* of ANNs, operating at a different level, performing different kinds of tasks.

Many control theorists have been impressed by the many theorems showing that supervised learning can approximate any well-behaved function f to an arbitrary degree of accuracy. They have been impressed by theorems saying that we can approximate even *ill-behaved* functions, like those required in some control applications, if we allow two hidden layers [1] or for simultaneous recurrence (which can emulate two hidden layers as a special case). But they argue—with justice—that real-world control problems (like those addressed by biological organisms) involve a *time dimension*. Instead of seeking the optimal mapping from $\mathbf{X}(t)$ to $\mathbf{Y}(t)$, we need to seek optimal maps of the form

$$\hat{\mathbf{Y}}(t) = \mathbf{f}_Y(\mathbf{X}(t), \mathbf{Y}(t-1), \mathbf{R}(t-1), W),$$

$$\mathbf{R}(t) = \mathbf{f}_R(\mathbf{X}(t), \mathbf{Y}(t-1), \mathbf{R}(t-1), W), \qquad (9.1)$$

where $\mathbf{f}_Y$ and $\mathbf{f}_R$ represent two vector outputs of a *single* network $\mathbf{f}$ and where $\mathbf{R}$ (for "recurrent" or "reality") is a kind of vector of memories. This is equivalent to the problem of system identification in control theory where we try to adapt a Model network that predicts $\mathbf{X}(t+1)$:

$$\hat{\mathbf{X}}(t+1) = \mathbf{f}_X(\mathbf{X}(t), \mathbf{u}(t), \mathbf{R}(t), W),$$

$$\mathbf{R}(t+1) = \mathbf{f}_R(\mathbf{X}(t), \mathbf{u}(t), \mathbf{R}(t), W), \qquad (9.2)$$

where $\mathbf{X}(t)$ represents sensor data observed at time t and $\mathbf{u}(t)$ represents actions we take after observing $\mathbf{X}(t)$.

Supervised learning is defined as the task of adapting simple static neural networks. *Neuroidentification* may be defined as the effort to adapt networks of the form shown in Equation (9.1) or (9.2) (with the possibility of additional time lags and noise models). *Neurocontrol* may be defined as the effort to build (or formulate) systems that include an adapted Action network:

$$\mathbf{u}(t) = \mathbf{A}(\mathbf{X}(t), \mathbf{R}(t), W). \qquad (9.3)$$

Systems such as Equations (9.1) or (9.2) are a variety of "recurrent network," but they are *very different* from simultaneous-recurrent networks such as Cohen–Grossberg or Hopfield nets. Much of the conventional wisdom about recurrent networks is unreliable, because it fails to distinguish between the these very different kinds of recurrence kinds of recurrence, and the many different ways of implementing each [2].

9.2 WHY NEUROCONTROL IS CRUCIAL TO INTELLIGENCE

The human brain, as a whole system, is clearly *not* a supervised learning system. It clearly *is* a "computer," an information processing system. The function of any computer, *as a whole system*, is to compute its outputs. The outputs of the brain as a whole system are *actions*. Therefore the human brain as a whole system is a neurocontroller. To understand the brain as a whole system, we must first understand *neurocontrol*; we must understand how it is possible to build (or to exist) a neurocontroller with the kinds of capabilities that the brain possesses. Clearly, these include very sophisticated capabilities, such as planning and problem-solving and foresight and the like.

Within the brain, we know that there are subsystems and phenomena such as memory and pattern recognition. But we cannot really hope to understand these subsystems until we know what their *functions* are. We cannot understand the functions of a *subsystem* until we know how it *fits in* to the design of the whole system; therefore, once again, an understanding of neurocontrol is a prerequisite.

From the viewpoint of control, the brain is living proof that it is possible to build a generalized controller that takes full advantage of parallel distributed hardware, that can handle many thousands of actuators (muscle fibers) in parallel, that can handle noise and nonlinearity, and that can achieve goals or optimize over a long-range planning horizon. This proves that neural net designs of *some* kind (known or unknown) could achieve substantially better performance than classical controllers today.

In summary, to understand or replicate true brain-like intelligence, the primary challenge to our community is to climb the ladder of ever more sophisticated neurocontrol designs. I will argue that we now can see the next steps of the ladder, far enough up to replicate all the capabilities mentioned in this section. (See White and Sofge [2] and Werbos and Pellionisz [3] for more details of the argument.)

9.3 A BASIC ROADMAP OF NEUROCONTROL

A chapter this short cannot give all the equations of all the basic designs, let alone all the applications. Neurocontrol systems in the real world can be understood at three levels of analysis: (1) at the *micro* level, where we discuss individual supervised learning modules (multilayer perceptrons, radial basis functions, CMAC, etc.) or other low-level modules *within* a control architecture; (2) at the *middle* level, where we describe how these modules are put together to build a general-purpose system methodology; and (3) at the *application* level, where we describe how general-purpose systems are used in stages, and in combination with application-specific modules, to generate a product. This may be compared to the three levels of building chips, putting chips together to make a computer, and figuring out how to use the computers.

This chapter generally focuses on the *middle level*. For a more complete discussion of the design options at all three levels (including equations, flow-charts, and subroutine structures) see White and Sofge [2]. For a discussion of how to use neurocontrol designs with fuzzy systems as modules, see Werbos [4]. Some of these designs are subject to a patent pending, in my name, through BehavHeuristics of College Park, Maryland.

At the middle level, ANN designs may be classified according to *what kinds of generic tasks* they perform. ANNs have performed four kinds of useful functions in control: (1) *subsystem* functions such as pattern recognition or neuroidentification, for sensor fusion or diagnostics and so on; (2) *cloning* functions, such as *copying* the behavior of a human being able to control the target plant; (3) *tracking functions*, such as making a robot arm follow a desired *trajectory* or *reference model*, or making a chemical plant stay at a desired *setpoint*; and (4) *optimization* functions, such as maximizing throughput or minimizing energy use or maximizing goal satisfaction over the entire future.

The first of these functions does not qualify as neurocontrol. ANNs for the second function are "supervised controllers;" they have been reinvented many times, usually by people who are supervised learning and base their system on a database of "correct actions" (often without telling us how they know what the "correct actions" are). The third function—tracking—is performed by "direct inverse controllers" and by "neural adaptive controllers." Some authors seem to assume that following a trajectory is the *only* interesting problem in control; however, the human brain is *not* a simple trajectory follower, and real-world engineering faces many other tasks as well. The fourth group of designs is clearly the *only* working group with any chance of replicating brain-like capabilities. Within the fourth group itself, there are two useful subgroups—the "backpropagation of utility" (i.e., *direct* maximization of future utility) and the "adaptive critic family" (broadly defined); only the latter has a serious chance of someday replicating true brain-like capability [2,3]. *Within* the adaptive critic family, we face a similar ladder of designs, from simple methods that learn slowly except on small problems, through to moderate-scale methods, through to large-scale methods requiring a neuroidentification component, to methods capable of true "planning" and "chunking" but requiring the use of simultaneous-recurrent modules [2].

In summary, we have a ladder here, starting from straightforward designs, easy to implement today, which can take us up step by step to a true understanding of intelligence. . .if only we have the will to climb higher.

9.4 WHAT'S NEW IN CLONING: SUPERVISED CONTROL

When people decide they will "simply use" ANNs in control, they often build up a database of sensor inputs $X(t)$ and "correct actions," $u^*(t)$, and use supervised learning to try to learn the mapping from **X** to **u**. Widrow's black-jack player in the 1960s was based on this principle. The intellectual challenge here is in building the database of "correct actions," which usually comes from a human being *already* able to solve the control problem.

Supervised control can be very useful when humans or computer programs are *already* able to compute an adequate control but are too slow or too imperfect to meet the needs of the application. A neural net clone (especially with neural net hardware) can solve the problem. For example, the National Aerospace Plane (NASP) will fly at a speed too fast for a human to stabilize in flight; under NSF support, Pap of Accurate Automation has developed a supervised control system on Silicon Graphics, which can replicate the reactions of humans in controlling a slowed-down version of a NASP simulator. In actual flight, the ANN could be run at electronic speed, or it could be used to provide the initial weights for a more sophisticated neurocontrol design. Jorgenson and Schley controlled an F-15 simulator years ago in a similar way [5]. Pap used a slight generalization of this approach, learning the map from $\mathbf{u}(t-1)$ and $\mathbf{X}(t)$ to $\mathbf{u}^*(t)$. The success of this preliminary work and the good human–machine interface have led to a large follow-on project supported by the NASP program.

McAvoy has used a similar approach to try to "clone" good chemical plant operators. McAvoy's Neural Network Club includes 25 paying corporate members, mainly large chemical process companies like Texaco; they have reported large savings from already-fielded applications of ANNs. Cloning the good operators is only one of many such applications [2]. The differences between the best human operators and the worst may be worth thousands or millions of dollars, because of their ability to maintain efficiency when the plants taken through transitions. However, good operators—like good adaptive controllers—pay attention to *past trends*, not just to $\mathbf{X}(t)$; therefore, to capture their abilities, it is important to treat this as a problem in *neuroidentification*, *not* as a problem in supervised learning. We try to predict the operators with a *dynamic* neural net model, not just a static map. Robust methods for neuroidentification are discussed in White and Sofge [2]. *Improved efficiency in chemical processing translates directly into reduced waste and large potential reductions in environmental pollution*; work on such applications could be enormously valuable to human society.

Supervised control is similar to expert systems, in philosophy, but we copy what an expert *does*, not what an expert *says*. It has similarities to "pendant" systems for training robots, but pendants do not learn how humans respond to *different input vectors* $\mathbf{X}(t)$.

9.5 TRACKING METHODS: WHAT'S NEW AND WHAT'S WHAT

Classical adaptive control—pioneered by Narendra [6] and Astrom—builds *linear controllers* whose parameters are adapted in real time, to control *linear plants* whose parameters are unknown, so as to make the plants follow a *ref-*

erence model. Tracking a trajectory or staying at a setpoint are special cases of tracking a reference model. Even when a stable controller is adapted in this way, the interaction between the plant, the controller, and the adaptation process can cause instabilities and breakdown; the crowning achievement of Narenda and Astrom here was the development of *whole system* stability proofs showing that this cannot happen for certain controllers. There are a few proofs for nonlinear systems as well, but they are difficult and limited in scope. Narenda has put major efforts into *neural* adaptive control, with NSF support, in order to achieve a more general nonlinear capability, which, in simulations, breaks down far less often than linear control does on realistic problems [2].

In neural tracking, as in classical adaptive control, there are two major design alternatives—the direct inverse approach and the indirect approach. Kawato has also developed a third approach [5]—feedback error learning (FEL)—which is essentially a hybrid neural/expert approach; it presupposes the existence of a *stable classical feedback controller*, which is then used in training the ANN.

Direct inverse control fits the biologists' notion of learning the mapping from spatial coordinates to motor coordinates—a subject often discussed by Grossberg, Eckmiller, and others. For example, given a two-degree-of-freedom robot arm, controlled by changing the joint angles θ_1 and θ_2, we may try to move the arm to the point with coordinates $x_1(t)$ and $x_2(t)$. If the mapping from θ_1 and θ_2 to x_1 and x_2 is one-to-one, then there will exist an *inverse* map from (x_1, x_2) to (θ_1, θ_2). Given a *desired* point $\mathbf{x}(t)$, we can use that inverse map to tell us the *angles* that send the arm to that point. We can learn the inverse map by first flailing the arm around at random and building up a database of *actual* $\boldsymbol{\theta}(t)$ and $\mathbf{x}(t)$; we can then use the supervised learning on this database to learn the map from $\mathbf{x}$ to $\boldsymbol{\theta}$.

Direct inverse control has many limitations. Neural applications to robotics typically have 3–4% error, far too much for practical use. Walter et al. [7] have done better, but only by using a highly accurate supervised learning method that limits the possibility of real-time readaptation. Miller [2,5] has done well by *modifying* the approach. He still uses $\mathbf{u}(t)$ as his target output, but he uses $\mathbf{X}(t)$ and $\mathbf{X}(t-1)$ as his input, using a differentiable version of CMAC as his supervised learning method. He reduced error to a fraction of a percent in using a real Puma robot to push an unstable cart around a figure-eight track; even more impressively, he changed the weight on the cart, and the system readapted more completely within three loops around the track. Nevertheless, it should be possible to readapt much faster than this to *familiar disturbances* like a change in weights, if we use time-lagged recurrent networks (as in Equations (9.1) and (9.2)) instead of supervised learning here [2].

In a more recent application under NSF support, AAC used direct inverse control [8] to replace the dynamic joint controllers *within* a more classical, hierarchical control design developed by Seraji. In simulation, this led to the first controller fast enough and robust enough and robust enough to control the main arm of the space shuttle, under human guidance. (Millions of dollars have been spent, unsuccessfully to use classical methods and AI in that application). NASA has authorized a large-scale follow-on, including tests on the full real arm within a year, and the NASA project officer expect that this will increase productivity of these activities in space 10-fold. The U.S. Navy is supporting a large follow-on in underwater robotics. AAC has also made an arrangement with a major U.S. robot manufacturer to market this technology.

Nevertheless, direct inverse control is not powerful enough to explain human arm movement. Uno and Kawato et al. [5] have performed many experiments proving that human arms do include an optimization capability. This can only be explained, in my view [3], by assuming that they are based on an *indirect* design.

In the indirect approach, we try to minimize a utility function, U, defined as $[\mathbf{X}(t) - \mathbf{X}^*(t)]^2$ plus terms for energy consumption, and so on. The tracking application tells us something abut the form of U but, beyond that, we simply move on to one of the optimization methods of the next two sections. In past applications by Jordan, Kawato [5], Narenda [2], and others, the backpropagation of utility was used, but biological systems presumably use adaptive critics here [2,3]. Narenda has shown that the indirect approach is more powerful than the direct approach and has even proved a whole-system stability theorem for a simple version of it [2]. The theorem can probably be generalized substantially.

Farrell of MIT Draper Labs (under NSF and Air Force support) has used *classical* adaptive control *together* with a neural net parameter predictor to control a simulated F-15 from an AIAA control challenge; however, the control did poorly when noise was added. This highlights the weakness of classical adaptive control with respect to noise—a problem solved by adaptive critic designs.

9.6 BACKPROPAGATING UTILITY

After we have a deterministic model of the plant to be controlled, the sum of utility U over all future time can be expressed as a function of our actions $\mathbf{u}$ (past and future) or as a function of the weights in our Action network. The task of maximizing future utility can then be treated as a straightforward problem in function maximization. Some people solve this problem by purely random search or by Hopfield nets (as in earlier work by Kawato), but we can do much better by exploiting gradient information. To get this information, we can use the *generalized* form of backpropagation, the form that I first applied in 1974 [9,10], which works on *any* sparse nonlinear structure (not only on the so-called "backpropagation networks," which are properly called multilayer perceptrons). To use the gradient well, we can use adaptive learning rates or sophisticated numerical methods, both of which are much faster than the steepest descent [2].

Actually, there are three ways to calculate the gradiant of utility: (1) backpropagation through time (BTT), which is highly efficient even for large systems but is basically an offline or batch method; (2) the conventional or forward perturbation method [10], which works in real time but grows in cost as N^2, where N measures the network size; and (3) the truncation method, which simply ignores certain cross-time connections. All three are implausible as models of biology (though truncation may exist in lower organisms).

BTT was first applied in 1974 [9], and by 1988 there were four working examples in control: Jordan's robot controller, Kawato's cascaded robot controller [5], Widrow's truck-backer-upper [5], and my official Department of Energy model of the natural gas industry used in their *1987 Annual Energy Outlook*. By now, there are many others, including McAvoy's (real-time) Model Predictive Controller for chemical plants [2], which has many imitators. Narendra's work uses forward perturbation. Many authors have reinvented truncation, which is useful only for the simplest tracking problems. Even though BTT is mainly an offline method, the possibility of using time-lagged recurrent networks lets us train *offline* a net that appears *adaptive* online, due to the recurrence [2].

The *failures* of backpropagating utility have mainly been due to *inadequate* models of the plant to be controlled; such models are often based on random perturbations or on supervised learning. McAvoy and I have used a more sophisticated neuro-identification method to solve this problem and reduced prediction errors by orders of magnitude on real-world data from a refinery and a wastewater treatment plant [2]. This is a crucial area for future research.

The use of forward perturbation in neuroidentification has given the false impression that time-lagged recurrent nets are expensive to use, at least if big. BTT is much cheaper, and new critic-based designs should permit low-cost real-time adaptation [2].

9.7 ADAPTIVE CRITICS/APPROXIMATE DYNAMIC PROGRAMMING

For a full explanation of the ladder of adaptive critic designs, see White and Sofge [2].

Adaptive critics are often seen as a type of reinforcement learning system, but they are more powerful than conventional reinforcement learning can be. Critic networks may be defined as networks trained to approximate the evaluation function (J) of dynamic programming, or something very close to J. The simplest useful systems include a Critic adapted by Heuristic Dynamic Programing (HDP) and an Action net adapted by Barto's Arp method. They have worked well in many applications but grow very slow on medium-sized problems. Klopf and Baird have shown that drive-reinforcement theory modified to incorporate Action-Dependent HDP (ADHDP) fully explains a wide variety of animal behavior experiments that were intractable to all other attempted models.

The next step up the ladder involves "advanced adaptive critics," which *combine* generalized backpropagation and adaptive critics in a unified way in a *fully* real-time system. In 1988, there was theory by myself [5] but no examples. Now there are at least four working systems, and AAC is working on a fifth. Here I discuss only one.

The most striking example comes from White and Sofge [2], when they were at McDonnell–Douglas (McAir). McAir was a world leader in making high-quality composite materials, which are stronger and lighter than other structural materials (for which the U.S. market is about $400 billion/year). Their market was limited because of high costs due to the lack of a continuous production process. For obvious reasons, McAir and others had spent millions of dollars on this problem, using the best classical and AI approaches, to no avail. After reading Miller et al [5], White tried neurocontrol. Direct inverse control did not work. Simple adaptive critics worked on a small test version but learned too slowly for the real thing. Using an *advanced* adaptive critic (really just the *second* step on the ladder, using ADHDP and backpropagation), he and Sofge developed the first workable system, which has been used to make real parts in St. Louis.

Essentially the same design was used in *reconfigurable* control for the F-15—a controller that adapts to conditions like a wing being shot off and reduces crashes about 100% to around 50%. This works with real-world noise, but the details of the application on a physical F-15 cannot be reported yet. White and Sofge—now at MIT and Neurodyne—claim that a prototype thermal controller for NASP, based on the same approach, looks very promising and may well be the only way to improve efficiency and reduce weight enough to allow NASP to reach orbit. A benchmark test problem representing NASP, developed by White and Ames, has been published [2]. The NASP office is working on an official version, to be used by AAC and by anyone else who asks.

Issues like exploration, learning speed, and "persistence of excitation" suggest that the next step up will do still better, if robust hybrid designs and robust neuroidentification are used [2]. For true planning problems, like "Star Wars" or robot navigation through *novel* cluttered space, the fourth rung of the ladder, given in White and Sofge [2], may be necessary. Naturally, it is this highest rung that now seems to fit mammalian brains [2,3].

REFERENCES

1. E. Sontag, *Feedback Stabilization Using Two-Hidden-Layer Nets*, SYSCON-90-11, Rutgers University Center for Systems and Control, New Brunswick, NJ, October 1990.

2. D. White and D. Sofge (eds.), *Handbook of Intelligent Control: Neural, Adaptive and Fuzzy Approaches*, Van Norstrand, New York, 1992,

3. P. Werbos and A. Pellionisz, Neurocontrol and neurobiology: new developments and connections, in *IJCNN-92 Proceedings*, IEEE, New York, 1992.

4. P. Werbos, Elastic fuzzy logic: a better fit to neurocontrol, *Iizuka-92 Proceedings* Kyushu Institute of Technology, Iizuka, 1992. See also P. Werbos, Neurocontrol and Elastic Fuzzy Logic, *IEEE Transaction on Industrial Electronics*, April 1993.

5. W. Miller, R. Sutton, and P. Werbos, *Neural Networks for Control*, MIT Press, Cambridge, MA, 1990.

6. K. Narendra and A. Anhaswamy, *Stable Adaptive Systems*, Prentice-Hall, Englewood Cliffs, NJ, 1989.

7. J. A. Walter, T. Martinez, and K. Schulten, Industrial robot learns visuo-motor coordination by means of neural-gas network, in T. Kohonen et al., (eds.), *Artificial Neural Networks*, North Holland, Amsterdam, 1991.

8. M. Adkins, C. Cox, R. Pap, C. Thomas, and R. Saeks, "Neural joint control for space shuttle remote manipulator system," in *Proceedings of the 1992 IEEE/RSJ International Conference on Intelligent Robots*.

9. P. Werbos, *Beyond Regression, New Tools for Prediction and Analysis in the Behavioral Sciences*. Ph.D. thesis, Harvard University, Nov. 1974, (Chapters 1–6).

10. P. Werbos, Applications of advances in nonlinear sensitivity analysis, in X. Drenick and F. Kozin, *System Modeling and Optimization* (Proceedings of IFIP 1981), Springer-Verlag, New York, 1982.

10

Neural Networks and the Human Mind

New Mathematics Fits Humanistic Insight

The past two years have seen substantial progress in artificial neural networks (ANNs). New ANN control designs, combining reinforcement learning and generalized backpropagation [1, 2], have demonstrated success on large-scale real-world problems which could not be solved by earlier designs, neural or nonneural. There now exists a ladder of designs, rising up from simple designs (of limited capability, but a good starting point), through to complex proven designs (which give more power and flexibility after they are mastered), up to new untested designs and ideas which should be able to replicate and explain human intelligence at the highest possible level.

After a brief review of neurocontrol, and an explanation of reinforcement learning, this paper asks *what implications* these designs have for our understanding of the human mind. It argues that this new mathematics is fully compatible with older deep insights into the human mind, due to humanistic thinkers East and West. One may therefore hope that this new view of the human mind may be of value in unifying important strands of human culture.

10.1 A REVIEW OF NEUROCONTROL

From an engineering point of view, the human brain is simply a computer, an information processing system. The function of any computer, *as a whole system*, is to compute its outputs. The outputs of the brain are *control* signals to muscles and glands. Therefore the brain *as a whole system* is a neurocontroller (a neural net control system) [3]. To understand the brain in functional, mathematical terms we should therefore focus on the subject of *neurocontrol*.

305

ANNs have been useful in four kinds of control task: (1) as subsystems of larger systems, where the controller itself is not an ANN; (2) in "cloning" applications, to copy what an expert *does* (unlike conventional expert systems that copy what an expert *says*); (3) in tracking applications, such as holding a plant to a fixed setpoint or making it follow a prespecified reference trajectory; and (4) in reinforcement learning or optimization *over time*. The first three of these four clearly have nothing to do with human intelligence.

Some biologists once argued that lower-level functions in the brain, such as the control of arm movement by the cerebellum, might be based on a simple tracking system; however, Kawato et al. [4] have done impressive experiments proving that these parts of the brain actually *optimize* movements over time. They do perform tracking, but only as *part* of an optimization task. A few authors have questioned these conclusions, but they still hold up quite well.

In brief, the *reinforcement learning* or *optimization* designs are the only designs of value in understanding the human mind. They are the only designs capable of meaningful planning or foresight. They are also the designs that have led to the most exciting real-world applications in recent years. Therefore this chapter focuses exclusively on them. To learn about other designs, stability, and so on see Chapter 9.

Within the field of optimization over time, two classes of design have proved useful in practice: (1) direct optimization, using generalized backpropagation to calculate derivatives of utility or performance or cost; and (2) adaptive critic designs, which approximate dynamic programming.

Direct optimization based on the backpropagation of utility was first proposed in 1974 [2]. By 1988, there were four significant working examples [4], including two model robot controllers, one controller of a simulated truck-backer-upper, and a U.S. Department of Energy official model of the natural gas industry [5]. By now dozens of examples have appeared, including a Model-Predictive Control scheme now used to improve efficiency and reduce waste in profit-making chemical process plants, and an optimal tracking scheme of Narendra [1]. However, none of these designs are plausible as models of the brain. Some of the designs require calculations *backward through time*; others require huge computational costs for large problems; and others simply cut off the key calculations that account for the long-term effect of present actions. These designs have great value in engineering (including an ability to reduce pollution while saving money), but they are not directly relevant to understanding the human mind; therefore, I do not discuss them here. Optimization methods derived from static function maximization are even less relevant here.

10.2 REINFORCEMENT LEARNING AND ADAPTIVE CRITICS IN GENERAL

Adaptive critic systems can perform "reinforcement learning." In reinforcement learning, an ANN system receives a vector of sensor inputs $X(t)$. It outputs a vector of control signals or actions $u(t)$. Then it receives a "reward" or "punishment" $U(t)$. In reinforcement learning, the system must somehow learn to output actions $u(t)$, which *maximize* future rewards U, summed across all future time, from $U(t)$ to $U(\infty)$.

Many thinkers throughout history have argued that the human mind is a reinforcement learning system. The behaviorist psychologist Skinner built his theory around "primary reinforcement," which is exactly like $U(t)$. Many ancient Greeks argued that the human mind maximizes "hedony" or "pleasure versus pain." Aristotle argued that the "telos" or organizing principle of the mind is simply the maximization of "happiness." John Stuart Mill and Von Neumann claimed that we maximize "utility."

In psychology, it is important to ask *what variables* actually enter into the $U(t)$ that we maximize. In biology, it is clear that there are fixed centers, such as the hypothalamus and epithalamus [3, 6], which generate primary reinforcement. From a Darwinian perspective, E. O. Wilson [7] has developed deep insights that suggest that $U(t)$—for a human individual—would represent some kind of *weighted sum* of the well-being of people whom the individual cares about. Wilson's insights fit well with ancient Confucian notions, which stress that well-adjusted humans give great priority to family values; however, they also allow for tribal feelings and for the possibility of explicit bargains [8] or social contracts, which permit cooperation at higher levels across different families or tribes, especially in "pioneer" environments that may permit growth. The Darwinian approach also suggests that humans do not really "discount" the intrinsic importance of U in the far future; this fits with the Confucian notion that wise and well-adjusted humans think ahead for many generations. These ideas (similar to some ideas from Christianity and Islam) can be reconciled with the requirements of a market economy, but they still have major policy implications [9].

Critics of reinforcement learning argue that humans often make suboptimal decisions and often put great energy into activities like exploration, which do not lead to direct rewards. However, *working, real-world* reinforcement learning systems share these characteristics [1,6]. In Darwinian evolution, one would expect nature to converge on systems that do the *best possible job* of maximizing some measure of success, *subject to the constraint* of what is actually possible for a physical learning system; in neurocontrol, we try to do the same. In addition, later parts of this chapter suggest that the true $U(t)$ of human beings may favor exploration more than simplified versions of it would.

In real-world engineering applications [1], we use adaptive critics to maximize $U(\mathbf{X}(t))$ rather than $U(t)$, because of the great efficiency we can get by exploiting knowledge of what we are trying to maximize. One would expect a similar arrangement in biological systems [6].

10.3 BACKPROPAGATION, FREUD, AND ADVANCED ADAPTIVE CRITICS

Adaptive critic systems try to approximate dynamic programming.

Dynamic programming is the *only exact* and *efficient* technique for maximizing U across future time, in the general case, where noise and nonlinearity may be present. To use dynamic programming, we proceed as follows. First, we, the users, must supply a utility function $U(\mathbf{X})$ and a model of the external world that we want to optimize. Then dynamic programming tells us how to solve for *another* function, $J(\mathbf{X})$, which can be used in choosing $\mathbf{u}$. $J(\mathbf{X})$ may be thought of as a *secondary* or *strategic* utility function. It represents a kind of *strategic assessment* of any possible situation $\mathbf{X}$. The basic theorem in dynamic programming is as follows: by picking $\mathbf{u}(t)$ at each time t so as to maximize $J(\mathbf{X}(t + 1))$, we *automatically* maximize the sum of U over *all* future times. Dynamic programming converts a difficult problem in *long-term* optimization into a straightforward problem in *short-term* function maximization.

Dynamic programming becomes impossibly expensive to use in its pure form, even for medium-sized problems. Therefore we cannot hope to solve such problems *exactly*; we will never play a perfect game of chess, and we should not expect our ANNs to do so either. To approximate dynamic programming, we can try to adapt "Critic" networks—networks that try to *approximate* the J function, or something similar.

There functions U and J show up very clearly in tasks like playing chess. In formal chess, the goal is to win; thus $U(\mathbf{X})$ is zero except at the end of the game, where it is $+1$ for a win and -1 for a loss. But beginning chess players often learn an old rule of thumb to measure their progress *before* the end of the game. They count 9 points for a queen, 5 for each castle, and so on. This is a simple approximation to J. Better chess players learn to place value on holding the center, and so on. Some analysts argue that the best human chess players really look ahead *only one move*; their apparent foresight may be due to a very careful, in-depth strategic assessment (J) of the near-term alternatives. In other words, their success may be due to a better approximation to the true function J.

In human psychology, the output of a Critic network corresponds exactly to Skinner's idea of "secondary reinforcement"—a *learned* reinforcement. Biologists have shown that the limbic system of the brain [1, 6] generates such reinforcement; the limbic system is often described as the "emotional" system of the brain. Just as U includes inborn feelings like pleasure and pain, J represents learned responses like hope and fear. When I argue that the human mind is an adaptive critic system, I am simply saying that the human mind is governed by hopes and fears that it learns through experience. The development of a more accurate J function is crucial to the development and intelligence of a human being; this corresponds to the Confucian idea that balanced judgment (J) is a crucial basic faculty for humans to develop.

Adaptive critic ANNs were first implemented by Widrow in 1973, and improved upon in a famous 1983 paper by Barto, Sutton and Anderson; however, neither of these designs can handle truly large, brain-like control problems [1, 4]. Figure 10.1 illustrates an advanced adaptive critic design that I proposed briefly in 1977 [10] and at greater length in 1981 [11]. In this design, the overall system is made up of *three* ANN components. One component, the Action network, actually generates the vector $\mathbf{u}(t)$. Another network, the Model network, is adapted to *predict* or *explain* the external world. The Critic net-

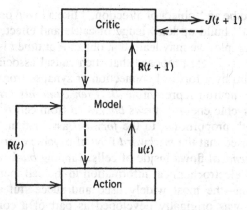

FIGURE 10.1 Backpropagated adaptive critic.

work, at the top, is needed in adapting the Action network. The upward arrows show how to predict $J(t + 1)$ for any given vector of actions $\mathbf{u}(t)$. See White and Sofge [1] for all the mathematical details. The vector $\mathbf{R}(t)$ represents an image of reality at time t, based on $\mathbf{X}(t)$ plus other information [1].

Figure 10.1 also illustrates how the Action network can be adapted through the *backward*, broken arrows, which represent the derivatives of J. These derivatives are important mathematically, but they also have great significance to psychology and economics.

In studying human values and fears, it is not enough to study functions like $U(\mathbf{X})$ and $J(\mathbf{X})$, which represent *global* measures of happiness, and so on. Humans also place values on specific *objects* and specific *variables*, values that are crucial in governing our behavior. For example, in economic systems, there are values or prices put on *specific* goods, which are crucial to the efficiency of such systems.

In economics, the value of a *specific* good, X_i, is defined by its "marginal utility." The marginal utility of X_i is defined as the proportionate *increase* in $U(\mathbf{X})$, which would result from a small increase in X_i. For example, the value of a peanut to you equals the increase in utility that would result from your consuming one additional peanut. Mathematically, the "marginal utility of X_i" is just a synonym for the *derivative* of $U(\mathbf{X})$ with respect of X_i. The value of a good to *society as a whole* over the *long-term future* is usually discussed in terms of "Lagrange multipliers," λ_i which are actually just the derivatives of $J(\mathbf{X})$.

Years ago, Sigmund Freud made a persistent effort to understand the underlying laws of human learning, laws that could explain the deep and rich experience he acquired regarding human thought over many decades. The theory he arrived at was essentially a neural network theory, motivated by his earlier study of neurophysiology in medical school. He argued that human behavior and human feelings are dominated by "psychic energy," by a system of emotional charge or values placed on specific *objects*. (An "object," in his terminology, could be an "object of affection," like a loved one.) He proposed that humans "first" build up knowledge of cause and effect, through experience; thus, for example, we may learn that object A at time t is associated with object B at time $t + 1$. He proposed that such causal associations are represented, in the brain, by a forward connection or synapse from the neuron representing A to the neuron representing B. *Then came his crucial insight*: he proposed that "psychic energy" flows *backward* from cell B to cell A, with a connection strength proportional to the *forward* association from A to B. At the time, he proposed that the *backward* flow of psychic energy is represented in the brain by *chemical* flows inside of cells, running *backward* compared to the usual flows of electrochemical information in the cell membranes.

Backpropagation—the most widely used and successful algorithm in the ANN literature— was originally developed as part of a conscious effort to translate Freud's theory into working mathematics [6]. Figure 10.1 illustrates the original idea. In this figure, the dashed lines represent the derivatives of J, which represent the "psychic energy." A *backward* flow of calculations— matching Freud's idea exactly—is used to work out the derivatives of J with respect to $\mathbf{R}(t + 1)$, then the derivatives of J with respect to $\mathbf{R}(t)$, then the derivatives of J with respect to $\mathbf{u}(t)$, and then—finally—the derivatives of J with respect to the weights in the Action network. These weights are adapted in response to those derivatives. This arrangement exactly fits the prescription of dynamic programming, which tells us to pick $\mathbf{u}(t)$ so as to maximize $J(t + 1)$.

Again, this idea was published in 1981 [11]. That same paper also discussed backpropagation in general terms (as in Werbos [2]) and proposed the use of differentiable model neurons to permit the use of backpropagation in adapting ANNs. It also discussed links to the brain. Over the years, I have also developed other ways to use backpropagation in adaptive critic systems [1].

As recently as 1990 [4], there were no published working examples of adaptive critic systems really exploiting backpropagation. (There had been delays, of course, even in simpler uses of backpropagation.) As of now, there are at least four, of which two are practical real-world systems with multiple applications. BehavHeuristics of College Park in Maryland has used a three network design, similar to Figure 10.1, to perform optimal seat allocation and scheduling, so as to maximize airline profits; a variant on this system has passed large-scale tests, and USAir has signed a contract to apply it to optimize their global network of flights. The system developed by White and Sofge at McDonnell–Douglas and Neurodyne has been used to make high-quality composite parts in a continuous production system, to build an F-15 controller able to adapt in 2 seconds to major changes in the airplane, and to develop a prototype thermal controller for an airplane (NASP) designed to reach escape velocity [1]. New applications by AAC of Tennessee are also important, but the reinforcement learning aspects are not yet published.

Some researchers argue that backpropagation has not been found yet in the brain. However, there are fundamental reasons why it would be difficult or impossible to build brain-like intelligence without such backward flows of in-formation [6]. There are many biological mechanisms that could implement such a flow, but no one has looked at these systems very carefully yet [6]. Recently, it has been discovered that nitric oxide does act as a "backward transmitter." Karl Pribram, in conversation, has suggested that his classical experiments on the limbic system may *already* demonstrate such a backward flow of information, inconsistent with classical neuron dogmas. Links to the cerebellum are discussed in [12]. There is a great need for new research to explore these biological issues, perhaps using new instrumentation.

10.4 LANGUAGE, PLANNING, DREAMING, AND CONFUCIAN ETHICS

Within the Confucian scheme, the first and deepest imperative is to be true to oneself. The most fundamental virtue is "integrity"—a state in which you tell the truth to yourself, and not just to others. However, to be true to yourself, you must make some effort to understand yourself in the most accurate way possible. This is one motivation for studying neural networks and other ways of studying the human mind.

If human beings are *born* as reinforcement learning systems, doing their best to maximize their personal sense of what seems good (U), how could they be capable of anything *but* integrity? Why should integrity be such a big issue for human beings, but not for other animals?

The answer comes from the role of language.

The adaptive critic systems now in use cannot replicate or explain language, because they are not even capable of high-order planning or "chunking," which is a prerequisite to language. However, recent research suggests that true planning and chunking emerge naturally and automatically from adaptive critic systems, which use *appropriate types of ANN* as Critic networks. In essence, one needs to use ANNs which settle down to an equilibrium, like the classical Grossberg/Hopfield nets, *but* are adapted so as to minimize error, with the help of backpropagation. (See [1, 17] for details.). Biological research suggests [1,12] that the brains of all mammals do use the appropriate types of network. Recent results also show that networks of this type can handle language pro-cessing tasks which were impossible with simple MLPs [20], and they have verified empirically [21] the arguments in [1] that they lead to faster learning when used as Critics.

Another prerequisite to language is "dreaming." In any kind of adaptive critic system, there is much to be gained by *exploring* or *simulating* possible future states of reality **R**, which have not been experienced yet as *actual* states. This point has been stressed [13] and demonstrated graphically by Sutton in his "Dyna" simulations [4]. Current sleep research appears to be fully con-sistent with this interpretation of dreaming as a kind of offline simulation [14]. In classical dreaming, of course, one would adapt the Critic network and the

Action network so as to handle the hypothetical states **R**; one would probably not adapt the Model network, because the Model network is the system used to *generate* the simulations in the first place. There is reason to believe that all types of mammal are capable of dreaming.

Even if we add dreaming and an appropriate form of Critic, the designs now in use would still not have a true ability to learn to use language. They would still adapt their components based on the *own individual* experience. They could respond to words as *sounds*, in a highly intelligent way, but this is not the same as *learning* from the experience of those who are talking to you. There would be a tremendous evolutionary advantage to learning from the experience of other animals, *as if* that experience were one's own experience. I have argued [6] that humans have evolved such a unique ability, very recently in evolutionary time, and therefore very imperfectly. (Studies by Jim Anderson in cognitive science have also made this point.). This ability may have begun with a kind of trance-like state, similar to dreaming, which allowed members of human groups to experience vicariously the memories of other group members returning from a hunt and dancing out their memories; *unlike* dreaming, this state would allow adaptation of the Model networks. The ability to use language led to another skill—symbolic reasoning—only in historical times.

If the ability to use language is new, it is not surprising that humans face transitional problems or instabilities in using language. These problems force us to *learn* certain skills through experience—such as the skill of integrity—without the biological support we have in learning older skills like vision. Still, the natural equilibrium of the system—the natural equilibrium state of a well-adjusted person—would involve a balance or match between the verbal side of our thinking and the nonverbal side; it would maintain the Confucian ideal of integrity. In matters concerning U—as in matters concerning visual perception—we would constantly be aware of what is coming to us from the nonverbal level, constantly ready to articulate those inputs as accurately as possible, and constantly ready to analyze what we see and feel by making full use of verbal and nonverbal skills, on an integrated basis. There is a close analogy here between the Confucian ideal of integrity and the Freudian ideal of sanity.

Social forces often encourage subtle forms of dishonesty and dogmatism, which make it more difficult for humans to learn effective symbolic reasoning and "integrity." Primitive corporate cultures (like animal societies) often do not value honest symbolic reasoning, or mental productivity in general [9]. Philosophers like Nietzsche and Ayn Rand have presented desperate (and valid) pleas for individual humans to overcome such phenomena, in order to achieve greater integrity. When the doors of perception and sensitivity inside the self have been locked and sealed, the emotional violence described by Nietzsche may be necessary at times to open them up; however, the reintegrated self need not be violent or antisocial. Irrational fears to that effect are one of the many factors one must overcome, in gradually developing more productive corporate cultures throughout the world, cultures that encourage individuals to live up to their full potential.

10.5 BEYOND THE BRAIN: HOW FAR CAN THE MATHEMATICS GO?

The preceding discussion in this chapter is fully consistent with the classical materialistic idea that the human brain and the human mind are essentially identical. ANN research—like modern neurophysiology—suggests very strongly that the brain itself can generate virtually all aspects of human intelligence, which are generally agreed upon. By Occam's Razor, this would tend to suggest that we should throw out classical views of the mind, which try to go beyond the brain. The logic of that viewpoint is unquestionable. The people who agree with that viewpoint should stop reading here, having found a mathematical framework that is fully capable of sustaining that view.

Nevertheless, the most creative ANN researchers (in my experience) do not all subscribe to classical materialism. As far as I can tell, their views seem to be similar in character to the views of the four most famous physicists of this century—Einstein, DeBroglie, Schrodinger, and Heisenberg. Like those four, they have a great deal of diversity. Like them, a majority seem to be open to the possibility that the human mind may possess capabilities or attributes that go beyond those of the known brain. This is paradoxical, since these are precisely the people most conscious of the points in the preceding paragraph. They are not the kind of people who believe things simply because their parents did. One might speculate that this surprising situation is due to these people observing capabilities or phenomena in their own unusually capable minds, which they find it difficult to explain. Or, as creative people, they may open themselves up to connections and feelings that more constrained technicians and apparatchiks may tend to block out. Or perhaps this is just a way of distancing themselves emotionally from the current state of what is known. In any event, a balanced and complete account of humanistic views of the mind must make some allowance for ideas and possibilities that are taken seriously by a significant portion of humanity.

Could the mathematics of neurocontrol still be useful in describing the human mind, if in fact the human mind *were* larger than the human brain?

There are two reasons to be optimistic here: (1) if the human mind *were* larger than the brain, then mathematical insights would be all the more important to help minimize the incredible confusion and chaos that this viewpoint would otherwise permit; and (2) the mathematical issues that led to our designs *are not limited* to systems made up of wet neurons and atoms; they should be applicable even to systems built up from other kinds of devices. Some traditionalists have argued that people should *believe* in concepts like soul, but should avoid using mathematics *or* experience or anything else (except submission to their authority) to understand them; however, this is not consistent with the notion of integrity as discussed in the previous section.

As an example, there is a large, old literature suggesting that individual human beings have some kind of symbiotic relation with or membership in some kind of large, collective intelligence. Hinduism and Buddhism have promoted the idea that we are all part of some great Mind. People like Teilhard de Chardin and Lovelock have promoted similar ideas in the West in recent decades. Carl Jung—borrowing heavily from Buddhism—has published very extensive studies of human psychology, supporting his notion of a "collective unconscious." Even the New Testament talks about a "true vine," which (to me) sounds like a neural network—a vast, invisible neural network, held together by invisible connections between people of all sorts across the world.

If those ideas were correct, I would predict that backpropagation in some form would have to play a crucial role in organizing this collective intelligence. Based on casual observation, I would claim that this collective intelligence would have to be in a relatively young or immature state; therefore, to understand or assist this intelligence, we would need to understand the forces permitting or encouraging greater maturation. We would need to reconsider Freud's discussion of the evolution of ego through appropriate flows of raw psychic energy, *as it would* apply within a larger intelligent system.

In the developmental process, the development of critical new gestalts or variables R_i plays a central role in channeling psychic energy in the service of the ego; it is particularly important for us to crystallize out new concepts that support greater foresight, greater subjective appreciation of the reality of a larger universe in space and time, and—in Freud's terms—the resulting ability to delay gratification (even in terms of budget deficits, investment [9], and welfare [15]). Just as specific memories or prototypes become assimilated into a global model or "ego" in Freud's theory [17–19], so too could Jung's archetypes become assimilated or absorbed into something more global and rational at a higher level.

When we as individuals participate in such a system, I would predict that the issues of symbolic reasoning and Confucian integrity would still apply, both on the personal and on the collective level, perhaps with much greater force. The evolution of the greater system from a purely nonverbal level to more (self-) conscious, symbolic communication within itself would be crucial to its maturation. (Some old Christian notions about The Word could be interpreted as guarded references to such a process.) As within a human individual, such internal communication would require a certain ability to detach oneself from the current flow of events, for a time, in order to focus attention elsewhere. As with any young intelligent organism, exploration and play and learning would be more important goals (in the U of this system) than they are for adults; however, practical issues of collective importance to all humanity [9,15] would also acquire great energy.

Traditional Taoist views of life and spirit on Earth also reflect the idea that invisible flows of higher-level psychic energy or ch'i, criss-crossing through multiple organisms, dominate the growth and adaptation of the greater system. (As I write this, I cannot help visualizing the biota of mountain streams.) Responding to these flows would be a natural behavior for a component of that larger system, at the preverbal stage of evolution. Even at the verbal level, these flows are the foundation on which all else is built.

In Hinduism and Buddhism, the fate of an individual is said to depend on "karma," an almost economic kind of action-and-reward system. In the back-propagation model, the adaptation of individual units or neurons is also analogous to market economics; each unit receives a kind of reward or punishment (i.e., the psychic energy used to adapt that unit and *also* used to adapt the actions of other units that affect that unit) directly proportional to the *value* of the output of that unit to the larger system, as determined through existing "local" connections in the network. Efforts to manipulate this system in "magical" ways could lead to substantial and effective negative feedback they seem harmful (deliberately *or* innocently) to the greater system; however, the Confucian notion of integrity and the Taoist notions of responsiveness and balance—if combined—could minimize such dangers. Minimizing negative feedback through detachment from participation on all levels is not a realistic option; as in the marketplace, it is the *net* balance between position and negative feedback that dominates individual units.

Unlike marketplaces in the real world, a well-evolved neural network would naturally avoid conflict of interest effects capable of corrupting the underlying system. Also, such a network would encourage independent ideas or exploration within components of the network, in order to develop new connections and insights; after all, such exploratory growth (sometimes via GA subsystems) is important even in today's ANNs, as a way of avoiding local minima (mental ruts).

Many physicists and Buddhists go even further and claim that the entire cosmos is one great Mind. Frankly, I do find it hard to assimilate *that* idea into neural networks or into any other idea I can make sense of or justify; however, the obvious alternative—the idea of a real, finite-dimensional physical universe, however weird and full of unknown forces—is currently viewed as a conservative heresy in modern physics. Many physicists now endorse the Everett/Wheeler notion of parallel universes or time-tracks; I find this notion very compelling intuitively, and it also fits certain notions from esoteric Taoism, but I am skeptical about any evidence for this notion coming from modern-day physics [16].

In summary, there is no real conflict between new ideas from neural network theory or physics and deep, classical ideas from Eastern and Western culture; in fact, the new ideas may provide a basis for helping us understand and appreciate the roots of the classical ideas at a deeper level.

REFERENCES

1. D. White and D. Sofge *Handbook of Intelligent Control*, Van Nostrand, New York, 1992.
2. P. Werbos, *Beyond Regression: New Tools for Prediction and Analysis in the Behavioral Sciences*, Ph.D. thesis, Harvard University, Nov. 1974.
3. W. Nauta and M. Feirtag, *Fundamental Neuroanatomy*, Freeman, San Francisco, 1986.

4. W. Miller, P. Sutton, and P. Werbos, *Neural Networks for Control*, MIT Press, Cambridge, MA, 1990.

5. P. Werbos, Maximizing long-term gas industry profits in two minutes in Lotus using neural network methods, *IEEE Transactions on Systems Man, and Cybernetics*, March-April, 1989.

6. P. Werbos, The cytoskeleton: why it may be crucial to human learning and to neurocontrol, *Nanobiology*, Vol. 1, No. 1, 1992.

7. E. O. Wilson, *Sociobiology: The New Synthesis*, Harvard University Press, Cambridge, MA, 1975.

8. T. C. Schelling, *Strategy of Conflict*, Harvard University Press, Cambridge, MA, 1960.

9. P. Werbos, Rational approaches to identifying policy objectives, *Energy*, March/April 1990. Reprinted in the *Handbook of Energy-Economy Modeling*, J. Weyant and T. Kuczmowski, eds., Pergamon, 1993.

10. P. Werbos, Advanced forecasting methods for global crisis warning and models of intelligence, *General Systems Yearbook*, 1977 issue.

11. P. Werbos, Applications of advances in nonlinear sensitivity analysis, in R. F. Drenick and F. Kozin, *System Modeling and Optimization* (Proceedings of IFIP 1981), Springer-Verlag, New York, 1982.

12. P. Werbos, Neurocontrol and neurobiology, *IJCNN Proceedings* (Baltimore), IEEE, New York, 1992.

13. P. Werbos, Building and understanding adaptive systems, *IEEE Transactions on Systems, Man and Cybernetics*, March/April 1987.

14. S. LaBerge and Rheingold, *Exploring the World of Lucid Dreaming*, Ballantine, New York, 1990.

15. L. Grant (ed.), *Elephants in the Volkswagen: Facing the Tough Questions About Our Overcrowded Country*. Freeman, New York, 1992.

16. P. Werbos, Chaotic solitons and the foundations of physics: a potential revolution, *Applied Mathematics and Computation*, Vol. 56, No. 2-3, p. 289–339, 1993.

17. P. Werbos, Supervised learning: can it escape its local minimum?, *WCNN 93 Proceedings*, Erlbaum, 1993.

18. D. Yankelovich and W. Bartlett, *Ego and Instinct: The Psychoanalytic View of Human Nature—Revised*, Vintage, 1971.

19. K. Pribram and M. Gill, *Freud's Project Reassessed*, Basic Books, 1976.

20. J. Munson and G. Berg, The tactical learning effect in recurrent connectionist networks, *WCNN 93 Proceedings*, Erlbaum, 1993.

21. P. Werbos and R. Santiago, Neurocontrol, *Above Threshold* (INNS), Vol. 2, No. 2, 1993.

Index